First published in Great Britain in 2010 by
The Derby Books Publishing Company Limited
3 The Parker Centre,
Derby, DE21 4SZ.

ISBN 978-1-85983-772-6

Printed and bound by Cromwell Press Group, Trowbridge, Wiltshire.

Susan Soyinka

FROM EAST END
— TO —
LAND'S END

THE EVACUATION OF JEWS' FREE SCHOOL, LONDON, TO
MOUSEHOLE IN CORNWALL DURING WORLD WAR TWO

DB PUBLISHING

In memory of my mother
Lucy Fowler née Smetana (1919–2003)
who made me all that I am
and of my aunt
Sonya Smetana (1927–1942?)
who went on a train journey in the other direction

T his book provides a significant insight into the evacuation of a group of children from the Jews' Free School, London, to the far west of Cornwall. A group who not only had to cope with the trauma of the evacuation process, but also had to contend with a journey to an unknown community where their presence may not have been welcomed. As it turned out their fears were unfounded and in the main they became, as the oral accounts would indicate, an important and treasured addition to the population of Mousehole.

While recognising the limitations of oral testimony and memory, Susan has managed ably to blend the recollections of evacuees and locals alike into an account which not only explains the experiences of both parties, but also puts the whole event into its historical, national and international context. As Susan points out, while some were making the safe journey to Cornwall, other Jewish children on mainland Europe were making one of an altogether different kind. I can commend this book wholeheartedly.

Dr Martin Parsons

Director of the Research Centre for Evacuee and War Child Studies, University of Reading.

CONTENTS

INTRODUCTION

In September 1939 about 650 children were evacuated with Jews' Free School (now known as JFS) in London, to Ely and the surrounding villages in Cambridgeshire. Within Jewish circles, this is a well-known and documented period in the school's history, with a substantial amount of information recorded on the JFS website and in other publications. Much less well known, indeed barely mentioned, is the evacuation in June 1940 of about 100 JFS children to Mousehole, a remote and at that time isolated fishing village on the tip of Cornwall, three miles beyond Penzance and more than 300 miles from London. In spite of my own Jewish background, and a 50-year association with Mousehole, I learned only recently of this interesting story and quickly became so fascinated by it that I decided to carry out further research, with a view to writing a book.

How did I become involved? By an extraordinary coincidence, I have connections with both sides of this story. My mother, Lucy Fowler née Smetana, was a Viennese Jewish refugee who came to England in 1938 to escape Hitler's clutches. The rest of her family were not so fortunate: she lost eight of them, including her parents, her only sister Sonya, three of her grandparents, her cousin and her uncle. Perhaps because of her trauma, she rarely spoke of her experiences and I knew very little of the family background. While conducting family research during 1995, I discovered that my mother's aunt and uncles, of whom I had never heard, had escaped with their children to Australia and America and that my mother had five first cousins still living in those continents, some of whom I visited. Wanting to connect with my new-found Jewishness, I took up an appointment as an educational psychologist working for Binoh, part of Norwood, a Jewish charity in London. This involved working with the children, parents and teachers of many Jewish schools in London. One of these schools was JFS.

On the other side of the story, I first visited Cornwall with my family some 50 years ago, and we have all been drawn to it ever since. Indeed, my brother Steve has lived in Cornwall for many years. In 1958, our mother arranged for us to attend a 'house party' organised by a fellow Austrian Jew, Erna Lowe, and held at St Clare's School in Penzance during the summers of 1958, 1959 and 1960. The school was used as a base to explore Cornwall, including Mousehole, with which we all fell in love. My other brother, Peter, spent two summer holidays working at the bird hospital there. Coincidentally, at a much later date, I married Andrew Trembath, whose father Edwin was born at 10 Fore Street, Mousehole, so my son Alex has a very strong connection with the village. Throughout the 1980s our family stayed during the summer at Harbour Cottage in Mousehole. We had such pleasant memories of these holidays that when the cottage recently became available once more for letting, I thought it would be wonderful to go there again, this time with my grandchildren as well as my children. And so we went back to Harbour Cottage in May 2007 and 2008.

During this time, I made friends with a dear lady, Greta Lewis, who sadly died in January 2009, and she told me of a friend of hers, Marian Harris, a distant relative of my son's whom I had not known, and now in her 80s. I visited Marian in May 2008, 50 years after my first visit to Mousehole. I received a warm welcome and learned many things I had not known about the Trembath family history. I was curious to see a photograph on the mantelpiece of an obviously Jewish family, which I learned was the family of Lenny Marks, who had been one of the Jewish children evacuated to Mousehole during World War Two. Thus unfolded the story of the evacuation of the children of Jews' Free School in the East End of London to what for them must have been the far ends of the earth. Given my own circumstances, I was amazed to be hearing about this remarkable piece of Jewish and Cornish history for the first time. Of course, I plied Marian with questions, many of which she was able to answer in astonishing detail.

According to Marian's account, the residents of Mousehole and their Jewish guests got on extremely well together, in spite of their very different backgrounds and experiences. Many of the evacuees maintained contact with their hosts, some even returning to live in Cornwall. I was treated by Marian to some charming anecdotes, but the story that most moved me was that of a man returning to Mousehole for the first time in 1999. After spending a week looking in vain for anyone who knew about the evacuation, he met Greta, who had not been in Mousehole during the war, so she sent him to Marian, who had. When this gentleman told Marian the name of the family he had stayed with, she asked 'you're not little Jacky Goldstein, are you?' Whereupon little Jacky Goldstein, now in his 70s and accompanied by his daughter, burst into tears.

Marian later wrote to me with the names of 22 evacuee children and some of their teachers, which was a very good starting point for my research. I subsequently obtained a copy from the Cornwall Record Office of the Mousehole School Register dated 5 January 1942, which showed that on that date 31 children had transferred from Jews' Free School Mousehole, to Mousehole School proper, indicating that Jews' Free School had existed in Mousehole from June 1940 to December 1941 and that a number of the children stayed on beyond that time. Sadly, the Jews' Free School Mousehole register, and also the evacuation records for the Borough of Penzance, have been lost, though some Truro records still exist. However, through my discussions with large numbers of people, I have been able to compile a list of about 100 children who were originally evacuated, together with the names of some of their siblings and family members who visited them. I have also been able to establish that the teachers who accompanied them were Mr David Levene, Mr Ralph Barnes, Mr David Nathan, Miss Cohen, Miss Haffner and Miss Rose Levene. The male teachers were accompanied by their wives and children.

In the course of my research, I have spoken with a number of historians, archivists and journalists in Cornwall and London, and members of Kehillat Kernow, the Cornish Jewish community. From these and other sources I have researched, I learned that some of the children originally evacuated with Jews' Free School to Cambridgeshire were not happy there and returned to London. Others were homesick, and since for the first few months of the war there were no bombs, simply drifted back home. Once the bombing started, however, some of the teachers in Cambridgeshire, including Ralph Barnes and David Levene, were sent back to London to collect these children and re-evacuate with them to Cornwall. One hundred or so JFS children, together with thousands of other evacuees, thus embarked on the lengthy and exhausting train journey from Paddington to Penzance, from where they were bussed to Mousehole. Here they were billeted with the villagers, and Jews' Free School Mousehole was established in the premises of Mousehole School.

This book is based mainly on the memories of Mousehole villagers and former evacuees, whom I have been able to contact via newspaper articles I have written and by word of mouth. In all, I have spoken with at least 15 villagers and 29 former evacuees to Mousehole, all of whom were interviewed by telephone during the course of 2009 and many of whom have corresponded with me. In addition, during February to May 2009, I met and recorded the stories of 11 villagers and 13 evacuees, while other informants, including two in America, have completed questionnaires. All 24 recorded interviews have been placed with CAVA, the Cornish Audio Visual Archive, and thus have become part of recognised Cornish history.

What is clear from the interviews is that most of the evacuees quickly integrated into village life and were accepted by the villagers as their own. They were introduced to swimming, sailing, sculling, fishing and mending nets, and they spent hours playing on the beach or walking along the spectacular coastal paths. The extraordinary coming together of these two vastly different communities was a life-changing experience for many involved on both sides. Seventy years on, they have been able to tell their stories, sometimes with tears, often with humour, and almost always with love and affection. Indeed, the striking feature of the interviews was the love felt between the villagers and the evacuees. One villager commented: 'I really, really loved them,' others regarded them as siblings and apparently several wanted to adopt. For the evacuees, it was 'magical', 'a fairyland', 'a wonderful, wonderful experience'.

It should perhaps be mentioned that, while the experiences of this particular group of evacuees were overwhelmingly positive, there were a very few sad stories. I understand that on a national level, the experience of evacuation was a very mixed one, with some evacuees, and even receiving families, experiencing long-term trauma. One JFS evacuee said to me: 'We couldn't have gone to a better place. We were fortunate; we hit on the place of places. Other children weren't so lucky.' Truly, this is a heart-warming and inspiring story, which deserves to be recorded for posterity.

What is particularly poignant about this story for me is that at the very time these children were travelling south-west to love and safety in Cornwall, my own Aunt Sonya – born like several of the evacuees in 1927 – together with thousands of other Jewish children, travelled on a train going in exactly the opposite direction from Drancy, Paris to Auschwitz in Poland, where a very different fate awaited them.

While this book focuses largely on the stories I have been told, I have wanted to place them in their correct historical context. For this reason, the first three chapters are devoted to the background history of the events which subsequently unfold. Although I have had to keep these histories extremely brief, I have found it fascinating to juxtapose the history of Mousehole with the history of the Jewish East End and the JFS, for what emerges is the story of two extraordinary groups of people, whose coming together was bound to be a remarkable event.

Given that the majority of the book is based on oral history rather than fully documented events, there are inevitably going to be some inaccuracies and inconsistencies, for which I apologise. I have had to rely largely on memories of events which took place long ago, and people's experiences of these events were often very different. I have tried wherever possible to back up what I have been told with the few archival records I have been able to obtain, and I have done my best to check out the facts. In the end, many of the accounts point in the same direction. The picture that emerges, although at times blurred at the edges, is rather like an impressionist painting which increases in clarity as you stand back from it.

Susan Soyinka

December 2009

PARTICIPANTS

The following people have participated in the writing of this book. I met and recorded interviews with most of those listed below, other than those marked with an asterisk* who completed written questionnaires, or with a cross+, who were interviewed by telephone only.

VILLAGERS

Jeanne WATERS, now Harris, born 1925
Marian HARRIS, born 1926
Percy HARVEY, born 1927
Jack WATERS, born 1927
Bertha POMEROY, now Waters, born 1928
Sylvia PENDER+, now Johns, born 1928
Lily POLGREAN*, now Grose, born 1928
Melvia CORNISH, now Williams, born 1929
Myra PHILLIPS, now Ellis, born 1930
Joan LADNER, now Richards, born 1932
Derek HARVEY, born 1933
Raymond POMEROY, born 1935
Anne PENDER, now Beeton, born 1938

FORMER EVACUEES

Evelyn GOLDSTEIN, now Edelman, born 1925
Vera GOLDSTEIN, now Lubin
Frances FROMOVITCH, later Frome, now Pomm, born 1927
Cyril HANOVER, born 1927
Ted LABOFSKY, now Leigh, born 1927
Maurice PODGUSZER, now Powell, born 1927
Mildred FROMOVITCH, later Frome, now Moore, born 1928
Jack GOLDSTEIN, born 1929
Jose MARKS*, now Kirby, born 1929
Anita GODFREY*, now Cohen, born 1930
Connie MELLOWS, now Stanton, born 1931
Miriam ROAR*, now Conway, born 1931
Arnold PODGUSZER, now Powell, born 1932
Betty POSNER*, born 1932
Millie BUTLER*, now Shulman, born 1933
Shirley SPILLMAN, now Drazin, born 1933
Malcolm HANOVER, born 1933

Esther POSNER*, now Estelle Kaye, born 1933
Pamela BARNES, now Fields, born 1940

Two new contacts were made at an evacuee reunion held at JFS in October 2009, Eddie Lazarus and Solly Lederman, now Sid Leader, who were subsequently interviewed by telephone. Other evacuees contacted via telephone and e-mail were Frances Cohen (now Ayrton), Gloria Cohen (now Goldberg), Maurice Delew, Daniel Frankel, Ronney Glazer, Shirley Woolf (now Adler) and Julius Kosky, who was in Newlyn. Two other evacuees preferred to remain anonymous.

Several Jewish evacuees to other parts of Cornwall also made contributions by telephone and correspondence. These were Hilda Dickenholz (now Alberg), Irene Harris (now Glausiusz), Sonya Harris (now Brett), and Ingrid Rosenbaum (now Savir).

In order to preserve authenticity, I shall be using the names of each of the above as they were at the time of the evacuation. These are the people who will be telling their stories in these pages.

Chapter One

SNAPSHOTS OF PRE-WAR
BRITAIN: MOUSEHOLE

There's magic afoot in Cornwall
As you who are Cornwall's know.
For she twines your heart in her fingers
And never can let you go.
You may think to forget in the city,
But a hurdy-gurdy's strain,
A beautiful face, a colour,
Or lamps that swing in the rain,
And the old strange spell is on you
And the world shrinks to be
A green cliff in the summer
A green cliff and the sea

Augustus Mann[1]

MOUSEHOLE, A HISTORY IN BRIEF [2]

The county of Cornwall is a long and narrow piece of land stretching south-west towards the Atlantic Ocean. At its far western tip, as if dipping its toe in the sea, lies the Land's End peninsula known as West Penwith. The south of the peninsula is indented by Mount's Bay, on the east side of which is located the village of Marazion and the stunning tidal island of St Michael's Mount, surmounted by a castle dating back to the 12th century. As one moves westwards around the bay, one reaches first the large town of Penzance, then a mile beyond the fishing village of Newlyn and finally, two miles further along the coastal road, the village of Mousehole, with its picturesque granite cottages built into the steep hillside. Snuggled around the almost semi-circular harbour and embraced on either side by an ancient quay, Mousehole looks back eastwards over the entire bay and south towards St Clement's Island, lying just outside the harbour entrance.

'For many centuries,' writes Margaret Perry, 'Cornwall, almost entirely surrounded by water and situated in the far west of England, seemed remote from the rest of that country, more easily accessible by sea than by land. Railways and improved roads changed this but even today there is a feeling, crossing the Tamar Bridge into Cornwall, of entering a foreign land. Or, if you are Cornish, of "coming home".'[3] Mousehole has been particularly isolated, since the coastal road to Newlyn and Penzance was little more than a treacherous cliff path until the late 19th century. Access until then was mainly via a road through Paul, a small village containing the parish church less than half a mile away and up a steep hill inland.

Mousehole's geographic location and physical characteristics are closely entwined with its history. A stream runs down the valley, through the centre of the village from Paul at a joint between two types of rock, granite to the west and greenstone, or blue elvan, to the east. Not only does this mean that there is a plentiful supply of fresh water, but also that the rocks provide a natural harbour, further sheltered by St Clement's Island. Although Mousehole was difficult to approach by land, it was in fact the first port of call for any sea traffic from the Atlantic, so while turning its back on England, it faced out to the rest of the world.

There is some evidence of settlement in the vicinity perhaps as far back as 4000 BC, in the form of stone monuments and early tools. According to tradition, the Phoenicians and Ancient Greeks of the eastern Mediterranean traded with this area for tin, possibly from about the 10th to the fourth century BC. The Romans certainly had some contact, mainly in the form of tax collection, from that time to about AD 1000. By the Middle Ages, farming and fishing had become well established, but the name of Mousehole did not appear in records until 1242.[4]

There has been much speculation about the derivation of the name Mousehole, pronounced 'Mowzel'. One possibility is that it is an English term referring to a nearby cave mouth; however, some locals prefer to think of it as of Celtic origin, one suggestion being *moweshayle*[5] or 'women's river' in Cornish. Interestingly, an alternative Cornish name exists, *Porth Enys* or *Porthennis*, meaning 'island cove'. The term *porth*, pronounced *por* and meaning 'cove', is still used by the older inhabitants of Mousehole today to describe the harbour. There is some evidence that Mousehole and Porthennis were once adjoining settlements, but at some point Porthennis became the Cornish term for Mousehole. Some of the young Jewish evacuees who arrived in 1940 added their own version, having become convinced that Mousehole was a derivation of *mazel*, a Hebrew word meaning 'fortune' or 'destiny', generally employed in the expression *mazel tov*, or 'congratulations'. The name *Mazel*, one of them insisted, had been imported by the Phoenicians. Cornish historians have discounted the possibility of a Phoenician connection, but it is intriguing to note that the place names Marseilles in France and Marsa in Malta apparently derive from the Phoenician word for port.

The Cornish people are of Celtic origin and their language is closely related to Breton and Welsh. The Celts arrived in Britain and Cornwall from across the Channel in around 600 BC, possibly earlier. Despite numerous invasions and conflicts over the centuries, the Cornish people have managed to retain their distinctiveness, if not their independence. The Cornish language developed during the medieval period and traces of it are still evident in place names today, most particularly in West Penwith. However, by the 16th century the indigenous Cornish language was already being gradually replaced by English and its fate was then sealed by the Reformation. It was last spoken in everyday use in the most westerly part of Cornwall, very probably in Mousehole, though some other villages lay claim to this honour. A Mousehole man called John Keigwin (1646–1716) made great efforts to record the Cornish language and build up a literature in it. He was said to have been the last educated man to speak and write Cornish; however, the last native speaker is reputed to have been Dolly Pentreath, also of Mousehole, who died in 1777. Another Mousehole resident of that period was William Bodenar, who died later than Dolly in 1789. He both spoke and wrote in Cornish and is believed by some to have a better claim to having been the last speaker of the language. Among the factors which contributed to the decline of the language were the refusal of the authorities to translate the Bible into Cornish and the fact that it became unfashionable to speak the native tongue, which came to be regarded as the language of peasants. Recently, there has been an enthusiastic revival of the Cornish language and identity.

As the first haven for trading ships arriving from the south and west, Mousehole, together with St Michael's Mount, became the first settlement and harbour of note at a time when Penzance and Newlyn were still unimportant. There is an early reference to a grant in 1266 of a market and fair held at Porthenesse. In 1292 Edward I granted a charter for a weekly market at Mousehole, and a fair of three days at the festival of St Barnabas in June, while in 1332 Edward III extended the right to hold fairs to seven days. Manorial records of the time show that Mousehole had Burgess status, indicating that it was considered to be a town. In 1337, annual payments were levied on all ports, based on the number of boats fishing, which had to be paid to the Duchy. In that year, the port of Mousehole was assessed at 100 shillings, second only to St Ives at 120 shillings. This compared with 12 shillings for Penzance and 10 shillings for Newlyn. At this time, Mousehole, Marazion and St Ives were developing more rapidly than Penzance and had superior status. This importance was further reinforced when in 1389 a grant of land was made to build a 'Key' in Mousehole.[6]

Over the next two centuries, Mousehole continued to develop, weathering such events as the Hundred Years War with France (1337–1453), the Black Death (1348–49), changes in feudal law and the imposition of the English language in church services. Nevertheless, Mousehole continued to flourish, with port books showing increasing trade. Records from 1524 showed payments of £12 3s for Mousehole against only £7 7s for Penzance. 'This was perhaps the greatest century for Mousehole, growing in size, prosperity and importance. But this was to come to an end in 1595.'[7]

The most catastrophic event in Mousehole's history was, without doubt, the Spanish Raid of 1595. There are two written accounts of this event, one by Richard Carew in *The Survey of Cornwall*, 1602, the other by the Spanish Captain, Carlos de Amezola, commander of the four galleys which carried out the raid. In the late 16th century, King Philip II of Spain planned to invade England, but in 1588 the Spanish Armada was defeated by the naval forces of Queen Elizabeth I. Tensions continued, and early in the morning of 23 July 1595, when Sir Francis Drake was with his fleet at Plymouth, the Spanish captain landed between 200 and 400 men in Mousehole and proceeded to burn the entire village. Most of the houses of that time were simple thatched dwellings which burnt easily. The only house to survive the raid was the Keigwin, which was of solid granite construction and still stands today; however, its owner, Squire Jenkin Keigwin, was killed in the raid, believed to have been protecting his home. Nettie Pender, a

Mousehole historian, writes: 'He died with his sword in his hand. This sword (and velvet coat) was later left to my family and I remember it in my house when I was a child.'[8] Having devastated Mousehole, the raiders moved on to Paul, where the houses and church, together with all its records, were also burnt. Undeterred, the Spanish then attacked and destroyed Newlyn and part of Penzance. Mercifully, Marazion and the Mount were spared, as the Spanish galleys fled at the prospect of Drake's fleet, which by this time had been mobilised. Sadly, Mousehole never really recovered from this tragedy, and from then on began to be overshadowed by Penzance. A final blow came in 1663 when Penzance was granted coinage town status, thus increasing its shipping trade – to the detriment of Mousehole.

Having been traumatised by the raid and other events, some members of the Mousehole community resorted to the traditional Cornish occupation of smuggling over the next century and beyond, the Mousehole Cave having been used, according to legend, for hiding contraband goods. Smuggling was often seen as a legitimate activity and was not confined to the poor classes. Nettie Pender recounts the story of a certain old smuggler 'who was brought before a Justice of the Peace to answer to a charge connected with his illicit occupation, but when he pleaded "not guilty" the Justice, assuming an attitude and a tone befitting of his station, said "You know you are guilty, for you have been carrying on this trade for years." "Yes," said he, "and please, your Worship, but if you'll believe me, the last keg of brandy I ever sold was that which I brought to your Honour on such a night for which you honestly paid me."'[9]

Over a period of time, the community settled down and started to rebuild its fishing industry. Crucial to this was the development of the harbour. A quay had been built on the south side of the harbour following the grant of land in 1389 (known as the south or great quay), and this was extended in the 17th century. There is evidence of a very early quay in Mousehole, a 'little low quay' jutting out at right angles from the northern end of the wharf, which appears in a map dated 1515. This was replaced in 1838 by a new quay going out from below the Ship Inn, creating an enclosed harbour, but it quickly became apparent that this was inadequate for the large fishing fleet. Plans were drawn up to remove the pier built in 1838 and to use stones from that one to construct a new quay. The south quay was also further extended at this time. The work was completed in 1870, giving rise to the present-day harbour. In spite of this, by 1880 the harbour was once again considerably overcrowded, with over 100 mackerel and pilchard drift boats, in addition to many smaller craft.[10]

Fishing had, of course, been the mainstay of the Mousehole economy for centuries and the basis for its community life. Indeed, 'over the centuries and probably until the 1920s, fish dominated the life of Mousehole. The pilchard season started in July and went on for about four months. During this time every available person would be needed to get the fish ashore and into the cellars'.[11] Here they would be salted, pressed and squeezed into barrels, tasks often carried out by women, who were also involved in the making and mending of nets, and the production of garments for their men-folk. The houses were built to serve these purposes, with living quarters on the first floor reached by outside steps, and ground-floor fishing cellars with storage areas above for nets and fishing gear. The cellars were often open-fronted, with massive pillars supporting the upper floor, the houses being built, together with the adjoining ones, around a cobbled courtyard.[12] The entire village was festooned with fishing gear, nets hung from poles leaning against the harbour rails, or spread across the beach, and ropes, barrels, baskets and pots strewn everywhere. Some of the fish, both fresh and preserved, was for domestic use, but much of the preserved fish was sent along the coast to London, or exported to the Mediterranean ports and beyond.

Like many fishing communities, Mousehole has suffered more than its fair share of tragedies and disasters. Numerous fishermen have lost their lives at sea, and ships from other shores have often been wrecked in the vicinity. In 1907, the *Baltic*, a Thames barge, ran aground on St Clement's Island. The crew managed to clamber onto the island and were rescued by a group of Mousehole fishermen, led by Stanley Drew in the *Lady White*. This was quite a feat as the *Lady White* had first to be hauled by crane over the baulks that close off the harbour during the winter months. A young crewman on the *Baltic*, Adam Torrie, remained in the village, married a local girl, Janie Blewett, and had many descendants. In 2007 a plaque was placed on the harbour to commemorate the 100th anniversary of the event. At the time of the wreck, the lifeboat was in Newlyn and could not be launched because of low tide. Following this, a new lifeboat house was built in 1913 at Penlee Point, just outside Mousehole, from where it was possible to launch a lifeboat at all times. A poem was often repeated in the village after these events:

> Oh, what became of the Lifeboat
> When the *Baltic* ran ashore?
> They took the *Lady White*
> And launched her across the por.[13]

Within a few decades, Mousehole was to suffer another great tragedy. On 19 December 1981, a coastal vessel, the *Union Star*, got into difficulty during a terrible storm, at the height of which the waves were 40ft high and winds were gusting at 100mph. The Penlee lifeboat, the *Solomon Browne*, with its crew of eight Mousehole men, went to the aid of the stricken vessel. 'Both lifeboat and coaster, with their crews, were lost, a tragedy too recent to consign to the pages of history, other than as a reminder of the many other acts of heroism down the centuries.'[14] The victims were personally known to the villagers interviewed in the writing of this book and also to some of the evacuees, who were at school with them in the early 1940s. Like the Spanish Raid, this was one of those catastrophic events from which it has been difficult for Mousehole to recover.

Fishing was not, of course, the only commercial activity in Mousehole and its immediate environment, though its coastal location has always been of huge significance. Agriculture has been, and remains, a major occupation, and many of the fishermen were also occasionally involved in the tin industry. There was at one time a mine between Mousehole and Newlyn, and the Mousehole fishermen also used to walk to St Just to work in the tin mines there, when fishing was out of season. Tin mining in Cornwall dates back some 3–4,000 years, but reached its zenith in the late 19th century. However, towards the end of that century there was a sharp decline in profitability due to competition around the globe, and the Cornish tin industry suddenly collapsed, resulting in a mass exodus. Many sons of Mousehole emigrated to America, Australia and South Africa at this time. Remains of the tin mines can still be seen dotted around the Cornish landscape and have become a tourist attraction; indeed, tourism is the industry which has predominated in Cornwall since the early 20th century.

Several factors contributed to the development of tourism. One was the spread of the Post Office. A Post Office was established in Mousehole in 1844, following a petition to the Postmaster General from the villagers.[15] No doubt the postman's task, as well as that of villagers and visitors alike, was made easier by the development of the coastal road between Mousehole and Penzance some 50 years later.[16] However, the journey between Cornwall and the rest of the country was still most strenuous. In 1792 it took 40 hours in a heavy stagecoach, the *Fly,* which arrived at Exeter, from whence it was necessary to proceed westward on horseback. The journey from London to Penzance usually occupied about five days.[17] This would not have been much different by the mid-19th century.

Another important event, therefore, was the arrival of the train. Penzance's first railway station was built in 1852, with a direct link to London following in 1859. As we shall see, the railway network plays a crucial role in the story that will unfold in these pages. The new railway link brought economic benefits to the area, as it enabled the transportation of fish, vegetables and flowers to markets that were hitherto impossible to reach. Farming was transformed and fishing developed from a largely local market.[18] However, the greatest change that it brought was tourism: social changes after World War One created an affluent and increasingly mobile population, and hordes started to arrive in Cornwall, first by train, then more and more by car.

Even with the rail link to Penzance, there was still the question of the journey between Penzance and Mousehole. In 1910, the first regular service to Mousehole was introduced in the form of a wagonette, which ran three days a week. The service was operated by a one-armed driver, Mr J. Henry Matthews.[19] Dorothy Yglesias, co-founder of the Bird Hospital,[20] describes her first-ever journey to Mousehole in that very vehicle just two years later:

> Having come down by train from London, we were met at Penzance Station by a horse-drawn wagonette, the driver of which had only one arm. This added greatly to the exciting final stage of our journey. Leaving Penzance behind, the wagonette jogged westwards for the three miles to Mousehole. The cliff road now followed close to the shore, and the impression still lingers of the beauty made by forests of wild mustard swaying in the breeze against the background of blue sea. When we came to the steep hill taking us down into Mousehole, the reins were held between the driver's knees while he applied the brake with his one useful hand. We clung to the sides of the swaying wagonette, our mother petrified, but Pog, Mary and myself were in such a state of happy anticipation that we felt no fear. Suddenly the hill ended in a sharp turn and there was the end of our journey.[21]

It was not until the late 1920s that a proper bus service was introduced, with a stop-off point at The Parade, and a final stop on The Cliff, overlooking the harbour.

Mousehole's beauty has made it attractive not only to tourists, but also to artists of all kinds, who have used it, like Newlyn and St Ives, for inspiration. The writer Anthony Trollope, who was a Post Office Surveyor in the mid-19th century, came to inspect the Mousehole Post Office in 1852. He held an amusing conversation with Betsy Trembath, the postmistress, which he later, reputedly, used in the writing of his novel *Small House at Allington*.[22] Dylan Thomas, the Welsh poet, visited Mousehole several times during the 1930s. He met his wife Caitlin through contacts in the area, and they married in Penzance in 1937. The couple lived briefly both before and after their marriage in Mousehole. He described Mousehole as 'the loveliest village in England'.[23] Some Cornish people would dispute that Cornwall is part of England! Mousehole was also the location for a number of films in the 1930s and 1940s. Bill Blewett, the village postmaster, had a starring role in a GPO film *The Saving of Bill Blewitt* (sic), which recounts the story of a fisherman saving up to buy a boat. Further roles came his way; he also appeared in several other films, including *The Foreman went to France* by Ealing Studios and starring many famous names of the time, such as Tommy Trinder, Clifford Evans, Constance Cummings, Robert Morley, Thora Hird and Gordon Jackson.[24] It was partly filmed in Mousehole in the early 1940s, to the delight of the local children and evacuees alike.

Dorothy and Phyllis (Pog) Yglesias, originally from London, were also interesting newcomers, whose first arrival in the village is described above. They came from an artistic family and Pog became a well-known sculptress. In 1928 they founded the Jackdaws Hospital. The two sisters had an amazing compassion for, and affinity with wild birdlife, and succeeded in communicating this to the local children. After the war, the hospital was renamed the Mousehole Wild Bird Hospital and Sanctuary, and in 1953 it was handed over to the RSPCA, but funding was withdrawn in 1975. Since 1976 it has been run by a local committee and continues to attract hundreds of visitors.[25]

In the late 1920s or early 1930s (accounts vary) Mousehole became connected for the first time to piped water and electricity supplies, though some dwellings remained without both until after the war. In 1934, Mousehole, Paul and Newlyn became part of the Borough of Penzance. This is important to our story as the billeting of evacuees in the area was undertaken by officials of the Borough. Charles Tregenza, a Mousehole man, was elected first Mayor of the enlarged Borough, and the first mayoral Sunday took place at St Clement's Methodist Chapel in Mousehole.

A history of Mousehole cannot be complete without reference to the religious life of the community. For centuries, Mousehole has been a part of the parish of Paul. The church at Paul dates back to the 13th and 14th centuries but was almost destroyed in the Spanish Raid, after which it was rebuilt in 1600. Worshippers in Mousehole came under the auspices of this church but, wanting a more local shrine, built St Mary's Chapel, probably some time during the 14th century. The building was close to the harbour and when damaged by storm the following century was never rebuilt.

During the 18th century the village became converted to Methodism following several visits to Cornwall by John Wesley, the Christian theologian who founded the Methodist movement. He first went to Mousehole in 1766, by which time Methodists were already meeting regularly in the village. A small Wesleyan Chapel was built in 1784 at the bottom of Raginnis Hill, and this was rebuilt on a larger scale in 1825. A separate Sunday School was built adjacent to it in 1875, with further renovations taking place in 1905. In 1932, the Wesleyan Chapel was renamed St Clement's Chapel. A chapel dedicated to St Clement once stood on the island, appearing in a map dated 1515.[26] In a separate development, the Bible Christians, who were teetotallers, built a church in 1844, which in 1932 became the Mount Zion Methodist Chapel. This eventually amalgamated with St Clement's Chapel. The Salvation Army also had a lively presence in the village, complete with a band and open-air services. These took place on Saturday evenings on The Cliff (the road just above the harbour) up until the late 1930s.

Closely associated with chapel life, there is a strong musical tradition in the village. 'There were plenty of fine singers in the congregation too. Sopranos, contraltos, tenors, altos, basses, they were all there, men and women, young and old, married and unmarried, a whole community joining in sacred song.'[27] Some of this musical ability was put to good use in the staging of several operas in the late 1930s; however, the most famous manifestation of it is the Mousehole Male Voice Choir, founded in 1909 to sing carols at Christmas time. The choir has, since that time, gained an international reputation. There is nothing more lovely than to listen to the choir on a cool summer evening as they stand in the harbour singing in the open air, with the sound of the sea lapping gently in the background.

There was at one time a thriving Jewish community in Cornwall, though this largely died out at the beginning of the 20th century when the synagogue in Penzance finally closed its doors. A Jewish cemetery still exists in Penzance. An ancient *mezuzah*[28] was recently found on a doorway in Mousehole, indicating that at least one Jewish family once lived in the village even prior to the arrival of the evacuees.

MOUSEHOLE SCHOOL

Central to our story will be Mousehole School, first built in 1848. The original schoolhouse was a large building on the left of Paul Lane, situated as you leave Mousehole to go to Paul. 'With the exception of Paul Church School (built in 1821), Mousehole School was the only school in the parish of Paul [...] [Other local schools] are all of a much later date. Children from Newlyn and elsewhere in the parish attended Mousehole School.'[29] This perhaps explains the surprisingly large size of the school for a relatively small village. The curriculum of the new school was reading, writing, geography, arithmetic, scripture, history, and needlework for the girls, all of this being provided for the grand sum of 3d per week.[30] Although the school was required to be conducted 'upon the principles of the Wesleyan Society,' interestingly, the children were not required to memorise the Wesleyan or any other catechism.[31] In its early days the school operated a pupil teacher system, whereby the best pupils were trained to teach. The 1851 Census lists three of them: Joseph Mitchell aged 14, Joseph Madron aged 16 and Martin Wright aged 16, who later became the second headmaster of the school.[32]

In 1880 school fees were abolished, and at the same time attendance was made compulsory. This produced an immediate increase in numbers, making it necessary to consider an expansion. A Mr John Birch became headmaster in 1893 and was still in the post when Nettie Pender started school in 1897. In 1902 a new Infant School was built on the opposite side of the road, on a plot of land purchased, with great foresight, at the same time as the plot on which the original school was built. The main entrance to the school was on Paul Lane, with another entrance at the top of Foxes Lane. This was followed in 1911 by a new Junior School on the same site, the two buildings constituting the present-day Mousehole Primary School. The headmaster at that time was still Mr Birch, assisted by Mr Freddie Ladner. Mr Birch was succeeded at Mousehole School in the late 1920s by Mr A.J. Elford, who was still in post during the World War Two years and is well remembered by villagers and evacuees alike. Freddie Ladner became the headmaster of Paul School, where he was also in post at the time of the evacuation. After his retirement, Mr Birch served as Mayor of Penzance from 1937 to 1940, and it was he who welcomed the evacuees at Penzance Station.

Over the last 80 years, Mousehole has witnessed enormous change, due largely to the increase in the number of second homes and holiday homes. In 1930 there were a mere handful of these, but by 1970 summer lets and second homes totalled some 70 properties, a figure which increased to 170 by 1990 and well over 200 at the time of writing. During the winter, the village is deserted. Grocers' shops have reduced from eight in 1930 to only one now, while other specialist businesses have decreased from 12 to one. These have been replaced by numerous art galleries and souvenir shops, as well as cafes and restaurants. In 1930, every outlet was owned or run by local families whose names had been associated with the village for many generations; indeed, many of them can trace their ancestry back 400 years. Most of the businesses are now owned and run by incomers.[33] Physically, Mousehole has retained its beauty, having changed very little in this respect, but some would say it has lost its soul.

MEMORIES OF A MOUSEHOLE CHILDHOOD

The villagers interviewed were unanimous in saying that they lived an idyllic existence in Mousehole before World War Two. Without exception, all emphasize the sense of freedom, safety and community that they experienced during their childhood. They also stress the importance of family, the high value placed on children and the elderly and the centrality of the chapel to communal life. Jeanne Waters, born in 1925, and the oldest of the villagers interviewed, recalls her early childhood thus:

'I was born in this house where we're sitting. I've lived in Mousehole all my life, and apart from 10 years after I married, always in this house. I had two brothers older than myself, so I was quite the baby of the family really. My father worked in the railway offices in Penzance and Mother was just keeping house. My grandmother lived with us by the time I was about four or five and she was a wonderful old lady with lots of wonderful old sayings.

'It was a very peaceful village, with a very happy, friendly atmosphere, quite large families in small houses but always an extended family, never turning anybody away if any member of the family needed shelter or help as they got older. And you had loads of aunts and uncles, that weren't really aunts and uncles at all but were friends of your parents, and you could go in and out their houses and chat to them. We were a very contented little village. There was no bustle, never seemed to be an awful hurry at all, a very leisurely sort of life until we grew older. It was a wonderful place in which to grow up, I always feel that, no violence at all, a bit of naughtiness from the boys but that's all.

'And our life centred round the church because there were very few other places you could go and meet up with each other. We had a choral society in the village and a very good male choir which is just celebrating its 100th anniversary at this moment. And it was just very cosy. I suppose some people might have found it dull, but you could always listen to wonderful stories from some of the older fishermen. They sailed all over the world, and we loved, as children, listening to the stories they had to tell of the places they'd been. We would often, if we could, get one of the older men to talk. We loved to hear their stories.

'No mains water in those days and in the early days before the war, no electricity. I can remember both of those coming to the village when I was seven. So we used candles and oil lamps in the evenings in the winter months, and no street lights in those days either. We became part of Penzance Borough and we had mains water brought to the houses and we had electricity and street lighting, which we thought was wonderful.

'Of course, living right on the sea, in the summertime our chief joy was swimming and the boys would dive off the pier and would have little rowing boats. They would have just one oar and use it at the stern of the boat and *scull*, as they called it, they *sculled* across the harbour and out through the Gap and into the open sea. And it was just lovely.'

Marian Harris was born in the village in 1926, in a house at the bottom of Raginnis Hill. There she lived with her mother, her great-grandparents, Mr and Mrs Richard Trembath, and their daughter, Florrie Trembath, Marian's great aunt, who was like a grandmother to her. Auntie Florrie subsequently married Vivian Johns and moved to the Gurnick, where, as we shall see later, they hosted two evacuees. Marian here describes her childhood and the games the children played:

'I lived in the house on Raginnis Hill until my great-grandfather retired from his business as a smallholder and then we moved down to a cottage he owned on the harbour front. I hated that. I wanted to stay where I was, but anyway, I spent the next 30-odd years there. When we moved down to The Cliff, the buses had only just started coming to Mousehole regularly, possibly about 1929, the Western National and a couple of local firms joined in as well.

'When the street lighting came in about 1935, we were allowed out a little bit later. And I think just about every street light in the village had a hopscotch drawn on the road beneath it, so we were able to play hopscotch late into the evening. Our play was very unsophisticated, but everything was so safe in those days. Our mothers thought nothing of allowing us to go up into the country and having a camp or climbing trees.

'Summertime, of course, we spent all our time on the beach. The girls, particularly, played shops and houses, and each little group had their own favourite place with a flat rock, which could be either a pretend kitchen table or a shop counter. We used to use the very thick stones, and the big long seaweed. If you got a nice blunt old knife from home, that was absolutely wonderful, you cut the thick stem into small sections and they were sausages. Bread was granite stones of round shape and butter was the green seaweed which you squeezed the water out of, and made into little pats. For money we hunted around for bits of slate and I used to have bottles of them, of different sizes for pennies, half-crowns[34] or whatever. We used to make drinks which we sold and I shudder now to think of how much wildlife we killed off, because if you found a piece of softish brick, you rubbed it along the side of a small pool and it coloured the water, and that was cocoa. But anyway, shops and houses was the favourite game, and we could play for days and literally we were like King Canute, down on the beach trying to force the tide to go out quickly so that we could get to our favourite rock.

'The boys, of course, were fishing with their pin hooks on a piece of cotton, catching *bullcats* as we called them. Practically every boy in the village would have had someone, a father or uncle, who was engaged in fishing. And if the boats were out at sea, the *punts* were available for the boys to mess about in. When it was fine weather, they were always on the boats doing something or down in the harbour playing cricket at low tide. The harbour then was just alluvial mud, and rather smelly. Girls weren't allowed to play on the *por,* as we called it, but the boys were. They had their own rules for cricket. I think if you hit the ball over the back of the quay you were out, but scored six runs. Once when we had film people here during the 1930s, a well-known actor joined in with the boys and he was very popular because he bought new cricket balls for them.

'Of course, the filming during the 1930s meant that locals got parts as extras. I remember my mother once had half-a-crown for spending a morning on the new quay looking over the railings down at the boat, and everybody had to look sad because the story of the film was that someone had been lost overboard. Half-a-crown was a lot of money in those days for literally doing nothing except standing on the quay and looking sad. Some people actually got speaking parts. The Post Office made a National Savings film in the 1930s here and our village postmaster, Bill Blewett, made his name as a film star in that and he went on to act in several films. One of the boys from school, Jack Gilbert, was in it, and he just had to swing on the railings, and as Bill Blewett went by on his bicycle he had to say "Hello, Mr Blewett". A little condemned cottage was turned into a shop, and village people were standing in the shop as customers. It was very interesting.'

Percy Harvey was born in Foxes Lane, Mousehole, in early 1927, just a few weeks after Marian Harris, and they were in the same class at school. Although his family had originally been of fishing stock, his grandfather suffered from seasickness and went instead into the building trade. Just as Marian had moved from downtown Raginnis Hill uptown to The Cliff, Percy moved at a very young age in the opposite direction from uptown Foxes Lane to downtown Chapel Lane. His father named the new house Floriana, after a town in Malta where he had stayed during World War One.[35] Here, Percy describes life in the village before the war. It is clear that the boys' activities were much more boisterous and involved much more rivalry than those of the girls:

'We were a very close community, and living downtown I was a downtowner, although the rest of my family were living in what we called uptown. The village at that time was divided between the people to the east of Fore Street, the uptowners and the people south of Fore Street who were the downtowners. It was a sort of a territorial thing and we had different gangs. Being a downtowner, I was a member of Leslie Hicks's gang. The gangs used to have fights up in the woods and in another place called Betsy Perry's Park. On one occasion, one of the boys was captured by our gang and tied to a tree, and it wasn't until about five or six o'clock in the evening that his mother came and asked, where was her boy? And we suddenly remembered what had happened so we had to go back up to Betsy Perry's Park and untie a rather frightened young lad, who was still crying when we got up there.'

Leo Tregenza made an interesting reference to such conflicts in his book:

When a lot of boys get together, especially in a place by the sea, you can look out for troubles and alarms. The Mousehole men were generally inclined to be indulgent to their escapades, even to the ringleaders, whoever they happened to be at any particular time, for the salt sea was perhaps beginning to run in their veins. And they would make good fishermen later on, fights would often take place, some of historic proportions.[36]

These were not the only divisions in the village, as Percy reveals:

'The village was also split between Wesleyans and the Methodist chapel at Mount Zion, and the children that went to the Wesleyan Sunday School were quite separate from the children who went to the higher chapel Mount Zion Sunday School. That was one of the dividing areas because most people in Mousehole were Methodist. Very few went to church.'

Although there are historical reasons for this split, connected with the development of the Methodist church, Marian gives an interesting additional explanation for the division in chapel affiliations:

'Most people in the village are chapel-going non-conformists. I was down-chapel, the Wesleyan Methodist, and the other side, Mount Zion, was uptown. I think possibly that was because at one time there were two separate little settlements either side of the stream which runs down from Paul. I think that was it. And one outgrew the other. But it was up-chapel and down-chapel and never the twain shall meet, in my youth.'

According to Marian's explanation, the religious divisions in the village were related to the fact that there were originally two villages. This could equally explain the different social groupings, such as the boys' gangs. As the boys grew into men, some of their gang rivalry persisted into adulthood. Jack Waters, born in 1927, here describes how the gatherings of men in the village were often also divided between uptown and downtown:

'The ones on The Cliff, they wouldn't mix with they that's down side the pub. They were completely different. Well, they'd walk up and down chewing tobacco, spitting a bit and chatting, and then there used to be another big group down on The Wharf, the other side of the village. They would never come up on The Cliff to walk and they that's down the bottom, they wouldn't go up the top to walk. But it was, you know, a community thing. They just kept their different patches and had their own mates, like.'

The men's social gatherings used to take place when they were not out fishing, for example when the weather was poor. Jack himself recalls helping out the fishermen when they returned from sea:

'When I was a lad going to school I worked in a fish cellar. There were three fish cellars open in the village here, which meant that when the pilchard drivers came in full of pilchards, they used to all take out the nets, count it into baskets and then Dick Eddy with his horse and cart used to go down, take them off the boats and put them in a fish cellar in big vaults. And then they used to put them in the brine and salt, pull them out from that and the girls used to pack them in caskets.'

Despite these various divisions and rivalries it is nevertheless clear from Jack's account that there was a strong sense of community which existed throughout the village before the war. For Jack, community was typified by being able to pop into the neighbour's for a cup of tea or a chat, and for Bertha Pomeroy, a year younger than Jack, it was being able to ask your neighbour for an onion if you ran short. For Bertha, life in those days was 'one big happy family'. Bertha has particularly fond memories of children being taken on outings to the various beaches and occasionally as far afield as Plymouth, which they all looked forwards to for weeks in advance. Sadly, this stopped during the war due to petrol rationing, but was made up for to some degree by the reintroduction of the old tradition of galas, during which children would dress up and parade around the village carrying banners and flags and singing. Singing was, of course, hugely popular in the village as Percy here relates, together with a further account of the boys' games:

'Both chapels had singing festivals during the Sunday School anniversary, the chapel anniversary, the harvest festival, and places would be full of people singing. There were always lots of people vying to become members of the chapel choir and eventually the Male Voice Choir. Before the war, the Mousehole Male Voice Choir, they were all Mousehole boys. Nobody outside Paul Parish was allowed to join the choir.

'This never applied, though, to the football team because we had two managers who were always on the lookout for talent, and that came from all over the place. The football team always went to play in a field above Love Lane called the Sloping Field. Football was very popular and all the boys tried to get into the Mousehole football side. Some did better than others, some even played for the county, but they learned their arts and skills playing across the Sloping Field. This was also a field used by animals and a local chap had a horse and cart and kept his horse in this field. He wasn't very struck on youngsters running all over it playing football, so he hid behind the hedge and when the time was right he would run down the field and chase the boys.

'Another thing before the war, my father made me a rather posh go-kart; everybody had one then. We went all over town with these go-karts, no cars to interrupt us, and gunned down Raginnis Hill at high speed. My go-kart was reckoned to be one of the best because it had pram springs built in, so it was a rather springy affair. Even when I went to the Grammar School I had it when I came home in the evening.

'And this is how we lived in Mousehole in those days. Everybody knew everybody else and the village was small and reasonably sort of contained. Everybody knew who you were so that no children ever got lost, people kept an eye on everybody and it was a very close-knit community. When my father decided to get married to a Newlyn girl, they said, "Oh, she's the one that went round the Point [ie Penlee Point]." It was something that happened to one or two families, but mostly the people were married within the Mousehole community.'

Because there was so much inter-marriage in the village, many people share the same surnames and are, at the very least, distantly related. Some of the villagers interviewed were able to describe in exact detail how they were related to others going back several generations. As Percy recounts, all this started to change when outsiders arrived:

'A lot of strangers started coming into the village. One, Augustus John, who was a famous artist, came to see my father and bought an old fish cellar out at the Gurnick and had it converted into a flat. I can always remember coming home one evening from school and my father said, "The people have moved in, you'd better take the keys." So I went down, knocked on the door, and somebody shouted, "I'm coming." I was standing outside with the keys and Mrs John appeared. She'd obviously just stepped out of the bath and she was quite *starkers*. So, this strange woman who appeared with nothing on was quite an experience for somebody who'd been brought up in a Methodist chapel!'

Despite the freedom the children were given, there were certain strict codes of behaviour which emanated from their Methodist upbringing. Melvia Cornish, born in 1929, describes the village as a beautiful place to grow up in, and she looks back with great nostalgia on the time when she played for long hours in the sunshine and knew people everywhere. She remembers children going down to the quay in the early evening during the pilchard or herring season to wave goodbye to their grandfathers who were sailing out of the harbour to fish in the evening. Nevertheless:

'There were so many things you just didn't do and we didn't need to be reminded, such as picking up people's washing left to dry on the beach. We were not absolutely perfect children but standards were very, very pronounced, and we all knew we weren't allowed to be rude to older people or to call them by their first name. It was Mrs or Mr, unless it was a very close neighbour and you might be allowed to call her Auntie and the man Uncle. The men in the village all had nicknames and once I got into trouble because I called a neighbour at the back "Mr Peggy" instead of Mr Jones.'

In fact, many of the villagers at that time had nicknames, for example, Edwin Trembath, like his father before him, was known as 'Nipper'. To add even greater confusion, at least to the outsider, second names were often interchanged with first names. Melvia was not herself, as she admits, a perfect child, sometimes misbehaving even in chapel:

'In fact, when my friend Augusta Dennis and I used to go to the service, we giggled like anything. Our collection, which was a penny, probably fell on the floor at least twice with a clatter, and then we were on our hands and knees down under, looking for it. And one Sunday, to our absolute disgrace, Raymond Pomeroy's grandmother came out of her seat and sat in the middle of us, one each side of her, and we weren't allowed to speak another word!'

Interestingly, it was quite permissible to admonish a child who was not a relative, something that could certainly not happen in today's world. Melvia also got into mischief outside, being one of the few girls to play almost as boisterously as the boys. Indeed, some of her games were those one would more commonly associate with boys:

'I was an adventurous child. I climbed the crane that was on one of the piers, I ran across the coping and climbed up the quay and swung on the railings, and climbed trees. I think I was a tomboy. Well, we were free, we could go for hours and nobody worried about us. If we didn't play on the beach we went up to the fields where we played roly-poly. There was one field that we called the roly-poly field, and we would roll up and down that until we got tired and then perhaps we would do a quiet thing next, like sit and make daisy chains. My friend and I never showed up at tea-time in case we were kept in for the rest of the evening after tea.

'We went galloping through the village like maniacs, playing cowboys and Indians. I was always the cowboy and said "you, you and you are going to be Indians." "I don't want to be Indians." "Well, you can't play if you don't be Indians." And we'd play hide and seek and *coosing*, up over the wall, short cut across Mrs Somebody's yard, through gardens, up over walls, to get away from the people who were chasing, because we had to hide away. Sometimes we'd climb over the door of the British Legion toilet. I could climb over the wall and the door and I'd open it for my friends and we dived in there. Sat there chatting while they were going all over the village looking for us!'

Generally, however, the boys' and girls' games were very different, and this was even reflected in the school playground, as Derek Harvey, born in 1933, recounts:

'We all joined together in class, but the girls had their own playground. The infants didn't, the infants had a mixed playground. But the boys had their own playground and the girls had their own playground, and we never met outside of the school. After school, we all went home. Never hung about up there, soon as the bell went at four o'clock, in three seconds flat it was empty!'

Grandparents were very important in all the children's lives. Joan Ladner, born in 1932, has particular reason to remember hers, and her story illustrates just how closely-knit the community was:

'It was idyllic really, it was just lovely. We were so free in those days, and everybody was just really friendly. I don't remember being unhappy at all. You could go in anyone's house, the door was always open for you. I remember my grandmother lived next door. Sadly, she died in 1940 at the age of only 55, and she left me this house, so I had this house left to me at eight years old, which was odd. Granddad sat me on his knee and said, "You've got a house." A bit awe-inspiring when you're eight. It was rented out for £3 10s[37] for a quarter and that was the same rent till we came here to live in 1954.'

One person who was a veritable institution in the village was Nurse Pender, here described by her granddaughter Anne, who, being born in 1938, was the youngest of the villagers interviewed:

'My Granny, Nurse Pender, was the General District Nurse and midwife in the village, and my father was born in Mousehole. Our family go back to the 13th century. The Penders all came from around Mousehole. In the late 1920s, Granny had an accident. She fell down the stairs and was unconscious for some weeks and the older people remember that they had to put straw outside the house where the carts came by so they didn't disturb her because she was in a coma. My mother had come over from Ireland and trained as a nurse in Plymouth, and she was sent down to replace her because she did midwifery as well as general nursing. So people at that time were either delivered by my grandmother or delivered by my mother, who was Nurse Kneafsey.'

The first child in Mousehole to be delivered by Nurse Kneafsey was Melvia Cornish who was born in 1929. Anne continues:

'Granny had clinics in the basement of her house. I remember fishermen coming in with fish hooks in their necks, and she would stitch them up. And yes, she did everything, I suppose like a minor accident department, really. There was no doctor living in the village; Dr Young, I think, was the doctor and he was in Newlyn or Penzance.'

'In November 1933, there was a terrible tragedy. My grandfather, Julius Pender, was a fisherman but he didn't own a fishing boat, he was one of the crew. The boat he was on set out from Mousehole on a long trip, but just after they went out he had a massive heart attack, and he was laid out on the deck of the boat, which turned round and came back. People knew that something was wrong because the boat was supposed to spend some days away, so when it came back early, they all gathered on the quay, and because Granddad was on that boat, Granny came running down and she could see him lying on the deck. She jumped from the quayside on to the boat and her skirt billowed out in the wind, and it probably saved her life, because otherwise she would have been unable to save herself. It was a story that rocked the people of this family and the fishermen. My grandfather was only 60 and she was working at the time he died.'

Aerial view of Mousehole harbour, showing the harbour safely enclosed by the two quays.

Mousehole Harbour, by Geraldine Underell, 1940s.

Mousehole viewed from the Gap, by Margaret Perry, 1949.

The Cliff, by Margaret Perry, 1949. The bus stop, where the evacuees first alighted, is to the left of the photo. The third house from the right is the newsagents owned by the Ladners, where Shirley Spillman was billeted.

Mousehole Male Voice Choir, singing in a boat in the harbour, by Margaret Perry, *c.*1950.

St Michael's Mount and Its Own Cloud, by Geraldine Underell. This would have come into view as the train carrying the evacuees pulled into Penzance Station on 13 June 1940.

The First Away from Mousehole Harbour, by Geraldine Underell. The view of St Clement's Island from the quay. Frances and Mildred Fromovitch once swam to the island.

Taking Home Supper, by Geraldine Underell. Jack Goldstein describes fetching mackerel for his foster mother and bringing it home to Duck Street, the entrance to which can be seen on the far right of this picture of The Cliff.

A Mender of Nets, by Geraldine Underell. Several of the evacuees were taught to mend nets.

Waiting For the Milk, By Geraldine Underell. This is likely to have been the Matthews' farm, from which Frances Fromovitch sold milk.

Washday At My Backdoor, by Geraldine Underell. Nets can be seen hanging over the harbour rails on The Cliff. Vera and Evelyn Goldstein recall spreading out washing over the rocks on the beach.

Mousehole School, 1936. Melvia Cornish is the first child on the second row.

Mousehole School, c.1937. Bertha Pomeroy is second from the left on the second row. Edwin Madron is fourth from the left, bottom row, and Jack Waters is seated fifth from the left, next to Edwin.

Foxes Lane, Mousehole. Left to right: Jim Rowe, Lizzie Downing and Miss Humphrys. Mousehole School can be seen in the background. Jim Rowe is standing at the shoot where the villagers used to get water.

The 'haymarket' in Aldgate High Street, 1920s. (Springboard Education Trust)

Wentworth Street in the 1920s, looking east from Petticoat Lane. (Springboard Education Trust)

King George V Silver Jubilee celebrations in Grey Eagle Street, 1935. (Springboard Education Trust)

Gardiner's Corner, 4 October 1936, where many members of the East End community, of all backgrounds, clashed with Oswald Mosley and his Fascist Blackshirts. (Springboard Education Trust)

Some of the back yards in East London, *c.*1936, typical of the homes where some of the evacuees lived. (Springboard Education Trust)

Brady Street Dwellings, 1960, where the Fromovitch family lived. Other than the high-rise in the background, the street looks much as it did in the 1930s. (Springboard Education Trust)

The Great Synagogue, Duke's Place, 1938. (Springboard Education Trust)

The blitzed ruins of the Great Synagogue, 1941. (Springboard Education Trust)

Charlie Saunders as a young man, caretaker of Jews' Free School in the 1930s and 40s, and married to the Fromovitch sisters' Aunt Mary. He lived at the school.

The Fromovitch sisters, wearing sailor outfits sewn by their mother on the occasion of the Coronation of George VI in May 1937. Left to right: Marie, Frances, Mildred, Ada and Irene.

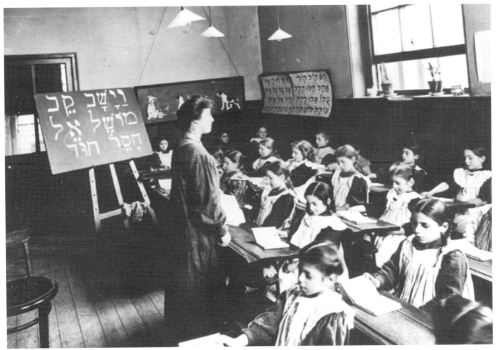

A girls' Hebrew class at Jews' Free School. (Springboard Education Trust)

Prize Giving Day at Jews' Free School, *c.*1930s.

Jews' Free School in May 1934. Ralph Barnes, wearing a white suit, is in the background, with his classroom above him.

Jews' Free School after the bombing in 1941. Dr Bernstein, the headmaster, is known to have clambered over the rubble, just like the man in the picture.

Jews' Free School, after the bombing in February 1941. The photograph was given by the caretaker, Charlie Saunders, to his niece, Mildred Fromovitch, and was possibly taken by him.

The evacuation of Robert Montefiore Senior School. Some evacuees think this school was used as a temporary school after their return from Cambridgeshire. The second evacuation may have started from here.

Young Nurse Kneafsey married Nurse Pender's son and they went to live in London, where their house was bombed during the war. By that time, Anne's father was fighting on the front line so her mother returned to Mousehole with Anne and her sister, Maureen, for the rest of the war. Melvia Cornish remembers the day when war was declared:

'We were at Sunday School and it was announced that we were at war with Germany. And then people were talking about bombings, men being called-up, older people were crying and we wondered what they were crying for. I can remember Jeanne Waters crying. But we couldn't understand what they were crying for because nothing had happened.'

Jeanne had very good reason to be upset:

'I was on my way from morning service at the chapel, and someone passing said, "War's been declared." My first thought was that Laurie and Eddie, my two brothers, would both have to go, that was the first thing I thought of. Eddie joined the Air Force, and my brother Laurie was in the Navy.'

Even the younger members of the village, such as Raymond Pomeroy, were affected by these events:

'Well, I was just four years old at the outbreak of war. I can remember some of the men that were going to war coming to see me in hospital because I had my appendix out at the end of 1939. Owen Ladner and Godfrey Ladner were going off to war and they came in to see me in the hospital. I always remember that.'

Like the Ladner boys and Jeanne's brothers, many young men in the village, fathers, husbands and sons, were called-up to serve in the war. This created a sort of vacuum in the community, both emotionally and physically. Not only did the villagers sorely miss their men-folk, but also many bedrooms in the cottages and houses became vacant, at least for the meantime. As elsewhere in the country, this was one of the factors that made it possible for the villagers to accommodate large numbers of evacuees. In the next chapter we shall examine the very different lifestyle of the children from London's East End during that same period. It is interesting to compare these two ways of life and to consider the impact on the London youngsters of being transplanted overnight into such a vastly different environment.

Chapter Two

SNAPSHOTS OF PRE-WAR BRITAIN: THE JEWISH EAST END

Pumbedita, Cordova, Cracow, Amsterdam,
Vilna, Lublin, Berditchev and Volozhin,
Your names will always be sacred,
Places where Jews have been.

And sacred is Whitechapel,
It is numbered with our Jewish towns.
Holy, holy holy
Are your bombed stones.

If we ever leave Whitechapel,
As other Jewish towns were left,
Its soul will remain a part of us,
Woven into us, woof and weft.

Avram Stencl [1]

ORIGINS OF THE JEWISH EAST END [2]

Jewish people have visited these shores since time immemorial, some would say as far back as biblical times. According to myth, King Solomon sent emissaries to trade for tin in Cornwall. As we have seen in the previous chapter, there is certainly a substantial body of legend which indicates that the Phoenicians, a Semitic people, traded with Cornwall. However, it was not until 1070, after the arrival of William the Conqueror, that the first Jewish community settled in London, initially in the City, having been invited by William to aid in his commercial activities. Banned throughout northern Europe from all other trades apart from medicine, the Jews had gained enormous expertise and capital in commerce but were entirely dependent on royal approval. Periods of a relatively peaceful co-existence were interspersed with years of severe persecution and cruelty, culminating in 1189 with massacres of Jews in London, followed in 1190 by a tragic event in York. Faced by death unless they agreed to convert, a group of 150 Jews fled for protection to the royal castle, where they committed mass suicide rather than give up their faith. [3]

In a sinister foreshadow of 20th century events, Jews in England throughout the 13th century were required to wear a distinguishing mark on their clothing. This was more strictly enforced in 1275 by Edward I, who stipulated that a piece of yellow taffeta had to be worn on the chest by every Jew over seven years of age. The end finally came on 18 July 1290, which coincided with the fast of Tisha B'Av,[4] when Parliament decreed that all Jews should leave England by 1 November of that year.[5]

During the next 400 years there were officially no Jews in England, though this was never fully enforced, as evidenced by the character of Shylock in Shakespeare's *The Merchant of Venice*, written between 1596 and 1598 which would suggest that Shakespeare had personal knowledge of Jews.[6] During the 17th century, Oliver Cromwell was favourable to the readmission of Jews and in late 1655, the Government agreed that it should be lawful for them to return. Following this, the first to arrive were Sephardim – that is, Jews of Mediterranean and Middle Eastern origin – who arrived from Spain and Portugal, but also Amsterdam and other parts of Europe to which they had previously emigrated. Again, this group was comprised largely of bankers and merchants. This time, the newcomers started to take up residence in the East End, where they opened a synagogue, a school and a cemetery. In the meantime immigrant Ashkenazim – Jews of central and eastern European origin – were slowly increasing in number. Unlike the Sephardim, the Ashkenazim were mainly poor and became involved in street trading, itinerant peddling and small-scale shop-keeping. The Ashkenazim also started to establish community charities; for example, in 1664, a communal physician was appointed at a salary of £10 per annum to attend to the poor, an office that continued until 1948.[7]

Over the 100 years following Cromwell, the rights of Jews in England became increasingly well established, and in 1753, a government bill was passed enabling Jews who had been resident for three years to become naturalised; however, this caused a public outcry, and later the same year the bill was repealed. Nevertheless, numbers steadily increased, and by 1800 there were about 10,000 Jews and four synagogues in the East End. Most famous were the Bevis Marks, opened by the Sephardi community in 1701, and an Ashkenazi synagogue erected in Duke's Place in 1690 but replaced with a more substantial building in 1722. This came to be known as the Great Synagogue. There was some dispute as to which rabbi had the right to the title 'Rabbi of London and the Provinces'. 'It was not until 1802, when Rabbi Solomon Hirschell was appointed by the Great Synagogue, that the matter was resolved. He became accepted and recognised as the first Chief Rabbi by the other London synagogues.'[8]

As the Jewish community grew, so did a whole range of charities, firstly among the Sephardi Jews during the 18th century, followed by Ashkenazi charities set up in the following century. Indeed, one of the most impressive features of Jewish communal development was the creation of a vast network of social, philanthropic and cultural organisations serving almost every aspect of the immigrants' needs. These included relief societies, provision of food, free dispensaries, hospitals and orphanages. The children's home founder, Dr Barnardo, although a Protestant convert, was the son of a Sephardi Jew who could trace his ancestry back in a direct line for 350 years.[9] In 1859, the Jewish Board of Guardians was established as a means of centralising relief efforts. It carries on its work today under the name of Jewish Care.[10]

In spite of a long tradition emphasising the importance of education, it was not until the early 19th century that the Jewish community started educating its children in any substantial number, the most notable school of the time being the Jews' Free School, whose history is outlined in the next section. One of the principle factors motivating this drive for Jewish education was the attempt by the members of various English organisations to convert Jews to Christianity, most particularly the London Society for Promoting Christianity among the Jews, founded in 1809. Although seeking integration and acceptance, Jews were determined to retain their own religious identity and found these attempts most distressing.

In spite of the social, educational and economic progress achieved by the first half of the 19th century, Jews in England were still deprived of many civil rights. Emancipation was perceived, to some degree, as a religious issue. Ever since 1534, it had been maintained that the Church of England was the only true religion, consequently Jews and non-conformists, including Roman Catholics, were barred from every avenue of public service, as they could not take the necessary oath on the Christian Bible. The Roman Catholics became emancipated in 1828,[11] but Jews continued to be excluded from sitting in Parliament, even though some had been elected. A number of Jews gained public office between 1833 and 1855 but it was not until an Act of Parliament in 1858 that they became fully emancipated. In 1858, Baron Lionel de Rothschild was elected and took his seat as the first Jewish Member of Parliament allowed to do so without taking an oath.[12]

For much of the 19th century, the Jewish rich and poor lived in close proximity and prayed in the same synagogues, but with increased acceptance, there was a steady move of the wealthy among them away from the East End and towards the more affluent areas of London, where the Jewish community gradually managed to become an established part of English society.

The situation changed drastically in 1881 following the assassination in Russia of Tsar Alexander II by a terrorist group which included a Jewish seamstress. The Jews were therefore blamed and, having been subject to considerable persecution in that region throughout much of the 19th century, now became the victims of a series of vicious pogroms which resulted in emigration on a massive scale. Between 1880 and 1914 there was an exodus of almost three million Jews from Eastern Europe, including two million from Russia and Poland and 450,000 from Austro-Hungary. Just over two million went to America, while 150,000 settled in Britain.[13] Those who came to England arrived by boat in London, dishevelled and disorientated, having survived an extremely hazardous journey during which they suffered yet further persecution. The East End was a natural destination due to its proximity to the London Docks and containing as it did an already established Jewish community, albeit of a very different nature to that with which the newcomers were familiar. The Jews who had worked so hard to gain acceptance in English society were alarmed that their own position might be jeopardised, and there were some unsuccessful attempts to deter the flow of immigration. Horrified, Chief Rabbi Hermann Adler implored his fellow Jews to welcome and support their oppressed brethren. There followed a 'crash course in integration', during which every available resource was mobilised – lay, ecclesiastical, philanthropic and educational. The schools, both Jewish and non-Jewish, were the main vehicles for integration, and, as we shall see in the next section, it was the Jews' Free School which came to play the most important role in this respect.[14]

The new immigrants lived in conditions of massive overcrowding. The home life of the majority of children attending school lacked the most basic of facilities. Privacy was unknown. Five or more children per family was common, with each family occupying just two or three rooms at most and the children frequently sleeping top-to-toe, several sharing one bed. Tailoring fathers and mothers used the living room as a workshop. Few people travelled far from home as poverty restrained them. Families lived close together, so that family visiting was the most frequently adopted form of recreation. As a result of this overcrowding, a large part of home life was lived out of doors. The more elderly sat in their doorways, enjoying the passing scene and chatting with relatives and friends. The smells of Jewish food wafted through the streets, and in the local markets every kind of Jewish food and goods was available: roll-mop herrings, *kosher* meat, salt beef, *cholla* and sweet pastries, as well as *menorahs*, candles and religious books. Adolescents searched the streets for excitement, no doubt getting into mischief, and the streets were the children's playground. During the last quarter of the 19th century a crime wave swept through England, and there were even suggestions that Jack the Ripper may have been Jewish. While this was highly unlikely, the involvement of some Jewish youth in criminal activities added to the call for increased educational opportunities.[15]

Work for the new immigrants was limited, and in order to secure employment they had to be prepared to work long hours in cramped conditions. One of the principal occupations was tailoring, which was undertaken in the most difficult of circumstances. When Jewish tailors went on strike in 1889, they were seeking a 12-hour day with no homework, an hour off for dinner, half an hour for tea and a six-day week. Other common occupations were cabinet-making, shoe-making and cigar manufacture.[16]

Despite all the hardships, and even a number of internal conflicts and disagreements, the Jewish East End developed into a vibrant community, its streets thronging with activity and excitement. Clubs were developed to keep young people constructively occupied: the Jewish Lads' Brigade in 1895, the Brady Boys' Club in 1896 and the Association of Jewish Youth in 1909. As people became more affluent, they moved out; however, following the Aliens Act of 1905, which effectively stopped Jewish mass immigration into the UK, there was a marked decline in the numbers of Eastern European immigrants.[17] By 1914, the Jewish population in the East End had declined to 100,000, from 125,000 a decade earlier, and by this stage the community had regained its stability.

Following the outbreak of World War One from 1914 to 1918, members of the Jewish community played an honourable part on active service, as they were determined to prove their loyalty to the country. In the years following the war, the community changed from being predominantly European-born to being predominantly British-born, partly because there was little immigration during and after World War One. The movement of Jews away from the East End continued apace, and by 1930 barely one-third of London's Jews lived there.[18]

During the 1930s, following Hitler's rise to power in Germany, there was a resurgence of anti-Semitism in Britain, and there were a number of clashes between East-Enders, both Jewish and non-Jewish, and Oswald Mosley's Blackshirts. By 1933, it was clear that events in Germany would be likely to lead to another wave of immigrants, and British Jews started making preparations for this eventuality. The sheer scale of events became apparent after the

German annexation of Austria in March 1938 and the events of *Kristallnacht* in November 1938, when 269 synagogues and 1,000 Jewish shops and dwellings were burnt. Thirty-thousand arrests were made and thousands of Jews were dispatched to concentration camps. Emigration escalated, and by the end of 1938 there were 38,000 German and Austrian Jewish refugees in Britain. By 1940, about 73,000 had been admitted. Some later moved on, principally to the United States, but it is estimated that 55,000 made Britain, and mainly London, their permanent home. Unlike previous immigrants, the new arrivals were largely middle-class and well-educated. Many had left a comfortable existence but now found themselves having to do menial work.[19] For example, the author's mother had been training to be a doctor in the Jewish Faculty of Medicine at Vienna University, but in 1938 she escaped to England, where she found herself faced with a choice of domestic work or nursing.

In 1939, the East End still had the largest concentration of Jews in London, some 60,000. With the coming of war in 1939, many young men served in the forces, and a large proportion of the children were evacuated. However, many servicemen and evacuees did not return to their homes, and by the end of the war the local Jewish community was reduced to 30,000. In 1940, the Blitz heralded the physical end of much of the East End. Many communal buildings were destroyed or damaged by bombing, including the Great Synagogue in Duke's Place and the Jews' Free School on Bell Lane. The last German rocket to hit London in March 1945 fell on Hughes Mansions, a residential block in Vallance Road, killing 130 persons of whom 120 were Jewish.[20]

The East End of London has for centuries been host to successive waves of immigrants from various parts of the globe. Following the war, the most recent immigrant community to establish itself in large numbers in the East End was the Bangladeshi community, living cheek by jowl with other immigrant groups. One building, more than any other, which symbolises the cultural and religious diversity of the East End is the London Jamme Masjid, at one time the largest mosque in the East End, which can be found on the corner of Brick Lane and Fournier Street. Originally built as a Huguenot Church in 1743, it became the home of The London Society for the Promotion of Christianity to the Jews in 1809, but was bought some 10 years later by the Methodists for whom it became their main chapel in the area. In 1898 it became the Machzike Hadas Synagogue, when 10 classrooms were built on the roof to accommodate over 500 children in the Talmud Torah. Finally, in 1975, it became a mosque.[21]

In the past two decades, developers have taken over and transformed the area beyond recognition: tenement blocks have been restored and are now worth millions; shops and warehouses have given way to vintage clothes stores and up-market bars, boutiques and restaurants. Despite some of its grim past, many former and current residents regret the loss of the vibrancy, character and neighbourliness of this historic area.

JEWS' FREE SCHOOL: A BRIEF HISTORY[22]

The Jews' Free School, London – or JFS as it is now known – is one of the oldest Jewish schools, if not the oldest, in existence and one of Anglo-Jewry's most important institutions. It has had a remarkable and colourful history: among its admirers was Tsar Nicholas I of Russia who in 1845 donated the sum of £50 to the school's funds.

The school started life in 1732 in Spitalfields, the Jewish quarter of the East End of London, as a Talmud Torah attached to the Great Synagogue in Duke's Place. Priority was at first given to religious and Hebrew teaching, but in 1788 the curriculum was extended to include English reading and writing and arithmetic. In 1817 a school, for boys only, was opened in Ebenezer Square close to Duke's Place, Petticoat Lane and Brick Lane, 'the heart of the then poverty-stricken, unhealthy and unwholesome surroundings of a dense web of courts and alleys'.[23] On the first day 102 pupils enrolled, aged from seven years upwards. For many years the school adopted a monitorial system which involved the teacher teaching selected pupils or monitors, who then taught the other pupils. Israel Zangwill, author of *Children of the Ghetto*, was a pupil teacher at JFS.[24]

The numbers rapidly increased, and pressure grew for the school to admit girls also. In 1822, land was purchased and a purpose-built school the size of a city block was constructed, making JFS probably the first purpose-built Jewish school of the modern era.[25] These new premises were in Bell Lane where the school remained until 1939, when all the children were evacuated. Close by was the Jews' Free Infant School, established in 1841, which became a main feeder school for JFS. The Infant School had two branches in Commercial Street and Buckle Street.[26] The Girls' School opened with 170 scholars, but by 1853 there were more than 500 girls in a department originally designed for 300. The emphasis for the girls was less on academic studies and more on domestic training. Furthermore, unlike the boys, the girls were made responsible for cleaning their classrooms!

As we have seen, during the latter part of the 19th century there was an influx of Jewish immigrants from Russia and Poland. By 1900, the school roll had increased to 4,250. At that time it was the largest school in Europe and probably the largest in the world. Between 1880 and 1900, JFS educated more than one-third of all London's Jewry of school age. This rapid expansion resulted in major alterations to the school's premises which were carried out in 1848, 1855, 1866, 1883 and 1898. The last addition was called the Rothschild Wing and opened onto Middlesex Street, better known as Petticoat Lane. So great was the demand for places that the police had to be called in to keep order on registration day. 'Despite its modern up-to-date buildings, JFS could not escape its surroundings. *The Sphere* described Bell Lane in 1905 as a "narrow and somewhat squalid thoroughfare…" Petticoat Lane was a bustling street, crowded with shops, stalls, men and horses, full of activity, set in a maze of narrow alleyways. The streets were teeming with musicians, vociferous street traders and market stallholders – colourful but rowdy, and not conducive to quiet study and teaching.'[27]

In the light of this background, the achievements of JFS have been many. For more than 100 years, the majority of its pupils arrived at the school unable to speak English. It provided them with a refuge, educated them in both secular and religious studies, anglicised them and sent them out into the wider community prepared to contribute to the well-being of society.

Anglicization was the process by which pupils were taught to 'adapt to English usages in speech, in manner, in mental attitude and in principles, in such a way as to enable them to integrate successfully into the wider community. This integration was a fundamental aim of JFS.'[28] It was regarded as the route to acceptance, and a means of avoiding the anti-Semitism which new immigrants, in particular, so often attracted. This was not seen as full-scale assimilation. Pride in being Jewish and observance of Jewish religious traditions were encouraged to the fullest extent. The speaking of Yiddish was, however, discouraged as it was perceived as an obstacle to anglicization, and this caused some rifts within the community.

At a time when it was difficult for a religious Jew to obtain teacher training experience, JFS operated as a teacher training college and played a significant role in countering the efforts of Christian missionaries seeking to convert the East End Jews. Most importantly, 'it furnished thousands of Jewish children with an escape route out of poverty'. 'JFS is an honour not alone to English Judaism' said the visiting Chief Rabbi of France in 1891, 'but to Jews throughout the entire world.'[29]

The school has had many distinguished teachers and supporters. Moses Angel (1819–98), headmaster from 1842 to 1897,[30] was one of England's most respected educationalists, despite being the son of a transported felon. When first appointed, he was given a salary of £140, a free house and free coals. He devoted himself tirelessly, almost obsessively, to ensuring that the pupils in his care received the highest standard of education possible. 'No matter how early you came,' said one pupil, 'he was there before you.' He was there when you left too. His tall figure was to be seen 'standing erect at the small door in Bell Lane, his keen eye directing the outpouring of the thousands of his charges in the narrow thoroughfare'.[31] He imposed no selection process. If a child was Jewish and poor, his claim to admission was recognised. Moses Angel and his two immediate successors, Louis Abrahams and Lawrence Bowman, covered an unbroken period of almost 90 years. In the past 187 years, there have been only 15 headteachers, though that does not include all those of the Girls' School nor the Boys' Central School.

The school has enjoyed the philanthropic support of the Rothschild family since 1817, the family providing the school with its presidents from 1847 to 1961. The women of the Rothschild family were as generous as the men, donating not only money, clothes and food, but also their time to working with children in the school. By 1939, 11 members of the House of Rothschild had taken part in the government of the school. Such continuity of staff and support has given the school an enviable tradition that has impacted on succeeding generations of pupils.

The Education Acts of 1902 and 1903 led to a more general availability of secondary schooling and provided for government assistance to voluntary schools. In 1905, the school came under the jurisdiction of the London County Council (LCC), which at first threatened the long-established independence of the school but was a necessary move in order to attract state funding. Two years later, the senior section of the school was reorganised to include a Boys' Central School, completely separate from the main body of the school, and occupying an upper floor with its own roof playground. In 1931, the Central School was officially recognised as a separate school, under the headship of Morris Buck.

The Jews' Free Infants' Schools provided for children between the ages of five and seven years, while Jews' Free Elementary School catered for the seven to 14-year-old age range, seven to 11 years being the Junior School and 11 to 14 the Senior School. With the advent of JFS Central, all the boys took an examination at the age of 11 and those who passed went on to JFS Central until the age of 16, while those who did not pass, as well as the girls, remained in JFS Senior School. The brightest children went to the Central Foundation School, which was the equivalent of a Grammar School, where they took the Matriculation Examination at 16.

Despite the declining Jewish population in the East End during the early part of the 20th century, accompanied by a fall in the school roll, the years between 1907 and 1939 in many ways represented a golden era of prosperity in the school's history. During this period, JFS was most certainly the finest-equipped elementary school in England, and a range of extra-curricular activities were developed. In 1907, Play Centres were opened, and in 1911, in keeping with the school's musical tradition, a brass band was formed.

In 1931, the newly appointed headmaster, Dr Enoch Bernstein, who had been a teacher at the school for years as well as being a former pupil, installed a pottery room. Other innovations included a machine-shop, a forge, a foundry, a printing room, a planetarium, a rock garden, an experimental farm, an aviary and an aquarium. This was in addition to improvements in the already existing science laboratories, museum and library. In 1938, a 5" gauge model railway was built in the playground. Dr Bernstein also presented film shows of his travels around the world. He built on a tradition of school outings, which had mostly been within London to museums, galleries and theatres, by starting to take the children further afield. One of the last outings was in April 1939, when Dr Bernstein and Mr Ralph Barnes took a party to Devon, accompanied by their 3in refraction telescope to aid them in their 'sky work'.

The Girls' School had a fully-equipped model house, which was opened in June 1936 and provided an excellent opportunity for teaching and practice in housecraft for the older girls. The bathroom of the flat was in constant use, and every school day 80 to 100 pupils, who had no bathroom at home, bathed during school hours. For, of course, it should be remembered that all this was achieved in the context of an impoverished local community.

In spite of this excellent work, by February 1938 the total school roll was down to 1,122 (270 in the Central School, 470 in the Boys' School and 382 in the Girls' School), due to a range of social, political and economic factors. The overwhelming majority of immigrants had arrived poor, few spoke English and they engaged in work that was irregular and low paid. As already seen, with the assistance of the better off in the community, a network of efficient charitable organisations was set up whose main aim was not simply to provide immediate relief, but relief accompanied by the means to enable the poor Jews to pull themselves up by their bootstraps. This they did, without compromising their religion or their Jewish identity. The part played in all this by JFS and the other Jewish schools cannot be exaggerated.

The beginning of World War Two marked the end of an era for the Jewish East End and for JFS. Pupils and staff (those not in the armed forces) were evacuated in September 1939 to Ely, Cambridgeshire, and the surrounding district and then, in June 1940, some of them went to Mousehole in Cornwall. In 1941, the school buildings, then occupied by the Fire Service, were severely damaged by bombing. By the end of the war most of the East End's Jewish population had left the area, not to return. It appeared to be highly unlikely that the school would continue after 1945, but through the foresight and determination of a handful of men and women, both its governing body, and equally importantly its assets, were kept intact. After an interval of 13 years, the Jews' Free School re-established itself in Camden Town in 1958.

After 43 years at Camden Town, the school, by then a mixed comprehensive catering for 1,500 pupils aged 11 to 18, outgrew its site and moved to Kenton in September 2002, where it now enjoys accommodation for 2,100 pupils in ideal surroundings and with first-rate facilities. The official opening of the new school on 14 October 2002 was attended, among others, by Mr Ralph Barnes, the last surviving male teacher of the original Bell Lane School, and one of the teachers evacuated to Mousehole in June 1940. He appeared in a photograph together with the Prime Minister Tony Blair, who was principal guest.

MEMORIES OF CHILDHOOD IN THE JEWISH EAST END

Almost all of the children evacuated with Jews' Free School to Cornwall were born and raised in the East End, many of them in very poor circumstances. A good proportion of them were the children, or grandchildren, of immigrants from Eastern Europe, and many of their parents carried out the traditional Jewish trades of shop-keeping, market trading and tailoring. This was a close-knit community, where extended family ties were of the utmost importance and where people tended to know one another. In this respect, the East End was more like a village than part of a city.

Some at least of their teachers also had their origins in the East End, but by this stage they had climbed the social ladder and moved out to more affluent areas. Mr David Levene, a very religious man who was the party leader, lived in Middlesex and commuted daily to Jews' Free School. His two teenage daughters attended Henrietta Barnett School, situated in Hampstead Garden suburb. Mr David Nathan lived in Hendon, and his son Bennet attended Finchley County School. Mr Ralph Barnes was the youngest of the male teachers, and both he and his wife Jean were originally of Russian stock. The family name had originally been Abrahams, and, like many Jews, this had been changed as part of the process of assimilation. His daughter Pamela, although not born till 1940, describes the early life of her parents:

'My father was one of eight. He was the eldest son and came from a pretty poor background, living in the East End of London. His father was a tailor so we were "working class", and from the stories I've heard over the years, times were tough. With eight children, his mother's work was just non-stop, day in, day out, and they lived, I think, in a very small house. They did have a back yard because I recall him telling me about having chickens.

'My mother was the elder of two sisters, and she was about eight years older than her sister, again not from a wealthy background. Her mother was third generation English, but her father had actually come over from Russia as a young man immediately after the pogroms, and he was working as a tailor in the East End. But very self-taught, my grandfather was, and the stories of my grandmother are that she was a wonderful home-maker and a wonderful cook.'

Pamela goes on to say that her father had an uncle who was a teacher, to whom he looked up and he decided, therefore, that he also would become a teacher. Ralph told the story in his own words in an article written in January 2003 to *Goldlink*, the Alumni magazine of Goldsmiths College.[32] At the time of submitting the article, he was 92 years old:

> I was a student at Goldsmiths from 1929–31. They were interesting and happy years…
>
> An uncle of mine, Mr Isaacs, advised me to apply for a teaching post at the Jews' Free School, Bell Lane in the East End of London, which I did. I was well aware of the school's reputation and its high standards of teaching. My father had been a pupil there in the 1880s and Mr Isaacs, my mother's brother, was teaching at the school. My application was successful, and my teaching career started in August 1931.
>
> I was given a first-year form of boys and I was responsible for teaching English, a comprehensive subject which included reading, writing, spelling dictation, composition, poetry and grammar. Also included were history, geography, arithmetic and PE, music and woodwork, which were taught by specialists. The headmaster, Dr E. Bernstein, was very resourceful. In addition to the main subjects taught he introduced a printing press, pottery, basketry, a model house and the model railway. Prior to going on a school journey to study the stars at night, the head asked me to accompany him, and had a telescope made in the metal shop. He also wrote a booklet on the constellations. I printed the book and still possess and treasure it today. In addition to my school work, I was also sports master. The school was my life, and I was very proud of it.

According to Charles Graham, widower of Pamela's sister Lydia,[33] Dr Bernstein, the headmaster, took Mr Barnes under his wing. Charles described Ralph as a great sportsman, and he knew also of his involvement with the printing press in JFS. Charles had himself been in the printing business, and he came across many people who had been taught by Mr Barnes and remembered him with affection. Many of the former evacuees also spoke of Mr Barnes' sporting abilities.

Ralph and Jean Barnes got married in 1935 and spent their honeymoon in Looe, Cornwall, so they were among the few people in the party to have visited that area prior to evacuation. It was after their marriage that they moved out of the East End:

'After Mum and Dad got married, they were very fortunate to get their own house in Palmers Green, North London. And so up until the time of World War Two, that's where they lived. Dad had quite a long journey to JFS, because I can recall him saying that in those days the trains ran like clockwork.'

A small number of the evacuees were also relatively affluent. Maurice Podguszer lived with his family just outside the East End, together with his older brother, Peter, and his younger siblings, Gloria, Arnold and Michael. Maurice describes his early family life:

'We were a family of five children, living in Old Street, EC1, and my father was a businessman, he ran an artificial flower and feather manufacturing company, mainly for the millinery trade. We had a very comfortable life and were probably considered to be rather an affluent family. There was a quite a big extended family including my father's brothers and his children, and my mother's family was even more extended with a great number of cousins. We met occasionally and we were a very happy and well-looked after family.'

At the outbreak of war, Maurice was attending Jews' Free School. He recollects that Dr Bernstein, the headmaster, was very much a public figure in the Jewish community. Maurice's younger brother, Arnold, remembers that, apart from playing in the local churchyard, his leisure time was spent mainly with his parents or visiting his grandparents at the weekends. In spite of the family's relative affluence Arnold reports that there was no bathroom in the house, so once a week the family went to the baths in Bath Street. With regard to religion, Arnold's recollection is that the family were not particularly observant other than during the main festivals, occasionally attending synagogue on a Saturday. The Podguszers changed their name to Powell in 1942.

Cyril and Malcolm Hanover's family were also better off than some of the other evacuee families, though Cyril recalls:

'I remember the Podguszers being richer than the rest of us. Their father was very well-spoken. His business was something to do with feathers, they were called the Davis Feather Mills Company.'

The name of the company was in fact *The Ostrich Feather Manufacturing Company*, but this comment nevertheless shows the extent to which everyone knew everyone else within the community. The Hanover family lived in Old Montague Street, described by Aumie Shapiro as being 'the very heart of the Jewish East End'. Their father was 'the one and only Jack Marks, possibly the most well-known fruiterer in the East End'.[34] Cyril Hanover describes his life thus:

'I was born in the London Hospital in Whitechapel, E1. My brothers were Malcolm, Ernest and Dennis, and I had a sister, Marie. They were my family. Even bigger families of seven or eight were commonplace in those days. We were well brought-up and our father was well-respected. Well, going back many years, my parents had a fruit and veg shop and were well known in London's East End. It was a very, very, thickly Jewish community in that area at the time. We had a wonderful family life and lived a very happy, contented and peaceful life until the war came.'

Anita Godfrey and her brother Irvine lived in Bell Lane, immediately opposite the entrance to JFS which they attended, and were also relatively affluent. Their father was a fruit and vegetable importer, born in England, but their grandparents were of Lithuanian or Russian origin. Most of the other evacuees were less fortunate in their circumstances, in spite of the fact that their parents were hard-working, industrious people. Ted Labofsky, who lived in Flower and Dean Street, describes his early family life:

'I was born in the East End of London, Spitalfields, which is very near to the Free School. My parents both worked in the tailoring industry. My father was a tailor and my mother was a felling hand. We had a very poor life really, before the war, though we never went short of food. We all lived in one bedroom and one front room and a very small scullery. Nothing really happened much before the war. I went to Jewish Lads' Brigade and went to camp a few times, and that's about it. We spent our free time mostly playing football and cricket in the playground in the tenement buildings where I lived. The buildings went round in a four square and the playground was in the middle. When we had the Coronation and the Jubilee parties, we would usually have them in the playground.'

But for Ted, like many Jewish boys, there was very little leisure time in those days:

'Mostly it was school. We went to school at eight, nine o'clock in the morning till four, came home, had some tea, and went to Hebrew classes, which we called *Cheder*, till eight o'clock at night. Came home and went to bed. And this was five days a week, and Sunday morning we went to *Cheder*. Free School had Hebrew classes in the morning, on Sunday, and in the afternoon we went to the *Cheder*, the Hebrew class in the synagogue. So the only real day we had off was Saturday. Saturday we spent most of the time going round to my grandmother, my *Buba*, and spent most of the day there. So we didn't go to services on Saturday morning.'

Living further to the east were the five Fromovitch sisters, three of whom, Frances, Mildred and Irene, went to Mousehole. Like other Jewish families with foreign-sounding names, the family changed their name to Frome in 1942. Mildred describes the hardships of their early life:

'We were a large family living in Brady Street Buildings. Our father was a tailor. There were seven in the one bedroom flat, no bathroom. Life wasn't easy, especially for my mother, a very dignified lady. It must have been very hard for her with a big family, and the facilities were appalling. But we were happy. One sister, Frances, was always helping but my oldest sister, Marie, was always reading, and the other ones were too young to help.
'When the war started my father joined the ARP [Air Raid Precautions] in Brady Street as he was too old to go into the army. My sister Ada went to a special school in London for handicapped children. She had problems with her back so for a year she had to sleep flat in a long carriage. She was born with a curvature of the spine. There weren't many toys, but we played and we made up games, as children did in those days. And we just got by.'

Mildred's older sister, Frances Fromovitch, elaborates:

'We weren't very rich, quite poor in fact, but we were lucky because my mother made all our clothes; she was very clever. We lived in a flat with one bedroom for the whole family. Two of us slept in the living room in a put-u-up. The others slept in the bedroom. So really we didn't leave much behind when we left.'

The girls played either in their flat or in the playground contained, like Ted Labofsky's, within their tenement building, as Frances recalls:

'We just didn't do much; played in the playground, went to the library which we all loved and that was all. This playground was in the middle of all the flats, and often we didn't need outside friends because we played with each other. There were five of us. We went to the pictures sometimes with one another, the pictures costing thru'pence each and sixpence for my mother.'

And, as we have seen with many other children of the time, visiting grandparents was an integral part of the weekly routine, as Frances recollects:

'My grandparents lived in Aldgate, which is not far from Whitechapel, and we'd go there to visit at different times. And on Seder night, on Passover, we'd go to my grandparents. The other grandmother lived downstairs, so she lived in the same building.'

The Fromovitch sisters did not attend JFS as it was too far away from where they lived. Nevertheless, they had a strong connection with the school as their uncle, Charlie Saunders, a non-Jewish man married to their Aunt Mary, was the caretaker at JFS and lived on the school premises. The caretakers of synagogues and Jewish schools are generally not Jewish to enable them to work on Saturdays, as it is forbidden for religious Jews to work on the Sabbath. The Fromovitch sisters' connection with JFS, through their Uncle Charlie, was to prove to be important. While many of those interviewed recalled happy childhoods, in spite of their impoverished circumstances, Frances was clear from a young age that she wanted a different life for herself:

'Although – what can I say? – you don't have to like where you were born. I never liked the East End and it's as though I knew about Mousehole. That's the strange thing. I never liked the East End of London. What is there to like? Rough sort of people, you know, drunk people, which we never saw in our home, but drunk people, little children sitting on the step waiting for their parents to come out of the pub. That was true because we saw it. No, it wasn't a wonderful place.'

The Goldstein children, Evelyn, Vera and Jack, also lived in rather difficult circumstances. Their father had a fruit stall in Petticoat Lane, and some of their aunts and uncles also traded there. Mr Goldstein had left the family, and their mother struggled alone to meet the needs of her children, in the process being obliged to move repeatedly from home to home. At the time of the war they were living in Cartwright Street. Evelyn is very clear that it was not a very happy childhood, and her sister Vera agrees:

'Before the war I lived with my mother, my sister and my brother. We were very poor. My mother had to work, and I belonged to the Girl Guides, and I used to get home early at night and do a lot of knitting and embroidery. I didn't go out much in the evening and we didn't have a lot of relations nearby, so it was more or less with my immediate family.

'We played games in the street, as kids did in those days, with balls and chalk and various things like that. But we didn't get out much because we lived in a tenement and it was very difficult to get down the stairs and then to come up again, so we more or less stayed in our home doing various hobbies. We liked to play games, Ludo, snakes and ladders, reading, things like that.'

Jack Goldstein tells a similar story and gives an interesting description of the kind of homes people lived in, referred to above by Ted and Frances:

'Well, we lived in the vicinity of the Jews' Free School in the East End and we were quite poor. And apart from school activities, we never had many other activities because we couldn't afford to do much, so there's not lots to tell really.

'Nobody that I ever knew had a house, they all lived in blocks of flats, called tenement houses. They were built in Victorian times, even earlier, and they were quite high and had about four or five floors, which were let out. On one floor there'd be a family, another floor there'd be another family. And there were hundreds and hundreds of those in the East End, and most families lived all their lives in them.'

For all three Goldstein children, life began to improve when they started attending Jews' Free School. Jack Goldstein has particularly happy memories of JFS, not least because it gave him opportunities to participate in activities that his family could not otherwise have afforded:

'I went to JFS. It was an enormous building with over 1,000 boys. One side faced Middlesex Street and the other Bell Lane. I remember the class I was in, in 1939; a Mr Rose, he was a lovely master. Before the war, Dr Bernstein was the headmaster of the whole of JFS. One thing I liked about him was that in the summer holidays he used to go to the United States. He had a very good cine camera and he used to take films of his journeys and show them to us on huge screens. I used to love it; it was like being in a cinema. Wonderful.'

Betty and Esther Posner, who lived in Chicksand Street, were also very poor. Their father worked in a millinery factory. Here they tell their story:

'Our mother came from Poland in the early 1930s to marry our father, who was Russian and 20 years older. She was illiterate. We spoke Yiddish as children. She didn't talk much about her experiences. We were very poor. Life was hard, food scarce and lacked variety, and we were thus undernourished. But we were happy children!'

Also of Polish background were Max and Ida Selner, whose parents came from the same village in Poland as the mother of Lily and Miriam Roar, showing just what a close community many of the evacuees came from. Lily and Miriam attended JFS Infant School on Buckle Street. Connie Mellows was of immigrant background too, her father having been born in the Ukraine. He came to London with his parents in 1898, but he did not become a British citizen until after the war. Connie did not learn about the original family name, Malofsky, until she married. She recalls her early life:

'I lived with my mother and father in Bishopsgate where my father worked in a shop and we lived in a flat on the second or third floor of the building. Consequently JFS was just around the corner from my home. The entrance to the Girls' School used to be in Frying Pan Alley. I had a very quiet life with my mother and father, but a family life. I had no brothers or sisters.

'I remember there was a girl friend who used to live round the corner in a flat in Middlesex Street. I knew her as Rica. I remember dressing up a lot, playing with dolls, and going to see my grandparents, who by then lived in Stoke Newington, going to the cinema occasionally, but nothing very, very spectacular.'

A little girl called Frederica White appears later in the story, and the child mentioned by Connie may well have been her. It was when Connie saw Frederica's name on a list of evacuees that she recalled her childhood friend, Rica. While a pupil at JFS, Connie says she learned to swim, a skill which would have been useful when she went to Mousehole. Another only child was Shirley Spillman:

'We lived in a tenement building in Commercial Road. Both my parents worked and I think, for them, life was relatively hard as making a living was hard in those years. I remember going into the shops, and the food and eating. Eating was very important. I think I spent a lot of time with grandparents because my parents were working very long hours. So I spent quite a bit of time with grandparents who were not born in England but were born abroad and were therefore quite foreign. I think they were Polish; certainly on my father's side they were Polish.'

Although many of the evacuees were later to give very full accounts of their evacuation, the descriptions of their childhood in the East End were quite sparse, particularly in comparison with the rich and nostalgic descriptions given by the Mousehole villagers of their early life. This was perhaps because of the limited facilities that some of them had beyond school and, for some at least, because this was a life they wanted to leave behind them. Nevertheless, one still gains the impression of a strong family and community life, which, with the help of institutions such as JFS, helped them to rise above their adverse circumstances and create a rich and diverse life for themselves. Thus many, like Millie Butler, do retain happy memories:

'I lived in the Wentworth Buildings in the East End of London with my parents, brother, sister and blind grandmother. I was a very happy child. I attended the Jews' Free Infant School and had friends who lived in the same area as I did. I remember the day that war was declared. I was with my girl friend's mother, Mrs Nardel, at the time.'

The day the war began was to change the lives of all these children forever.

Chapter Three

PREPARATIONS FOR EVACUATION AND EVACUATION ONE

Who was it robbed the apple trees? Evacuees!
Who drove away the honey bees? Evacuees!
Who was it set the mill alight
And gave the villagers a fright? Evacuees!

Who was it trampled down the beet? Evacuees!
Who was it littered down the street? Evacuees!
Who was it terrified the cows
Threw sticks and stones at fattening sows
And even tried to draw the ploughs? Evacuees!

But who have crept into our hearts? Evacuees!
And of our families now are part? Evacuees!
When peace is made and they have flown
And we are left here all alone
We'll always think of them at home. EVACUEES!

JFS fourth year group in Soham[1]

THE GOVERNMENT EVACUATION SCHEME[2]

With memories lingering of the horrors of World War One, the governments and peoples of Western Europe watched anxiously as the Nazi Party rose to power in Germany throughout the 1920s and early 1930s, culminating in 1933 in the appointment of Adolf Hitler as Chancellor. With the creation in Germany of a new air force, ever-increasing military expansion, the rise of fervent nationalism and the persecution of Jews throughout the country, a second world war seemed inevitable. Attempts to appease the dictator were doomed to failure, such was Hitler's thirst for expansion. On 13 March 1938, Austria was annexed. The author's mother watched with foreboding from her balcony in the heart of Vienna as Hitler paraded triumphantly along the boulevard before her, greeted enthusiastically by the Viennese crowds. Atrocities began in earnest on 9 November 1938 throughout German-controlled territories when hundreds of synagogues, businesses and homes were destroyed, and thousands of Jews were arrested and deported to concentration camps. This was *Kristallnacht*, the 'Night of Broken Glass'. The prospect of war drew ever closer.

Despite the talk of 'peace in our time', the British Government had been secretly preparing for war. One of the major concerns was that Britain's cities would be subject to heavy aerial bombardment and that a mass evacuation of large sections of the population would be necessary, in order to alleviate the expected chaos and possible panic. As early as February 1931, the Government started to prepare plans for the movement of women and children away from the industrial cities to the relative safety of the rural areas. The plan was appropriately code-named 'Operation Pied Piper'. The subject of evacuation was debated in Parliament throughout the 1930s, and on 28 November 1934, Churchill declared to the House of Commons: 'We must expect that under pressure of continuous air attack upon London, at least 3,000,000 to 4,000,000 people will be driven out into the open country around the metropolis'.[3]

In May 1938, the London County Council (LCC) approved, in principle, the evacuation of all schoolchildren within its jurisdiction in time of war. At the same time, the Anderson Committee was established under the chairmanship of Sir John Anderson. The Committee met a total of 25 times, during which time they called 57 witnesses and other representatives from 26 government departments and private organisations. One of the first responsibilities of the Committee was to divide the country into three separate categories:

- Evacuation or high-risk areas, large industrial and commercial cities, docklands and centres of communication such as London (which was given priority), Birmingham and Manchester.
- Reception areas deemed safe to send evacuees at the outbreak of war, including rural counties such as Cambridgeshire, Cornwall, Devon, East Anglia and also Wales.
- Neutral areas, medium risk towns such as Cambridge, which were a reasonably safe distance from the main industrial areas.

In June 1938 a decision was taken that children would be evacuated school by school, with their parents' consent, to mainly private houses. Siblings were to be evacuated to the same area on the same day, with the younger ones accompanying the school of the eldest. Since teachers were to play such a prominent role, close liaison was established with the National Union of Teachers (NUT). Teachers were strongly in favour of billeting children in private homes rather than in camps, hostels or boarding accommodation, 'simply because it would place some of the responsibility for the care of the children on the host families and less on the teachers'.[4] From a modern childcare perspective, one would also have hoped that the billeting of children in private homes would, at least in the best instances, give the children a semblance of normal home life, rather than being institutionalized, though it has to be said that this did not appear to be a consideration of the Anderson Committee, judging by the comments of Penny Starns.[5] The Women's Voluntary Service (WVS) was established at this stage and was asked by the Committee to help with the planning of the scheme.

The question of transport was also considered in detail. The Committee 'needed to plan how to evacuate an estimated several million adults and 750,000 children from the Metropolitan district.

In the event 827,000 primary schoolchildren [...] were the ones eligible. Also evacuated were 103,000 teachers and helpers, a pupil teacher ratio of 8:1.[6] The committee proposals on transportation were sent to the major railway companies, who 'calculated that they could move 3,600,000 persons in 72 hours if they just ran a skeleton service'. [7] After detailed discussions, the Anderson Committee produced a report in July 1938 (but not released until October) stating that:

- Evacuation would not be compulsory.
- Billeting would be compulsory.
- Teachers would be responsible for supervising the movement of schoolchildren into reception areas.
- Central Government would be responsible for the initial costs.

By November 1938 the Government had begun 'secret' preparations for the evacuation scheme, though overall responsibility was delegated to the Ministry of Health and the Board of Education. Sir John Anderson was given a new role of co-ordinating Civil Defence, of which evacuation was just a part.

A major issue still to be resolved was that of deciding on reception areas and calculating how many billets could be provided. One source of information was the 1931 census, but this was insufficient for the purposes intended, therefore more up-to-date information needed to be obtained. A request was sent in September 1938 to the clerks of all the housing authorities in England and Wales asking them to provide information about the amount of accommodation available. An extensive domestic survey was carried out in January 1939 by 100,000 volunteer interviewers called 'visitors', which covered five million houses.[8] 'When all the returns were collated and analysed, the results showed that on a basis of one person per habitable room, there was enough space for 6,050,000 people. However (taking various factors into account) [...] the final billeting figure was reduced to 4,800,000. One very interesting feature to come out of this 1939 survey was that 18 per cent of the available billeting accommodation in England and Wales, amounting to 1,100,000 rooms, had already been reserved by private evacuees [...] seven months before the war was declared! [...] the Government [later] realised that although 1.5 million had been evacuated under the official scheme, nearly 2 million had made private arrangements.'[9] Naturally, it was largely the more affluent members of society who were able to afford to do this. Many of these 'private evacuees' left the cities in July and August 1939.

During 1939, it was established that priority for evacuation was to be given to:

- Schoolchildren.
- Younger children with mothers and guardians.
- Elderly, disabled, the sick and pregnant women.

In March 1939, plans for evacuation were sent to London schools, and it was anticipated that 20,000 teachers would be needed to help the children leave London. The LCC co-ordinated the evacuation schemes for its own area plus 11 adjacent boroughs and districts in neighbouring counties. By August less than 70 per cent of those children in the LCC area eligible for evacuation had registered and it was estimated that only 35 per cent of those eligible left in the first phase of the scheme.

Meanwhile, throughout the country, many precautions for the protection of civilians were being put in place: gas masks were issued and use of them was practiced in schools, provision for black-out was made, and public and private shelters were being built as rapidly as possible. Three types of air-raid shelter became available: the Anderson shelter, a rather flimsy steel structure which was nevertheless strong when put into the ground because of its arched design; a concrete structure which councils offered to build in people's gardens, in school playgrounds and down the centre of some streets; and the Morrison Table, a metal structure with a solid roof and base, for indoor use. Eighty underground tube stations also became shelters for thousands of Londoners, who took them over in spite of initial Government fears about their use.

The Government issued a number of documents in order to prepare the public for what to expect with regard to evacuation; for example, parents were sent a list telling them what they needed to pack for their children.[10] In addition to a gas mask, identity card and ration book, children were expected to carry the following items in a small suitcase:

BOY	GIRL
2 vests	2 vests
2 underpants	2 liberty bodices (if worn)
2 shirts	2 knickers
2 pyjamas or night shirts	2 nightdresses or pyjamas
2 pairs socks	2 pairs socks or stockings
2 pairs boots or shoes	2 pairs shoes
1 Wellingtons (if possible)	1 Wellingtons (if possible)
1 warm coat and/or macintosh (if not being worn)	1 warm coat and/or macintosh
1 pair knickers or trousers	1 warm dress or tunic and jersey
1 pullover	1 cardigan
6 handkerchiefs	2 cotton frocks
1 toothbrush	6 handkerchiefs
1 face flannel	1 toothbrush
1 comb	1 face flannel
2 towels	1 comb
	2 towels

In the early months of 1939, it was becoming apparent that Germany and Italy were preparing for war by rapidly increasing their air forces and submarine fleets. Finally, following Germany's invasion of Poland, it became clear that war could no longer be avoided, and on Thursday 31 August 1939, three days before the declaration of war, the order to evacuate was issued. Operation Pied Piper was put into immediate effect.

Between 1 and 4 September 1939, more than 600,000 Londoners, including 393,700 unaccompanied schoolchildren, as well as thousands of mothers with children, left London.

Chaotic scenes ensued at the railway stations. 'Leave was cancelled for all railway men and every available passenger train was assembled at main line railway stations. [...] Extra metropolitan police were drafted in to cordon off the streets. [...] More trouble was caused at the station by distraught parents than by the children themselves, many of whom felt it was like going on holiday, some of the younger ones even brought buckets and spades. [...] From September onwards evacuation ceased to be merely a matter of administrative planning, instead becoming a massive problem of human relationships.'[11] There were even more problems in the reception areas, where in some cases more than double the number of evacuees arrived than was expected, causing a huge headache for the billeting officers.

Despite the declaration of war on 3 September, the much-feared gas attacks did not materialise and bombing did not take place for many months, leading to the period being called the Phoney War. As a result, many evacuees started drifting back home, where there were now no schools as they had all been evacuated, and many were being used for ARP Centres and other purposes. Some children spent months wandering the streets, though from November 1939, some schools began reopening in some of the evacuated areas. Children were able to go to any school within three miles of their home if their original one remained closed. Notices such as the following started to appear on some of the vacated schools:

LONDON COUNTY COUNCIL
NOTICE
AN ELEMENTARY SCHOOL IS NOW OPEN
ON THESE PREMISES[12]

By January 1940, about 177,000 evacuees had returned home; however, the war became a reality as countries in mainland Europe fell to Germany's advance, and in May 1940 British and Allied forces were successfully evacuated by boat from the beaches of Dunkirk. These events resulted in the development and implementation of plans for further large-scale evacuation of children. This time mothers with young children were not included in the scheme, as this had proved problematic during the first evacuation.

In June 1940, 160,000 children were evacuated from the LCC area, this number including many children who were being re-evacuated. Large numbers were sent to the South West, including almost 30,000 to Cornwall alone. Throughout the following months, schoolchildren continued to be removed from those areas considered to be within the main target areas for enemy bombing. Within the year more than 60,000 further evacuees were moved. Among these numbers were children who were evacuated abroad; however, official overseas evacuation was suspended because of the lack of naval protection for convoys, and they were stopped altogether following the tragic sinking in September 1940 of the SS City of Benares, with the loss of 77 evacuees and 170 adult escorts and crew, though private evacuees could still travel overseas.

There was a final evacuation during June to September 1944 when the VI and V2 flying bombs, or Doodlebugs, as they became known, were launched from Germany causing people to move out of London and other cities. Throughout the war, some evacuees gradually returned home from the reception areas, reaching a peak in October 1944. In London, the South East and the other main target areas, this return process was a slow one as many of their homes had either been destroyed or were structurally unsound, and, of course, some children had been orphaned. By July 1945 almost all the evacuees in the UK had returned home, although more than 5,000 remained in the reception areas and 29 children were never claimed, even though their parents were alive.[13]

Following the war, the Government evacuation scheme was generally regarded as a resounding success. Certainly, it was an unparalleled feat of logistics. More recent studies, most especially by Martin Parsons, have brought to light the long-term effects of evacuation and criticism has been raised at the lack of foresight regarding the human impact of such a massive movement of people and especially children.

Certainly, there can be no question that the operation was planned along military lines. Penny Starns, co-author with Martin Parsons, has commented '[Sir John Anderson] brought in a lot of male military or ex-military officers to talk about the planning, which is one of the reasons it was codenamed "Operation Pied Piper" [...] They hadn't thought of the emotional impact that this would have on the families. I think these officers were from a class where all the children were used to going off to boarding school anyway and leaving their mothers at the age of seven or eight, so what was good enough for them was good enough for the rest of the population.'[14]

Martin Parsons has written extensively about the trauma suffered by many evacuees. He writes: 'It is very apparent that little, if any, notice was taken of the views and opinions of parents and indeed children and other evacuee groups who were to take part in the process, basically because of a desire to keep the planning and implementation "secret". There was a certain dehumanising element inherent in the organisation. These recommendations came from a bureaucratic procedure which ostensibly ignored the feelings of the individuals concerned both in the designated reception and evacuation areas, relied on the unquestioning co-operation of teachers without whom the scheme would have collapsed before it was instigated, and thought fit to create a billeting scheme which required no expert supervision and monitoring from outside agencies both before and during the whole evacuation process.'[15] During the course of his research, Dr Parsons spoke to many evacuees who 'mentioned sexual and physical abuse which has scarred them, in some cases physically, for life [...] There is a need to look beyond the jingoistic journalism that went on at the time, born out of propagandic expediency, which has influenced the images many people had, and still have, of the Government Evacuation Scheme.'[16]

THE JFS EVACUATION TO CAMBRIDGESHIRE[17]

Like vagrant seed far tossed upon the blast,
On distant soil, in strange surroundings cast,
Ancient creed, a Babel of strange tongue,

The strangers with the strange to them among;
The offspring of the ever-wandering folk,
Who have long suffered persecution's yolk.
In Ely here, beneath the ancient shrine,
Where countless men have found uplift divine,
Which God has graced since distant Saxon days,
For nature's gifts to give Him grateful praise,
We folded are, 'mid Fenland's open charms,
We humbly praise the Shepherd of all souls,
Who led us to the door of Mrs Knowles.

Mr J. Bourn, JFS teacher evacuated to Ely[18]

After these extensive preparations, the day had come. 'On Thursday 31 August 1939 the order to evacuate arrived. The next day the [JFS] pupils, some tearful, some excited, all duly labelled and carrying gas masks, sandwiches and their Singer's Prayer Books,[19] were marshalled at Liverpool Street Station and taken by train to Cambridgeshire [...] 150 were billeted in Ely, and 500 distributed among nine nearby villages, including Littleport, Chatteris, Sutton, Pymore and Prickwillow. The Central School boys were divided between Fordham, Isleham and Soham [...] A new chapter in the school was opened up by the evacuation, and the fullest opportunity was taken of continuing Dr Bernstein's work in a country setting.'[20]

The first duty for teachers on the day of arrival was to write to parents giving a name and address for the foster parent of each child, no easy task after a long and stressful day. In an interesting account of the first JFS evacuation, Dennis Adams told the story of one JFS teacher, billeted in a flat above Lloyds Bank in Ely, who wandered about, exhausted, during the early hours of the morning with an armful of letters looking for a post box. In the blackout, she had completely missed the box immediately outside the bank.[21]

During the first few days, not all placements proved to be compatible and billeting officers had to re-allocate some of the children. Nevertheless, on 29 September 1939, this glowing tribute to the conduct of the evacuation was published in *The Jewish Chronicle*:[22]

EXODUS OF THE CHILDREN

Social Worker's Tribute

High tribute to the LCC and the teachers in connection with the arrangements which were made in the recent evacuation of children from London is paid by that well-known social worker, Miss Miriam Moses, JP, warden of the Brady Girls' Club in Hanbury Street, in the area of East London with which she is concerned, the percentage of the Jewish children evacuated was seventy-five.

> The organisation of the LCC was 'simply marvellous', and the help of the teachers was beyond praise. As to the Jewish mothers themselves who are known for their great attachment to their children, they controlled themselves very well indeed. She herself was present at the exodus of the children from the Jews' Free School (Central); the Robert Montefiore, Senior, Junior and Infant Schools; Buxton Street School; and the Commercial Street Infants' School.
>
> As Chairman of the Managers of the Robert Montefiore and Buxton Street Schools Miss Moses has [been] told that the children were all settling down very nicely indeed [...]Those who have come in contact with these children have been highly impressed by their behaviour as Jews, by their general eagerness to be of help to their hostesses and, in fact, by their conduct all round.

It is interesting to note that although JFS was the only designated Jewish school in the area, all the other schools mentioned here had a high proportion of Jewish pupils, as evidenced by Miss Moses' involvement with them. Two weeks later, a letter appeared in *The Jewish Chronicle*[23] full of praise for the manner in which the evacuees had been received in Cambridgeshire. Once again, a comment is made about the behaviour of the children as Jews, showing just how important the issue of acceptance was at that period:

> ### JEWS' FREE SCHOOL
>
> I recently had the opportunity of staying a few days with my brother, who was evacuated with the children of the Jews' Free Central School 'somewhere in Cambridgeshire' and soon remarked upon the hospitable manner in which the villagers entertained the children, some of whom had been separated from their parents for the first time in their lives. The evacuated children and the local boys played together and were on terms of warm friendship. Everything was done to make the children comfortable. The New Year and Sabbath services were held in the village school. I was told by one of the local billeting helpers that, with the exception of one or two very minor alterations in billeting, no complaints had been received and that the villagers had grown quite fond of the youngsters, who, I might add, were behaving in a manner befitting a pupil of a school with such a great tradition as the Jews' Free School. The boys were making themselves generally useful about the households, and many of them were rendering valuable service and assisting on farms and allotments.
>
> *Mr Alan Silverman, E3*

In spite of this optimism, there were, in those early days, frictions and misunderstandings between the evacuees and the local population, to the degree that there were complaints from some of the locals about the scale and nature of the influx; indeed, some members of the local councils sent a petition to the Government demanding that 'no more foreigners be sent to the area'.[24] It is not clear why this particular destination was chosen for the JFS children, though the evacuation of the East End to this area was determined largely by the fact that the nearest railway station, Liverpool Street, served this part of the country. In addition, it seems likely that the reason, at least in part, was associated with the fact that James de Rothschild, a major benefactor to JFS, was Member of Parliament for the Isle of Ely. Certainly, it seems that he received the brunt of the criticism. Fortunately, these difficulties were largely ironed out with the encouragement and support of the local Christian ministry, most particularly the Dean of Ely, the Very Reverend L.E. Blackburne, with whom Dr Bernstein established a firm friendship. The wife of the Vicar of Ely, Mrs Hinton-Knowles, was also extremely supportive of the Jewish evacuee community and a poem, quoted at the beginning of this section, was written by one of the JFS teachers expressing gratitude for her efforts.

Her role was instrumental in sorting out the difficulties which arose regarding the billeting of some 70 refugee boys who arrived with JFS, accompanied, among others, by Mr Podguszer, father of two of the evacuees who ultimately went to Mousehole. The refugees had been rescued from their homes in Austria, Germany, Czechoslovakia and Poland and brought to England on the *Kindertransport*. These children were severely traumatised, having witnessed first-hand Nazi atrocities, including the murder of their own family members. For them, being frog-marched to a railway station and herded onto a train brought back frightening memories, and they were in a deeply distressed state. Furthermore, they did not speak English, so it was almost impossible to offer them any explanation or even words of comfort. It quickly became apparent that they could not be billeted in foster homes like the other JFS children, so Mrs Hinton-Knowles arranged for them to be accommodated in a large house in Ely. The empty building was filled with furniture and equipment brought from the school in Bell Lane, and thus became a hostel, known as the Ely Jewish Boys' Home. An article about the home appeared in *The Jewish Chronicle*[25] in December 1939:

ELY JEWISH BOYS' HOME

Dr E. Bernstein, Headmaster of the Jews Free Boys' School, writes to place on record the admirable work done by the East London Refugees Committee on behalf of the refugee children evacuated with the Jews' Free School to Ely. The Ely Jewish Boys' Home owes its creation to one of the best-known public workers in Cambridgeshire, Mrs Hinton Knowles, wife of the Vicar of Ely, aided by Mr James De Rothschild, MP, and the Bishop of Ely. The Home provides a strictly orthodox Jewish life for 50 refugee boys, and has its own Synagogue – the first to be established in Ely since 1290. The Ministry of Health has from the outset taken a special interest in what it regards as a unique effort in community billeting, and has expressed keen satisfaction with all the arrangements.

Further misconceptions arose when a large oven was delivered to the hostel, which fuelled all manner of speculation. Local residents became concerned about what might be happening behind closed doors. Dr Bernstein invited the Dean of Ely to inspect the offending equipment and he was able to confirm that it was in fact a kiln to be used to make pottery. The Dean was also impressed by the excellent behaviour of the young refugees, and was thus able to put an end to the unpleasant rumours which had been circulating.

More generally, the JFS children were perceived to be 'people who are ignorant of the most elementary system of living', a view expressed publicly by a leading local figure.[26] Certainly, many of the evacuees came from overcrowded and impoverished backgrounds, and it is to be expected therefore that a number of them suffered poor health. 'Bathing disclosed problems such as scabies and head lice which later spread to the local children. The teachers were just as horrified as the foster mothers, who set about a cleansing programme with puritanical zeal.'[27] The problem may not only have been on one side. As we shall later see, some of the Mousehole evacuees who had participated in the original evacuation complained that they became infested in Cambridgeshire and that this, together with other factors, was one of the reasons for their early departure.

Almost half of the JFS children who were evacuated to Cambridgeshire in September 1939 returned to London by December 1939. One of the unfortunate consequences of this early departure was that some of those children retained a lifelong negative perception of their experiences in that area. This is a pity since, for those who remained, the experience became a largely positive one, as is demonstrated in the following poem written by a JFS teacher one year after evacuation:

> When Stepney came to Cambridgeshire
> A long, long year ago,
> The Town boy and the Country Boy
> Found each so hard to know.
> The talk was hard to understand;
> And odd in many a way
> The Town boy found the Country boy,
> At home, in school, at play.
>
> When Stepney came to Cambridgeshire
> Each reckoned each so strange;
> The Town boy eyed the Country boy
> Who eyed him in exchange.
> But ere a dozen hours sped by,
> They grew less scared and coy,
> For Town and Country both found out
> A boy is still a boy!
>
> And so throughout a year of War,
> In sun and stormy weather,
> The Town boy and the Country boy
> Have worked and played together.
> The mists of strangeness blown away,

Let light of friendship through
To bless both Town and Country boy
In all they say and do.

S.M. Rich [28]

Once the initial difficulties were sorted out, JFS became a thriving and accepted community living within the local community. Dr Bertha Tilly, headmistress of Ely Girls High School, with whom some evacuees shared premises, wrote in 1940, 'that evacuee girls have become in all things our sisters, sharing our building and our playing fields, exchanging with us dramatic performances, meeting us in matches and have entered as far as possible into the kind of life we lead here in the Fens'.[29] Mr Burgess, headmaster of Needham School in Ely, considered that the brighter evacuee boys stimulated his pupils to achieve higher standards than might otherwise have been the case.[30]

The issue of school premises was potentially a fraught one, but it appears in most instances to have been resolved amicably. Normal classroom arrangements had to be drastically changed, and following his arrival, Dr Bernstein and his staff worked for many hours with local teachers to try to resolve an almost impossible situation. Where space was available, evacuee pupils were simply enrolled directly into already existing classes. Elsewhere, village halls, church halls and meeting rooms were requisitioned; however, in many instances facilities had to be shared due to lack of space, such that local pupils used the classrooms in the mornings while the evacuees used them in the afternoons, a frequent arrangement throughout all reception areas. Dr Bernstein preferred the latter arrangement as it enabled his pupils to continue with a Jewish style of education with their own teachers, though it did, of course, cause disruption to the local community. The refugee boys were taught separately at the hostel.

Even with his pupils scattered over a wide geographic area and with a variety of classroom arrangements, Dr Bernstein succeeded, against all the odds, in retaining many of the school's former traditions and activities. With the situation of the refugee boys resolved, he then proceeded to transfer from Bell Lane all the school's printing and basketry equipment, together with the games and billiard tables from the Play Centre. A print room was installed at the home and, within a short time, a magazine was produced entitled *JFS Evacuation News Sheet*. The first edition appeared in December 1939 and the 23rd and last edition in July 1942.

Play Centres, run on the lines of those in Bell Lane, became the focus of the children's recreational life and operated in most of the JFS reception areas. The school's musical traditions were brought back to life. The JFS Operatic Society was re-launched and over 70 boys and girls rehearsed *The Pirates of Penzance*, giving two public performances in March 1940. Hundreds were turned away from the doors and the grand sum of £25 was raised for the Red Cross. In July 1940, a public gymnastics display was given in the hostel garden, to which local dignitaries were invited. This was followed by an open-air concert for the benefit of local children, who packed the garden around an improvised stage. Comments were made about the improved complexion and health of the evacuees, most especially the refugee boys, which was attributed to the open air and balanced diets of life in Cambridgeshire.

Indeed, in addition 'to the usual Bell Lane activities were added country pursuits – hay-making, currant and gooseberry picking, pea-picking, beet-singling, beekeeping and allotment work'.[31]

For Dr Bernstein, this idyllic country life was shattered by a tragic event. 'The JFS school buildings in Bell Lane were severely damaged in February 1941 during one of the worst nights of the London Blitz. Dr Bernstein was in Spitalfields at the time, he was absolutely distraught and spent the next day clambering about the rubble of the school that had been his whole life. He returned to Ely a broken man to share the news with his pupils and staff. The Dean [of Ely] tried to comfort and counsel him and maybe in an attempt to lift his spirits he offered to let JFS occupy a part of Hereward Hall, part of the King's School'.[32] This meant that, from September 1941, many of the JFS children in outlying villages were able to continue their Jewish education all under one roof. The girls also attended Hereward Hall, where they were taught in separate classes from the boys and had their own dining room. Dr Bernstein wrote in the *Evacuation News Sheet*:[33]

> The transfer to this wonderful home is a most gratifying happening, and we entertain the deepest gratitude to The Dean of Ely for his kindness. Our school is the oldest Jewish school in the country and we feel most proud that we are being given a home in the oldest Public School in the country. We are opening a new chapter in the history of Jews' Free School and we have every confidence that our record here at the King's School will be worthy of the high traditions of both great schools. With its lofty spacious rooms, so airy and well lighted, our school work is being carried on under most pleasant conditions. No longer do our schoolrooms look upon the vistas of brick and mortar we knew so well in London. Instead we have the pleasant view of the beautiful Cathedral Park...From the raucous cries of Middlesex Street to the trills and full-throated song of the birds of a cathedral close – from the grime of London streets to the heart-quickening colours of the glorious English countryside – how fortunate are we to have such a wonderful transformation effected on our school life!

The stage was now set for Dr Bernstein to rebuild his school to its former glory; however, he never quite recovered from the shock of losing his beloved school at Bell Lane, and in August 1942 Dr Bernstein applied for retirement on the grounds of ill-health. He later settled in America, but he continued to correspond with former colleagues and pupils until his death in 1966. At the end of 1942, Miss Lipman was appointed the first female headteacher of all the JFS pupils, a position she held until her retirement in November 1944. The JFS Central School, which by 1942 was at Isleham only, had made every effort to keep the Jewish spirit alive, by holding regular religious services and celebrating many Barmitzvahs. Gradually, however, the numbers fell and it closed after the summer holiday of 1943. 'The war quickly took its toll on numbers in Ely; ever more teachers went into the armed forces, others drifted back to London and children returned home despite the bombing. In December 1942 there were 158 on the roll; in June 1943 134; and in May 1944 just 115.'[34]

Thus, an extraordinary episode in JFS history came to a close. Meanwhile, even as this story was developing, an even more unusual and much less well-known episode in JFS history was unfolding several hundred miles to the south-west of Ely.

MEMORIES OF THE FIRST EVACUATION

As World War Two drew closer, government preparations, which had hitherto been conducted in secret, were becoming increasingly visible to the public. The sense of foreboding is captured here by Maurice Podguszer:

'I can remember the preparations for war where windows were being taped with brown paper to stop glass from shattering. There was a great deal of fearfulness about what war would bring, and it was explained that the children would have to be moved out of cities in order to protect them. A great deal of news was being broadcast at that particular period of time, and of course parents were busy talking about it, and you could see preparations in the form of air raid shelters being dug in the streets and in small park areas. You got this fear, this aspect of fear being generated from what was going on round you.'

This atmosphere is perfectly conveyed in a poem written by one of the evacuees in Cambridgeshire:

THE BLACKOUT

People bang into one another;
Where's my sister, where's my brother?
Father! Mother! Are you there?
Hark! The siren fills the air.
Here come Germans circling round.
Run to shelter underground.
There the people wait to hear,
The sound that tells that all is clear.

H. Hyams, 10 years [35]

This general state of public anxiety made it difficult for parents to decide what was best for their children, even though they were being advised to allow them to be evacuated. This anxiety about what to do is typified in the actions taken by Ted Labofsky's parents. At the time, Ted was attending JFS Central School, but did not go with JFS to Ely; however, as events rapidly unfolded, his parents quickly changed their minds:

'I didn't go with Free School on the first evacuation, on the Friday, 1 September, because my mother and father didn't really think there was going to be a war. But on Sunday morning, 3 September 1939, when the air raid warning started at 11 o'clock in the morning, my mother grabbed me and my sister, put a few things in a carrier bag, and took us round to the Jews' Free Infant School. And they sent us away on a different evacuation; we went to Hunstanton in Norfolk, which was diabolical. There were four of us, three boys and my sister, billeted with a family. My sister was 13 and they thought she was going to be a scullery maid, and we only stayed there for 13 days. We weren't very happy. By the time I came back, from the end of September 1939 until we went again in June 1940, I never went to school.'

Ironically, the family Ted stayed with in Hunstanton was Jewish, which demonstrates that difficulties which occurred during billeting were more often along class lines rather than religious ones.

Many of the children who ultimately went to Mousehole were first evacuated with JFS to Cambridgeshire; however, some were evacuated elsewhere, like Ted because of initial indecision, sometimes because they attended schools other than JFS, or in the case of some young JFS pupils, because they were evacuated with older siblings who did not attend JFS. All five Fromovitch sisters, Marie, Frances, Mildred, Ada and Irene, were evacuated together to Aylesbury with Mile End Central School, which Marie and Frances attended prior to the evacuation, as Frances recalls:

'We took our rucksacks and our gas masks every day to school. You always had to have them with you, as you might go straightaway. You could have gone any day without even telling your parents. They might say, "Come along, we're going today," and off you'd go. A woman took five of us in 'cos they couldn't get anyone else to take five. They did try and keep us together. And well, we didn't like it, and I remember my oldest sister Marie crying and I was laughing because there were feet that way and feet that way. All five of us were sleeping in one bed, and that's why I think I was laughing. The woman had a lodger, a male lodger, it's so funny, and he had to walk through our room to get to his room.

'We stayed there about six weeks. Then my mother and my aunt came to pick us up because I kept writing home, "we don't like it and we're not getting enough to eat. We're hungry." They came one day, and my mother said, "We've come to take the children home," and the woman said "Well, I tried to do my best." And they wouldn't talk to her because they were angry and they waited for us to come home.'

This story illustrates, not only the pressure which children often put on their parents to take them home, but also the tensions that could arise between the parents of evacuees and foster parents, where parents felt that their children were not being properly looked after. When the girls arrived back in London, there were no schools left as they had all been evacuated. When arrangements were made to reopen some schools, Frances believes they started attending Robert Montefiore School. Mildred also has memories of being unhappy in Aylesbury. She remembers that when they returned home, their eldest sister, Marie, was not evacuated again. This was probably because, by then, she had reached the school leaving age of 14 years. Her younger sister Ada was re-evacuated separately:

'She had a back problem and went to a special school in Oswestry and stayed in a castle. Eventually she had an op there, a pioneering one, one of the first in the country, and it was fantastic. She says to this day, if she'd never had that operation she wouldn't have lived a normal life.'

This was an instance where evacuation clearly had a very fortunate outcome. Pressure on parents is likely to have been the reason for Millie Butler's return to London:

'I do remember that my mother made clothes for me to take on a journey. She told me I was going away with my cousins but I did not understand what she meant. I was sent to Fordham near Ely in Cambridgeshire. I was very unhappy there, I cannot remember why, and my mother came to collect me and to take me home to London.'

Although Maurice Podguszer was a pupil at JFS, he was evacuated with his elder brother Peter, who attended Central Foundation School (CFS) in Cowper Street:

'I can remember having to have all clothes put into a rucksack, and having to take sandwiches with us for the journey. We were all wearing labels attached to our lapels, and we were assembled at the school and then marched to a station to board a train that would depart for wherever we were going. Well, it was a journey of excitement and it was as if we were all going on a great big outing. We wound up in Newmarket. I can remember being de-trained and then we were all allocated different places to be fostered. We lined up in front of desks and various people said, "You're going here." Myself and my brother, we went to what was Lord Rothschild's stable, where the horses had once been, which had been converted into a dormitory with folding beds, and this was our billet. We remained there for about two months and were looked after by the staff of Lord Rothschild's estate. And then from there the whole school was re-evacuated to Fakenham.'

The reason for the re-evacuation was because the boys of CFS got involved with gambling, in competition with the local stable boys:

'And literally within a very short time the stable lads had been deprived of their wages, and the CFS boys were full of it. On top of that, racing was still going on at Newmarket and it was nothing unusual for part of the school to play truant and go and watch the races. There was a deputation from the Newmarket authorities that said that this had got to stop, and it was decided the easiest way to stop it was to re-evacuate the whole school and so we wound up in Fakenham, where both my brother and I were re-billeted.'

Clearly, this was not a very suitable location for vulnerable and, apparently, unsupervised young people! One wonders how many other children were billeted in such inappropriate locations. Maurice did not like the schooling in Fakenham and returned home in December of that year. Meanwhile, the younger members of the Podguszer family, including Arnold, were evacuated to Prickwillow, as part of the evacuation of the younger parts of JFS even though they were not at that time pupils there. Maurice thinks that their evacuation with the school was probably arranged by their father. Here, Arnold describes his first evacuation experience, and the reason for his return to London, which was again due to an unsuitable arrangement:

'I was evacuated possibly on 3 or 4 September with my younger brother and my sister. We went to Cambridgeshire, a place called Black Horse Grove, and there we stayed with a railway crossing minder and his wife, who were childless. It was a small cottage and had no mains electricity or gas, but there was a water pump in the kitchen and there were two bedrooms. We helped mind the railway crossing, which we thought was great fun. But my parents took great exception because it was too onerous a responsibility for children of five, seven and nine to be working a crossing gate, and so they took us home at the end of the first week.'

Arnold goes on to describe his father's subsequent attempts to provide his children with an education since there were now no schools available:

'Father now had three young children on his hands and he attempted to find a tutor. There were other children in the area who had either not been evacuated or like ourselves had returned, so he tried to start classes for them also. This went on for a while but it wasn't successful. He then enrolled me in what was called the Robert Montefiore School and I was probably a part-time student there because I recall going in the mornings, but not every morning, certainly not in the afternoons. I can't remember what I actually did with myself at the time but I do know that I wandered around London. I saw them filling sandbags and it was quite an exciting time, but certainly there wasn't much education going on. I mean, so far as I was concerned school was an encumbrance. I preferred to be free and not have to attend school.'

Mr Podguszer, according to Maurice's account, was obviously very actively involved in the welfare of Jewish children during that fraught period, having first participated in the reception of Jewish refugee children fleeing from Europe, including those arriving on the Winton train.[36] He was then involved in the supervision of the *Kindertransport*[37] refugees to Cambridgeshire, and subsequently in the organisation of education for the returning evacuees. By the time Maurice returned to London, towards the end of 1939, he was able to attend one of the part-time schools which had by then been put in place to try to establish some form of education:

'I had to go to school again, which was the Jews' Free School as that had originally been my school. At that time, pupils of Jews' Free School, such as they were, collected together and were sent to a school which was in the Vallance Road area. I'm pretty certain it was Buxton Street School because my mother had said she'd been a pupil of that school. But it was a temporary, *ad hoc* arrangement. From my understanding, it was made clear that although this school was running, they weren't prepared to continue to run it and that the children would have to be re-evacuated. There was no provision.'

Maurice believes that one of the JFS teachers, Mr Barnes, may have taught at the temporary school in Vallance Road, as he has a clear recollection of him prior to the second evacuation. In normal circumstances, Jews' Free Senior School was a segregated boys' and girls' school, though the younger boys and girls were taught together. However, in the prevailing circumstances, Maurice remembers that even the older boys and girls were no longer segregated.

Like many of the other JFS pupils, Cyril and Malcolm Hanover were also evacuated to Cambridgeshire. They went to Soham with JFS Central School, which Cyril attended, but returned after only two weeks because of the circumstances in which they found themselves. Malcolm Hanover explains why:

'I can remember being unhappy where we were billeted. There were caterpillars on the wall, even the bedroom walls. Dad came and saw us and was dismayed and disgusted at the state, and we were then returned to the East End.'

Cyril thinks that they may have gone to a temporary school at some point, but this could not have been until long after their return, since they came back so early on. It is likely therefore that, like Ted, he and Malcolm spent many weeks, possibly months, roaming the streets of East London. Another JFS pupil, Jack Goldstein, also had a very upsetting experience, which he describes in vivid detail:

'I was evacuated two or three days before the war started. We went to a place called Prickwillow which was near Littleport in Cambridgeshire. We were all assembled at the Jews' Free School, which was then in Bell Lane, and we were all lined up and tagged with our names and addresses, on a kind of a label thing hanging from our coats, and we were just marched along in file up Middlesex Street towards Liverpool Street Station. It wasn't far, only about a 10-minute walk. There were lots of mothers and fathers and the next thing we knew we were on the train, waving goodbye, going we didn't know where to. In those days, very few East End kids went out of London, so we could have been going to the end of the world. We were just told to get on the train and I remember we were given, I think, a bar of chocolate and little bits and pieces to eat, maybe a bit of fruit, and we just sat back until we were told to get out when we arrived. I was doing something that I'd never done before. It was all a bit strange, you know, here we were in the middle of nowhere, and we were taken to a particular place and told, "Right. Go in there, you're going to live there." Lots of children were separated and some went one way, some the other. My sister went to Littleport and I went to a village called Prickwillow. I wasn't told where she was. I didn't find out till afterwards where she was. Littleport wasn't far from where I was, but I was never given the geographical location.'

Jack's story illustrates very graphically how children were shunted from one place to another with little thought for their feelings, and how the lack of information given contributed to their confusion and unhappiness. Had he known that his sister was living just nearby, and been able to visit her, this might have enabled him to settle down much more easily. He continues:

'I stayed in a small cottage outside Prickwillow called Railway Cottage because the man worked on the railway, and in those days they got a place to live, when they lived in these remote places. I remember it was on this kind of desolate looking road and alongside the road was a big dyke. A dyke was a place where rainwater gathered, something to do with the fact that it was very flat Fenland. I don't remember anything at all about the people I stayed with. I was not there very long; a few weeks maybe. The evacuation turned out to be a complete fiasco. Nothing warlike happened in the first six months, so most parents thought "what have we got our kids there for?" Most kids didn't like it anyway. I left because when my mother came down to see me, it was discovered that I was running alive with fleas which I never had before I went there, and the other boy that was with me, Monty Pirelly, he also was running alive with fleas, and word got around to all the mothers and fathers that we didn't like the place, we didn't like the people and we didn't like the food, and before I know where I was, I was back in London and so were most of the others.

'When I came back, JFS was closed. We were back a few months, and I think I went to a local school, but I can't remember which one it was. It seemed to all go past in a flash, you know.'

Meanwhile, Jack's sister Vera, although just a short distance away, had a much more pleasant experience, showing what a lottery the billeting process was:

'I stayed in a place called Littleport with a very nice lady. But there was nothing happening much in London and a lot of the children were returning home because there was no activity, no bombs. So a lot of us got back to London somehow or other. I was there only about six weeks.'

There were all kinds of reasons for leaving the reception area, some more unusual than others. Although many evacuees who remained in Cambridgeshire came to appreciate the attractions of country life, for many the pull of London was irresistible, as is captured in another evacuee poem:

I have been evacuated
From dear old London Town,
And now I am in the country
It makes me sulk and frown.
For, though I love the country
I had to leave my home
And now instead of London's streets
The country-side I roam.

But someday I'll return again,
And see my home once more.
Then I'll hear the pleasing sound
Of London's traffic roar.

Betty Hyams [38]

For many it was simply that parents, quite understandably, wanted their children back home, as was the case with Anita Godfrey and her brother Irvine, who went to Ely. Ronney Glazer went to Isleham for three weeks and was billeted to a home on the side of the river. The river overflowed and he was then sent to Soham, where he did not like the people. He stayed for a total of only nine weeks. Some children never went to school, as was the case with Jose Marks:

'We met at the Jews' Free School everyday for a week expecting to be evacuated. We were told to be ready for safety's sake. When we were finally evacuated, I stayed on a farm in Ely for a short time, where I helped out on the farm with another girl, and there was no schooling, so I left because it didn't work out. I was sent to Soham in early 1940, but I did not stay long as there was no school there either. I left Soham and came home to London in the spring of 1940, and in less than two months we were on our way to Cornwall.'

Jose's case suggests that there was a considerable lack of coordination between billeting and education authorities. A few children who eventually went to Mousehole did not travel with the original evacuation. One of these was Evelyn Goldstein, Jack and Vera's older sister. Having been born in 1925, she had left school by that stage, and, in any event, she wanted to stay home with her mother, who was on her own. Other children who were not evacuated for a variety of reasons were the Posner sisters, Shirley Spillman and Connie Mellows. Connie was away on holiday at the time of the first evacuation:

'When war broke out we were in fact on holiday in Clacton, and my mother and I stayed there for a while, then later we went down to the south coast where my father's sisters had taken a house. I lived there with my mother and my aunts and my cousins until, of course, the south coast was evacuated. My mother and I then came back to London and I went to a temporary school in Toynbee Hall.'

The evacuation scheme was dependent for its success on the commitment and co-operation of teachers. For the thousands of teachers who participated in the evacuation, their lives were just as disrupted as those of the children they travelled with, though they had a little more information about what was happening and where they were going. They were also more capable of analysing and understanding the situation they found themselves in, which must have made it easier for them to deal with than the children. Nevertheless, they had little choice but to go along with the flow of events.

In spite of all the settling-in difficulties in Cambridgeshire, and the departure of so many children, the situation did ease to a large degree for those who remained, due largely to the staunch efforts of the teachers. The name of Mr Levene, who ultimately went to Mousehole, appears in the first edition of the news sheet,[39] and it is clear that he was very actively involved in the life of the evacuated Jews' Free Central School. In his comments, Mr Levene is keen, like others, to emphasise the good behaviour of the pupils as Jews:

Evacuation News Sheet no. 1 December 1939
JEWS' FREE SCHOOL MAGAZINE
CENTRAL SCHOOL
EVACUATION NEWS SHEET
Issue No. 01 DECEMBER, 1939

WE CREATE A GOOD IMPRESSION. It must be borne in mind that very few of the inhabitants in our area had ever come in contact with Jews. The following report by Mr D. Levene from Soham, is typical of all three areas.

'From the very first our boys made a good impression on the villagers, and time served only to enhance the good reputation of the J.F.S. Central School. From all, one hears Golden opinions in most cases of their excellent conduct in billets and out of doors. The boys have shown an adaptability which reflects great credit on them, and the harmony existing between the boys and the villagers has greatly assisted to ease the work of the teachers in what would otherwise have been an almost impossible task...'

With regard to the Play Centre, Mr Levene wrote in his report:

'Very few boys do not attend regularly. As I watch the boys I often think that it is just a bit of the J.F.S. transplanted; the same faces, the same cheery voices, and (dare I whisper it) the same nicknames. The foster parents are very grateful for the relief thus afforded.'

The article also indicates that Mr Levene conducted services on Saturdays and Holy Days in the Church Hall and taught classical Hebrew as well as mathematics to boys preparing for their matriculation; however, Mr Levene's sojourn in Cambridgeshire was cut short when he was asked, with regret, to return to London, 'owing to so many children being called back to London by their parents'. The event was recorded in the *Evacuation News Sheet* of Spring 1940,[40] where the following exhortation was given to the pupils who remained:

'You, who are now settled in your billets, know that you have done your duty by making the work of the Government easier by remaining at your posts [...] We are living in

> historic times, and it will be of extreme interest to look back, when peace is restored, on what we did in the reception areas.'

Little could the author have known that his words would be read with interest some 70 years later! Ralph Barnes was also one of the teachers evacuated with JFS. Like Mr Levene, he was sent back, as he recorded in an article published in 2003:[41]

> 'Sadly, on 1 September 1939, two days before the outbreak of World War Two, we were evacuated to Cambridgeshire. My stay was shortlived because a number of children had returned to London, which had not yet been bombed and I was told to return to the capital.'

His daughter, Pamela, though not yet born by this stage, heard many stories during her childhood about that first evacuation and is able to give a graphic account of those events:

'My parents settled in the village of Sutton with a family called Baden-Powell. Not Lord Baden-Powell, but he was related, one branch of the family from the famous Baden-Powell of the Scouting Movement. Years later, after the war, when I was a young teenager, my parents took me back there and we met the family. Of course, they were quite elderly by then, but they were absolutely charming and had remembered my parents, and my parents had very happy times with them.

'They lived in a marvellous house, very well appointed for those days, owned most of the village and people paid rents to them. He was a major land-owner, as well as, I think, being a farmer. He was the sort of man that if he walked down the high street, everybody would doff their caps to him. And I recollect my father telling me that when he spoke to a road sweeper one morning, the road sweeper was taken aback because no one used to talk to him, or even look at him. I found that quite astonishing, that there was this total class division.

'I know I was conceived while they were staying there, because that was something my father related to me years later and I could have worked that out, I suppose, for myself!'

Pamela was born in October 1940, by which time her parents were in Mousehole. The date of her conception is interesting, as it pinpoints Ralph and Jean Barnes to a particular place and time, and means that they were still in Cambridgeshire up until at least February 1940. Conceived during one evacuation and born during another, Pamela was indeed a true product of the evacuation, and hers is a very special story.

For the children who returned from that first evacuation and were subsequently evacuated to Mousehole, this was to be but the precursor to what for many of them became one of the most remarkable and memorable episodes in their lives.

Chapter Four

JOURNEY TO CORNWALL

'We were home from Cambridge for only a short time and then were put on a train at Paddington Station going to Penzance and then a bus to Mousehole. The adventure begins.'
Jose Marks

'We went on the Cornish Riviera, 9.30 special.'
Cyril Hanover

PREPARATIONS IN CORNWALL

Like the rest of the country, Cornwall had been preparing for evacuation since early 1939 and Cornwall County Council had been receiving Government instructions since that time. One of the remarkable features of the Evacuation Scheme is that it was conducted within the context of a very limited communication system by today's standards. Almost all contact was by letter, since the telephone system was not yet in wide use. Letters would have been sent to Cornwall via the railway network, and since the train journey to Penzance was extremely long, post would have taken a minimum of two days to arrive at its destination. Replies to letters could not be expected to be received within much less than a week. Ministers and other officers from London also had to make the journey down to Cornwall to consult with local officials, which must have been a time-consuming process.

In January 1939, a meeting of the West Penwith Rural Council[1] noted that, having received instructions regarding the Government Evacuation Scheme:

> ...a preliminary letter should be sent to each Householder in the District setting out the proposals, and that following this, a Register of all houses, hotels, camping grounds, etc., had to be prepared, followed by books for use of visitors who would visit each house and record what accommodation was available on the standard basis of one person per habitable room [...] and a return made to the Ministry and to the County Council by 28 February next, the Council having then on the information available to make a provisional decision as to:
>
> a) the number of unaccompanied children
> b) the number of teachers and helpers
> c) the number of others which each house could accommodate.

Following this exercise, it was reported that further instructions had been issued by the Ministry of Health stating that 4,500 persons could be accommodated in the district,[2] and asking the Council to proceed with the working out of their detailed plans on this assumption. By the summer of that year, billeting arrangements were well underway in Cornwall. In August 1939, *The Cornishman*[3] reported that the power of appointing Billeting Officers for Penzance had been delegated to the Mayor and that he had appointed the Town Clerk as the Chief Billeting Officer. It was emphasised that the duties of the Billeting Officers extended only to those persons involved in the official Government Scheme, including teachers, voluntary helpers and other persons engaged in carrying out the plan. This was a reference to the fact that private evacuees were not to be included in this scheme. This is relevant to our story as a number of members of the families of the Mousehole evacuees came to stay in Mousehole and Newlyn at various times during the war, on a private basis. The article went on to outline the prices payable for accommodation under billeting notices:

> For children provided with board and lodging, 10s. and 6d.[4] per week where one child is taken, and 8s. 6d. per week for each child where more than one child is taken.
>
> For persons provided only with lodging (with the use of the water supply and sanitary conveniences) 5s. per week for each adult and 3s. per week for each child.
>
> For voluntary helpers from the evacuation areas working full-time in the reception areas, 21s.[5] per week for each person to cover board and lodging.

The first evacuees arrived in Cornwall in early September 1939. At this stage, they did not travel as far as Penzance and West Penwith, the furthest south-west having been St Ives. On 4 September 1939, *The West Briton* newspaper reported[6] that train 116 arrived in Truro, bringing with it a contingent of 619 mothers and children. The following article in *The Cornishman*, dated 6 September 1939,[7] describes in evocative terms the arrival of evacuees in Camborne on the previous Saturday, which would have been 2 September, the day before war began:

> ### EVACUEE CHILDREN AT CAMBORNE
>
> ### MANY SMILING FACES; A FEW SAD
>
> It was a rather dreary scene which greeted the evacuee children at Camborne on Saturday afternoon: rain-sodden pavements, a leaden sky and a steady downpour of rain formed the scene with which these poor war-tossed children had their first glimpse of Camborne, where perhaps they may have to reside for, maybe a few days, a few weeks, or perhaps for months or years.
>
> In spite of this very dull and dreary outlook, most of the children seemed perfectly happy, and to look upon the great matter of evacuation as some big adventure or another holiday.
>
> There were, however, a few sad-eyed and tearful children, and for those one felt extremely sorry, nor could one help thinking of the hundreds of homes which this week-

end will be without the happy carefree voices of these children and of the parents who would so sadly miss them.

No fewer than 960 mothers and children arrived at Camborne Station at 4.25 p.m., which was 20 minutes before they were expected. There were 800 children and 160 mothers and children. A teacher said that they assembled at Maida Vale at 5 a.m. and got to Paddington at 8.30., whence they left for Camborne. When they left they did not know where they were going…

It is clear from this account that the journey was in excess of 12 hours, and this does not include the time taken to get to the meeting point in London, or to billet the children to their foster homes on arrival. For the children who were later to go to Mousehole, they would have had to wait for children disembarking at Camborne and other stations, then the train journey to Penzance was an extra 30 minutes, followed by the time to disembark from the train, plus at least another 30 minutes for the bus journey to Mousehole. With billeting, it must have been a minimum of 16 hours, at the very least, from the time the children left home in the morning until they were found a bed in the evening.

For the September 1939 evacuees, arrangements were made for their education which replicated arrangements being made in other parts of the country. These were to disrupt the lives of the local children as much as those of the evacuees, as reported on 7 September 1939:[8]

EDUCATING THE EVACUEES

Schoolchildren received in Cornwall from evacuated areas are being sorted out this week, and the Cornish schools are reopening next Monday […] eventually a total of 34,350 evacuees are being received in the county […] the schools will be run on the double shift system. One week Cornish children will go to school from 9 to 1, and the evacuees will go to school from 1 to 5. The succeeding week, they will turn about.

In spite of the welcome they received, many evacuees returned to their homes during the period of the Phoney War, as we have seen was the case with the children who went to Cambridgeshire and other parts of the country. This was in spite of the poster campaign mounted by the Government aimed at encouraging parents to keep their children in the reception areas. In Cornwall, this campaign was supported by the local press, the following headline appearing in December 1939[9] being typical:

DON'T RUSH CHILDREN BACK TO DANGER

BE THANKFUL FOR SAFETY AND KINDNESS IN THE COUNTRY

CORNWALL'S ATTITUDE TO EVACUEES FROM THE TOWNS

The writer of this article, H. Hartley Thomas,[10] was editor of *The Cornishman* and a keen proponent of the evacuation scheme, having served in the Royal Air Force during World War One. He pointed out that even though the actual war in progress was not the war expected, and that it was natural for families to want to be reunited, attack or even invasion by the Germans nevertheless remained a real threat. He considered that it was therefore unwise for parents to remove their children from the security of the countryside to cities that were in grave danger of being bombed. Indeed, he said, parents should reflect upon the experience of those populations in European countries overrun by conquering Germans and Russians, and should 'count their blessings', including peace, good beds, wholesome food and friendly assistance by voluntary helpers in many parts of the country.

As events unfolded in Europe, it quickly became apparent that further arrangements for evacuation would need to be made. On 22 February 1940, Cornwall County Council's Civil Defence Committee[11] reported that a Conference of Reception Authorities was to be held at County Hall in Truro on Thursday, 29 February 1940, when the proposed arrangements under the new Government Evacuation Scheme would be considered. On the same morning as the conference, the Civil Defence Committee met again in the Council Chambers in Penzance,[12] when the clerk reported that the quota of unaccompanied children to be sent to the area in the event of further evacuation taking place after the development of air attack would be 2,000[13] and that arrangements had been made for Mr Warren, the assistant clerk, to attend the conference and to receive the necessary instructions. The clerk also reported that the conference in Truro would discuss the following:

1) Detraining arrangements
2) Road transport to dispersal points
3) Billeting arrangements
4) Educational arrangements
5) Co-operation between Billeting and Education Authorities

Such was the urgency of the situation that meetings such as these were scheduled simultaneously. Mr Warren was not present at the meeting in Penzance presumably because he was attending the conference in Truro. The conference was given full coverage in *The West Briton* on 4 March 1940.[14] This article is worth recording at length here, as it raises a number of interesting issues, in particular the numbers of evacuees to be distributed throughout the county, and the thorny issue of compulsory billeting:

IF WAR NECESSITY SHOULD ARISE

Cornwall has been scheduled to receive 28,200 children under the Government's revised evacuation scheme. This was revealed to a conference of local authorities held at Truro, on Thursday, when Mr L.G. Hanuy,[15] Ministry of Health evacuation officer for the South-Western area, described the plans which had been made for dealing with the problem in the event of intensive bombing. The Lord-Lieutenant of Cornwall, Colonel E.H.W. Bolitho, presided.

The local authorities and the number of persons to be accommodated in their areas are as follows:– Bodmin borough, 400; Launceston borough, 500; Fowey borough, 300; Helston borough, 500; Liskeard borough, 600; Lostwithiel borough, 200; Penryn borough, 400; Penzance borough, 2,500; St Ives borough, 800; Truro city, 700; Camborne-Redruth urban district, 3,000; Looe urban district, 200; Newquay urban district, 800; St Austell urban, 500; St Just urban, 800; Camelford rural, 200; Kerrier rural, 2,000; Launceston rural, 800; Liskeard rural, 2,000; St Austell rural, 2,500; St Germans rural, 2,000; Stratton rural, 500; Truro rural 2,500; Wadebridge rural, 1,500; West Penwith rural 2,000.

Mr Hanuy stated that evacuation would only be carried out in the event of air raids, and it would relate only to unaccompanied children; there would be no mothers and young children. The department would expect them, if necessary, to use full compulsory powers, but it was hoped they would be able to obtain the billets required without having to use compulsory powers. They might also be required to have a little overcrowding in order to get the children in [...] He stressed the necessity for cooperation between the billeting and education authorities [...] He asked authorities to get their schemes on paper and submit them to the Ministry as quickly as possible.

Mr Hanuy said the object of the roll of householders which they were asked to compile was to ensure that there was an equitable distribution of the burdens of billeting. It might be that the roll would not be sufficient to enable them to meet their requirements. It was unfair that householders who were willing to receive children should be penalised merely because they were willing, and the burden should be shared by those who were able to bear it. It was in respect of those people they should certainly use compulsory powers [...]

The arrangements for the transport of the evacuees were outlined by Mr F.E.G. Reed, representative of the Ministry of Transport, and representatives of the Great Western Railway and Southern Railway companies gave particulars relating to the arrival of trains at the de-training stations.

There was also a discussion about the particular difficulties experienced by reception areas which were sea-side resorts, and whether or not boarding-house keepers should be expected to take children with the billeting allowance, thus depriving them of their normal income. The chairman said he believed a great deal could be done by goodwill and common sense, and he was sure Cornwall abounded in both! A great number of other issues were also raised, such were the concerns of those attending.

The article conveys how massive an undertaking evacuation was, and also the sense of urgency and anxiety experienced by all concerned in its organisation. One can imagine the buzz of conversation immediately following what must have been a lengthy and exhausting meeting, and once the article was published there must have been talk of little else in the area. An abbreviated article was re-run two days later in *The Cornishman*[16] under the following heading:

EVACUEES FOR CORNWALL

PENZANCE ALLOCATED 2,500

An interesting comment appeared in *The Cornishman* in March 1940[17] in relation to the representative of St Just at the Truro meeting:

> St Just District Council on Wednesday night discussed a matter of importance to many residents in that area – the evacuation scheme.
>
> Mr G.J. Richards, vice-chairman of the council, outlined what had taken place at the County Conference, which he had attended.
>
> 'I may say,' he remarked, 'that the object I had in mind in going to the meeting was to get a revision of the numbers allocated provisionally for billeting in St Just, but I found that among all the members present, representing many or most of the places in the county, there was not one single request for a smaller number of evacuees to be sent to them. In view of this I thought it would put St Just in a rather bad light if I made such a claim.'

In all likelihood, many other participants at the conference had similar issues, but such was the climate of the times, and such was the pressure being placed on all concerned by the Government, that most people would have felt uncomfortable if they should appear not to be contributing to the war effort.

The issue of costs to participants in the scheme was discussed in March at the West Penwith Rural Council.[18] Particularly noteworthy is the difference in remuneration between men and women. It is also interesting to note that the costs were to be borne by the Government. The officers of the committee unanimously recommended that:

> [...] Mr Warren be paid immediately the sum of £25 to cover the cost of putting his car on the road and the sum of 3d per mile travelling expenses in respect of the same; the whole cost to be charged to the Ministry of Health Evacuation Scheme Account [...]
>
> As most of the preliminary work will of necessity have to be done after office hours, the committee recommend that Mr Warren be paid at the rate of 1/6d[19] per hour for this work, and that he be empowered, if found necessary, to employ additional assistance at the following rates:
>
> 1/6d for a male, and 1/3d for a female.
>
> The committee considered the report prepared by Mr Warren as to the [...] particulars of the Billeting Scheme which would be based on the education facilities available [...]

The comment about the billeting scheme being based on the education facilities available is interesting, as it would suggest that the 100 or so children in the Jews' Free School party were billeted in Mousehole because that number of places was considered to be available in Mousehole School, a school whose pupil numbers at that time were probably in the region of 100.[20]

Inevitably, these plans gave rise to much anxiety and confusion in the area. In April 1940, *The Cornishman*[21] reported that thousands of West Country households had been sent leaflets in connection with the Government Evacuation Scheme, with a view to obtaining a list of West Country householders willing to look after evacuated children, but that many people had refused to complete the forms. The Cornish people were urged to adopt the slogan 'a Roll of Honour of the Home Front' as this was what this list of householders was felt to represent.

These exhortations appear not to have been too effective, as *The Cornishman* reported on 12 June[22] that the responses to the appeal for voluntary offers to take in unaccompanied schoolchildren under the evacuation scheme had been most disappointing. The number of voluntary billets was less than half the 2,500 figure allocated to Penzance borough. It was therefore stated that compulsory powers would have to be exercised for the remaining half. Quite clearly, the enthusiasm to receive evacuees was not universally felt, though there can be no doubt that many Cornish people did their utmost to take in evacuees and make them feel welcome, as indeed is evidenced by the Mousehole evacuation recounted in these pages. In fact, an article appearing on the same day[23] reported that preparations in Mousehole were well underway, coinciding, significantly, with the return of a number of young men in the village from Dunkirk:

MOUSEHOLE

Quite a number of our young men, attached to various branches of H.M. Navy, were engaged in saving hundreds of lives from the beaches of Dunkirk.

Homes are being prepared for the reception of evacuees expected to arrive this week. Miss L.M. Humphrys has been appointed hon. secretary to the committee.

Many Mousehole residents rejoiced with parents and other relatives on Monday of this week when the glad news was received from Lce Cpl Jack Pender and Jack Richards attached to Ambulance Unit BEF that they had arrived safely back in England; also to learn that Cecil Thurban has returned safely to his base after being engaged in bringing back numbers of men from Dunkirk.

One of the people in the village who remembers these preparations is Jeanne Waters, who was 15 years old at the time:

'I think the WVS did a lot to tell people what was going to happen and where to be at the time, and all we knew was that children were coming from London, and of course it was fully expected that London was going to be bombed. And this was our great fear for the children: we thought, well, at least they're coming somewhere safe. I think the feeling of the adults was, let's see what we can do to help them, because everyone was conscious of the fact that they needed to be made welcome and needed to feel at home because they were coming to perfect strangers.'

A much younger Derek Harvey, then seven years old, was told about the forthcoming evacuation at Mousehole School:

'At the school we were read the riot act about what not to do and what to do. We were told that these poor children had been bombed out of their houses and their houses had fallen down and all the rest. We were forewarned a bit, by parents as well I suppose, that we mustn't sort of mock them or whatever, because it was our village and for a load of children to come to stay, in a way upset things really, altered our lives a bit, because we would have children in the village that we didn't know.'

Clearly, the adults in the village recognised that the arrival of so many evacuees could cause difficulties for the local children and took steps to prepare them for this. Melvia Cornish remembers hearing about the evacuation and also some of the apprehension she felt at the time:

'I don't know whether we were told at school or whether it was Sunday School that some children were coming down from London to stay here and they were going to be billeted with families, and all the families that had spare rooms were going to be asked to take them. This was very important because it was going to be very dangerous in the cities. We were very excited about this but viewed it with mixed feelings, really. We thought, we don't know about these children and will we have room in our school, because there was going to be quite a lot of them.'

Meanwhile, in London, the Jewish community was also considering the prospect of further evacuation, together with the problems which could arise for Jewish evacuees. On Friday 14 June 1940, an article in *The Jewish Chronicle*,[24] probably written a few days earlier, expressed the anxieties of the community:

THE SECOND EVACUATION

With the creeping of the enemy ever nearer to these shores, and the actual start of bombing operations, the Government have come to the wise conclusion that a further evacuation of schoolchildren from the Greater London areas must begin this week. Among the 120,000 children affected there will certainly be a proportion, perhaps a considerable number, from Jewish homes, and their dispersal into parts of the country as distant as Cornwall, Devonshire, Somerset and Wales may add materially to the difficulty of the Jewish problems raised by the earlier exodus. These problems can be shortly summarised as: first, the provision of religious instruction; and, secondly, the possibility of replacing, however inadequately, the atmosphere of Jewish home life of which the children will be deprived. Something, but only something, has already been accomplished in both these respects by the Jewish Emergency Committee and the Central Jewish Committee for Evacuation Problems [...] It would be a disaster all round if it produced a young Jewry more or less completely estranged from its faith [...]

The Jewish Chronicle bemoaned the fact that arrangements were not being made for grouping Jewish children into hostels, as, in the writer's view:

> Such a plan would at least make it possible to dispense with non-Jewish accommodation for the evacuees, and to provide, if only partially, distinctively Jewish surroundings and atmosphere. Obviously, too, it would ease the problem of providing religious education seeing that the evacuees would not be scattered over wide areas.

Although some hostel accommodation became available in Penzance, this would have been too far for the children destined to attend Mousehole School, who would need to be billeted in the village. The day before this article appeared in the London press, there was a huge heading in *The West Briton*:[25]

28,000 CHILDREN TO BE EVACUATED TO CORNWALL

BIG INFLUX BEGINS TODAY

Commencing today and continuing until next Tuesday, children evacuated from possible danger areas will arrive in Cornwall. Altogether, Cornwall is scheduled to cater for 28,000, but it is not known whether this number will be billeted in the county within the following six days.

This was Thursday 13 June 1940. The second evacuation had begun.

WE MEET AGAIN

Telling their stories in their late 70s and early 80s, the former evacuees' memories of the journey to Cornwall are patchy and inconsistent. Many of the children involved were very young, and this second evacuation was even more fraught than the first, as the Phoney War had now become a real war. Just a few weeks earlier the Germans had invaded France and the Low Countries, and the evacuation of Dunkirk had taken place between 26 May and 4 June. On 10 June, Italy declared war on France and the United Kingdom. The signs of war were all around and public panic was mounting.

The children being evacuated to the South West must have left their homes at a very early hour in the morning to embark on a lengthy journey going they knew not where and not arriving at their final destination till the evening, for some late evening. In these circumstances the day must have been a complete blur for many of them. For this reason, many of the former evacuees are unclear about where the journey that day began. It was not possible to assemble at JFS, as the school was by this stage being used by the Fire Service. A number of other schools were mentioned as possible starting points, including Buxton Street School, Deal Street School, Vallance Road School and Robert Montefiore.

These schools were all in close proximity to one another and, as we saw in the last chapter, some of them may have been used as temporary schools when evacuees drifted back to London. At that time, Buxton Street and Deal Street were feeder schools for Robert Montefiore Senior School. It is likely that Vallance Road and Robert Montefiore were one and the same school. All these schools had a very high proportion of Jewish pupils.

Two of the older evacuees, however, Ted Labofsky and Maurice Podguszer, both born in 1927, were able to recall these events in some detail. Here is Ted's story:

'The children who went to Mousehole were the ones who had never been away, or who had come back. It was a very quiet time between September 1939 till maybe June, and then they started [...] Dunkirk was happening, and they expected raids any time, so then my parents said to me, "You're going to have to be evacuated". The Fire Service had taken over JFS, so they took us round to Buxton Street School, just off Vallance Road. They had a gathering of children there from different schools, but mainly from Free School because Free School was the biggest school round there. A good percentage was JFS, but there were also children from Robert Montefiore School which was in Vallance Road. Some of the children were very, very young. We had no idea where we were going. They just put us in a bus, took us to a station, and I don't remember much except the journey down, a long journey on a train.'

Maurice Podguszer has a slightly different version of events, though the details are broadly the same:

'A group of children from the East End of London assembled at Vallance Road School, and from there we were evacuated as Jews' Free School. We were predominantly children from a previous JFS register, and they took those JFS teachers who were available, but there was a separate grouping of children from around Vallance Road. We were all Jewish children who had returned to London and got rounded up to attend school. JFS was closed so the children got taken to Vallance Road. There were 60 or 70 of us, possibly more, and we were 80 per cent JFS, no question about that. There was just the one block of children, we all came down together at the same time. Alongside our children were a lot of children who joined us from other schools who were not Jewish and who were dropped off on the way.

'I went with my younger brother, Arnold, and the instruction that I had as the older brother was that under no circumstances could we be separated. So I can remember marching again through the streets of London. There were crocodile lines of children marching first of all to Liverpool Street Station, where we were put on a train, and by some means or other it went all around London to get to the West Country Station, Paddington.'

The JFS 'block' described by Maurice comprised pupils not only of JFS Junior and Senior School, but also pupils of the JFS Infants Schools and the JFS Central School. Maurice believes that Liverpool Street was a collection point for groups of children arriving from different locations, to be transported to other locations.[26]

'At that time trains could easily go round London without any bother whatsoever from Liverpool Street, through the rails that were running alongside Farringdon and all that way. So there was no difficulty of getting out to the Paddington area.'

This is an important piece of information, as it indicates that even though the children had to reach Paddington Station, which was some miles away, they were able to walk first to Liverpool Street, as they had done for the first evacuation. However, the distance from the Vallance Road area to the station is greater than the distance from JFS in Bell Lane, from where they had walked for the first evacuation. Hence, it is also possible that some children were bussed, particularly the younger ones. Maurice's brother Arnold, born in 1932, tells this story:

'I do remember on the day we were going off that I was given a stamped addressed envelope and was told by my mother that I had to put the address that we were going to on the back so they would know where I was. My parents didn't know what our destination was to be and I assume my brother had the same instructions. I did know at the time that I was going with my brother with the Jews' Free School, but more than that I didn't know, I didn't know any students in that school. I remember wearing a raincoat which was really far too large for me, but I was going to grow into it. We started off at Robert Montefiore School carrying, I believe it was, a rucksack. There were several dozen of us and we went off in pairs and walked through the streets of London.

'I remember one instance en route, in fact we passed my Uncle Bert and I saw him with other men filling sandbags and putting them outside a bank or some other major building. And I remember he greeted us and we greeted him, but we were just walking and couldn't stop and chat. It was sort of "Hello" and "How are you?" and "You're off to evacuation?" and "Yes", and that was it. We walked, it wasn't quite Indian file, but we were two by two, we walked along the street, until we finally got to a station and boarded a train.'

Betty and Esther Posner, born in 1932 and 1933 respectively, also remember leaving from a school, though interestingly they name different ones. Esther thinks it may have been Robert Montefiore and remembers crying when their mother waved them goodbye. Betty thinks it was Deal Street:

'We left the East End from a local school, Deal Street, I remember it well. You could reach this school from Vallance Road. The school there at the time was Robert Montefiore. It was a very Jewish area. Mother saw us off at Deal Street. A double-decker bus took us from there to the train station.'

Vera Goldstein remembers that the re-evacuation was advertised, so that everyone knew where to go, but she does not recall where that was. Before Vera left for the journey, her older sister, Evelyn, who did not go with them on this journey, recalls:

'When Vera and Jack went at that particular time, they had to get their bits and pieces together quickly, and I remember giving Vera a coat I had, because they never had all that much to wear. We never knew what type of climate it would be and so I gave her my coat because she didn't have one.'

Many of the other evacuees must have been in a similar position. Certainly the Mousehole villagers remember that a number of them arrived with very little. Vera's brother Jack Goldstein, born in 1929, recollects that:

'The other children were talking, and one said to the other, "Are you going on the evacuation?" and so word went round we were going on an evacuation again. The Jewish children were spread around, they had got scattered. JFS got taken over by the Fire Service, so I don't know where we assembled. We were all marched off again up Middlesex Street to Paddington, I think. But I wasn't aware we were going to Cornwall, I wasn't aware we were at Paddington. All I remember was getting on a train.'

Information about the re-evacuation appears to have been spread via the local 'grapevine'. Cyril and Malcolm Hanover, born in 1927 and 1933 respectively, believe that they did know they were going to Cornwall. Possibly their father, Jack Marks, being a well-known figure in the community, may have learned of the destination. They know that they left from a school, but they cannot remember which one.

Frances and Mildred Fromovitch, born in 1927 and 1929 respectively, also knew what their destination was to be. Their circumstances were somewhat different to the others as they were not JFS pupils. Together with their three sisters, they had originally evacuated to Aylesbury with Mile End Central School. On their return they learnt that Mile End Central was due to re-evacuate to Wales, and that is where they were due to go; however, they were told by their Aunt Mary, wife of the JFS caretaker Charlie Saunders, that JFS would be travelling to Cornwall, and it was suggested to them that this might be a better destination for them.

It is interesting to note that in spite of all the apparent secrecy, some people in the area did have knowledge of where the schools were to be re-evacuated, though it certainly seems that most of the children were kept in the dark. Aunt Mary's preference for Cornwall may have been because the Saunders had visited Cornwall a few years before the war. Clearly somewhat more affluent than their relatives, they had travelled by car to Portreath, taking with them Frances, who was then aged 10. Frances was likely, therefore, to have been the only child in the group to have previously visited Cornwall. All that her sister Mildred remembers of the second journey is getting dressed and being taken to a station by their mother. Frances believes they went directly to Paddington:

'[...] because I remember my mother standing, waving us off. And that was a bit sad. She was just waving to us and we were on the train, just the three of us [Frances, Mildred and Irene]. Not Ada and not Marie, just the three of us, and the train packed with evacuees.'

One person not on the 'grapevine' as she had not been on the first evacuation was Connie Mellows, who was born in 1931. At the beginning of the war, she had spent some time on the south coast and on her return to London had started attending a temporary school at Toynbee Hall. She learned about the second evacuation from her former JFS teacher:

'One day my mother was walking me to Toynbee Hall through Petticoat Lane market and we met Miss Cohen, my teacher when I was at JFS. She said to my mother, "What's Connie doing in London?" and my mother explained and she said, "Well, you know there's another wave of children being evacuated with JFS. Why don't you let Connie go on that wave?" My mother must have gone home and spoken it over with my father, and they agreed that I should be evacuated out of London. I remember my mother buying me a soft-top suitcase and I remember her putting my clothes in it, but apart from that, not a lot.'

Miss Cohen was one of the teachers who eventually went to Mousehole, though possibly not in June 1940, as she does not appear in a photograph taken in Mousehole in July 1940.[27] It is likely that the reason that she was in London at this time was because she was teaching in one of the temporary schools for returnee evacuees. Connie still recalls her distinctive appearance:

'I remember this lady was quite tall, but then, of course, all adults to me then were tall. But she had white hair and she had an Eton crop and had glasses.'

Later descriptions of Miss Cohen by other evacuees tend to confirm that this was the same lady who went to Mousehole. A brief but interesting account of the journey was given by Ralph Barnes, another one of the teachers, in the article which appeared in his alumni magazine:[28]

A few days elapsed (after my return to the capital) and I was ordered to report at Paddington Station, where I met up with a group of boys and girls and four teachers – two ladies and two men! We entrained for Penzance in Cornwall. On arrival we were bussed to Mousehole. We obtained some classrooms in the local school and were able to do some basic teaching.

Ralph Barnes' daughter, Pamela, born in Cornwall in 1940, thinks that her father and the other teachers in charge of the party were informed of the destination, on a need-to-know basis, prior to the journey. Also, as a JFS teacher, she thinks he would only have been responsible, at least in the first instance, for the JFS children, even though he must have been aware at some stage that a few children from other schools were included in his party. She believes, too, that her parents did meet up with children at a school rather than at Paddington Station, as her father writes, though she has no knowledge of which one. Certainly, this is likely to have been the case, since it is clear from all the accounts that the majority of children started their journey at a school, and it would have been the job of the teachers to supervise them. Pamela recounts:

'I don't know how much notice they were given but I know from both my parents that it was quite an ordeal from the point of view that people in those days didn't do a lot of travelling, and they knew they were going to undertake this long train journey; although, quite by chance, my parents had actually honeymooned in Cornwall in 1935. I know that it was quite an exercise organising all these children and gathering at Paddington station.

'I don't know whether they were told exactly where they were going before they set off, or somewhere along the route, but I remember my mother saying that when they saw this name Mousehole, they said, "What a strange name." The name was just so funny, no one had ever heard of it. They were told that they were going to this village in Cornwall. And all they knew was that they had to go to the furthest station, Penzance.'

THE LONG JOURNEY

For most of the Mousehole evacuees, the journey itself remains a complete blur, other than the memory of the overwhelming fatigue and exhaustion that they experienced. For a number of them, a few fleeting images remain burned in their memories forever. The layout of the train played an important part in the way in which the journey was experienced. Train coaches at that time consisted of a number of individual compartments, each capable of holding about a dozen people, with a long corridor down the side, enabling movement between compartments and coaches. The JFS party would therefore have been grouped into several compartments on one or more coaches. Few evacuees remember the presence of adults, but one assumes that the five teachers involved must have patrolled up and down the corridors to supervise the children. Another important factor was the way in which the various school parties were organised onto the train. Maurice Podguszer is the only evacuee to recall something of how this was carried out:

'It was a long and tiring journey, and we started out very early in the morning, about nine o'clock or earlier. We took the *Old Cornishman* from Paddington, and the train was divided into sections getting off at different points. It wasn't a continuous journey. After several hours the train would stop and children would disembark. Of course, everybody thought that was their turn to get off, but the group of children that I was part of, we stayed on the train. Somebody must have had the instruction that our group was going to Mousehole, that there were x number of places in this town called Mousehole where so much of the population would take the children.'

Maurice remembers Mr and Mrs Barnes and other adults being on the train, but he cannot recall any officials supervising the operation, apart from railway employees. He believes that when the train stopped and some children disembarked, they were told to do so by:

'Whoever was marshalling the train; that is the only way I can put it. I think that the way we were put on the trains was the blueprint for how we were going to get off the trains. If you were in the first carriage, as we were, then you got off at Penzance. Further back you were de-trained in other parts of the West Country before getting to Penzance.'

In other words, those travelling furthest, including the JFS contingent, were placed towards the front of the train. There were, of course, a number of schools who finally disembarked at Penzance. This clearly was the kind of military-style operation that has been alluded to in the previous chapter. Despite his young age at the time, Arnold Podguszer has a good recollection of the journey:

'The journey itself was very long. There were women dressed in grey uniforms at the station, I don't know if it was the WVS, and we got on the train and it went on and on. We were in our own little compartment. I remember adults coming along the corridor but I don't remember anybody being in our little compartment with us. We stopped en route at least once or twice. At those times we were not allowed to get off the train. I do remember drinks being passed in through the carriage windows to the children there, and I do know that groups of children did get off the train. Where they went, or which children they were, I've no idea, but our group stayed on the train. You know, there was always a conjecture, "Where are we going?"'

Arnold remembers catching glimpses of the sea well before they reached their final destination:

'It was very long, very tedious, and we were all very, very tired, but I do remember the thrill of seeing the coast, the sea and the sandy beaches, and wondering, "Hurray, this looks like a holiday. Are we going to stop here?" But we didn't stop, it went on and on and on and on and on, and we were really quite exhausted until we got to...I didn't know it was Penzance. By the time we got off, coaches were waiting.'

For Frances Fromovitch, her abiding memory is of seeing soldiers at Newton Abbot:

'I know we all had haversacks, and probably some clothes and underwear. And when we got to Newton Abbot – I've remembered it all these years – all the soldiers were lining up. I don't know where they were going, but they were standing there, all looking at us and laughing and handing in comics and sweets. These poor soldiers were giving us sweets and comics. So, Newton Abbot – where could they have been going? Years later, I wondered how many of them came back.'

For Frances's sister Mildred, the only memory which remains of that journey is of carrying a gas mask, and a bag with chocolate and corned beef. Two other sisters, Betty and Esther Posner, also recall seeing soldiers coming over to the train and handing them bars of chocolate, which they thought was when they reached St Ives. The fact that the sisters both remember soldiers shows how childhood memories can be reinforced by sharing them with siblings. The train would not have passed through St Ives, though it may well have been signposted on the way. Children destined for St Ives would have disembarked at St Erth.

For Cyril Hanover, the journey was like going on holiday. Malcolm, Cyril's younger brother, in spite of being only seven years old at the time, thinks he remembers the journey very well:

'I may be wrong, but the journey was then, I think, about nine hours, it's speeded up now. The Cornish Riviera they called it. The evacuee train arrived at Penzance at 6pm. And also, I remember the most horrendous sight, and I stand to be corrected, but I can see the funnels of ships sticking out of the water in Plymouth harbour as the train went through Plymouth and then over the Saltash bridge. Then you were in another county, you were in Cornwall. You left Devon and you were in Cornwall. But that was vivid. Now, I don't think I imagined it, although I was only six and a bit at the time. I remember that terrible sight, the Germans had bombed Plymouth and the West Country and the funnels of the ships sinking has stayed with me forever, sticking out of the sea in the harbour.'

In fact, the bombing of Plymouth did not take place until a year later, so Malcolm must have witnessed these events on his return journey. Also, Malcolm was just turned seven at the time of the second evacuation. The age he gives here is that of when he went on the first evacuation. Thus his recollection here is of three separate events. This illustrates how easily childhood memories can become merged one into the other.

For many of the children, the journey was a very stressful experience, particularly as they did not know where they were going, or when they were going to arrive, as recalled here by Vera Goldstein:

'It was only JFS there. I don't remember other schools being on it. The train journey was very, very long and we didn't know where we were going. A lot of the kids were crying because they wanted Mummy and it was very traumatic. I do know that, and it seemed to go on for ever and ever. But finally, when we did arrive in Mousehole, we were treated with the utmost love and care.'

Jack Goldstein has similar recollections and, like so many of the evacuees, has no memory of being supervised on the train:

'We were on a train and we weren't told where we were going, and it seemed to us that we were on this train for God knows how long. It all seems a blank, all I know was I was on a train with a bunch of other children, and the train was jogging along, jogging along. I remember when we finally arrived it seemed as if we had been on it for ages and it was dark. As far as I know, there were teachers with us but I don't recollect seeing them. All I remember about it, it was a hell of a long journey and I was pleased it was over. It was dark anyway and we couldn't see where we were. I didn't know I was at the seaside or anything.'

Other children do recall seeing the sea, but it is likely that many of them were sound asleep on the latter part of the journey and were totally oblivious to the landscape they were travelling through. Even when they disembarked, many of them must have been so exhausted that they were not able to take anything in by that stage. Since it was June, it is unlikely to have been dark at the time the train arrived, but it could well have been so by the time that billeting was completed and the children finally were given a bed to sleep in. Despite his good recollection of the morning's events, Ted Labofsky remembers little of the journey itself, other than that someone came round and said they were going somewhere to the West Country. Of course, this would have meant little to most of the children.

For other evacuees, memories of these events are fleeting and confused. Connie Mellows remembers the journey as being long and tedious. She did not know anybody on the train and, like so many other children, has no recollection of teachers being there. Shirley Spillman recalls the confusion she felt on their arrival:

'I remember having a postcard stuck on me with my name and address and who I was. I can't remember an awful lot about the train journey, it was a very long train journey, and when we arrived at our destination, I didn't really understand where we were.'

Jean Barnes, wife of teacher Ralph Barnes, must have had a particularly arduous journey as she was five months pregnant at the time with Pamela:

'I recall my mother telling me that it was a long train journey, which nowadays takes five and a half hours, but I think in those days it was a lot longer. And it was ghastly conditions, as you can imagine. You know, it must have been just hellish, that's all I can think of. I can remember her saying it was such a relief to finally get to Penzance. It seemed like they'd gone to the end of the world at that point. And I'm not sure, but I think they arrived in the evening, so it had been a long day, and then they still had the whole thing of sorting out who was going where. It didn't stop there, because people had to be bedded down that night, didn't they?'

Long though the journey was, there were children travelling to Cornwall that month of June 1940 who had come from even further afield than the East End of London. Ingrid Rosenbaum, a German Jewish refugee born in 1934, had fled Germany with her mother in early 1939 and within a short while had been evacuated to Northampton, where she was kept in a coal cellar before being rescued once again. Now aged six, she travelled to Bugle near St Austell, where she was billeted with the Trudgians, who treated her 'just beautifully' and accepted her as one of the family. Paul Ritter, another Jewish refugee from Europe, had started his journey in Czechoslovakia and spent some time in Cleethorpes on the north-east coast of England before finding his way to a home in Gulval, near Penzance. Paul, by now 15, was admitted to Penzance County School, where only one year later he passed the School Certificate examination.[29]

One person who did not travel to Cornwall on that day was Evelyn Goldstein. She stayed on to witness some of the terrible events which took place in London during the following months:

'And then came the time when my sister and brother were re-evacuated and I stayed home with my mother, which was a one-parent family at that time, so I didn't go down on the train. We had some terrible experiences staying in shelters in the East End. The bombing had started and we were going back and forth to various shelters. One in particular was originally a horses' stable and it smelled terrible and was very damp from urine. We couldn't lie on the cobblestones, so my mother managed to get two deckchairs and we slept on those.

'Then we moved again and we joined another shelter, a pre-fabricated one which was more or less on the street, and, of course, the bombing was going on. When we came out I saw various limbs lying around and my mother and I were in a terrible state. At that time I had a violent cough, from bronchitis, and my mother then said that she would love me to be with my sister and brother, to be safe and to be in a better environment. So she then went to the Jewish Board of Guardians and she told them that I needed to get away and was it possible for me to do so. So they said providing the person who Vera was staying with was able to take me, they would be willing for me to go, but we had to find our own way there.

'So my mother decided to get me evacuated to where my brother and sister were in Mousehole. We corresponded with Auntie Minnie [Vera's foster mother], and she said I would never have bronchitis again. I went on the coach with mother, it took 10 hours.'

Evelyn already had knowledge of her destination, but for the children who arrived before her on 13 June 1940, Mousehole was a great unknown. In retrospect, it was a huge gamble for the Government to send so many children to such a distant location, so totally unfamiliar to them and where the distance and cost of transport would mean that parents could not check up on them on a regular basis. Everything hinged on how they would be received and cared for in their new homes.

Chapter Five

ARRIVAL

'I can remember the evacuees coming, the very day they arrived. Mousehole was a closed shop, outsiders were viewed with suspicion.'
Derek Harvey

'I remember vividly we went into a hall and people came in and chose the children, and I held onto my sister's hand.'
Betty Posner

ARRIVAL IN PENZANCE

As the train drew near to Penzance, St Michael's Mount and the whole of Mount's Bay came into view. At this point there must have been complete commotion on the train as the children stood up to gaze in astonishment at the scene. Some evacuees recall this moment, one being Frances Fromovitch, for whom this marked the start of a lifelong love affair with Cornwall:

'The journey must have been very tiring. But I remember seeing St Michael's Mount, and I thought, "It's a fairyland." When I said that to my sister Mildred the other day, she said, "Well, it was." And that's how it struck me. We all hopped off the train and there were buses there, green buses that picked us up and then we went all along the coastal road. We were looking at the sea and couldn't believe it. Wonderful coloured sea. And when we got to Mousehole, there was really lovely scenery there too.'

Arnold Podguszer also remembers this moment:

'I remember before we actually arrived there seeing this castle-like thing in the distance which was obviously, we learnt later, St Michael's Mount. And we saw sandy beaches there in the distance as the train pulled into the station. We got out of the train and thought it was like being at the seaside and we could get ice cream and so forth, but none of this happened. I vividly recall that there were two or three coaches waiting for us, and we boarded them, and then again started what seemed like an interminable journey, onwards and onwards, as it got darker.'

Little could the children have known the astonishing reception that was awaiting them at Penzance Station. This was reported in great detail in *The Cornishman* the following week on two successive days, 19 and 20 June 1940.[1] The event was given full page coverage under the massive heading:

WEST CORNWALL WELCOMES EVACUEES

There then followed a blow-by-blow account of everything that happened on that remarkable day, which is worth recording here at some length, such is the atmosphere conveyed. The article speaks for itself, praising the triumphs, but also dissecting the pitfalls of this extraordinary exercise. The children were met at the station by, among many others, John Birch, former headmaster of Mousehole School and by this time Mayor of Penzance.

HUMOUR AND PATHOS

LONDON CHILDREN ARRIVE AT PENZANCE

THE SCENES AT THE STATION

Never have such scenes been witnessed at Penzance Station as occurred there on Thursday evening.

Long, long before the train from London bearing the evacuee children was due to arrive every available vantage point overlooking the station was crowded with spectators. One section, composed in the main of children, lined the Cliff, overlooking the arrival platform, waiting to give their visitors a welcome. Outside, in the station approaches, great crowds had to be controlled by the police and traffic wardens. There was an air of expectancy about, a feeling of curiosity mingled with sympathy for these children sent so far from their own firesides.

Inside the station, there were equally busy scenes. The Mayor and Mayoress (Ald John Birch, JP, CC, and Miss D.P. Harvey, JP), were there with members of the Town Council and Corporation officials [...]

Indeed, it is quite impossible to mention all the people who were there, playing their part in giving a welcome to the visitors. Suffice it to say that it seemed that half the population of Penzance was assembled either inside or outside the station [...]

THE TRAIN ARRIVES

A puff of smoke in the neighbourhood of Long Rock; the Mayor goes down the platform, accompanied by the station marshall, Cllr. P.T. Johnson; Mr H.E. Tucker, the station-master, presiding genius over the great arrival, sees that every last-minute detail is in order. The stage is set, and now, with much waving and clapping from the onlookers, the train glides slowly to a halt opposite to where the Mayor is standing.

The Londoners have arrived.

The Mayor advances and shakes the nearest teacher by the hand, and bestows a pat on the head for the first head leaning out of the window. Nothing formal – just a homely greeting from the civic head of the borough.

And here, a word for Ald Birch alone. The manner in which he received these children, the way in which he was to be seen helping them from the carriages, picking up forgotten articles or chatting with the kiddies excited a feeling of the deepest admiration. He was not acting as the Mayor of the Borough, but as a human, kindly-disposed man, and one felt proud that he should represent Penzance on an occasion such as this.

And what of the children themselves? What did one expect to see? Whatever it was, it was eclipsed by the actual scene at the windows, crowds of eager, happy faces, with not a single tear anywhere. True, they were very, very tired, for it had been 12 hours since they had assembled at their London schools [...]

'Please, Mister, can we get out?' 'Are there green fields where we're going?' 'Can we swim and is there a bathing pool here?' These and thousands of other questions were flung at anyone who went near the carriage window.

They were thrilled beyond measure at the sight of the sea, with its wonderful blueness. Many there were who had not seen the ocean before – the most they had ever done was to go for a day to Margate or Southend.

And, in connection with the sea, one small boy – he could not have been more than seven – made a remark which, for its sheer cockney accent, could not have been bettered; indeed, it almost sounds as if it was made up for the occasion, but it's quite true. Turning to an equally small companion, he exclaimed: 'Cor blimey, I ain't never seen so much blooming water in all my blooming life.'

[...] what of the London teachers themselves? They looked nearly 'dead beat' – far more tired than the children, but they kept a cheery face and had a kind word for everyone [...]

The children arrived with a variety of luggage, ranging from small hand-cases to great suitcases, army kit-bags, paper parcels and every conceivable type of receptacle. A great number of these, of course, were left in the carriages, and had to be retrieved and their owners found. Incidentally, the carriages themselves looked as if half the stock of Covent Garden had been eaten on the way down.

Of course, there were a few very minor tragedies, as when Tommy or Suzie lost her big brother or sister, but everything was soon put to rights, and reunion took place in a wreath of smiles [...]

And so, to St John's Hall. Here, the children, and there were over 1,000 of them, in addition to teachers and helpers, were given tea or milk and bread and butter and jam, to take off the first pangs of hunger after the journey – if there were any after all the fruit and chocolate that had been eaten.

Here, among the chattering, noisy crowd, there were some children who fell asleep over their food, worn out by their experience. For so many of them this was their second evacuation. This was by far the longest journey they had ever made.

There is evidence that the JFS evacuees arrived on that day and not on one of the trains arriving over the next few days, as Mousehole is mentioned in the article as one of the destinations. Remarkably, therefore, none of the JFS evacuees remembers this reception at the station. This may have been because they arrived on a later train that day, by which time many people in the crowd may have dispersed. Also, it is clear from their accounts that they were not taken to St John's Hall like most of the other evacuees, but were immediately put onto buses to take them to Mousehole. Or, they may have been too utterly exhausted to know what was going on.

The author of this article, H. Hartley Thomas, goes on to give more detail about subsequent events. Whereas he is full of praise for most of the people involved both in the organisation of the reception and the foster parents who took children into their homes, he is highly critical wherever he thinks that insufficient attention is given to the needs of the children. He criticises officials at St John's Hall who, for reasons of 'red-tape', kept children waiting for an unnecessarily long time, so that it was approaching midnight before some children were found a home. Eventually some Penzance people, exasperated at the wait, 'besieged the officials, and took the children away bodily', an act to which H. Hartley Thomas gives the greatest credit.

He is particularly scathing about people who took steps to avoid having children, and he reserves his most venomous remarks for a village which, apparently, turned children away, though he refrains from mentioning the name of the village:

In addition to Penzance, the children were taken to such places as Sennen, Sencreed, Mousehole and Newbridge. Wherever they may be, whether it is by the sea or in the country, these London evacuees, fleeing from the terror of Hitlerism, will find a safe haven and happy 'holiday' here in West Cornwall.

They have come out of possible danger into safety, out of darkness into light, and although difficulties in individual cases are bound to occur, it is safe to say that they will find happiness and peace in their new surroundings.

SOMETHING YOU SHOULD KNOW

THIS CAN HAPPEN IN CORNWALL

PENZANCE, SATURDAY

On Friday, we paid a well-deserved tribute to the people of [...] Penzance for the magnificent way they received the London evacuee children into their homes.

Today, we repeat that tribute in the main to those who yesterday made a home for still more children. On the whole the same splendid spirit was there, but regrettably enough there were black spots which are a smirch on the reputation of Cornwall as a county famous for its hospitality.

While many women were besieging the billeting office begging for children to be allotted to them, I had five small children in a car for an hour and three quarters, unable to find homes for them.

The first householder refused to take two small boys, yet he is a great believer in brotherhood!

At the next house the people were not at home, and at the third house, the people were away from Penzance. Back to St John's Hall again, where it took nearly an hour to get new billeting forms issued, including one for the wife of an army officer who took pity on these mites as she saw them in the car, and said she would take the two boys.

Then to another address for the little brother and sister, who sat weary, but patient, while I discovered that the occupants of the house had deliberately gone out (so a neighbour informed me) to avoid taking the children.

Finally, a Treneere resident offered to take the children and they at last found rest.

Then there is the incredible case of a bus-load of evacuees who were sent several miles by bus to a village, which refused to take them, and they were brought back to Penzance.

THIS REFUSAL IS ALL THE MORE REVOLTING WHEN I TELL YOU THAT THERE IS A VICARAGE IN THIS VILLAGE

SUCH IS CHRISTIANITY IN 1940

Another black spot was the man who said he would not give evacuees the same food as he ate himself; why should they live in luxury? Yes, my readers, that statement was made. I have my opinion, and so have you about that man, whoever he may be.

Let him visit the poorer districts of the town and see the way those grand women are feeding the children.

After the rush of billeting children is over, the police should expose by prosecution, those who have deliberately given false information or who have refused to take these unfortunate children into their homes. I know there are many genuine cases where ill health or other reasons make it impossible, but there will be many cases deserving of prosecution.

These are people in this Hell War of 1940, who regard [those] working for hours on end without a break [...] as individuals who are enjoying themselves, and have no responsibilities! Thousands of men have seen the interior of Hell at Dunkirk, and others have given their lives to defend the homes of all those described above.

There is a lot more I could say about these people, more I could say moved by the tragic fall of Paris, but a feeling of nausea is already coming over me.

These examples illustrate the people who, at the first sign of invasion and danger to their homes and skins will come cringing and grovelling to the troops and the LDV; the fathers of the evacuees, maybe, to save them from the machine gun bullets of Hitler.

Thank God, they are the exceptions.

And now I am going to transport some more children, which will cleanse my thoughts.

H. Hartley Thomas

The more negative stories told here by H. Hartley Thomas are examples of the darker side of evacuation, of the kinds of reaction to evacuees which the Government had clearly not foreseen, and yet, as we can see in hindsight, were inevitable. Prosecution was one course of action against such people, but no amount of prosecution would change them into individuals who would receive children lovingly into their homes. The success of the Government Evacuation Scheme hinged on the willingness of people to take children in. Sadly, such stories were commonplace throughout many reception areas, though happily not, it seems, in Cornwall.

BILLETING IN MOUSEHOLE

The exuberance and optimism of H. Hartley Thomas and the people of Penzance was not at this point matched by the mood of the evacuees, for reasons that H. Hartley Thomas would himself have understood. The children arrived in Mousehole tired, dishevelled and confused, and many of them were in a state of distress. They were not at this stage familiar with the layout of the village, and therefore when they disembarked from the buses and were led into a building, they had no means of knowing where they were. Some thought it was the school, but others, including some villagers, have mentioned the British Legion Hall or St Clement's Sunday School, both of which also have large halls. The most likely venue is the school since the education authorities were involved in the billeting process. A couple of the evacuees also remembered going through gates, which could only have been the school gates. If they did indeed go to the school, they could have alighted from the buses at either The Parade, near the Coastguard Hotel or on The Cliff, above the harbour. Had they gone to the British Legion Hall or the chapel, they would have disembarked at The Cliff. Given the number of children who arrived, there is the possibility that they were taken to more than one venue, which would explain the variations in different people's accounts. One of the villagers, 11-year-old Melvia Cornish, remembers going up to the school to watch the evacuees arrive, and she recalls the initial uncertain reaction of the village children:

'When the day came, we all trooped up to the school to await the arrival. They arrived, I think, in a couple of buses, maybe three, and we were out at the gates. We weren't allowed to go into the reception area, but we stood back and let them all pass through and looked at them, they looked at us and we were all giggling and wondering all about it. They were clutching very small parcels of clothing. Some had little paper carriers and some had small paper parcels and one or two had tiny little attaché cases. And lots of parents were up there to receive the children.'

Billeting was such a traumatic event that at this point, some of the children appear to have awoken from their daze, and whereas the journey was a blur, they have vivid recollections of the dreadful process of selection. Some of the village children were old enough and mature enough to recognise the condition in which the children would be arriving. One such person was Jeanne Waters, 15 years old at the time:

'I was down on The Cliff with a number of other people, who were waiting to get these children and take them home and make them feel welcome, really waiting to love them a bit, I think. Everyone was so concerned about how they were going to fit in – were they going to find it difficult? So we must do our best to make them feel wanted and take away any fears they had, about coming to strangers and bombing in London. So at least they would know they were safer here. I think there was a general feeling of great concern for the children. That was the overwhelming feeling that I remember.'

The 'closed shop' mentality, mentioned earlier by Derek Harvey, and the tendency of this ancient village to look inwards, was for the time being set aside in order to welcome these city children fleeing danger, just as in times gone by they had welcomed the victims of shipwrecks. Jeanne recalls the arrival of the evacuees:

'They got off the buses down on The Cliff, above the harbour, which would have been totally alien for them, to see boats in the harbour and the sea. They looked so lost and tired and as grubby as can be, poor little souls. They were probably scared to death. They looked in need of love and attention.'

Jeanne is unclear about where the children were taken, perhaps because her family were not involved in the billeting process on that day, as they did not have an evacuee immediately. This was probably because her grandmother lived with them, but eventually they did take a little girl:

'We had Frederica White, she was six or eight. She had lovely almond-shaped eyes. Her father was a taxi driver and her mother made clothes. Frederica didn't come directly to us. She came to a couple who were friends of my parents, Mr and Mrs Rob Stanley, living down in Coastguard Road. I think Mrs Stanley wasn't very well and found it a little bit too much to care for her, and my mother said, "Look, she can come to us because the boys have gone and there's room." And that's when she came to us, a very short time after their arrival. She called my mother and father Auntie and Uncle Waters.'[2]

Many of the evacuees recall being the last to be chosen, which of course they could not all have been. This was apparently a common phenomenon among all evacuees, the belief that they were last. It indicates just how excruciating it was for them to watch others being chosen, while they were kept waiting and wondering when it was going to be their turn. In general, boys were kept waiting longer than girls, as many people preferred to take little girls, who presumably they felt would be less trouble. It was also difficult for siblings, of whatever gender, who wanted to remain together, as many people were unwilling to take more than one child. The only person who actually recalls being picked early on was Shirley Spillman who, significantly, was only seven years old and was alone:

'It was dark and we went into what appeared to be a village hall. We were grouped round the hall in a circle, standing against the wall with our little suitcases, waiting to be chosen by the people who would be our family and would be looking after us. People looked at you and I think there was a distinction if they wanted a boy or a girl. I was chosen fairly early on by Mr and Mrs Ladner, who lived at Vanguard House, right on the front. They had a little shop in the front, with a library, and sold newspapers and cigarettes, and at the back Mr Ladner had a men's barber's shop. They lived at the back and above the barber's shop. The views that they had, in the centre of the harbour actually, looked straight out on to the harbour.'

Some of the other little girls were chosen with relative ease, but those in pairs or threesomes took longer. Millie Butler, also seven years old, gives this account:

'I went to stay with the Tonkin family, a widowed mother, Mrs Gertrude Tonkin, and her son, Jack, who was the village wheelwright/carpenter and had a shop on Fore Street where he plied his trade. I lived with them at 10 Duck Street and stayed there until I was 11 years old when I returned to London. My cousin took me back to London at one time, but the bombing was very bad and I was sent back to Mousehole after a few days.'

Millie had gone on the first evacuation with her cousins and, it appears, travelled with her cousins again on the second evacuation. The cousin she mentions here was Barney Green. She remembers that he had a friend whom everyone called 'Mac'. This was probably Danny Macintosh, someone who appears to have gained something of a reputation for himself, as he is remembered by evacuees and villagers alike, as we shall later see. He was billeted with Mr and Mrs Richard Ladner on Chapel Street. Millie also recalls that another JFS evacuee was Leila Touchinski who was the sister of actor Alfred Marks.

Ten-year-old Jose Marks, sister of Lenny Marks, gives this description of her arrival in Mousehole:

'All of us, perhaps 100, were taken to Legion Hall to be assigned foster parents. I was chosen by the Madron family to live with them. Their daughter, Stella, chose me out of the remaining children. The Madrons were a big fishing family. I was very happy at the Madrons', but, being young, I was sometimes homesick.'

Jose had to move after some months because the Madrons' grandfather moved in with the family. She then went to live with a Mrs Trembath on Regent Terrace, whose husband was the driver of the local bus and whose daughter Susan was a children's governess. There was already an evacuee living with Mrs Trembath, who, according to the Mousehole School records, was Marion Hewson. Jose recalls that her friends Ida and Max Selner went to live in Vivian Terrace with Mrs Webber, while the Selners' friends, Lilian and Miriam Roar, were billeted with another Mrs Trembath and her daughter, Joan Young, at Portland Place. Yet two more sisters, Betty and Esther Posner, aged seven and six respectively, were billeted with the Drews, as Esther here recalls:

'Most people wanted only one child, and we didn't want to be separated. We were the last to be given billets. We stayed with Johnny and Pauline Drew, he was the lifeboat mechanic of the *Solomon Browne*, which was lost in recent years, and lived at 2 St Clement's Terrace. Minnie Harvey was his sister, who lived on the harbour front. She was a very nice person who always asked us to go to tea.'

Living close to Johnny Drew in St Clement's Terrace were Mr and Mrs Waters, the parents of Jack Waters, and like the Drews they took in two little girls, Celia and Rosita Reiderman, who are well remembered in the village, partly because of their striking appearance – they apparently had fuzzy hair – but also because they remained throughout the war. One villager describes Rosita as being like a little doll, 'everybody fell in love with Rosita'. Sisters Desiree and Elaine Frischman, who were about eight and 10 years of age, were billeted with Ernest Ladner, who was the butcher, and his daughter Lizzie, who lived in Brook Street. Derek Harvey remembers how two other young sisters were placed and also recalls the arrival:

'They arrived in the evening, but it was still light, so it must have been summer. They arrived by bus up at The Parade, and they were all marched down to the Sunday School next to the Methodist Chapel. And all the ladies of the village congregated and they were allocated whoever they could take. Most took one, but some took two. My aunt, Mrs Katie Harry, had a girl, one of two sisters, Betty Konyon, and across the street from her, Mrs Blewett, had Betty's sister, called Deborah. My mother was a tailoress and made clothes, so they were well-clothed and well-shod. A lot of them were; a lot of people in the village took them to heart and really looked after them.'

Myra Phillips, living in Paul, did not witness the arrival, but she remembers people talking about the distressing scenes:

'We didn't see the evacuees arrive, but I heard stories of them just being picked out like a cattle market. People were crying. Anita Godfrey was billeted with us and her brother was at Todden Coath with a Mr and Mrs Taylor who were farmers. Anita was a very shy, quiet little girl. She shared my bedroom with me; in fact, she shared my bed. I didn't mind because I felt that she was lonely and sad. We made her as much at home as we possibly could. My parents were very kind, caring people, and, a little girl coming from home, I mean she could have been homesick. Her brother was always very bright and cheerful but I didn't see him all that often. And David Levene, he lived in Paul, he was a happy little fellow, he had short black curly hair and was a very nice boy, and he lived with the Harding family in Paul pub.'

Records indicate that Myra's first evacuee was a Londoner called Gladys Bartrop, so it seems likely that Anita went to live in Paul at some later stage, though her brother Irvine does seem to have been in Paul from the outset. Also billeted in Paul, at Mount View, were two 11-year-old little girls, identical twins Betty and Doris Fishman, who went to live with another Mrs Waters. They are remembered by many of the evacuees simply as 'the twins'. Another pair of twins, only five years old, were Rose and Philip Chapman, billeted with Mrs Tregenza in Dumbarton Terrace in Mousehole. Not all siblings were billeted together, however. David

Evacuees on the beach in Mousehole, July 1940. The adults seated at the front are Miss Haffner, holding Lydia Barnes; Miss Levene; and (no relation) Mr Levene, with Shirley Spillman on his knee. Back row from the right: Ida Selner, Max Selner, Jose Marks, Betty and Doris Fishman, and the twins.

Evacuees on the beach in Mousehole, July 1940. Mr Levene is standing on the right. Jack Goldstein is seated in the front centre, just behind a little girl.

Evacuees at Paul, July 1940. The group is standing in front of the King's Arms, Paul, which is adjacent to Paul Church Hall, where the Sabbath services were held on Saturdays.

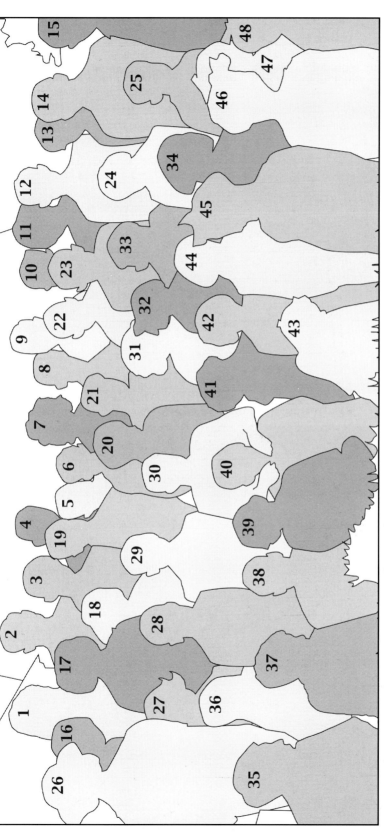

1 Ena Kosky 2 Mr Barnes 3 ? 4 ? 5 ? 6 Jack Joseph 7 Frances Fromovitch 8 Ronney Glazer 9 ? 10 Daniel Frankel 11 Vera Goldstein 12 Bernie Warman 13 Aby Baruch 14 Ronny Smolovitch 15 Danny Macintosh 16 Ruth Coleman 17 Jose Marks 18 Connie Mellows 19 Lenny Marks 20 ? 21 ? 22 Maurice Podguszer 23 Cyril Hanover 24 Malcolm Hanover 25 ? 26 ? 27 ? 28 ? 29 Monty Pirelly 30 Eddie Lazarus or Harry Fireman 31 Mildred Fromovitch 32 ? 33 Ted Labofsky 34 Elaine Frischman 35 ? 36 Arnold Podguszer 37 ? 38 ? Pirelly 39 ? 40 Lew Lazarus or ? Fireman 41 Irene Fromovitch 42 Frederica White 43 Lydia Barnes 44 Desirée Frischman 45 Betty Posner 46 Esther Posner 47 ? 48 ?

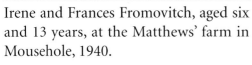

Irene and Frances Fromovitch, aged six and 13 years, at the Matthews' farm in Mousehole, 1940.

Irene, Frances and Mildred Fromovitch, aged seven, 14 and 12 years respectively, in Mousehole, 1941.

Betty and Esther Posner, with their foster parents, Johnny and Pauline Drew, in St Clement's Terrace, 1940–41.

Lily and Miriam Roar on a picnic with their foster mother Mrs Trembath, June 1940.

Lily and Miriam Roar playing at 'school' with their foster mother Mrs Trembath, August 1940.

Millie Butler and Miriam Roar, Mousehole, 1944.

Anita Godfrey and her brother Irvine.

Maurice and Arnold Podguszer in Mousehole, *c.*1940.

Elaine and Desirée Frischman on arrival from London in 1940, billeted with Joan Ladner's grandfather, Ernest Ladner, and her Auntie Lizzie.

Joan Ladner, with her evacuees Harold Lazefsky and Daniel Frankel, *c.*1940.

Ted Labofsky on Mousehole beach, c.1940.

Mr and Mrs Harvey, Ted Labosky's foster parents, c.1940.

Ted Labofsky on Mousehole beach with his foster family, the Harveys, c.1940.

Rosita Reiderman, Mousehole, *c.*1940.

Mrs Reiderman, Mousehole, *c.*1941.

Frances Fromovitch, Mousehole, *c.*1940.

Jack Goldstein, Mousehole, *c.*1941.

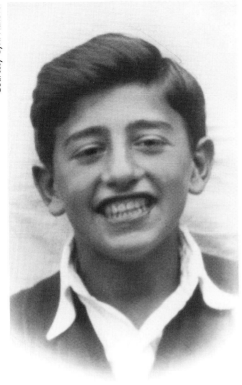

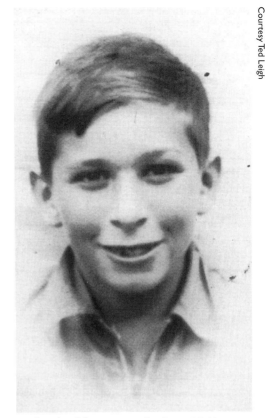

Cyril Hanover, Mousehole, *c.*1940.

Ted Labofsky, Mousehole, *c.*1940.

Evelyn Goldstein in her late teens.

Vera Goldstein in her late teens.

Jack Goldstein with his mother on Mousehole beach, August 1941.

Jack Goldstein (wearing a cap) with Harry Fireman in Duck Street, 1940.

Nurse Pender, Anne Pender's granny, who was District Nurse and delivered over 1,000 babies in Mousehole and district. She held a daily clinic for the evacuee children.

School's Out, by Geraldine Underell. The children would have revelled in their freedom, once released from their school desks and able to go to the beach or harbour.

Pat-a-Cake, by Geraldine Underell. The girls' games were rather more sedate than those of the boys.

Men About Town, by Geraldine Underell. The building on the left is the Keigwin Arms, Mousehole, the only house to survive the Spanish Raid. The local children and the evacuees loved wandering about the village, and it was considered entirely safe for them to do so.

Sea Dreams, by Geraldine Underell. Many of the evacuees, like the village children, enjoyed standing at the harbour watching the boats.

Curiosity, by Geraldine Underell. The ever-fascinating harbour. The boys wearing caps are likely to have been evacuees.

The Landlubber, by Geraldine Underell. Mousehole children in Percy Laity's boat *c*.1944. Left to right: on the steps, David Grose; in the boat, Donald Waters, Raymond Pomeroy (one of those interviewed) and Gordon Prince; in the water, Alan Paris, one of the London evacuees. The name 'Landlubber' is likely to have been used to describe the boy on the steps.

Sea Pups, by Geraldine Underell. Many of the evacuees learnt to 'scull', along with the local boys.

Last Paddle of the Day, by Geraldine Underell. The village boys enjoyed playing in the harbour and were often joined by the evacuees.

More Fun in the Harbour, by Geraldine Underell, *c.*1944. The boys, left to right, are Raymond Pomeroy, Gordon Prince, Donald Waters, Alan Paris, Philip Worth and Russell Quick. The boys had been 'playing boats' in the harbour when the picture was taken.

Mousehole Carnival, 1946. The May Band that year was organised by Joan Ladner, aged 14 years. Mousehole School is in the background, on the right.

Levene's brother Ralph was billeted with Mrs Lugg in Wellington Place, while his sister, Frances Levene, was billeted with Mr and Mrs Harry, on The Wharf. She is well remembered in the village because she stayed until after the war.

Vera Goldstein was billeted with Johnny Drew's sister, Minnie Harvey, and clearly remembers the distraught atmosphere:

'We landed in this village hall, and we were all crying, all tired and bedraggled. My friend Ena Kosky and I, and Frances and Mildred, were the oldest in the group. I remember sitting on the floor in the hall, and then various ladies came in and they were selecting who they would like to have with them. I was chosen with Ena by Mrs Harvey, and we went to this beautiful house called Waterbury. We were very poor in those days, and here I landed in a lovely house. She was lovely.

'Mr Harvey had died in the Great War and their son William was also away at war. I stayed with Mrs Harvey all the time, but Ena didn't stay with us very long. After she left, my sister came down and she had bronchitis. And Mrs Harvey said, "If you can get her into school, I will gladly have Evelyn," which she did.'

Meanwhile, the three Fromovitch sisters, Frances, Mildred and Irene, aged 13, 11 and six respectively, were having difficulty as they wanted to be billeted together, and when Frances and Irene were finally selected, it appears that they were not the first choice of their new foster father. Here is Frances's account:

'When we got to Mousehole we went to the school, I'm sure it was the school, because I remember some village boys sitting on the gate watching us. The villagers had laid on a nice tea for us, of sandwiches, cakes and lemonade, I remember, which was lovely. We'd been on the train a long, long time. Then, after tea, we had to wait around for the local people to take us to their homes. We were left to nearly last as they tried to keep my sisters and I together. The first person I really saw was Stella Madron. She was very pretty, the grown-up sister of Edwin, Jimmy and Joey Madron, and she was smiling all the time. I thought "what a nice lady".

'But I wasn't very pleased with how we were chosen, and that's always struck me because most of the children had gone, and we were still there. I think that they were trying to keep the three of us together. And then Irene and I went with Wright Matthews who lived in a dairy farm on Commercial Road, just before the school. I think we got chosen by him as we were the last ones left. I'm sure he said, "Oh, I wanted another two, but they've gone." I never forgave him. And I put a spell on one of his cows. But we were all right, Irene and I, with Wright Matthews. His wife and his daughter Lenna were lovely. Later on, Miss Oliver would take the three of us, which was good.'

The memory of the hurt at being told she was not first choice has stayed with Frances for seven decades. It is quite probable that this was just a throw-away line on the part of Wright Matthews, and certainly not intended to cause such hurt. When a child finds herself in such a powerless position, unable to answer back, revenge is often carried out in silence, as when Frances said, albeit tongue-in-cheek, that she put a spell on the farmer's cow. Frances's sister Mildred vividly recalls her distress when she was left alone:

'We were standing in the school and lots of people came in and took the children home with them. Two came and took Frances and Irene. I just remember standing in the playground, it was definitely a school playground, and most of the children had gone. I was standing there with one other child, and we were the last two and I stood there, crying "I'm being left here and Frances and Irene have gone." And then this lovely, smiling man came over to me and said, "Come on love, I'll take you, come home with me." His name was Mr Warren. Mr and Mrs Warren, they were lovely people.'

Mildred remembers her feelings at the time, especially when she was finally chosen:

'You were overwhelmed by it all. How it must have been for Irene I don't know, because she was younger. But when I got chosen, I was wanted. I remember feeling wanted.'

Here, she describes her new billet, and two further changes of home:

'Mr Warren, he lived in Commercial Road, when you come in to the village on the main road, leading up to the school. He sold fruit and vegetables to the outlying farms. He had a son who was in the Army and lived in Newlyn and another son in the Navy. When his son came home from the Navy they needed his bedroom, and so I had to leave and stay somewhere else. Now, the second place, I cannot remember the name, he was a shoe repairer and they lived the other side of the harbour. He had a little girl and they were lovely people. And then why I left there I don't know. You just do as you're told, don't you? Then I went to Miss Oliver, and then Frances and Irene came to Miss Oliver.'

Some of the boys, and especially the younger ones, found the billeting process just as upsetting as the girls. Jack Goldstein, who was 11, was in the difficult position of being with two other boys and found the whole episode very distressing indeed:

'The first thing that's in my memory, and I shall never forget, we were standing in what looked like a school hall, and there was all us kids there, and there was all ladies, mostly local ladies, standing around. These ladies were picking kids out and were discussing before and saying, "Who would want two boys?" or "Who wants two girls?" And the ladies would step forward and look at a certain child and say, "I'll have that one," or "I'll have those two," or whatever.
'I was with my friend, Monty Pirelly, and his younger brother, whose name escapes me. I had been in the same class as Monty in JFS. And being as we were three, not many people wanted three little boys. I think we were the last ones standing, and we were crying and tired and falling asleep and we felt shattered. I heard some ladies saying, "What are we going to do? Nobody wants three boys," because most of them never had big houses, most people lived in fishermen's cottages. Anyway, this lady stepped forward and said, "I will take those three boys."'

Although he did not know it at the time, Jack was in fact staying in the home of Joe and Lylie Madron. In spite of being in a good home, however, these were not the end of his troubles, as he was to leave the Madrons shortly in what he calls 'unusual circumstances'.

'Well, we were wonderfully looked after by this lady, and we got wonderful food. The billet was on Raginnis Hill, it was the harbour master's house, and it was in a very good position to see over the harbour, which in those days was full of fishing boats. Very busy little fishing port, you know, and that's why they had that location. They even had a special telescope. Anyway, she used to sit us by this window in the kitchen overlooking the harbour and we had a lovely view, and she used to give us our meals there by the kitchen table. On one occasion this boy, he was a bit cheeky I found out, one day she gave us food and he looked at this food and the next thing he picked up the plate and said "I'm not eating this rubbish," and he threw it out of the window.'

The consequence of this behaviour was that Mrs Madron, quite understandably, did not want to have any more evacuees, and all three boys were re-billeted. Jack continues the story:

'I was then billeted with Mr and Mrs Richards in No. 1 Duck Street, near the harbour, just opposite my sister. She lived I think at No. 2 or No. 4. Mr and Mrs George Richards were an elderly couple in their 60s who offered to take me in. He was a retired fisherman with two grown-up daughters.'

Some of the boys, particularly the older ones, seemed less distressed by the billeting process than the girls. Ronney Glazer, aged 13, was happily billeted with Mr Pender the milkman, on Raginnis Hill. He later moved to Mr Thomas, who had a farm between Paul and Mousehole. Malcolm and Cyril Hanover, who were seven and 13 years old, feel that they were very lucky with their billet. They quickly became part of the family, who provided for them very well as Cyril here recalls:

'I do remember vividly, we were taken to Mousehole on a coach and all put in the British Legion Hall. Well, the authorities were there from the school and the local council and the villagers were there and we were being separated to go to our foster parents, the Cornish people. A lady and her husband came forward, and we were allocated to them. We were very fortunate, Malcolm and I, we had a lovely – well, they were all lovely people – but we were given to a Mr and Mrs Mary and Dick Sampson, who lived in Keigwin Place. They got a pittance, I think, as far as billeting money was concerned. I was 13, but I can remember what five shillings was, in those days, and it was a very small amount. I thought, "how could they manage?" They were so kind, giving up their beds for some of us, and giving us pocket money as well. We had two families. Mary and Dick Sampson idolised us.'

Two other very lucky boys were Lenny Marks, 13, and Bernie Warman, probably of a similar age, who were billeted with Marian Harris's Auntie Florrie and Uncle Vivian Johns in Gurnick Street. Marian and her mother, who by that time were living on The Cliff, were not able to take in an unaccompanied child evacuee as Marian's mother was working full-time, though they did at various points have a mother and baby, and other adult evacuees. Marian does not remember seeing the evacuees arrive, as she was not home from her school in Penzance by that time, but she does recall that:

'They hadn't a clue where they were. It could have been Timbuktu for all they knew. They were just very tired and getting a bit hungry I think by then. My aunt and uncle had two boys, Bernie Warman and Leonard Marks. I believe Bernie's forbears came from Poland. Auntie Florrie went up in the evening to get two little girls. She thought she could manage two little girls, but she was a bit late in getting there for some reason or other, and there were only boys left. So she came home with two boys, much to the delight of her husband because they had no children, and to have two 13-year-old boys, oh, he was thrilled because he could teach them how to fish, where to fish and equip them with hooks and lines. He used to take them out fishing with him. Lenny particularly liked that.

'The boys slept in the back bedroom. Auntie Florrie let the front bedroom, and she and Uncle Vivian slept in the middle room. The boys went upstairs at the back, and they washed in the bedroom with a china basin and jug, using cold water. They had to come down for hot water.'[3]/[4]

Several villagers recollect that members of their family, like Auntie Florrie, arrived late for the billeting. This was probably because they had been to work during the day, or were otherwise engaged, and were, therefore, unable to go until after they had arrived home. This late arrival of some of the villagers must have been a factor affecting the billeting of the children, contributing to the fact that it carried on until late into the evening. It also meant that most of the latecomers had to take boys. Mrs Harvey, Percy Harvey's mother, was also one of those to arrive late, as Percy himself, then 13 years old, recalls:

'The bus stopped on The Parade, up by the Coastguard Hotel, and these little children got out with their cardboard boxes. They walked down Parade Hill, around the corner and up Commercial Road to Foxes Lane, up to the school. And then there was some arrangement for the women in the village to go up and well, just to take their pick because they knew nothing of the children. If they saw somebody they liked they would say, "Well, we'll have that little girl or those two girls or that boy." But I do remember, from what my mother said, that when she got up there most of the girls had been allocated to houses and there were a number of boys that were left to be sorted out. And we had Ted, Isadore Labofsky, and a very nice chap he was too. We got on very well together and he soon settled into our family.'

Ted Labofsky, then aged nearly 13, also remembers being picked out by Mr and Mrs Harvey:

'The next recollection I've got really is being in the school hall. We were all lined up there and people were coming round picking out children, just picking us out. And naturally all the girls went first and most of the smaller children went first, and then at the end there were just a dozen or so boys about my age. By then it was late evening. Well, then Mr and Mrs Harvey came along and said, "We'll have him."

'They lived in Floriana, which is a house behind the chapel at the bottom of Raginnis Hill. Percy Harvey Snr had two sons: Percy, who was very nice and who was one year older than me, and Billy who was younger.'

Another two boys of Ted's age were taken in by Joan Ladner's mother, Janie Ladner. Joan was an only child and remembers her excitement:

'I was told that there were going to be two young people living in our house and I didn't mind whether they were girls or boys. So, we were all just prepared to welcome them and I was thrilled to bits when they came. They came home in the night. Mum went up to the school and brought Daniel Frankel and Harold Lazefsky home. She said the boys were looking very forlorn and everybody was choosing girls but Harold and Dan wouldn't be parted. They were friends and they wanted to stay together. They were older than I was, so from then on they became my brothers really. Well, we just all thought they were wonderful. Of course, they were welcomed at all the houses, even with my granny and granddad and my great-granny, who lived to be 102 and seven months and died in 1950. We were all treated the same.

'And Elaine and Desiree Frischman, who were with my grandfather Ernest Ladner, were also like sisters, and they used to always have lovely clothes their mother sent down. I think their mother was a dressmaker. I also remember their mother playing the piano when she came down here, very well indeed.'

Joan remembers other members of her extended family taking in evacuees.[5] A very young Raymond Pomeroy, only five at the time and living on The Cliff, remembers sitting on the wall opposite the Sunday School and watching the evacuees arrive with their little bags. His family did not have an evacuee, but he remembers that Alan and Tony Paris were allocated to Charlie Jeffery, the shoemaker who lived close by in Fore Street, and that Billy Wright went to live with Mr and Mrs Oliver in nearby Duck Street.

Another two boys to be left to the end were Maurice and Arnold Podguszer, as Maurice, then 12 years old, recounts:

'It was very late afternoon, and we went to a hall in the lower part of Mousehole. And once we were there we were given tea and more sandwiches, and then they decided how they would disperse the children and we were possibly the last two children to find a billet. I can remember distinctly at one point where Arnold and I were going to be split up, Ralph Barnes said, "No, they mustn't be split up." He was there supervising who went where and how, and was very much involved from what I can remember.

'We were finally selected, I should say, round about seven o'clock in the evening, eventually by a person who then became known to us as Nanny. She worked for the Cromptons who we were billeted with and were descendents of Cromptons, the lamp people. It was a very wealthy family. They had a son and she was the Nanny to this son, but the son was away at either

Harrow or Eton. This woman introduced herself: "I'm Nanny, and you will call me Nanny," and took us back to a house at Penlee Point. Mrs Crompton was there and we saw her but Nanny was looking after us. She was, if you like, the boss.'

Maurice's brother, Arnold, although only eight years old at the time, recalls what happened in remarkable detail:

'When we arrived in Mousehole, we pulled up outside what was a stone wall. There were gates there and, just beyond it, maybe 5 or 10ft in, was this large stone building and we went in there. I remember there were curtains at the entrance. It was lit up in there and there were scores of us going in. They had tables or benches set up and there were drinks of hot chocolate. I remember that very vividly because one thing I loathed was hot chocolate, which I declined and therefore I went thirsty because there was no alternative.'

Other children do recall getting refreshments, including Arnold's brother Maurice, so perhaps Arnold was too tired and distressed to realise that other refreshments were available. He continues:

'And gradually people came in and they selected children, and the children were taken. There were two ladies sitting at a desk registering the names, and then they went out through the curtains and out into the street. I remember my brother, Maurice, and I were there almost until the very end, perhaps because my parents had insisted we should stay together. One of the things I do remember was one of the villagers coming round feeling my legs. I was a very thin, spindly child, with a big mop of dark brown hair, and I don't know if they were feeling to determine whether they could make a profit out of feeding me or not. We were almost like Hansel and Gretel and the witch really; children being fattened up.'

It seems more likely that the person was checking to see if Arnold was strong enough to work on the land or on a boat. Clearly this must have been an unpleasant and frightening experience for him, which reminds one rather of the time of the slave trade in America or even of that other ominous selection process going on at the very same time in Eastern Europe. Again, the person who did this could never have imagined that such an action would remain in that child's memory for a lifetime. Arnold continues:

'But anyway, we were almost the last to leave this room and we were really tired. And a lady came and introduced herself as Nanny. I don't know who took our luggage – I am certain we were much too tired and exhausted to take our own, but we must have done. We walked to Penlee Point, along the coast, it was dark and we got to their home and were taken up to bed and we just dropped off to sleep. We were absolutely exhausted.'

As we have seen, most of the children were billeted with Mousehole villagers; however, there were two girls who, like Arnold and Maurice Podguszer, were billeted with wealthy outsiders. Connie Mellows, who was nine at the time, was billeted, together with another girl whom she had not known before, with a Mrs Rose and her married daughter Mrs Lewis, who lived in a very large house on Cave Lane, off Raginnis Hill. Mrs Rose was connected with the Rose's Lime Juice family. Connie has no recollection of the billeting process itself, but her arrival at the house made a lasting impression on her:

'I just remember going there with Mrs Rose who at that time seemed terribly old to me, and her daughter, Mrs Lewis, and being shown our bedroom. I was absolutely gobsmacked, I suppose you could call it, because we had this lovely bedroom with two little beds in it with blue silk throws and on top of those blue silk eiderdowns, with a small chest-of-drawers in between. It was to me like princesses in a castle. The window in the lounge overlooked St Michael's Mount. And it was such luxury as I had never experienced before. Apart from anything else, when I lived at home with my mother and father I didn't have my own room, I was sleeping in the same room as my parents.

'Our bedroom didn't overlook the sea but faced Raginnis Hill, at the back, and the other great luxury for me was the fact that we had a bathroom because we didn't have a bathroom in Bishopsgate. We used to go to the public baths, so that, of course, was the wonder of wonders. But we never used to see a lot of Mrs Lewis or Mrs Rose because there was a maid, whose name I can't remember, who used to care for us and give us our meals.'

Clearly, from Connie's description, this was a much more wealthy family than was usual in Mousehole, and what she could not have known at the time was that these were outsiders to the village who apparently were not integrated into village life, as one of the villagers, Marian Harris relates:

'Mrs Rose lived in the second or third house in Cave Lane. She had something to do with Rose's Lime Juice. They were total strangers who came here and built the house. They had nothing to do with the village and did not socialise with the Mousehole people.'

As a consequence, Connie and her fellow evacuee had a very different experience from the other evacuees, which, we shall later see, sadly led to an early departure for both of them. Connie describes it this way:

'It wasn't that I was unhappy, but it wasn't what I was used to, there wasn't the warmth there that I was used to. There wasn't any warmth.'

The last to find a bed that night among the weary travellers were, of course, the teachers, who like the evacuees had had a very long day indeed.

Mr Levene stayed in Wellington House, the home of an elderly couple, Mr and Mrs Thomas, who had a grown-up married daughter. His family were with him in Mousehole, but may have joined him at a later date. They had their own living room and two bedrooms upstairs and shared a bathroom, but otherwise they lived separately from their hosts.

Mr Nathan and his family, including his son, Bennet, then aged 15, initially stayed with Freddie Ladner, the headmaster of Paul Church School, who lived at Coronation Villa. According to the villagers, the Nathans later moved to a house on Raginnis Hill.

Miss Haffner and her elderly father, Mr Haffner, went to live with Mrs Bodinar on Gurnick Street, though it is not clear whether Mr Haffner went down with the evacuees or whether he joined his daughter at a later date.

Mr and Mrs Barnes and Lydia were given the home of Miss Humphrys, a retired school teacher, who was in fact in charge of the billeting process in Mousehole. Their daughter Pamela tells the story:

'I think she took it upon herself to come over to us as a family – remember it was my father, my mother and my sister – and she could see my mother was heavily pregnant, and she said, "You know what. I've got a cottage, I don't need it. I'm only on my own." I think she went to live with a sister, and she said, "I'm very happy to let you rent the cottage for however long it takes," which was just fantastic. So from day one my parents were in Brookland Cottage in Foxes Lane.'

For Joan Ladner, just eight years old, there was another very important and special arrival that day, who also came on a bus:

'I was just with my widowed mum then, and the day the evacuees came we had our first kitten, he came in a shopping basket from Heamor. And because of the evacuees coming that day, I called him Vaccie, and we had him for nine years.'

A NEW ARRIVAL

There was to be another important new arrival that year in the form of baby Pamela Barnes. Within a short while after the party's arrival in Mousehole, Ralph Barnes received his call-up papers but was given compassionate leave and allowed to stay for the birth of his child. A lovely story about Mr and Mrs Barnes is given by villager Lily Polgrean, 12 years old at the time, in her book about her childhood in Mousehole:[6]

When the evacuees came during the war years, they were from the East End of London. They were the Jewish Free School, and their teachers came with them. They were billeted in local homes and took over the whole of the Infants School, where they were taught. One of the teachers' wives was expecting a baby at the time [...] They often came to the beach at the Boys' Cove and I noticed that the husband was very solicitous towards his wife. He settled her on cushions by their favourite rock, which was a perfect shape for resting her back, and wrapped rugs around her against the sea breezes. I watched with great interest – it was so romantic!

Pamela Barnes was born on 11 October 1940, which that year was Erev Yom Kippur, the eve of Yom Kippur, the Day of Atonement. Pamela here tells the story which was passed down to her by her mother:

'I was actually born in Bolitho Nursing Home in Penzance, which later became the Pirates Hotel. She had a gorgeous room, and said it was total luxury, considering it was wartime. In those days, fathers weren't in at births, and it was a day later that he was now allowed access to come. My father literally walked that day from Mousehole to Penzance, which is a journey of about three miles or so along the coast road there. It was because it was Yom Kippur that he walked.

'Yom Kippur is the holiest day in the Jewish calendar, and my father came from quite an Orthodox background. The Jewish law is that you don't ride on the Holy Days, and that goes for the Sabbath every Saturday, every Shabbat, and it goes for all the high festivals and holidays for Orthodox Jewry.'

At some point, Jean Barnes and baby Pamela returned to Brookland Cottage in Mousehole. Another person to arrive later in the year was Evelyn Goldstein, who had not been part of the original party to Mousehole. Here she describes her own arrival some months later, by which time she was 15 years old:

'We managed to get a coach and we travelled on that coach for about 10 hours, and it was just horrendous because we went over the River Severn, I believe it was, and saw the bombed out areas. Vera and Jack had written to tell me that it was lovely and that you can hear the seagulls and it was very close to the sea, and I visualised it, and I was dying to get there. Eventually we arrived in Mousehole, and Mrs Harvey, who we called Auntie, was so thrilled to see me, and she said I won't have a cough once I'm living there, with a bedroom which would be mine and Vera's to share and be our own. And that's what happened – it was just like living in paradise.'

Chapter Six

FIRST IMPRESSIONS

'My first memory is of watching the fishing boats coming and going all day long.'
Jose Marks

'I'd never seen the seaside before. Well, I thought it was beautiful. To me it was like a wonderland.'
Jack Goldstein

LOCAL REACTION

Trains continued to arrive over the next few days, and H. Hartley Thomas, writing in *The Cornishman*, continued to berate those who fell short of expectations with regard to the treatment of evacuees, but he remained full of praise for those whom he considered to be doing their duty. As we saw in the last chapter, full page coverage was given in *The Cornishman* on 19 and 20 June 1940, which were a Wednesday and Thursday. The first train to arrive had been on the previous Thursday, 13 June, with further trains arriving until Tuesday 17 June. For this reason, it was possible for *The Cornishman* to cover the entire event in one edition, which it did to very great effect. In one of the later articles of the same edition,[1] H. Hartley Thomas was particularly scathing when children were kept waiting for long hours, so that the cars which had come to collect them were kept idly waiting when they could have been deployed in helping distribute other children. He did not blame the voluntary workers, many of whom had been on duty for many hours, but rather the system; indeed, it is hardly surprising that such hitches occurred given the enormity of the exercise and the speed with which it had been arranged. He went on to describe some of the more positive stories:

> Everywhere one is hearing stories of the kindness extended to the visitors. Of course there are exceptional cases, where the children are not wanted. But it is quite safe to say that both in the Penzance and West Penwith area there is not the slightest need for any child to be in a house where he or she is not wanted, or they will not be well cared for [...]
>
> The Mayor of Penzance (Ald John Birch) is still indefatigably meeting every train, and is working like a 'brick' to give the children a sunny and cheery welcome.
>
> The Mayoress (Miss D.P. Harvey) is working herself to a standstill as head of the Women's Voluntary Services. She and all her helpers are doing a wonderful job.
>
> The arrangements for the billeting of the children in the West Penwith area have worked quite smoothly, and it is understood that everything has been settled and every child found a home before a late hour at night [...]

Throughout the weekend, on the sands, in the sea, and in the fields, the Londoners were enjoying themselves to the full in their surroundings. Sights that they had never seen before were causing them untold delight [...]

And finally, one story of kindness at the station. One of the children dropped a sixpence which lodged behind the door, and could not be reclaimed. The services of a railway porter were enlisted, and what did he do? Did he grumble? Not a bit of it. He fetched the necessary implements and removed the back of the door, placing the sixpence into the hands of the child who, but a few moments previously, had thought that its fortune had vanished forever [...]

One mother of 14 took away 12 from one centre. It took three cars to convey them and their belongings. Mothers like these are the salt of the earth.

The same article also related the story of a number of Catholic children being re-billeted within the area so that they could come under the care of a local Catholic church. Clearly, the authorities were prepared to take account of children's religious needs, but since there was no synagogue in the area, the Penzance synagogue having closed early in the 20th century, it would not have been possible to make similar arrangements for Jewish evacuees.

Appearing in the same edition of the newspaper, and on the same page, were articles and letters from a number of readers expressing concerns about the welfare of the evacuees billeted in the area, some of which were to be of particular relevance to the Mousehole evacuees.

WARN THE CHILDREN

Will all our readers and their friends who have evacuee children billeted in their homes please make them understand that the Penlee quarry blasting is harmless.

Many of these children are liable to become hysterical, if they suddenly hear these detonations – which occur four times daily.

Maurice and Arnold Podguszer, who were billeted in a house opposite the disused quarry at Penlee Point, just outside Mousehole, were to have an adventure there, as we shall see in a later chapter. Betty and Esther Posner were clearly unaware of the warning below when they later got stranded on the beach at Mousehole:

EVACUEES AND THE SEA

Sir, I have been told that a large number of the Penzance evacuee children who have recently come to the Penzance area never saw the sea before they came here, and had no idea of what it was like. These children are crowding our beaches, but know nothing of tides or currents. Would it not be a good thing if their guardians and the general public warned them of the danger of going into the water beyond their depth, lest what was intended for pleasure might end in disaster.

Herbert Richards, Penzance, 18 June 1940

It was common throughout this entire period to see appeals for clothing for evacuees in the newspapers, such as the one below, again in the same article:

CLOTHING FOR EVACUEE CHILDREN

MAYORESS'S URGENT APPEAL

We are requested by the Mayoress of Penzance, Miss Dorothy P. Harvey, to make an urgent appeal to the people of Penzance to provide clothing for evacuee children in the borough. Many of the children have arrived with only the clothes they are at present wearing. The stock which the Mayoress had in hand is exhausted, and a fresh supply is urgently needed.

Many of the evacuees did indeed come from very poor homes and had little clothing of their own. It is also true to say that they were only allowed to bring a small amount of clothing with them, which is unlikely to have been sufficient for those children who ended up staying for a long time, in some cases throughout the war. Foster parents varied in their levels of generosity, but it is certainly the case that a number of Mousehole families clothed the evacuees billeted with them out of their own pockets.

LETTERS OF GRATITUDE

A number of letters from teachers who had accompanied evacuees billeted throughout the area, again written in the first few days, also appeared in *The Cornishman* on 19 and 20 of June 1940, expressing their gratitude for the manner in which they had been received. Many of these letters are fulsome indeed in their praise, and it is clear that these expressions of gratitude are not just a mere formality. A St Buryan resident quotes one London headmistress as saying: 'this is how we dreamed that it might be but never dared hope it would be'.

Several more letters of gratitude were published in *The Cornishman* a week later.[2] The following letter, addressed to the Penzance Town Clerk,[3] is of particular significance, as it is written by the chairman and secretary of a committee representing the leaders of school parties. The speed with which this committee appears to have been formed suggests that the teachers involved had learned from their first evacuation experience of the need for such co-ordination:

Dear Sir, On behalf of the recently formed committee representing the leaders of the school parties and all London teachers evacuated to Penzance and district, we wish to express our deep appreciation of the generous reception accorded to us and our pupils by the local authorities and foster parents.

Most of us have had experience of the previous evacuation in September last, and can assure you that our reception by Penzance folk compares very favourably in warmth and sympathetic understanding with anything we have met elsewhere. We should also like to express our admiration for the way in which this very difficult task has been tackled by the officials and voluntary helpers. The organisation has presented a very difficult problem, but by the enthusiasm and spontaneous expression of goodwill of all concerned it has been carried through very happily and successfully.

It is our sincere hope that on further acquaintance we and our charges will be found worthy of the kindness and hospitality we are receiving in such liberal measure. Yours faithfully,

A. K. Horwood (Chairman)
C. Walshe (Hon. Secretary)
Penzance, 22 June 1940

Three further letters appeared in the same edition of *The Cornishman*,[4] from teachers billeted with their parties. A Mrs Frances Arkwright, leader of Party iv/140 billeted in Newlyn, wrote:

Everyone was most friendly and the kindness of which you and all the people receiving us was almost overwhelming. Nothing at all that would contribute to the happiness and well-being of the children seems to have been overlooked. It will be a great relief to the parents in London to know that their children are getting such wonderful treatment. The teachers and myself thank Penzance and Newlyn people most heartily.

A Mr R.C.C. Brown of Edmonton School, now domiciled in Goldsithney, wrote:

Sir, I feel we cannot let the opportunity pass of thanking all who have even the least share in our welcome to Cornwall, and more especially in our welcome to and settlement in and around Goldsithney. Even nature itself seemed to invite with the people in its welcome, gorgeous skies, long fine days and marvellous blue seas, inviting us to revel in their sparkling waves.

From the moment we reached Penzance, at about 5pm on 14 June, we realised we were at home. Every consideration was shown us there [...] and [then] we were off by coach for the picturesque village of Goldsithney.

Here we were right royally received; a very welcome tea was waiting us [...] When I say most of us had been up at 4 or 5am, you can understand that the tea and rest were doubly welcome.

After tea, a fleet of privately owned motors arrived to take us to our new homes, and [...] soon after 7pm we were all really 'At Home'. [...] many of our party have had from 3 to 5 months in billets, [and] the people of this village and its environs seemed determined to make us forget the word billets and substitute 'home'.

What a tragedy that it needed a war to bring the children of our greatest town to this aptly named Cornish Riviera! Finally [...] I do hope [...] that our stay here will only be the commencement of many lifelong friendships.

A teacher billeted with his party in Marazion also wrote a letter, which may have particular relevance to our story:

Sir, I am writing on behalf of my colleagues and myself for the really magnificent manner in which Marazion welcomed our children. One word can aptly describe it. 'British.'

True humanitarian Christianity was shown. No one thought of creed, race, colour, wealth or poverty. There were children – the future of the British Empire.

What did the children think of the spread? I think that some did not believe it true. One incident will describe what I mean. A child pushed a penny into a Girl Guide's hand and said, 'A penny jam cake, please.' She had to be persuaded to take the penny back! Marvellous, all free!

I should also like to express our thanks to a few of the helpers whose names I managed to catch and remember [...] Also, there were many car folk who 'took the children for a ride' – home. Oh, I mustn't forget the wonderful Girl Guides…

I want to close this already rather long letter with one request. Men and women of Marazion, when our school is set going, visit the 109 new babies of your village, and you will be proud of them – and pleased with yourselves. I am, yours faithfully,

J. Bourn (teacher in charge)
Marazion Hotel, 23 June 1940.
PS They are not 109 perfect angels!

The name of the teacher in charge in the letter above, J. Bourn, is most interesting, as are his comments about humanitarian Christianity and the lack of thought for creed or race, which leads one to believe that he may not himself have been Christian. There was a JFS teacher called J. Bourn who was evacuated with JFS to Cambridgeshire and wrote a number of articles and poems in the *Evacuation News Sheets*. One of his poems is quoted in Chapter Three at the beginning of the section on the first evacuation. This could well have been the same J. Bourn, as there are reports that there were quite a large number of Jewish children in Marazion, and he may well have been assigned to be in charge of them.

An article also appeared on that day about how well the Mousehole evacuees were settling down,[5] though interestingly, no mention is made of the fact that they were Jewish, an indication of the way in which they were accepted without question.

MOUSEHOLE

Practically the whole of the evacuees have settled down in the district, and boys' and girls' glowing letters to their parents have called forth replies of heartfelt gratitude with also numerous letters of appreciation to foster parents [...]

On Monday evening, in a field lent by Cllr A.W. Matthews, boys and girls of the school and a number of evacuees assembled, the latter sharing with local children a programme of sports.

EVACUATION SNIPPETS

Also appearing in *The Cornishman* on 19, 20 and 26 June 1940 were a number of amusing anecdotes, often inspired by the Cornish fascination with the cockney accent.

One little humorous story. Two kiddies were billeted in a house, where there was a budgerigar. Says one to the other 'Ooo, look, there's a coloured sparrer!' 'Garn,' said the other with scorn, 'that ain't a sparrer, that's a baby owl.'[6]

...And then there was the lovely, blue eyed, golden-haired little girl, aged five years, who though extremely happy in her new home uttered never a word.

She was dressed, bathed and given some biscuits and milk, but still the couple she was going to live with had not heard her voice.

Then, as she was laid between the sheets, in a loud cockney accent, the 'doll' spoke, and her first words were 'Oh! Boy. What a bed!'[7]

OVERHEARD

Sir, You have recently published very amusing sayings by the evacuee children now at Penzance:

Girl to boy: are you an evacuee? Yes.

Boy to girl: are you an evacuee?

No, I am an evacushee.

Guardian to friend: My two children are named Greygoose.

Friend: And I have two Partridges.

Herbert Richards, Penzance, 23 June[8]

THE FIRST FEW DAYS

The arrival of 100 or more evacuees in Mousehole resulted in a doubling of the child population overnight. Even given the willingness of the villagers to host the evacuees, this must have felt like an invasion. Many of the evacuees were very quiet on arrival, such was their fatigue, but this changed rapidly as they started to explore their new environment, as Marian Harris recalls:

'They weren't particularly talkative when they arrived, I think in a way they were too traumatised. And they were certainly overcome at the sight of the sea. But the very first morning after they'd arrived they were all up early and were all down on the beach, the harbour, the quay; the places seemed to be black with them. I think I'm right in saying that our local lads then didn't go into long trousers until after they left school, but all these boys from the East End had long trousers on, and I think that was something that we'd look and say "Oh goodness, they're all wearing long trousers."

'To use a modern phrase, we were gobsmacked, because there seemed so many of them, and they were all so different, and all with what we used to call a cockney accent. We hadn't come across that before and they were everywhere. Whereas Cornish children, possibly, taken somewhere else would have been a bit slow to explore, these children were all over the place. It was as though they'd suddenly been let out of prison, and I think possibly they hadn't seen the sea before. It was all very exciting for them. Some of them got very tired of it very quickly and wanted to go home, and they did go home. But quite a few stayed and the friendships that they made endured for many, many years; a lifetime.'

Understandably, some of the village children initially felt some resentment towards the children who were invading their village in this way, as did Melvia Cornish:

'Well, at first, we were absolutely overrun. It seemed to us they were going in all our favourite places, and going out on our beach, bathing where we usually bathed, and we weren't sure about that. I don't remember any rows with them, but certainly we might have had a few arguments about, "You're not going on that bit, that's our bit," and that sort of thing, but of course they wouldn't know which were our bits or not. Gradually we just took it in our stride really; I mean, children do.'

Young as he was, Derek Harvey recognised the trauma that the children must have suffered:

'The evacuees, they were a rather woe-begotten lot, which was fair enough really, because they'd been turned out of their home and turned out of their place of living. As far as they were concerned they'd come into a strange land, because we children of that age, we were free as the air, we wouldn't know a war was on really, because there were no restrictions on where we went.'

Jeanne Waters recalls, in particular, the way children spoke, as well as their new-found freedom:

'The main thing, I think, was the different accent. Instead of a sort of laid-back West Country burr in the voice, there were these sharp little cockney voices, like little cockney sparrows, you know, calling to each other. They settled in very quickly and you could hear them calling to one another. There wasn't a great deal of traffic in those days in the village, and they were able to run about on the beach, they could run in the harbour and they could run in the street. They weren't as restricted, I think, as they probably were at home, so they must have had a sense of freedom when they came here. But the greatest thing I found so strange was the accent.'

Another villager, Melvia, also commented on the strange accent of the evacuees:

'Next day, which was their first day, I remember being down in the middle of the village under the clock, and there were all these children. We looked at each other and when they spoke, and we spoke, we didn't know what they were talking about, their accent was just completely foreign to us. We thought they'd come from a foreign country, and they didn't understand us at all because we were speaking our natural dialect in those days. But gradually we did talk to them and gradually we got to know them.'

Such was the Cornish interest in the cockney accent, already noted in the newspaper articles above, that one evacuee, Ronney Glazer, was called upon to carry out a very unusual duty for his foster father. Luther Pender asked him to visit his mother once a week because she was so fascinated with Ronney's accent! Of course, the evacuees also must have found the Cornish accent difficult to decipher at first, as Ronney here recalls, though eventually many of them delighted in learning typically Cornish phrases:

'On the first morning we had to walk down Raginnis Hill to register at the school. People all said "good morning" in that strong accent. It felt like being in a foreign country, but they made you feel welcome. It was very uplifting since leaving home as a youngster was a bit of a tear.'

Ronney's comment about the children being required to register at school on that first day is interesting, as it is only mentioned by one other evacuee, Arnold Podguszer. It certainly seems likely that the JFS teachers would have needed to check the numbers and billeting arrangements of all their charges, and that they and the Mousehole teachers would have needed this information in order to make the necessary arrangements for the schooling of the evacuees. However, as we shall later see, schooling did not begin immediately.

In addition to the difference in accents, some of the evacuees had names which were unfamiliar to the Cornish people, which lead to difficulties for Percy Harvey's evacuee, Ted Labofsky, as Percy here recalls:

'Well, this chap was called Isadore Labofsky, and I think it probably was during his time in Mousehole that he decided that he would rather be called something else, because I know we then started calling him Ted. Whether this had anything to do with it, I'm not too sure, but we had a butcher who used to come up with his basket of beef every weekend, as we always had a joint on Sundays. And he would look around the door and say, "Is Isadore there?" and if Isadore was there he would say, "When is a door not a door?" Ted didn't take too kindly to this thing happening repeatedly, and I think it was then that he perhaps decided that Ted was a better name than Isadore. But I know that before he left we'd forgotten the name Isadore and he was Ted to us and one of the family.'

In actual fact, Ted had always been known as Ted, but his official name, Isadore, must have appeared on the evacuee record form and therefore become known to his foster family. This was harmless banter, no doubt, but is perhaps an example of why many Jewish people felt it necessary to anglicize their names; indeed, Ted also later changed his surname from Labofsky to Leigh. Percy soon started to learn about Ted's life in London, and came to realise what a different life he and the other evacuees had there:

'He talked about his parents and how his father was a tailor. To somebody who lived in Mousehole in those days, talking about London was like now talking about Vietnam or somewhere. It was certainly unknown to us what London was like. But we soon learned that when they came down, many of them hadn't seen a cow, they didn't know where the milk came from and they didn't know very much about country life. But this was part of our life and they soon learned that there was another existence other than the back streets of the East End of London. I think they probably learned more than we did because they came to us and lived in our community, and I don't think that there was any difficulty at all in them joining in with life in the village. They fitted into the village remarkably well.'

As Percy indicates, in spite of the issue regarding his name, Ted quickly learnt to appreciate village life:

'Well, I thought it was very nice because we had a nice garden, the two boys were very friendly at the time. I thought the village was beautiful. I still do.'

Sadly, there were in those early days a few forms of unpleasantness arising due to the evacuees' different religious backgrounds. A number of them recall that, because they were Jewish, a few local children thought that they must have horns. This may well have been part of the reason for the early departure of some of the evacuees; however, for those who remained, this was soon forgotten and forgiven as the evacuees became accepted into the village. No doubt the misconception that Jews had horns was a myth which was easily dispelled once the local population were in contact with real Jews. Unfortunately, in many other parts of the country, this belief that Jews were in some way devilish was far more widespread and was quite an issue for Jewish evacuees in those areas.[9]

Some of the younger children found it more difficult to settle in than the older ones, as they were, naturally, missing their parents. Malcolm Hanover remembers his first day in Mousehole:

'I was very sad our parents weren't around, they were back in London. I remember I must have been crying, and Auntie Mary looked at these two evacuees, one of six and one of 12. We were in a sitting room with the stairs going up to the bedrooms, like in a ship. Sitting in this lounge with the radio on, and us very sad and me probably tearful. And – Cyril remembers this – Auntie Mary said "Bugger Hitler!"

'She really felt for us, for what he'd done, taken these kids away from their family, their parents. She was marvellous, she was wonderful, as was Uncle Dick. He was just an ordinary fisherman in his boat going out to sea. I went back to stay with them several times in later years.'

Most of the other younger children also quickly recognised what a lovely place they had come to. Betty Posner remembers the nice, kindly people who made them welcome, while her sister Esther remembers the beautiful harbour and coastline, and the lovely walks up Raginnis Hill. Jose Marks remembers watching the coming and going of the boats and the friendliness of the villagers. Arnold Podguszer gives a very full account of that first day and the impact it made on him:

'I do remember the following morning the thrill of going down onto the beach. It wasn't a sandy beach, there were rocks, large rocks and little pools of water where you could see fish and other sorts of marine life. To me it was a wonderful thrill to see this and to clamber over the rocks. When I had been to the seaside with my parents it was always a seaside where there was sand and you didn't see much of the buildings. But this was a really beautiful and quaint village and actually it was a lovely little place. It was delightful!

Arnold is clear that, even at the age of eight, he recognised the beauty of his new surroundings. Most of the older children were also unequivocal in their praise of Mousehole and its people right from the outset. Malcolm's older brother, Cyril, settled in very quickly:

'It was lovely because it looked like we were on holiday. Lovely harbour, small fishing vessels. Everybody there was a fisherman, practically, except for one pub, one barber, a couple of fish shops and a Post Office run by a lovely couple, the Blewetts. Wonderful, wonderful village, wonderful, friendly people. Right from the start!

Maurice Podguszer also remembers the first few days as feeling like a holiday:

'This was a wonderful trip to the seaside. The bedroom we had overlooked the sea and the Penlee lifeboat slipway. Penlee Point is about a quarter of a mile outside Mousehole, no more than that, and it was an easy walk down. This was where the lifeboat was kept, and opposite Penlee Point was a disused quarry.
'In the first few days, it was a question of excitement, apprehension and a great holiday. It wasn't a question of we were going to school or anything. It took some days before we had the reminder that we were schoolchildren, and we had to attend school!

For Mildred Fromovitch, also, the village captured her imagination from the moment she arrived there:

'It was like a place of magic actually, because it was a place I'd never seen before; the boats, the people and the sea. It was like a place that wasn't real!

In spite of her resentfulness at not having been Wright Matthews' first choice, Mildred's sister Frances immediately fell in love with the village:

'I thought it was wonderful because of the water, the sea. I couldn't believe it. I mean, when you come from the East End of London to a place like that, it's magical. I couldn't get over it. And we had a good old time on the beach. I think it took about six weeks before they could get us into the school. They had to work it out, because there were all these extra children. But I loved it straight away.'

Jack Goldstein, who had had a difficult start due to the change of billeting, was nevertheless tearful in recounting how much he loved the village. His older sister, Vera, was also fulsome in her praise of the village and its people when describing her early days there. Like so many of the evacuees, she commented on how unreal the situation seemed, so far removed was it from the reality of their own lives back in London:

'My thoughts were, obviously, worried about the three of us leaving my mum. Well, at that period it was Jack and I, but the lady was so hospitable to us, she was so lovely, and then for the first time in my life there was a bathroom there. She had a piano, and her daughter played the piano beautifully. Mrs Harvey was a piano teacher and she played the piano, and everything was so new and exciting. From the kitchen window we could see right down the harbour and it was just like another world. It was wonderful. I was just absolutely...I couldn't believe it. I thought I was on another planet.'

Having already visualised Mousehole from the letters she had received from Vera and Jack, Evelyn Goldstein's expectations were all fulfilled when she arrived in Mousehole later in the year.

'I thought it was just as I saw it in my mind's eye. I was just thrilled to be going there, to this cottage which was in a little Ope, along the quay. They called it the Ope because that was where we walked through and then you were on the little main road near the quay, where the harbour was, and the bus used to stay there. Mr Harvey was dead and her son was a Japanese prisoner-of-war, and her daughter was a school teacher and worked in Penzance. And so, of course, she was living in the cottage with us.

'On the corner there was a shop, I think Mrs Ladner was there. That's right, and she had two sons and we all became very friendly, like we'd been there forever. Auntie was so proud, she used to take us all over the village and say, "Look at my two pretty maids," and we went with her everywhere. She used to like us to hold on to each arm and she would take us everywhere, all over the village to show us off.'

A charming memory of the children's first week in Mousehole comes from a surprising source, Dorothy Yglesias, founder of the Mousehole Bird Hospital, in her book about her work.[10] Although several of the evacuees remembered visiting the bird sanctuary, Dorothy is the only person to have mentioned that the local children were given a week off school:

If the sanctuary had more birds during the war, then Mousehole certainly had more children. In 1942 *(sic)*, numbers of young evacuees were sent to the district and many from the poorest parts of London came to live in the village.

The local children were given a week's holiday in which to get friendly with the newcomers and show them the 'sights'. We came under the latter heading, and one day a whole gang came up to visit us. We did our best to explain the why and wherefore of everything. They listened in silence.

Then one little girl piped up, 'Any reward?'

'None whatever, except that you will have saved a bird's life,' we told her.

A fat little boy with the look of a future city alderman then said solemnly, 'A beautiful idea, I think, meself.'

In the coming weeks, the evacuees had plenty more opportunity to see the 'sights' and to settle into village life. One factor which helped them in this process was that the summer of 1940 was a particularly good one, with long, endless days of sunshine, right through to the autumn of that year. What better place for children to be, during that period of war, than the beautiful village of Mousehole?

Chapter Seven

VILLAGE LIFE

'We were part of village life, of course. You couldn't avoid it. They took us in and they were really warm, very friendly. It was a whole different culture, going away from London. You got the ocean, you got the fresh air, and the wonderful atmosphere and people. Just wonderful, country folk, marvellous. We couldn't have gone to a better place. That's why people kept going back.'
Malcolm Hanover

THE RHYTHM OF VILLAGE LIFE

By all accounts, the children adapted very quickly to village life, a process which was frequently described using such terms as 'they integrated well', 'they were part of the family', or 'they became part of village life'. In addition to the good weather, this process of integration was assisted by the fact that village life was governed by a distinct pattern, centred on the one hand around chapel life and on the other hand around domestic routine, which in itself was underpinned by the fact that this was a fishing community. This way of life was something that was familiar to the Jewish evacuees, since Judaism also revolves very closely around religious, family and community life. In fact, Judaism is sometimes described as not just a religion, but also a way of life, which impacts on every aspect of daily routine. Even those evacuees who came from families which were not particularly religious would have been very familiar with the routine of Jewish life, because of their attendance at JFS. For both communities, therefore, there was a pattern to each day, each week and each season, throughout the year. For both communities a great importance was also placed on children and the elderly. Marian Harris describes how quickly the children fitted in:

'After a time we accepted them, so that in spite of coming from the Jews' Free School, they became part of a village which was 95 per cent Methodist. And the foster parents simply took the children to chapel and they lived as village children. The ones I think who didn't fit in quickly went home. I suppose we just became one community. Any disputes we had wouldn't have been anything more than you would have had with a local lad or girl. We just accepted each other. I mean, they were different, but over the months that disappeared and we just accepted their presence. There were differences because they were Jewish, but the headmaster, Mr Levene, because his children were so happy and well-cared for, made no objections to them going to chapel, as long as they went to synagogue on Saturday. They all had to do that, and they had to observe the fast and the religious festivals.'

Jeanne Waters spoke of the way 'village life very much had a routine to it. That was the way of life here.' Living with Mrs Harvey, Evelyn Goldstein, the oldest of the newcomers and the same age as Jeanne, was quick to recognise and appreciate this routine and to participate in it with enthusiasm:

'Everything was a pattern, everything was the same. In the week we attended school, where I helped out, and we'd come home lunch-time and look forward very much to the meals. It was just wonderful and then we'd go back after lunch and come back home about fourish and we would have tea. After tea, Auntie used to say, "You can go out, walk up and down the quay there," which we did, and see other children. We knew everybody and everybody knew us. So it was really great fun and life went on every day, it was just wonderful.

'On a Saturday we used to go with her into Penzance, which was a lovely treat. Minnie was engaged to John Nicholls and on Sunday he would come and visit, regularly every Sunday. After tea we would go into the living room and John would perform on the piano and Auntie used to say, "Now come on, girls, sit up tall and listen," so we'd sit up like two soldiers, Vera and I, and we'd sit there with a straight face trying not to burst out laughing.'

Evelyn and her sister Vera became part of Auntie Minnie's extended family; for example, they frequently called in on her brother, Johnny Drew, at the Penlee lifeboat, where he was coxswain. Family visiting was very much a part of village life. And as members of the family, they were taught the skills that Auntie Minnie taught her own daughter:

'I had always loved sewing and I remember at one time Auntie went into Penzance and brought home some navy blue serge, and she said, "Now Evelyn, I'm sure you're able to make yourself a little skirt." We cut out the pieces, and I sat and joined it altogether with running stitches, and then Minnie cut a band and I sewed the band on, all by hand, because we never had a machine, and put the zip in. I used to think I was the cat's whiskers when I went out in this lovely navy blue serge skirt that I made myself, with a navy corduroy jacket that my mother had managed to get for me.'

Even at the time, Evelyn was always conscious of their privilege and good fortune, and constantly reflected upon this:

'We had our own bedroom, my sister and I; it was paradise. Waterbury was so close to the harbour. We used to go out on to the quay and on a clear day you could see St Michael's Mount, and always when the fishing boats came in every afternoon, the seagulls would be hovering over the boats. And then Johnny always came every afternoon with a bucket of seawater and he would bring in pilchards to Auntie and say, "These are for the two girls. My gosh, they're such pretty maids." We would love it because before then we'd never even tasted pilchards, you see. Auntie Minnie treated us like her own two children, because she loved us, she really did, and we loved her. It was marvellous. I can always recall lying in the bed and thinking to myself, "I haven't coughed so much since being here, the coughing's stopped." I would lie awake and listen to the seagulls, it was like music. It was wonderful to listen to them and to watch them all on St Clement's

Island, where they would collect. And it was a really lovely time, you know, it was a lovely, lovely time being there, and we learnt many things.'

Evelyn's younger sister Vera talked about her time spent at Auntie Minnie's with equal enthusiasm, and she also learned many new skills. Although Mrs Harvey was rooted in the village, it is clear from Vera's description that she was of middle-class standing:

'When we arrived in Mousehole, Auntie Minnie earned a living playing the piano. And during that time, Minnie Junior, who was 27, taught at Lescudjack School in Penzance and was engaged to John Nicholls, who had a hardware shop in Market Jew Street. He was in the Army and was a French interpreter. Minnie was getting her trousseau together, and Evelyn and I, we did a load of embroidery, tablecloths, chair backs. We also started knitting for the troops. Minnie took us in hand and taught us so much: how to knit and to sew, how to cook and to wash and to iron. She taught us such a lot, and a lot of common sense, a lot of general knowledge, because though we were at school we weren't getting much education at that time. In the evenings we went out with Auntie Minnie, to visit Uncle Johnny. She was very protective of us because we were teenagers and used to say "these are my two beauties". It put Mum's nose out a bit.'

One can understand how Mrs Goldstein, left on her own back in London, felt rather excluded and rejected by these euphoric descriptions of the wonderful new life her daughters were experiencing without her. These feelings must have been replicated by other parents in similar situations around the country, who felt no longer needed or wanted and powerless to do anything about it. This must have also left them feeling very ambivalent, as of course they were also concerned for their children's safety, otherwise they would never have allowed them to be evacuated.

Betty and Esther Posner were billeted with Mrs Harvey's brother, Johnny Drew, and also became involved in visiting family and friends. Like the village children, they heard stories of long ago, as Betty recalls:

'Johnny's favourite song was *I'll Walk Beside You*, and he used to sing it while he was combing his hair. He told us stories about the pirates and about the Spaniards who came to Mousehole centuries earlier. I can remember where Minnie Harvey lived, she was the sister of Johnny Drew with whom we were evacuated. There was a little arch near the harbour.'

The little arch was called the Ope, an open space between some of the houses on The Cliff, and referred to by many of the evacuees. Although the two families clearly visited one another on a frequent basis, remarkably the Goldsteins and the Posners do not remember one another. They were of different age groups, and as we shall see in a later chapter, the children tended to play with others of the same age. There was also a marked tendency for children to become caught up in the bubble of life within the family in which they were billeted. Jeanne Waters' description below shows the degree to which the experience of each evacuee was determined to a large extent by the family they were billeted with. Like the Goldstein sisters, Frederica White had come from a working-class family and entered a clearly middle-class home:

'Frederica's father was a taxi driver in London. She said her grandmother's name was Mrs Lipschitz, and my father used to tease her about it, but she knew it was just teasing. She must have been about seven, I should think, and she came with no toys and very few clothes. In fact, it was a very small suitcase she had. My parents were very generous people and Frederica was often getting little gifts and presents given to her and she loved that. She and I shared a bedroom and we had two little white painted iron bedsteads. On one occasion I went upstairs and could hear her talking and wondered what she was saying. I heard "My snow white bed, I love my snow white bed," and when I looked round the corner she was stroking the honeycomb counterpane on the top. She was really delighted with her snow white bed.'

It seems that bathrooms and comfortable beds were a cause of astonishment for some of the children arriving from the poorest homes, as we have seen in the case of Connie Mellows and in some of the stories recounted in *The Cornishman*. There were other ways in which Frederica was introduced to a whole new way of life, including books and new clothes, which she could never have imagined for herself:

'If she wanted to read I was always there to help. There were always plenty of drawing and writing things in the house. And always books, this house was always full of books when we were young. She was just welcomed as one of the family and could use anything there was really, to amuse herself.

'When we had a Sunday School anniversary every summer, everybody had a new dress for the occasion and a new hat. We all wore hats in those days to chapel. It was decided that Frederica should have a new dress for the anniversary, so Mother and I took her into Penzance to a big store there and we chose the material, a beautiful sky blue – I can see it now – and we got one of the seamstresses in the village to come for the day to the house and make it so that it could be tried on Frederica. She thought she'd like a pair of patent shoes, so she had black ones with an ankle strap on, and she was very proud of those. She also chose to have a panama hat because I wore one to school, and I think she felt a bit more grown-up in a panama hat.

'We chatted, and she asked innumerable questions, why this and what that. But she wasn't a demanding little girl, she always seemed to be very delighted and grateful with what she had.'

For a small fishing community, there appear to have been a surprising number of relatively affluent families in Mousehole at that time, though in almost every case, there were strong ties with the village. Another child who came from a working-class background into a middle-class home was Shirley Spillman, who quickly got drawn into the life of her foster family, as their home was in some respects at the centre of village life. Like many of the villagers, the Ladners' two sons were away at war. Shirley tells her story:

'The Ladners had a newspaper shop right on the front. It was a very modern house, it had a bathroom and a toilet. In the back they had a barber's. I don't know where the females went for their hair. They weren't the most fashionable.[1] The barber's shop was the meeting point for a lot of the men in the village.

'Routine took over. Mousehole was very self-contained. The connection with Penzance was for shopping or market day. People went there once a week on Saturdays to do the shopping, not necessarily food shopping, but clothes and bits and pieces. Chapel was a very big thing, as it was the social centre for most people. On a Sunday there was Sunday School, then you had the service and you came home for lunch. Then you had a bit of a rest in the afternoon and then you'd go back about 6pm for the evening service. You put on your best clothes. The pub was definitely off limits. I wasn't of an age, but if you were a churchgoer you didn't go anywhere near that pub.

'It was a very low key existence, the horizons were not exactly limited but you didn't have horizons. You just lived within that very bubble. Mrs Ladner used to go to Mrs Waters' most afternoons. She had two or three sons who worked on a farm. I don't recall going to other people's homes that much, you were never kind of invited out for tea. I didn't find that connection.'

Shirley is unusual in stating that she did not find that there was a lot of social intercourse in Mousehole, as this is certainly not the account given by villagers, or indeed other evacuees. Perhaps being a little girl as well as an only child from a very different background, she did not realise that, in Mousehole, invitation was not needed; people simply called in on one another without formality. It may also have been that the Ladners kept more to themselves than other villagers or were too busy with their newsagent's shop to participate as much as others in village life. In fact, much of their social life was obtained through their work, as Shirley here acknowledges:

'They were friendly and also being in a shop you were the centre, the focal point for a lot of people coming and going. And it had a little library there, and the books or magazines were changed once a fortnight.'

Shirley is, however, clear that she was treated extremely well, even to the degree that she was taught to play the piano, which must have been paid for by the Ladners, though to her regret she did not persevere, as she preferred to be out playing on the beach:

'I was looked on like a little princess. I was clothed and fed irrespective of whether there was money there or not. They spent far more than the evacuee allowance on me. I was clothed beautifully, I didn't have any hand-me-downs; I had new clothes every season when the seasons changed. I had a winter coat and summer stuff. I really was looked after, very well cared for. I was loved I am sure. But I wasn't disciplined. You came as a child and you grew up with it. You joined the family.'

Millie Butler, who like Shirley remained in Mousehole throughout much of the war, certainly participated in every aspect of daily life, developing a routine very much like any other village child:

'I loved the village and its people. I went to the beach every day when the weather was fine, with my friends from school. I used to go to the Post Office every day on my way home from school to see if there was any mail for me. I knew everyone in the village, especially the fishermen who used to love to sit with us children and tell us stories of the sea and about St Michael's Mount. I used to watch them making fishing nets and listen to them talking.'

Another person unequivocal about his love of the village and its people, in spite of his earlier traumas, is Jack Goldstein. Like Millie, he got drawn into the village life which unfolded on his doorstep:

'When I lived with the Richards – they were in their 60s at the time – it was near the bus stop on a very narrow street called Duck Street, so narrow I used to stand in the middle and put two hands out. I lived on the corner house facing the harbour, I could just step out the door and I was right on the harbour – they called it The Cliff. And I remember looking at all the boats coming and going and all the fishermen, and everybody was very friendly. I remember going to school, coming back, and strangely I can't remember seeing my sister Vera for a long while.'

The fact that Jack saw very little of his sister who lived next door is further evidence that children got caught up in the life of their own foster family. Cyril and Malcolm Hanover were also very happy living within their foster family, the Sampsons, who became a second family for them. For the Sampsons, listening to the radio was a regular activity. No doubt they were eager to hear news of their two sons, Ronnie and Richard, who were away in the war. Cyril remembers that:

'Keigwin Place we were, yes. And the people were so kind, they made us so comfortable, and every night we used to listen to the radio. At nine o'clock there used to be the news with the radio announcers, so we used to try and guess who they were, Malcolm and myself and the Sampsons. There were four radio announcers at the time, Frank Phillips, Bruce Belfrage, Alvar Lidell and Stuart Hibberd, and when they used to come on and say, "This is the nine o'clock news," we used to try and guess which one was reading it.

'Everybody knew everybody, and they were so friendly and loving. Being Londoners we'd never experienced anything like that. There wasn't a bad apple in that village. They adopted us, you see, they were civilised, they were lovely. We were fortunate, we hit on the place of places. Other children weren't so lucky. Coming to complete strangers, you're building a new life. It was unbelievable. Your family's your family and these are strangers, but they finish up being like your family. You never wanted to leave there.'

Living a little way outside the village, at Penlee Point, Arnold Podguszer was also getting to know the family he was living with, and to some degree he entered into village life, though to a lesser extent than other evacuees. The Cromptons were a well-to-do couple and it seemed to Arnold that Mr Crompton was a man of leisure, although occasionally he dressed up in a special policeman's uniform. His wife did not work either and the person to whom the care of Arnold and his brother was entrusted was Nanny. Shortly after their arrival, Arnold had his first taste of village life:

'On my first or second day there, Nanny took me to the hairdresser, a man called Ladner, and I think for four-pence, that was the price of a haircut. He simply got clippers and I was virtually shorn of all my hair. That was the first experience of going to a hairdresser there.'

This event is recorded for posterity in a group photograph taken in July 1940, where Arnold's shorn head is clearly visible. His brother, Maurice, remembers that Mr Crompton had come to live in Mousehole with his second wife:

'Mousehole was a lovely place to be and he was very keen on fishing. There was no need for him to work, he was that wealthy. Mr Crompton had a terrific motor boat, and he was involved in the Dunkirk rescue. I can remember being taken out when they had fuel to run the boat. He'd also landed the heaviest tunny, that's a fish, some years before, and there was a wonderful picture of him with this fish, which he'd landed by rod and reel, being hoisted out of the water by crane which was used to seal the baulks of Mousehole harbour. It was huge, I mean really huge, something like 690-odd pounds in weight. He certainly was somebody who was used to a very fine standard of living. So we were very lucky to be billeted with them. Nanny, she'd been with the family when they were in the north of England. It was more like they were the gentry of the area. But we were really isolated, there's no question about that. We were in a situation where we were outside of the village and were very much under the thumb of Nanny.'

Clearly, Arnold and Maurice's evacuation experience was very different from that of other evacuees, both because their foster parents were so wealthy, but also because they were outsiders, which meant that the boys had less opportunity to become integrated into village life. There can be no question, however, that materially they were well taken care of. Over on the other side of the village, Connie Mellows, also living with a wealthy outsider, describes Mrs Lewis sitting in splendid isolation, overlooking the village:

'Mrs Lewis was Mrs Rose's daughter, and I think Mr Lewis must have been some sort of officer in the Army because there was a head and shoulders photograph of him on display in uniform. I remember Mrs Lewis's bit for the war effort was going round Mousehole with a little galvanised iron wheelbarrow collecting waste paper. The rest of the time she used to sit in their sitting room-cum-lounge doing a gigantic jigsaw puzzle of the Pied Piper. That window overlooked St Michael's Mount because we could see it through the window where she sat.'

The name of the jigsaw was somewhat ironic, given that the evacuation scheme was code-named Operation Pied Piper. Mrs Lewis was hardly a Pied Piper figure, as events will later show, and she did not show any interest in her two evacuees. Any contact that Connie was able to make with village life was through her own efforts and not through the family she stayed with. Fortunately for her, she was quite a forward little girl who had often sung on the stage and won talent contests since she was five. Her outwardness enabled her to make her own relationships with the villagers.

In contrast to Connie, Frances Fromovitch became so much a part of the village that she can still clearly visualise the harbour, and she recollects exactly where various people's homes were situated in the village. Even though her first encounter with Wright Matthews still rankles, she recognises how good his wife and daughter were to her and her sister Irene:

'I don't know if I ever forgave Wright Matthews. But his wife was lovely, and Lenna, his daughter, was lovely. She gave up her nursing career to stay at home and help her mother to look after us, Irene and me. They fed us and even bought some clothes for us.'

It is extraordinary that one of the villagers should have sacrificed a career to help care for evacuees. Frances helped Lenna and her mother by bathing her sister, Irene, every evening. This developed into a routine which came to have huge significance for Frances:

'Before Irene went to bed, I bathed her every night. She was six and I was about 13, see, so I used to bath her. And then they said, "Oh yes, you can go out. Come in at nine o'clock," which I did. I raced down the road and Edwin Madron was there on his bike, near the harbour rails. He used to wait for me every day; every day by the pier. He always liked me. I don't know why, but he did.'

This was to be the beginning of a youthful wartime romance.

CORNISH PASTIES AND GEFILTE FISH

For both the Mousehole and the Jewish communities, food was of paramount importance and played a large part in their respective cultures. For the villagers of Mousehole, food was based largely on two components: home baking, including the famous Cornish pasty, and fish, which was available fresh on a daily basis. Most of the village women cooked on large ranges, called 'slabs', described by Jack Waters as 'a combination of a fire with an oven on top'. Somewhat unusually, Jeanne Waters' mother had her own electric cooker and also had her shopping delivered from a shop in Penzance. Jeanne here describes the importance of baking in the village:

'The women all did their own baking. We had at that time three public bake-houses in the village, and in the summer months you didn't light up the big Cornish range which was huge and ate a lot of coal and was far too hot. You carried your baking to one of the bake-houses.'

Bertha Pomeroy used to take the family Christmas cake to the bake-house near the Ship Inn and remembers being fascinated as she watched the cake being pushed into the oven on a large flat object. Evacuee Millie Butler also remembers being sent on errands to one of the bake-houses:

'Mrs Tonkin did not have an oven so one of my jobs was to take the saffron cake every week to the village bakery to be cooked, and then I would go back to collect the finished product.'

Anita Godfrey also remembers the importance of food and baking, which even her mother enjoyed when she came on visits:

'As you come into Mousehole, a little way along was a sweet shop. Just past the sweet shop were three houses, one with a big opening. There was a baking house called Rowe where they used to make beautiful cakes and Cornish pasties. My mother used to go and buy them.'

The sweet shop she refers to was in fact Ladners, the newsagent's, so clearly it was sweets rather than newspapers which drew her attention to the shop. Evelyn Goldstein here recalls how baking formed part of the weekly routine in the Harvey household:

'Auntie would be busy Friday and Saturday making beautiful cakes and scones. And we used to look forward to Sunday like you can't believe because we used to scoff everything up in two minutes. We loved the saffron cake. I had never had it in my life but it was just wonderful. And the little tiny sandwiches, which we'd never seen before, you know, with the crust cut off the edge.'

Even in the Rose household, Cornish food must have been appreciated. Connie Mellows was sent on an errand to collect some 'splits', or scones, with amusing consequences:

'I can remember being sent down the road to a grocery shop at the bottom of Raginnis Hill to collect a bag of "splits" and a bowl of cream in a glass bowl. I was carrying it back and I looked down and it looked like a sponge was floating on the top. I thought half a split had fallen into it, and that I'd get into trouble. So I poked my fingers in and I fished it out and I ate it – and it was solid cream!'

In fact, quite early on in the war years, making clotted cream on a commercial basis was banned, but this must have been after this episode, which occurred during the summer of 1940. Shirley Spillman also remembers the importance attached to food, and the way in which it formed part of the routine of village life:

'Food was quite a big item. Although it was wartime we never wanted for anything, although some fruit, bananas and that type of thing we didn't have. But we had poultry, and obviously Cornish pasties, and there was saffron cake, which was very popular. Meals were rather regulated. You had a certain meal this day, a certain meal the next.'

Fish was the other major staple food. It was also a godsend to the Jewish evacuees wanting to eat *kosher*, that is, in accordance with Jewish food laws, as it meant they could avoid eating meat. There are reports that the fishermen always ensured that the evacuees had fish available for this very reason. Pamela Barnes clearly remembers how her mother's friend, Agnes Gruzelier, used to prepare pilchards:

'She used to marinate pilchards. That was her kind of signature dish. She would have these vats of little containers of pilchards in her little cottage, and she would marinate them in brine, onions and black peppers, and that's how they ate fish. You could preserve the fish over the winter months. We were still living in times when nobody had refrigerators, so they had to think ahead for the winter months. Pilchards were very much a delicacy.'

Fish was the food that Maurice Podguszer most remembers:

'There was no shortage of food, no rationing. And fish, the most magnificent fish that one could think of, was always at the table. Later, in Luton, I was aware of the rationing. There was also a local fish and chip shop which we regularly attended and had a pennyworth of chips or whatever it was in those days. It was a wonderful thing.'

While it may have seemed to Maurice and others that there was no shortage of food, Mousehole was, in fact, subject to rationing like the rest of the country.[2] Joan Ladner recalls that her grandfather, who was the butcher, and her mother, who had a grocery shop above the butcher's, kept strictly to the rationing laws:

'We always had fish on a Friday in those days. Everything was very traditional, pasties on a Wednesday, and of course there was meat rationing. My granddad was the butcher but he wouldn't give us a pennyworth more because they were afraid not to abide by the rules, and my mother was serving rations obviously in her grocery shop.'

Percy Harvey remembers that there were occasionally food problems, but his father would bring home food from farms where he carried out building work. Raymond Pomeroy describes how some of the villagers managed to cope with food rationing:

'I can remember in the war the Army being at the top of Raginnis Hill in a couple of fields and going up there as children, and one of the cook sergeants there gave me a container full of lentils. I remember bringing them home to Mother and she said it was a godsend because of the rationing. Also during the war my grandmother and grandfather had a chip shop which was another godsend to people for a meal, really, as that was unrationed. And also rabbits, my father used to go rabbiting, which was another source of food. All these things were helpful with the food supply.'

Marian Harris's ration book was in the possession of her aunt, with whom she took her meals together with her aunt's two evacuees:

'My mother had a housekeeping job, so where she worked, they had her ration book, and she had breakfast and most of her meals there before she came home. So when my mother went to work I came here to Aunt Florrie's to have breakfast, and she had my ration books. I came here and had my tea. Apart from sleeping here, I was always here for meals. I was part of the family.'

One evacuee put his foster mother's rationed margarine to an unusual use, as Derek here recalls:

'Billy Wright was one of the evacuees and he was the biggest rogue who ever came down here. He lived across the road with Mrs Oliver, and Billy used to plaster his hair with margarine. Mrs Oliver, poor soul, it was rationed, and she lost her ration in Billy's hair.'

However, one person who did not enjoy the food was Arnold Podguszer, Maurice's younger brother:

'Well, Nanny was quite a strict person but I think that was all to our good. Maybe as young children we needed some discipline, but it was quite a pleasant life. The only thing I found unpleasant was I was always a finicky eater and you were required to eat everything that was on your plate. There were certain things I loathed and hated and I had to contrive different schemes whereby I didn't eat it, such as putting it in my pocket handkerchief and then emptying it out afterwards and throwing it away. Because we were told if we didn't eat it, it would be served up at the next meal, and I believed these things. Plus there was a man called Lord Woolton who was the Minister of Food, and we were told that he would be informed if we didn't eat our food and all manner of terrible dire punishments. But otherwise I think we had a thoroughly enjoyable time there.'

Nanny was not a Mousehole person, but had come from 'up north' with the Cromptons. Although well meaning, and wanting to do the best for her two charges, she probably had a different attitude towards children than did most of the villagers. Nevertheless, her warnings of dire consequences for children who did not eat up their food were probably echoed up and down the country during that period.

Of course, eating Cornish food could have been problematic for anyone wanting to keep strictly *kosher*. Although only a teenage village girl at the time, Marian remembers one such case. And even though most of the young evacuees enjoyed the Cornish diet they were offered, in the main, there would have been a strong hankering for food with which they were familiar. Equally, Jewish parents back home were keen to keep their children in plentiful supply of Jewish food, as Marian here recalls:

'I can remember one Orthodox lad, Max Davis, who lived along the street here, and there were great difficulties at his foster home because he wouldn't eat anything which wasn't *kosher*. I think his parents used to send him quite a lot of things. Our boys also sometimes had food parcels. Bernie used to get some sort of salmon rissole that his *Buba* used to make and send down to him. She spoke no English at all. I presume she spoke Yiddish.'

Marian used the Yiddish term *Buba* for grandmother completely naturally. When asked about this, her simple reply showed the degree to which the two communities learned from each other:

'Yes, *Buba* and *Zaide* [grandfather]. He always spoke about his *Buba* and I don't think of saying anything else now if I'm talking to Jewish people. And Lenny's father had a market stall and he used to have quite a few parcels sent, sometimes with fruit and things like that. And a delicious Jewish sweet called, I think, *halvah*.[3] But Lenny was very good, he shared everything. He was very open, he was the least talkative probably, more reserved of the two boys, but when he had a parcel he shared it with everyone. But Bernie didn't. He used to take his upstairs and put it under the bed and I don't think he even shared it with Lenny. Well, his *Buba* used to make those especially for him.'

It is probable that the Jewish teachers living in the village would have cooked some Jewish food within their homes. Certainly this was the case in the Barnes family; indeed, it was Mrs Barnes' responsibility to obtain *kosher* meat for the evacuee community.[4] Perhaps the one respect in which Pamela's childhood may have been different from that of other children in the village was the Jewish food cooked by her mother, and which Mrs Barnes introduced to some of the villagers, who, like Marian, came to appreciate Jewish cuisine. In Jewish homes, the Sabbath meal is eaten on a Friday evening and Pamela recalls her mother's preparations:

'My mother was a very good cook and I remember every Friday lots of cooking smells and kids coming in. She didn't want to have meat or bacon in those days, so she kept *kosher* in that sense, and the diet I got used to is what I prefer to this day. We had a lot of fish and eggs. We bought fish from the mackerel man who came up on his horse and cart, with fish all freshly caught that day. Milk and eggs we were able to get across the road from the farm. And you could get a few bits and pieces from the Hockins, who ran a little grocery shop down near the front. Mum used to give away her meat and bacon coupons, or trade them for butter, and occasionally the grocer, as a favour, would give her a tin of salmon, which was like gold dust.

'I remember Mum made *gefilte fish* [a typically Jewish dish] every Friday, and that was one of her specialities. She liked the white fish and would mince it up with onion and then bind it together with egg and boil it. Other people also fried it. It's not a particularly attractive looking dish, but it is absolutely delicious. Our friend Agnes Gruzelier would always recall, "Oh, we used to come up the lane and this lovely waft of cooking would be coming out." Mum let them try it and they all began to like it, and that was definitely the Friday night speciality.'

Pamela also remembers sitting on the windowsill of Brookland Cottage eating little baby tomatoes like sweets. Fruit and vegetables were largely unobtainable during the war, except for those grown locally. A very big treat, therefore, came in the form of boxes of fruit brought down from London by Jack Marks, father of Cyril and Malcolm Hanover, and shared among all the village children, both local and evacuee. This is remembered by many of the villagers and evacuees.

A HELPING HAND

A number of the children became involved in helping out their foster mothers. This was particularly true of the older girls, and even the younger ones remember happily running errands. Evelyn helped Mrs Harvey with the washing:

'On wash day particularly, which was a Monday, we would take the basket, Vera and I, and we'd lay the washing out on the rocks and it used to dry beautifully, and I used to say to Auntie, "Is it safe there? Will they take my things?" "My gosh, they would never touch a thing, they've been there for years." And we used to go and collect the washing from the rocks and everything smelt beautifully of the sea and everything was dry and crisp and lovely.'

The freshness of washing in the sea air, contrasting as it did with the grimy atmosphere of London, was something that Frances also remembers:

'The wife of the farmer at the top of Raginnis Hill had a cousin who came over from the other side, the Lizard somewhere, and she helped her in the house. And she hand-washed everything with a scrubbing board, and she would turn pillowcases inside out to do the inside, make sure it was all clean. Everything, you can't believe, it was so brilliant, so white.'

A number of the evacuees also helped in the work of their foster parents, something which they clearly enjoyed. There is no sense that this was in any way exploitative; the evacuees were engaging in tasks which had previously been unfamiliar to them, and which they now found fresh and exciting. In any event, sending village children on errands, and teaching them tasks involved in farming and fishing, was a normal part of village life, a way of training them for their future occupations, and would have been carried out without question. Since the evacuees were accepted into the village, they would naturally have been expected to do the same as the village children. The Fromovitch sisters both helped their foster fathers, as Mildred here recalls:

'When Mr Warren used to go out and about selling his fruit and veg, and it was holiday time from school, I'd go with him and drive round all day with him; he had a van. And we went once to a farm and the farmer's wife had made a blackberry and apple tart, an enormous one, on a big platter, and with lovely clotted cream. We had some, it was wonderful.'

Her sister Frances sometimes helped Mr Matthews with his work as a dairy farmer:

'Wright Matthews had this little dairy farm up near the school. He had his cows and some chickens up there. I used to go to feed the chickens, which terrified me as they were running around my feet as I was looking for eggs. And then I used to serve milk to the locals, and was told if they wanted a pint, give them a pint and a little bit extra, or whatever they wanted in their jugs. I put the steriliser on, fixed it on, wasn't difficult, I mean, because I was only young. I'd do that and then they'd come in for their milk.'

Jose Marks, one of the younger evacuees, remembers going around the corner to a dairy farm, most probably the Matthews' farm, to collect milk. She also remembers that one day her brother, Lenny, went out to help on a fishing boat and made £11. However, he was warned never to do it again because of the possible danger of mines in the bay. Like a number of evacuees, Jose recalls helping 'Uncle Joe' and other fishermen to mend nets with her brother. He was the harbour master whom Jack had originally stayed with and was the brother of Edwin Madron Snr, Jose's foster father, whose family owned a big fishing vessel called the *Renovelle*. Even Connie Mellows, who only stayed in Mousehole a short time, got involved in this activity:

'I used to go down to the harbour and help make the fishing nets. The fishermen used to make nets by winding string up and down with a shuttle, knotting it at the points where the strings crossed. They showed me how to do it, so I used to help them make the nets.'

The making and mending of nets were tasks which must have required considerable patience, and it is clear that this patience was extended towards the children of the village, including the evacuees, when teaching them how to do it. Children were often sent down to the boats to collect fish for their families, and again, the fishermen treated the children with kindness and patience, as this story by Jack Goldstein portrays:

'The fishing boats came in after they'd been out two nights, when they'd got the amount of catch they wanted. Most of the boats used to catch pilchards and mackerel. All the men on the fishing boats lived in the village, and they all got to know the evacuee children. In the beginning, when we weren't known, Mrs Richards looked out and saw the fishing boats come in with their catch, and she used to say, "Go down to the so-and-so number boat," which was one of the boats that she was friendly with – they all had their numbers on the front, on the bows – and she said, "Tell them your Mrs Richards' boy".'

At this point, Jack became very tearful in his telling of the story, so emotional was he about the sense of belonging that Mrs Richards had given him in calling him 'her boy'. He went on, still tearful:

'She was like a mother. They were both like a mother and father. Anyway, she used to say, "Tell them you're Mrs Richards' boy and can we have some mackerel or some pilchards," or whatever she wanted to cook. We went down and within a few days, it was marvellous, they knew us by name and we got to know them by name, and they never questioned you. As soon as you came down and said, "Can I have mackerel or pilchards for so-and-so," they knew the lady you were living with had sent you down. And this is what the local boys used to do, nobody went and bought fish in a shop or anything. There were never no shops that sold fish because there just wasn't no need for it, was there? Didn't pay for them. And I remember doing that every time she wanted fish, going down and bringing them back, lovely mackerel and pilchards, about a foot long, and she'd cook them. Terrific, beautiful. I'd never eaten any fish like that, nor ever seen a live fish before.'

In fact, the boats would have landed their catch at Newlyn before returning to Mousehole. Distribution of fish was strictly controlled during the war years but it was accepted practice that fishermen would retain some fish from their boat's catch, and it was this fish that would have been brought back into Mousehole when the boats returned to their home port. This would particularly apply to pilchards and mackerel during the season for these fish.[5]

Of course, many of the village children also helped their parents in a number of ways and this was often part and parcel of the training for their future occupation, as was the case with Derek Harvey:

'My father was a carpenter and I think I was going to be a carpenter from day one. When I was four years old we had a cellar, a lot of houses in Mousehole had cellars, and my father used to do a bit of work in the evenings for different people. In fact, my father built two boats in the cellar, one for ourselves and one for other people. And I spent many, many, many, many hours with my father with a hammer and a bag of nails and a bit of wood, and when I was old enough, my father used to do quite a lot of work in the evenings and I used to go with him.'

Several evacuees remember taking injured birds to the Bird Hospital, and one little boy in particular became actively involved in the work that was done there, as Dorothy Yglesias recalls in her book:[6]

Amongst these evacuees was a poor-looking boy about 10 years old with rather a sad, wistful expression, who seldom said anything, but he brought more birds than any of the others while they were here. It was he who came running up the hill one evening with a scarlet face and breathlessly said to me, 'Please come at once and break a window to release a jackdaw.' It seemed that one had fallen down the chimney of an empty cottage, that all the doors and windows were blocked and fastened and the owner away.

'We'd better try to get the key,' said I.

'It's the bird or the window and it *ought* to be the window,' said the boy.

Completely squashed, I called Pog, knowing she would enjoy the job. Armed with a hammer she and the boy went off to strike the blow for freedom and out flew the bird quite uninjured. Having broken the law and the window, they proceeded to present a policeman with the bits, an apology and a promise to make good the window.

The same boy later brought a seagull that was in a very bad way. I could see there was no hope, and told the boy so; but pointed out that nothing could now hurt the bird any more. The boy rebelled at the thought of death and said, 'No! He must be called Strongheart.'

The bird died in the night. Next day I met the boy running full tilt down the hill; he stopped dead: 'How is Strongheart?' I told him he had died in his sleep. 'Damn,' said the boy, and he went on running.

ACCIDENTS, EMERGENCIES AND MISHAPS

The Government had given careful consideration to the medical needs of evacuees and had accordingly issued instructions to the reception areas. The following article appeared in *The Cornishman* in June 1940:[7]

MEDICAL TREATMENT FOR EVACUEES

In cooperation with the Central Medical War Committee of the British Medical Association, arrangements have been made for the home treatment by general practitioners of unaccompanied schoolchildren in the reception areas. The treatment will be given, without charge, to the householder with whom the children are billeted, and the local authority should make these facilities known to householders in their area. The practitioner will look for payment to the Local Medical War Committee and not to the local authority.

An interesting entry in the Paul Church School log book shows that on 16 July 1940, a Nurse Simmonds employed by the London County Council visited Paul School to examine the evacuees there.[8] No doubt she also paid a visit to the evacuees in Mousehole School. This aside, medical care in Mousehole was largely in the hands of the formidable Nurse Pender, who at the time of the evacuation was 62 years old and probably about to retire. Her granddaughter, Anne Pender, tells the story:

'My granny was District Nurse Emily Pender and she held a clinic every day. Her house was around the corner from the old Post Office and was called St James's Place. It was a two-storey house and my sister Maureen remembers quite clearly the queue which went round from her basement clinic at the bottom of the house, winding right around the old Post Office. And these were the evacuee children who needed care and attention because they had various illnesses such as impetigo and scabies, and some of them were in a very poor state of health.'

According to a footnote in Percy Harvey's book,[9] Nurse Pender reported to the 1940 AGM of the Paul and Mousehole Nursing Association that she had seen 307 patients with 3,104 visits during that year. Infestation was a common problem, and Jose Marks remembers that she and many other children had to visit the nurse because of that: 'One of the girls got nits and we all got them.' Another of the evacuees who also suffered from this problem was Arnold Podguszer, much to his own chagrin:

'In spite of having my hair shorn off, not many weeks later I got nits, I don't know how. My mother would have been absolutely devastated to learn that this had happened to her child, but that's what happened, and then we got rid of it with a tooth comb. I don't think there was any medication, just frequent combing got it out. I suppose Nanny did it.'

It is likely that Arnold also visited Nurse Pender at this time, not the only occasion he was to do so:

'I also had an infection, somebody had scratched my finger and I got a very nasty ulcerated finger, and I remember going to the nurse and had quite a major sort of lesion there and gradually it healed under her supervision. I remember one of the little boys had impetigo – we constantly picked up these things – and had to have this sort of purple dye put on his skin. It looked quite horrible.'

Infectious and contagious diseases were not at all uncommon in those days, not only among evacuees but also village children. There must have been an outbreak of diphtheria at that time, as Joan Ladner sadly recalls losing her two best friends that year to this distressing illness. Derek Harvey's sister was also affected:

'I remember one occasion we were coming home from Sunday School, and my sister had diphtheria. My mother came to the corner and told us to go back because that was a contagious thing and I stayed up at my Auntie Katie's, with Betty Konyon for a couple of nights until the house had got fumigated and bedding had been changed.'

Arnold appears to have been particularly unfortunate that year with regard to his health, as he recalls also getting tonsillitis:

'I do know that somewhere in 1940, I had to go into hospital and have my tonsils removed, and I remember it was a very sad occasion for me because there was nobody to visit me. I was taken there and at the end when they collected me, I was collected and that was it.'

It seems remarkable that neither Nanny nor the Cromptons visited Arnold while he was in hospital. Although at a material level he was receiving excellent care, it seems he was not treated like a child of the family in the way that many of the other evacuees were. Arnold's older brother, Maurice, also had to be rushed to hospital at one time, an account which attests to the fact that the Cromptons did in fact go beyond the call of duty, in some respects at the very least, in the care they gave to their evacuees:

'The heavy raids on Plymouth in 1941 took place simultaneously with me going down with acute appendicitis and being taken by ambulance to the hospital in Penzance. And I can remember being driven around Mount's Bay with the searchlights in the distance. The operation was carried out privately and paid for by Crompton, and then I was taken back to the house for convalescence. This is one of the reasons why I probably didn't get very much schooling, because of being convalescent.'

Betty and Esther Posner, Johnny Drew's evacuees, had a terrifying experience on the beach, one of which a correspondent to *The Cornishman* had forewarned, as we saw in the last chapter. Esther tells the story:

'One time we were stranded by the sea reaching the rocks we were playing on. The tide came up to our waist and we were very frightened. We got sent to bed without supper as our punishment when reaching home.'

This was not to be Johnny Drew's only experience of evacuee children getting stranded on the beach, as is clear from another article published in *The Cornishman* in August 1941.[10]

MOUSEHOLE

A little evacuee boy, residing in the village, became stranded on a rock between the Cave and Point Spaniard, Mousehole, early on Sunday evening. On his predicament becoming known, Mr Johnny Drew, engineer of the Penlee lifeboat, secured a punt and rowed to the lad's

rescue. When he got there, however, he discovered that the boy had swum to the mainland, leaving his clothes on the rock, and walking to a nearby house. Although there was some 'tumble', Mr Drew rowed on to the rocks and brought off the clothes.

Frances and her sisters were also subject to a boating mishap:

'Ada, who was on holiday, Irene and myself went out on Joe Madron's boat to collect his lobster pots. It wasn't a happy journey as we all fell ill. My youngest sister Irene was tied to the mast in case she fell in the water, because she felt so ill. I looked to my right at one time and saw the back of a whale. Terrified, I pointed to it and Joe said "It's only a baby whale." As we all felt ill, Uncle Joe, said "as soon as I turn the boat to go home, you'll all feel better." That really happened. On the homeward journey, we stopped feeling ill.'

In another incident involving a boat, it would seem that the spell that Frances had put on one of Farmer Matthews' cows materialised one memorable day:

'I was on the quay in Mousehole, when suddenly I saw a cow, one they were taking to market, running along the harbour. It ran down the slope on to the beach, with Wright Matthews, the owner, chasing after it. When Mr Matthews got near the cow, it butted him in the chest and he fell over on his back in the harbour.'

One of the villagers, Joan Ladner, although much younger than Frances and knowing nothing of the 'spell', actually remembers this incident. Her grandparents saw the cow running down Dumbarton Terrace, where they lived, onto The Parade, from where it careered across the village and down into the sea, looking as if it intended to swim all the way to St Michael's Mount. It was then pursued in a boat by the harbour master who had to lash it to the side of the boat, with great difficulty, and drag it back to shore. Marian Harris also watched with amusement from her bedroom window on The Cliff as events unfolded in the harbour below.

WHAT'S IN A NAME?

As the children settled into the village, they became intrigued with all things Cornish, and, of course, top of the list was the name of Mousehole. For some, they came to feel so at home that they wanted to look for a Jewish connection, and hence speculation was rife about the origin of the village's name. Maurice Podguszer tells this fascinating story:

'One way and another we had a great time, and also had explained to us how the name Mousehole had come about, which was rather intriguing especially as we were Jewish. Apparently, so we were told, the name Mousehole was a corruption of the Hebrew word *mazel*. How this corruption came about was the cave that we used to frequent was actually an ancient tin mine opening, and the Phoenicians used to sail all the way across the Mediterranean and through the Channel and made landfall at Mousehole. Having made that landfall at the tin mine it was *mazel*, it was good luck that they made this huge journey in order to get tin.[11]

'We were told this story by Mr Haffner [father of one of the teachers], who apparently had done a certain amount of historical research and he produced this story for the children. He was quite an elderly man but quite learned. I think he came to the school to talk to us about it.'

The belief in the Hebrew origin of the name of Mousehole was widespread among the evacuees. It is unclear where Mr Haffner obtained this information, since there is nothing in historical records to verify it, according to present-day Mousehole historians. And yet it remains an intriguingly plausible possibility.

The evacuees were not alone in looking for a Hebrew connection with Cornwall. Writing about his childhood memories of Mousehole, Leo Tregenza twice refers to a surprising myth which apparently existed among Cornish fishermen. Here he describes watching them from the headlands, as they went about their fishing below:

There was a strange, spiritual element in the activity (for me); but no less so, I am sure, to some of the fishermen themselves. It was not for nothing they liked to be thought of as the lost tribe of Israel, and there must have been times when they saw themselves on the Sea of Galilee within the limits of Mount's Bay.[12]

Thus the evacuees spent the summer of 1940 learning about their new environment and becoming part of village life. As the long hot days came to a close, however, they had to turn their thoughts to the far more mundane issue of school.

Chapter Eight

AT SCHOOL

'I don't think I took a lot of notice of school, I was so enamoured of what was going on around me.'
Vera Goldstein

'It's the village life that has stuck with us, going to the British Legion Hall, we enjoyed that, or climbing up Raginnis, all around the fields, seeing the ships come in.'
Frances Fromovitch

'I cannot remember real schooling. I can remember clambering round the cliffs; I can remember walking towards Land's End; across to Lamorna Cove one way, and going up through Paul and then coming right the way round and then coming down through Raginnis Hill. I can remember all the wonderful colours, but I can't remember school.'
Maurice Podguszer

INITIAL ARRANGEMENTS

While the evacuees loved their new environment, they were less enthusiastic about their education, which suffered because of the prevailing circumstances. Many of the accounts of their life in the village are as vivid and as fresh as if the events they describe happened yesterday. By contrast, the stories of their school life in Mousehole are often hazy, confused, and sometimes even appear contradictory. Probably the main reason for this is that their experience of village life was fresh and exciting, and therefore imprinted itself on their memory, as is perfectly expressed in the comments above. School life, on the other hand, was something that was familiar to them, albeit in a different setting and in very different circumstances. Furthermore, their schooling, in some respects, was a continuation of what had gone on previously, in as much as many of them were with their former classmates and had some of the same teachers, as Jack Goldstein here makes clear:

'You know, I can't remember those details because it didn't seem important. Well, I mean I liked school, I always did like school, but it's just the fact that although we were in a strange place and a strange school, we had teachers that we'd seen before and children that we knew from Jews' Free School in London, and that was sufficient.'

The fact that some of the evacuees were there with children, and some teachers, that they knew did, of course, make the settling in process easier for them, which may have been part of the Government's plan in evacuating schools as units. The Jewish authorities also took the view that it was better for Jewish children to be taught together, so that they could continue with their Jewish education and lifestyle. It is possible that Mousehole School was chosen for JFS because it contained two separate buildings that lent themselves to accommodating both an evacuee school and the local children as separate units. There was the Infants' School, or lower school, a single-storey building with two classrooms. Then there was the main part of the school called the upper or big school, which had four classes and four teachers, Mr Elford being the headmaster.[1] The big school had two large classrooms which had sliding doors so that they could be partitioned off into four smaller rooms, and there was an additional smaller room at the back.

However, it appears that it took some time to make the appropriate arrangements to accommodate all the evacuee children, given that the school population had now doubled. Many of the evacuees think that they spent the entire summer without going to school. Connie Mellows, who spent only three months in Mousehole, thinks that she never went to school there. It seems more likely, though, that the children did go to school in July 1940, but because they had already had a two-week break, followed by just a few short weeks in school and then the summer holidays, this felt like one long holiday.

The jumbled anecdotes did eventually emerge into a coherent picture, supported by an interesting and last-minute find at the Cornwall Record Office. The most likely scenario is that during the first few weeks following their arrival in June 1940, and after a two-week break, a large group of evacuees attended the upper school with the local children for a short while, possibly in a separate room, during the period in which alternative arrangements were being made. However, a number of children, most probably the ones of junior school age, were sent up to Paul School.

Eventually, arrangements were made for Jews' Free School to occupy the Infants' School and at this point, all the evacuees were brought together again and taught separately from the local children in their 'own school', Jews' Free School Mousehole. This arrangement stayed in place until the end of 1941, when JFS Mousehole closed and the remaining evacuees were integrated with the local children. The only person who remembers temporary arrangements being made, while the teachers were sorting out what to do, is Mildred Fromovitch, who thinks that the evacuees and local children were taught together for a while:

'From what I remember, there were two buildings there. We were in one building to start with, with the local children, and then we were moved to another building, and we were there, just the evacuees were in that building. I'm sure at the beginning we were together. There was more than one entrance, but if you come in up Commercial Road to the school, there was a big building on the right. We were there first and then we moved to the other building. Whether it was infants and juniors and they took all the infants out I don't know, but that's the one we went into, the lower building.'

The school entrance that Mildred describes is the bottom entrance. Jack Goldstein remembers going to school via the top entrance:

'If you walk up towards Paul, the school is on the hill. I used to walk up Duck Street, and it more or less led you to the hill that went up to Paul. I used to scoot up this. And when you got there, the school was on your right and you walked down into the entrance to it.'

Putting all the evacuee and local children together must have resulted in massive overcrowding. Jose Marks says that this issue was dealt with by sending some of the children up to the school in Paul. Miriam Roar,[2] whose older sister Lily had been a friend of Jose, also remembers going to school in Paul:

'We attended a school in Paul, and I remember walking back to Mousehole from Paul School with a group of other children. On one occasion, one of the group hurt their knee, and the others had to carry her. We all went along singing *I'm a wounded soldier, can you see to me.*'

The author was initially puzzled by these isolated references to Paul School, since all the other evacuees had talked about going to school in Mousehole; however, on her very last visit to Cornwall Record Office in August 2009, she came across the log book of Paul Church School. A fascinating entry in the log book on 1 July 1940[3] confirmed the story given by Jose and Miriam:

> *Admitted 45 children: – 1 local boy, 11 from L.C.C. Schools, and 33 from the Jews' Free School. The afternoon assembly will be at 1.25 and the Registers will be closed at 1:30pm. The Time Table will be adjusted accordingly. Mr D. Nathan, BSc, will teach the Evacuees.*

Paul was a much smaller school than Mousehole and took children from four to 11 years of age, after which they either went to Mousehole, Newlyn Board School or one of the other secondary schools in Penzance. The headmaster at that time was Mr Freddie Ladner, who lived in Mousehole, and with whom Mr Nathan and his family stayed for a while. Mr Nathan's qualification was clearly entered at a different time to the rest of the entry, suggesting that a check was made before committing it to permanent record. In spite of his BSc, Mr Nathan appears to have spent his first few weeks either taking children swimming, or taking them on nature walks; indeed, these are the only activities he is recorded as doing between 1 July and 1 October 1940, with a four-week break in August. During this period, it seems that Mr Nathan took his class on no fewer than eight nature walks and went swimming with them five times, presumably to the beach in Mousehole. Anita Godfrey remembers doing 'nature study walks up Paul Lane', which suggests she was one of the children in Paul. Jose Marks also recalls these early days:

'Daily life was going to school in Paul for a half a day, and then we would go to the beach where they would teach us about botany and how to swim. The teachers were more interested in singing and swimming. One teacher, a man, would go up to Paul, sit in the classroom and sing *On Ilkley Moor bar t'at.*'

It seems the teachers also were enjoying their new-found freedom! In point of fact, the probable reason for so many outings was the overcrowding in the school. There is no record to the effect that schooling for evacuees was officially arranged on a half-day basis, but this seems in effect to have been what happened.

JEWS' FREE SCHOOL MOUSEHOLE

The situation was eventually resolved towards the end of September 1940. An entry in Paul Church School log book[4] on 30 September reveals the following:

> *Received notice from the Education Office that the children of the Jews' Free School, Party 19, will be transferred to the Mousehole Infants' School premises to join the other members of the Party as and from Tuesday 1 October. Mr D. Nathan will be transferred to Lescudjack Boys' School on 1 October.*

There are several interesting features to this entry, not the least being that it identifies Jews' Free School as being Party 19. Mr Nathan's departure to Lescudjack is surprising as he definitely reappears at Mousehole School at some stage, where he was remembered by both evacuees and village children. It is unclear whether the other JFS children in the party were in the Mousehole Infants' School premises prior to 1 October, after their brief period of integration with the local children, or whether that was the date that the entire party moved in there. One of the things making this arrangement possible was probably the fact that some of the evacuees had left by that date, so that there were not quite so many children to squeeze into the building. Another factor causing the delay was the decision about what to do with the Mousehole infant children, who had their own toilets and playground. Again, it is not clear what happened to them, but it is likely that they moved up to the big school, though this could have been problematic, as Jeanne Waters points out:

'The Infants' School had infant toilets, little ones, and there was a level playing area outside. Once you went up into the Senior School, you had a very sloping playground at the back and a bank on the top there. It would have been difficult for the little ones to go up into the Senior School.'

Once the children of JFS had their own separate school premises, the next issue was how to organise them into classes, given that they spanned a large age range. Since there were two classrooms, the most likely arrangement is that the children of infant and junior school age, that is those from five to 11 years of age, were in one classroom, while the older children of 11 to 13 or 14 were in the other room. Arnold Podguszer recalls being in the junior class, while Millie Butler, who sat next to Arnold in school, recollects the evacuees being taught 'in accordance with their age' but separately from the local children. Ted Labofsky, who would have been with the older group, remembers there being two classes:

'There were only two classes of children of all ages. There was the junior class, which was the youngsters till about 11, and then the 11s to 14s were in another class. We were separate from the local children and we didn't really learn anything.'

Vera Goldstein recalls that there were different arrangements at different times, and that at some point, she was asked to help out with the younger children. Her older sister, Evelyn, had by this stage officially left school, but she nevertheless went to school in Mousehole and was also involved in helping out:

'Every day I went to school and I used to sit there and watch, take part sometimes in some of the things they did. As I was a little bit older, they said "You can stay and try and teach the little ones something" and that's what I did, I stayed and helped with the little ones, the Jewish children. It was just a little room with all the little children.'

Ronney Glazer also remembers being taught separately from the local children and has a rather unusual and pleasant recollection of his life at Mousehole School, which must have somewhat distracted him from his studies:

'Opposite the school was a little hut where the Mousehole Male Voice Choir used to practice. We used to hear them singing from school.'

Parents back in London, together with the Jewish authorities overseeing the welfare of evacuees, would have been enormously proud to read the following article which appeared in *The Cornishman* in January 1941.[5] As far as can be ascertained, this is the only reference in the local press to the evacuees in Mousehole being Jewish:

MOUSEHOLE

In comparison with other places in Cornwall, Mousehole may congratulate itself on having a generally respectable lot of evacuees, the larger proportion being of Jewish parentage, from the Metropolis. Accommodation has been provided in the infants' department of the Mousehole school buildings, where the children are very comfortable, and taught by their own efficient staff. The headmaster (Mr Levene) and teachers reciprocate the sociability of local residents, whilst boys and girls are equally friendly – with good manners. Foster parents deserve a mead of praise for doing their best to make them very happy.

Not all evacuees to Cornwall were such models of good behaviour, however. It would seem that the Cornish authorities found it necessary to establish a hostel for difficult children to house evacuees whose foster parents could not cope with them. In an interesting forerunner to modern behaviour management courses, a training course for the staff of such hostels was held in Exeter in September 1941.[6]

THE JFS TEACHERS

Although accounts vary, it seems certain that Mr Levene was the most senior of the evacuee teachers and, therefore, the headmaster, as is confirmed in the article above. In any event, he remained in Cornwall a year longer than Mr Barnes. Having taught at the JFS Central School in London, he taught the older children in Mousehole, the 11 to 14s, and was probably assisted in this task by Miss Cohen. It is probable that Mr Nathan also taught the older children, though it is not clear when he left Lescudjack School to come and teach in Mousehole. It is not known which age group Miss Levene taught. Mr Barnes taught the younger children, though probably the older ones in that group, the eight to 11-year-olds, while Miss Haffner taught the very youngest children.

In spite of remaining in Mousehole only six months, Mr Barnes became well known by the villagers as well as the pupils, among all of whom he was extremely popular. Two village teenagers, Jeanne and Marian, were struck by how handsome he was! Indeed, he was so active in all aspects of the children's lives that a substantial number of the evacuees thought that he was the headmaster. Maurice Podguszer says that 'he handled every problem', and was of the view, therefore, that it was Mr Barnes who took overall responsibility for the children. Even some of the local children thought that Mr Barnes was in charge of the evacuees, as Joan Ladner here recalls:

'Well, Mr Levene was a little bit more awe-inspiring, but Mr Barnes was absolutely lovely and he was, I think, assumed to be their headmaster. He seemed to be in charge really. The Barnes seemed to be a very happy family. I think they sometimes used to go up to my Aunt Emmie's, where their landlady was, for tea, to the Trevetho Villa. That was where their landlady, Miss Humphrys, was staying.'

Jack Goldstein describes both Mr Levene and Mr Barnes as 'wonderful men', but he also thought that Mr Barnes was the headmaster; however, Pamela Barnes says that her father was definitely not the headteacher, though it is likely that he and Mr Levene shared many responsibilities. Ted Labofsky remembers that he was taught mainly by Mr Levene:

'Well, mostly Mr Levene was my teacher because he was from the Central School and he was a maths teacher, and Mr Barnes was from the Junior School; he took sport and was good at cricket and things like that. But we did swap teachers at times.'

Among the older pupils, Frances is clear that her teachers were Mr Levene and Miss Cohen, and that she was not taught by Mr Barnes. She tells this anecdote about Mr Levene:

'There was a boy called Lazarus who argued with Mr Levene. I don't know what was going on, but a little fight broke out and the boy scratched Mr Levene's finger. The boy said, "I'll tell my brother of you, he's a boxer", and there was a Lazarus boxer. I was sitting near Mr Levene at the time, and I saw what happened.'

This was in fact Eddie Lazarus,[7] who did indeed have an older brother, Harry, who was a boxer. Eddie also had a younger brother, Lew, who was in Mousehole with him and later became the well-known boxer Lew Lazar. Frances remembers Vera Goldstein sitting at the back of her class and being joined there by her sister, Evelyn, when she came down. Vera and Evelyn both remember a number of the teachers and some of the things they were taught:

Evelyn: 'Mr Levene was very nice and friendly, he was such a lovely man and he would teach us various things about Jewish life. He wrote in Hebrew in my autograph book. He used to say at the time, he doesn't mind if the children go to chapel with their ladies as long as they remember that they're Jewish. I remember Miss Cohen from the Jews' Free School in London, I think she was my teacher in London.'

Vera: 'I remember all the teachers. And Mr Barnes' wife was lovely, we knew her, she was pretty. Miss Cohen was a very formidable lady. She had a parting in her hair with a grip. She taught us how to make gloves with gussets in them, with chamois leather. I think her name was Leah or Lilian. I can't remember actual schooling as such, like reading, writing and arithmetic.'

Judging from the comments, Miss Cohen seems to have made quite an impression on a number of the children. Some of them remember that she had to take to her bed once for some weeks, due to a problem with her leg. Interestingly, some of the villagers also remember her, which suggests that she stayed on after JFS Mousehole was closed and taught the local children, among them Joan Ladner:

'We had one of the evacuee teachers, a Miss Cohen. I was a bit frightened of Miss Cohen, I must say. She was a bit strict.'

Cyril also remembers all the JFS teachers in Mousehole, and like Jack he recollects that some of them were his previous teachers in London. As one of the older pupils, he would also have been taught by Mr Levene, but it is Mr Barnes who he remembers best because of the sporting connection:

'Mr Barnes, I remember him very well because he was also into sport; he was a lovely guy. He was a cyclist and our sports master as well. And he favoured me because I was a good all-rounder, footballer and cricketer, and I represented the Jews' Free School for Mousehole, me and a friend of mine, a boy called Deswarte. I know his wife was with him, and his daughter Lydia. In fact, his wife was pregnant – I knew about the birds and the bees when I was 13! She was a nice woman.'

The Barnes family lived close to the school in Foxes Lane and Frances remembers a task she was asked to do by Mr Barnes:

'I used to have to run down to Mrs Barnes and get the tea tray and take it back to Mr Barnes in the school. She made his tea, so he must have been there then. It must have been before he was called into the Army.'

Miss Haffner almost certainly taught the youngest children, aged from five to seven. Arnold Podguszer remembers only being taught by a female teacher, probably Miss Haffner, as this is a name he recalls. Malcolm Hanover also remembers Miss Haffner being his teacher, and he makes some interesting comments about Miss Haffner's father, who many children remember:

'Yes, Miss Haffner, she was a nice kindly lady, and I got friendly with her late father, who was a foreign-speaking Jewish man, I'd say East European. He was quite elderly then, but he lived with a lady down the Gurnick.'

Cyril described Mr Haffner as a lovely old man, 'like Moses over the Red Sea'. Villager Sylvia Pender also remembers Mr Haffner as a lovable figure whom the Hanover boys used to talk about. From Maurice Podguszer's account in the previous chapter, it seems Mr Haffner sometimes had involvement with the children at school.

Mr Nathan appears to have been remembered more by the village children, including Myra Phillips and Melvia Cornish, suggesting that his return to Mousehole School was at a later stage and that he stayed on in Mousehole after JFS Mousehole closed. However, he is remembered by Maurice as the Podguzers and the Nathans were acquainted.

Derek Harvey, who would have been eight years old by the time the evacuees joined his class, remembers some of the Jewish teachers very well, and he makes an interesting comment about their teaching capabilities:

'I can remember being in Miss Levene's class and I know the actual class, I can go to the class now and see where I was. I didn't get on with her very well. We had good teachers of our own and we never had any homework and we were quite laid back, but she was a bit bossy really. And Mr Nathan and Mr Barnes and the rest of them, we liked them, and we changed from our own teachers because they had a bit more knowledge, I think, than what our teachers did.'

Given Derek's description of the female teacher, it is possible that he was referring to Miss Cohen rather than to Miss Levene. Derek tells a lovely story about one of the Jewish teachers:

'I remember Mr Nathan, I don't know whether Mr Nathan or Mr Barnes, but right up the top end of the boys' playground, and it's still there, there's a concrete ledge, one or two feet above the playground level. He used to put a coin, a sixpence I believe, on the ledge of the wall and if you could walk along that ledge, which was sloping, you could have the sixpence. But the trouble was, nearly all the boys from here, we wore hobnailed boots and couldn't take them off. One boy, who never wore boots and had rubber-soled shoes, was the one who managed to get it, though not every time, and so a sixpence would be up there and might be there for two, three or four days or even a week or two until somebody got out to it.'

INTEGRATION

Jews' Free School Mousehole continued to operate as a separate school from Mousehole School throughout 1941. Mr Barnes had been called-up and left by January 1941, so this could possibly have been a time when an extra teacher was brought in, Miss Cohen and/or Mr Nathan. Towards the end of December of that year, records show that Mr Levene's two daughters left Penzance Girls' County School, which they had been attending. It would seem, therefore, that the Levene family left at this point, and that Jews' Free School Mousehole was closed. The reason for Mr Levene's departure is not known, but it may have been associated with the fact that many of the older JFS children had left by then. One factor contributing to the large number of departures was that many of the evacuees in Mousehole were born in 1927 and would have reached their 14th birthday during 1941. For children not attending Central or County schools, 14 was the school leaving age at that period.

There is evidence that a small number of evacuees who left school at 14 remained in Mousehole to work, but most of them would have returned to London at this point. Some also needed to return for their Barmitzvah. Nevertheless, more than 30 Jewish children remained in Mousehole and these were transferred in January 1942 into Mousehole School. This transfer of children is recorded in the Mousehole School register[8] on 5 January 1942.

ADMISSION.						NAME IN FULL. *(Enter Surname first).*	Date of Birth.			Whether Exempt from Religious Instructi'n	NAME OF PARENT OR GUARDIAN.
	Date of Admission.		Date of Re-admissi'n								
	D.	M.	Year	D.	M.	Year		D.	M.	Year		
2081	5	1	42				Fishman, Doris	25	2	29	Yes	Mrs. Waters
2082	5	1	42				Fromovitch, Irene	30	1	34	Yes	Miss Oliver
2083	5	1	42				Fromovitch, Mildred	27	11	28	Yes	"
2084	5	1	42				Godfrey, Anita	29	1	30	Yes	Mrs. Phillips
2085	5	1	42				Godfrey, Irvine	7	4	33	Yes	
2086	5	1	42				Hewson, Marion	2	12	28	Yes	Mrs. Trembath
2087	5	1	42				Levene, David	21	1	34	Yes	Mrs. Harding
2088	5	1	42				Levene, Frances	5	4	35	Yes	Mrs. Lugg Harry
2089	5	1	42				Levene, Ralph	1	12	31	Yes	Mr. Lugg
2090	5	1	42				Paris, Thomas	1	11	31	No	Mr. C. Jeffery
2091	5	1	42				Reiderman, Celia	4	9	29	Yes	Miss Hicks
2092	5	1	42				Reiderman, Rosita	24	2	35	Yes	Mrs. S. Waters
2093	5	1	42				Selner, Ida	16	12	28	Yes	Mrs. Webber
2094	5	1	42				Selner, Max	5	5	31	Yes	Mr. Webber
2095	5	1	42				Swager, Phyllis	3	5	36	Yes	Mrs. Swager
2096	5	1	42				Swager, Sylvia	1	7	29	Yes	" ?
2097	5	1	42				Spillman, Shirley	2	8	33	Yes	Mr. R.
2098	5	1	42				Wright, Betty	24	10	31	No	Mr. Bennett
2099	5	1	42				Wright, John	26	3	35	No	"
2100	9	1	42				Podguszer, Arnold	16	4	32	Yes	Mrs.
2101							Podguszer, Michael	6	3	34	Yes	"
2102	27	1	42				Taylor, Walter Ernest G	25	11	31		Mrs Grazelier owner Mrs. Taylor Tenant
2103	3	3	42				Stephens, Rona	22	12	32		Mrs. Williams

There is much interesting information contained in the register: date of birth, name and address of guardian, home address and date of departure. There is a column called 'Name of Last School', which for the entire group is listed as Jews' Free Mousehole, the most compelling documentary evidence that this school did indeed exist, even though the register is no longer available. Interestingly, there is also another column entitled 'Whether Exempt from Religious Instruction' and almost all of the children are entered as 'Yes', presumably because being Jewish they were exempt from Christian instruction; however, a very small number of the children were listed as 'No' in this column, presumably because they were not Jewish, even though they were listed as having attended Jews' Free Mousehole. This issue is discussed further in the next section.

The transfer would have meant moving all the children into the upper school, while the young Mousehole children moved back into the Infants' School. Shirley Spillman remembers that the move from the Infants' School to the main school happened suddenly, apparently without any warning or explanation:

'We went to school going up the hill. It was large, there were a couple of big buildings, very large grounds, but what I took in or what I learnt, I think would have been minimal. We were segregated, I think, and we weren't part and parcel of the mainstream of the school. I think we were in the smaller building on the front and there was a bigger building at the back. Later we transferred into the mainstream. It just happened, I think just one day you walked in and instead of walking that way, you were told to go in there and you walked that way.'

Arnold also remembers the transfer happening in this way, and he has very good reason indeed for remembering the very day:

'That happened, so far as I am aware, in January 1942, and I remember it very vividly because that was the first and only time I've ever been caned at school. The reason was that we were in the playground and I was unaware, as a new person, that there was one particular part of the playground for girls and another part for boys, and I was playing in the girls' playground, unaware that there was some sort of segregation. I was caught, and the punishment for being in the girls' playground when you shouldn't have been was six of the best. And I thought, how unjust, nobody ever told me, and here I was being punished for something I didn't know about. I assume it was the headmaster. No, having a cane across the palm of your hand wasn't very pleasant.'

The register shows that Arnold started school four days later than the other children that year, which was because he had been home to London for a brief time. He may therefore have missed any instructions given to the other children following the transfer. Nevertheless, one can understand his resentment at the way he was treated, which clearly still rankles all these years on. In spite of this unfortunate incident, Arnold does have some pleasant memories of his time in Mousehole School:

'I remember it was very pleasant at that stage. Not only were you in classes then, but when the weather was good we'd go on hikes along the coast, to see the flora and fauna and so forth, which I always found very interesting.'

It may not be much comfort for Arnold to learn that corporal punishment of this kind was not reserved for evacuees. Percy Harvey clearly remembers Mr Elford's cane, even though he left the school at the age of 11:

'I was never taught by Mr Elford. He used to keep a cane in his room – he had a separate room – and you had a thrashing every time you misbehaved. Some of the boys saw more of his room than I did.'

Derek Harvey is another villager who has good cause to remember Mr Elford's disciplinary methods:

'He was in World War One, and we had the cane a few times, we had the cane every day, nearly. I don't know whether the evacuees had the cane as well, but we certainly had the cane almost every day; there was always something wrong, maybe because we antagonised the evacuees, and because of that we were dragged into what we used to call the "private room", and we'd have a whack or two across the hand with the cane. A lot of children, the boys, had the cane a lot of times. I met Mr Elford years after he retired, because his son married a cousin of my mother, and he said, "You felt the back of my hand a few times." "I know," I said. "But it didn't hurt really, did it?" he said. "I don't suppose so really, because we didn't turn out too bad," I replied. But we never had any problem; we must have done something wrong, you know, we were smacked for some reason.'

Derek is very generous in finding a justification for Mr Elford's behaviour. It perhaps needs to be said, though, that at this period corporal punishment of this kind was not at all unusual and, indeed, was considered by many to be good for children. This is not to excuse it, but rather to place it in its context. Derek tells another story about his headmaster:

'We never had school lunches. We left school at 12 o'clock, everybody out, even the headmaster, and back again at half-past one. At four o'clock, the bell would go and it was everybody out, including the masters. No homework, nothing after four o'clock, the first person out through the gate was the headmaster usually, Mr Elford.'

Frances also remembers being taught by Mr Elford, and she had a very different reason to visit him on one occasion. She had been given a rude note by one of the boys in the playground and took it to Mr Elford so that he could deal with it. She is unwilling to reveal its contents, no doubt because it contained some schoolboy naughtiness! Frances still has a school report card signed by Mr Elford in June 1942, describing her as 'polite and reliable' and recommending dressmaking as a suitable occupation for her.

By all accounts, the evacuees and the village children had no problem getting on once they were taught together, as Derek here recounts:

'But we all integrated and some of them were good as gold, very well behaved, and at school we had classes that were altogether. Up the big school, then, there's one classroom which is off the corridor independently to the rest. The back room, which is the single room, I was in there, probably when we were with the evacuees altogether. And that's the classroom that Miss Levene used to be in.'

Although no longer attending the village school at that time, this is also the way that Jeanne Waters remembers it:

'But you know, in the village I can't ever remember there being any feeling that there were evacuee children and local children – they were all children together. And that was a happy integration. There was never any animosity, they played well together and they lived well together. They were just absorbed into village life really. It must have been a very different life for them.'

OTHER EVACUEES AND REFUGEES IN MOUSEHOLE SCHOOL

The JFS pupils were not the only visitors whom the Mousehole people accepted into their midst; indeed, there was an incredible mix of children who attended Mousehole School during the war, thus changing the nature of the school dramatically. An examination of the school register for that period[9] reveals the names of children from as far afield as Bath, Barnstaple, Blackpool, Bristol, Dartford, the Isles of Scilly, the Isle of Wight, Sheffield and Southampton. Some of these children had obviously Cornish names and were probably visiting family. The length of their stay, in some instances several months or more, suggests that they were using the opportunity of their visit to Mousehole to be in a safe place. In fact, some of them were listed as unofficial evacuees, for example Elizabeth Tregenza, who was admitted to the school on 1 July 1940 and stayed until 25 July 1941, when she returned to Brighton. Others also had connections with the village, for example Sally and Susan Eustace, who were the nieces of Miss Ross, partner of Major Bryant[10] who owned the Coastguard Hotel. Susan Eustace[11] eventually settled in the village. Elizabeth, Sally and Susan were among 12 unofficial evacuees who were admitted to Mousehole School between 25 May and 8 July 1940.

Nine official evacuees, who were not Jewish, were also admitted to the school at this time, three on 24 June and six on 1 July 1940. These probably arrived on the same train as the Jews' Free School children, as they were all Londoners, although only one of them, James William Wright, lived in the East End. Interestingly, six of these children left the school by 25 July 1941, when the remaining three children, Betty and Jean Merritt and J. William Wright (as he was now recorded), transferred to Jews' Free School. The reason for this is not clear, but it may have been felt that the three would feel more comfortable being taught with their fellow Londoners, or possibly it was done for administrative reasons connected with the evacuation scheme. J. William Wright, who became known to the villagers as Billy Wright, may have known some of the Jewish evacuees in London, as he attended Buxton Street School, and, it would seem, his brother and sister, Betty and John Wright, were already in JFS Mousehole.

These five children, Betty and Jean Merritt and Betty, John and Billy[12] Wright, together with one other child, Thomas Paris (known as Tony Paris), were listed among the 31 children who transferred from Jews' Free School Mousehole to Mousehole School on 5 January 1942, but they were also listed as not being exempt from religious education. The implication of this is that, not being Jewish, they continued to receive Christian instruction with the village children. The fact that Betty and John Wright were not admitted to Mousehole School in July 1940 along with their brother, suggests that they were admitted immediately at that time to Jews' Free School Mousehole. This raises the possibility that they had previously attended Jews' Free School in London, even though they were not Jewish. There is some evidence that there were a small number of non-Jewish pupils at JFS before the war. Frances recalls that there were some non-Jewish children with the party, one name she remembers being that of Peggy White, whose name is also remembered by one of the villagers in Mousehole, Joan Ladner:

'My Gran and Granddad had a Gentile and she came with them. She was Peggy White from Whitechapel, who was a bit older than our boys and lived with my Gran and Granddad in Dumbarton Terrace. I think she probably lived there at least 18 months to two years. Because she was lovely and was, again, like another sister, really.'

Vera Goldstein remembers Peggy White attending JFS at Bell Lane, so it would appear that a few non-Jewish children were allowed to attend the school. The fact that Peggy's name does not appear on the Mousehole School register also suggests that she must have been on the JFS register from the outset, together with Betty and John Wright.

There were two other significant influxes to Mousehole during the war, which have been frequently mentioned by the villagers, though neither of these is on the scale of JFS. The first was the arrival in early 1941 of a number of Belgian refugees, though most of these settled in nearby Newlyn, only three families with six or seven children staying in Mousehole.[13] The second was the arrival in May and June 1941 of 22 children evacuated from Plymouth following the heavy bombing raids on that city, almost all of whom returned home by the end of that year. Although only six years old at the time, Raymond Pomeroy remembers the arrival of the Belgians:

'When I came home from school one dinner-time, the harbour was full of Belgian trawlers, and then when we came home after school they were all gone to Newlyn. That would be when Belgium fell to the Germans.'

The Belgian refugees were Catholics and since they were also non-English speakers, they constituted an even more distinctive group than the JFS children, as Derek Harvey here recalls:

'Of course, what confused things a bit afterwards, in 1941 when France and Belgium fell, we had a lot of refugees in school as well, and mostly they were Catholics, so we had a right old mixed-up school really. Quite a lot went to Newlyn; but here there were quite a few, the Dhoores, the De Waeles, the Vantorres; Lisette De Waele lived just across the road here, and she was quite a clever girl.'

Such was the level of integration of the Jewish children into the village by this stage that, in spite of the obvious differences that had been evident on their arrival a year previously, they were seen as part of the village, which was now being host to yet more outsiders.

EDUCATION, WHAT EDUCATION?

Quite a substantial number of evacuees expressed strong views about the poor quality of education they feel they received; indeed, this seems to have been their only real complaint about their time in Mousehole. Arnold feels particularly strongly that he suffered educationally:

'My perception is that most of the time we were given little cards, which had poems or other writing on them, and we were required to copy them. So far as maths was concerned, I really don't recall that we ever did anything, and if we did it was nothing more than simple addition and subtraction. There was no multiplication or division. We were never encouraged to read books or anything of this type, and I think that was a very sad reflection of mine so far as my education was concerned. There were no examinations, there was no sort of pushing; we were left so much more to our own devices, which I felt was to my detriment. I didn't realise this at the time, but when I returned to London I realised how much schooling I'd missed. Others would talk of Dickens or Chaucer or other things, but I hadn't a glimmer of these things. I felt it very keenly.'

Clearly, Arnold was taught by Jewish teachers as well as local teachers, and was quick to recognise that the local children probably suffered as much from the prevailing conditions as did the evacuees:

'Oh, I'm quite certain. You know, this was a difficult period for the Government, for the country, for the people, and they did the best that they could and the prime concern was the safety of children, and I understand that.'

Interestingly, Arnold's story about the use of cards in the classroom is similar to that told by Percy Harvey, who recalls spending much of his time in the Infants' School, either making raffia mats or singing. Percy here describes his own education in the infant class, which must have been some seven or eight years earlier. Clearly, methods and materials had not changed a great deal in that time!

'In Miss White's class the only thing I remember doing anything very much other than some arithmetic was, she had a series of cards and there were four pictures on each card that made up a story. We would be given a card and we'd have to write the story that was depicted in the four scenes on this card. The next week they'd shuffle the cards up and you'd have another one.'

Arnold was certainly not alone in mourning his loss of education. Jose Marks also felt this very strongly, in spite of the fact that in all other respects, she loved being in the village. She felt that she had no education. Shirley Spillman felt, like Arnold, that she was not sufficiently pushed and stretched:

'I don't think the education was particularly good, because we were treated as a little bit delicate, if you like. Perhaps it was me; I needed to be pushed, to be disciplined. I wasn't. It was pleasant. Nobody told me to do anything. I can't even remember having any homework, to be honest.'

Arnold's brother Maurice shared this view, although he also realised that one reason he did not remember having much of an education was his absence from school during the period of his illness and convalescence at the time of the air raids on Plymouth in 1941. Maurice later became a teacher and is surprised that the experience did not put him off teaching for life:

'The only thing that I can remember was the fact that there was this playground and that through it ran the stream coming off of Paul Hill. So I must have spent a lot more time in the playground than in the classroom, where it would just have been the rudiments of numeracy and literacy. But you see, again, there was this problem, we were all different ages. I think that the teachers' hands were full with what was going on around them.'

Ted Labofsky, also someone who loved his life in Mousehole, was equally critical of the poor education, which he felt was due in part to the insufficient number of specialist teachers which they had been used to at JFS Central School. His comment suggests that Mr Nathan, who was a mathematician, had not returned to Mousehole School before Ted's departure, which was probably during the summer of 1941:

'We were just sort of revising what we were doing before the war. We never did mental arithmetic and geometry and geography and things like that. I was on to trigonometry before we went away, but we never did anything else like that. No, there were only the two teachers, Mr Levene and Mr Barnes.'

It seems there was a small amount of specialisation within Mousehole School. According to Melvia, Mr Elford took the older children for history while Mr White taught geography. Nevertheless, villager Jack Waters agrees that the education they received in Mousehole was not always satisfactory:

'Teaching was a bit vague, I think; we weren't blessed with good teachers.'

Another villager, Derek, holds similar views about his early education and makes an interesting comment about the lack of educational materials, which had clearly been a long-standing issue for many years prior to the war:

'We never had great education really. The school was run by the county and they didn't have any money, so we never had any books. We used to even take Christmas cards and any paper we could scrounge home back to school to use to draw on, because the text books we had, had been used over and over and over and over. I can never remember any new text books being bought while I was in school; they'd been there since my mother, probably.'

Thus, in addition to a lack of specialist teachers, there was also a considerable lack of educational resources, greatly exacerbated by the increased number of pupils and consequent overcrowding. Given the lengthy and arduous journey between London and Mousehole, it is unlikely that the JFS teachers would have been in any position to bring much in the way of books and other materials, though there is evidence of prayer books having been brought. Hence, they would have had to rely largely on the educational materials already available in the school, which had to be shared out among local children and evacuees. In all probability, the reason that reading appeared not to be encouraged in school was due to the fact that there were insufficient books there; though, as we have seen, some of the Mousehole homes did have books, and some were also available through the small library at Ladner's shop. Again, it is important to understand all these events in the context of the times.

One person who was happy with her education in Mousehole was Joan Ladner:

'Well, I think we were taught well with everything really, I mean even from sewing, in Miss White's class. You'd get taught all of the different stitches, it was quite comprehensive. I left school at 14 but I think I did as well as anybody.'

Ted was amazed to find just as he was leaving Mousehole that he could have gone to the Penzance County Boys' School, where there can be no doubt that he would have received a far superior education. As a Central School boy he was one step up from the ordinary Senior School and not quite at County School level, or Grammar School as it was later to become. In the circumstances he would probably have been able to make the transition from Central School to County School, had some thought been given to the situation. The fact that he was not told about this can only be attributable to the febrile mood of the times, which made planning and organisation very difficult. There must have been many other instances throughout the country where children's educational needs were overlooked. Ted was understandably annoyed.

'I remember when I was 14 I had to leave school. I went to Mr Levene and said that I was going home. He said, "Why?" I said, "Because I'm leaving school," and he said, "Well, you could go to the Grammar School in Penzance, you know." And I said, "Well, why didn't you tell me that when I first got here?"

Frances, like Ted a former Central School pupil, also had the opportunity of going to the County School but did not do so, although in her case this was her own decision. Mousehole obviously held too many attractions for her:

'I went to Penzance Grammar School for a while but I didn't like it so I asked to go back to Mousehole School. I even had a grant of some kind which I lost.'

As a teenager, Frances was unaware of, or perhaps unconcerned about, the benefits of a County or Grammar School education. There was an enormous gulf between the education received by the vast majority of children who left school at 14, and that received by those children who attended the higher-level schools for which there was usually an entrance exam. These schools had a much broader and more formal curriculum, the pupils did vast amounts of homework, as was the case with Marian, Jeanne and Percy, and worked towards the Matriculation examination, which gave them much better prospects in life. Of course, the paucity of education received by the majority of children was greatly worsened for those affected by evacuation, not just for evacuees but also for children in reception areas. It is probably these issues, among others, which gave rise to the Education Act of 1944.[14]

Percy here talks about the selective process he underwent, prior to the war, to gain admission to the County School:

'By this time we were approaching 10, so we took a scholarship to get into the County School. Most people weren't interested, they were going fishing, but they reckoned that there were two scholars who were going to pass for the County School, and that was Marian Harris and Percy Harvey. And they were "certs"; they were going to go to the County School. Anyway, we took the exam, but Marian passed and I failed, which was very much to everybody's surprise. If you passed, like Marian, I don't think you paid anything very much, but I think if you didn't pass and you wanted to go to the County School I think it was £3 a term, which doesn't seem very much these days. Anyway, my father was just about able to afford it.'

Percy readily acknowledges that children less fortunate than himself were deprived of a good education and greater opportunities:

'But the rest of them stayed on with Frank White and were taught by the headmaster, Mr Elford. So that is where most of the education of village people ended. There were some good scholars there that never went to the Grammar School, they never really had the chance. I mean, today they would have gone to the Grammar School. They would have made a name for themselves.'

Percy received a further and unexpected benefit from his attendance at Penzance County School, which was host to Devonport High School following the bombing raids on Plymouth. It was decided that the County boys would go to school in the mornings up till one o'clock, and that the Devonport High School boys would take over the school in the afternoons. As a consequence, Percy found himself free in the afternoons, which gave rise to an unusual and pleasant experience for him:

'I do remember spending a lot of time at home in the garden in the afternoons listening to classical music. I remember that we had a hammock in the garden and just above our house, there was a biggish house up on the top of the hill, in Love Lane, and there was a woman there, Miss Cumberland, who was very well-off, and she used to invite Walter Barnes and two others musicians from Penzance to come over two or three times a week to join her in string quartets, playing Haydn, Mozart, etc. I found that most interesting actually. I would lie in the hammock listening. Miss Cumberland was not a local person but she was interested in music, obviously, and they had her as president of the Male Voice Choir for many years.'

Blissfully unaware of all these issues was Pamela Barnes, who did not start attending Mousehole School until 1944, at the age of four. The account she gives of her first year at Mousehole School is vastly different from that given above, whether because by this time the situation in schools had changed, or whether because the mood of the time had changed. Or it may simply have been that Pamela entered school with that freshness and enthusiasm of the very young child:

'I just remember being really pleased at being able to go to school because it made you feel very grown-up. I literally had to walk out of the cottage and in two minutes I was in this lovely school. And the first thing I can ever remember was that they had a wonderful hand-made wooden Noah's Ark up there. It was a beautiful thing, quite a large ark with all the animals carved out in wood, and one of the first things I ever did in school was play with this ark.

'The other thing they had around the walls was all the times tables, starting with two times two, right up to probably the 12 times table. And this is how you learnt, you used to just recite it, so one of the first things we did every morning was to chant the times tables, and I wish they did that now. Because, although I was never brilliant at maths, one thing I can do is add up and subtract. I just have total recall of these beautifully printed tables, probably done by one of the teachers, all round the walls, and we'd all take turns to chant. Mrs Legge would say, "Today, Pamela, you can do the four times table," or whatever it would be, so it'd be your turn to do that, and that's how you learnt.

'Obviously reading was part of the curriculum. I remember we were able to sit and read books, do sums, and this Noah's Ark just rears up. And obviously, I remember playing in the playground.

'If I recall, Mrs Legge had been widowed at a very early age during World War One, never re-married and I don't think she had her own children. So many men were lost in World War One, and a lot of women of her generation bore that all the rest of their lives, didn't they? They didn't meet other partners and they just carried on with their lives, and teaching was her life. That's right, yes, dear Mrs Legge.'

Indeed, the backdrop to all these events is that another World War was in progress. It is the impact of that war on the daily lives of the villagers and evacuees to which we turn in the next chapter.

Chapter Nine

AT WAR

When fisherfolk are brave enough
To face mines and the foes for you,
You surely can be bold enough
To try fish of a kind that's new![1]

WAR, WHAT WAR?

It was easy for the evacuees in Mousehole to forget that the reason for their presence in the village was because a vicious war was in progress and that they had been sent there, away from their families, for their own safety. Cornwall did not suffer the intensive bombing that was experienced in other parts of the country, and for most of the evacuees, occupied as they were by their new life in the village, war became a distant echo. Their few direct experiences of war served only to add to the excitement, as in this event described by Arnold:

'I remember also, it might have been 1941, an autogiro crashed on the hill. This was not a fixed wing plane, it had a rotor and an engine, not quite a helicopter. I remember the pilot coming out and being cut and bloodied, but he survived it. Just above Mousehole, as you left the harbour going slightly south, there it was.'

The younger evacuees and village children experienced war as a vague fear, rather than an ever-present danger, as this story by Derek demonstrates:

'My gran and my grandfather lived in Newlyn, and we used to walk up Paul Hill and go through the fields to get there. I remember going up one day with my father, I wasn't very old, maybe eight or 10, and there must have been a raid on somewhere. I remember we hid under the hedge. I don't know what good it would have done, but we thought we'd better stop and we kind of got in, underneath the hedge, and then it went quiet and we carried on.'

ON BEING PREPARED

The presence of war was nevertheless felt in Mousehole and the local area, the most visible manifestation of this being the use of blackout and air raid shelters, though surprisingly, these are mentioned by only a few evacuees. One of the villagers, Derek, remembers the blackout:

'We had blackout in the houses and we didn't have any street lights either. They weren't on at all. The people were going round with torches. So the village was black on a moonless night, and no chinks of light from people's windows. In our part of the village, we knew exactly where we were. We could walk round in the dark and wouldn't have any problems. You knew where the steps up and down were, and at my mother's we had four steps up, and you could walk up the four steps as if they weren't there, you got so used to it. But also during the war, at least half the houses in the village, like my gran's, never had electricity, because before the war the electric board began doing what they called a cottage scheme, they put in lights in each room and one plug. And then the war came and that was stopped, the ones that never had it didn't have it until the late 1940s. And the street lights came on again in about 1947, 1948.'

Mildred remembers the moment the lights were briefly restored at the end of the war:

'The only time I saw lights in Mousehole was when the war in Europe finished and they put the lights on up the hill, it was like a fairyland. Today it's a normal thing but then to suddenly see lights, it was fantastic.'

The lack of street lights meant that people did not go out much in the winter evenings, which clearly curtailed social life, though not, it seems, chapel life as Derek recalls:

'The only place you went out was anything on down-chapel or up-chapel, like Sunday evening service. We had a Christian Endeavour movement at the other chapel, which I used to go to as a child, and that was Friday nights, and everything was blacked out. I remember they had a big green curtain inside the door so you could get in quickly if we had any lights on. And the fire was lit, an open fire up there, and that was very nice. But apart from that we stayed in, unless you had relatives to go to. I probably spent some time up my auntie's with Betty Konyon, and my sister did, because we were all children together, all the same age.'

Some of the families had shelters, usually the indoor Morrison shelter, as most private homes in the village would not have had the space for an outdoor one. Millie remembers that Mrs Tonkin had one of these, as did the families of Percy Harvey and Sylvia Pender. Mr and Mrs Pender used their shelter as a bed when they had visitors. Up in Paul, Myra also remembers the family using an indoor shelter:

'I can remember having a table shelter in our middle room and my brother, not wanting to come in, just put his head in. My mum told him he'd got to bring his whole body in and he said "You can have my head as a souvenir." My dad was out on special constable police duty that night, and we were left in, very frightened.'

Derek remembers that the school had outdoor air raid shelters and also a siren:

'I remember in the early part of the war, when the evacuees were here, the air raid siren was put up on the front of the school and they used to test that every so often just to see if it worked. It was up on the school for several years after the war finished. We had two Anderson shelters up school, one in what we used to call the quadrangle, and another one at the girls' end, because the girls and boys playground was segregated. We used to have air raid practice with the teacher who gave us a piece of brown paper to put on the floor in the corridor to sit on, and then we filed out into this shelter, which was down a couple of steps. It was dark and would always have six inches of water in the bottom, so we used to make sure the teachers were in first.'

Some members of the village were actively involved in the ARP.[2] Jack Waters was an ARP runner, which involved taking messages from one place to another and generally keeping a look-out:

'We had to go around checking the lights and checking the windows and if there were any lights on, knock on the door. When there was a warning the sirens used to go off, if there was going to be any likelihood of any foreign planes going over, and then the ARPs would go out and just walk around and see if anybody was being parachuted down or if there was a bomb or a fire. Well, I just went around and if there was anything, like, then you had to run and tell somebody else at headquarters. I don't know where the headquarters was.'

The headquarters was, in fact, in Duck Street, where agreement had been made for the establishment of a Wardens' Post.[3] It seems that the wardens were to be allowed leisure activities while on duty at the post.

WARDENS' POST, MOUSEHOLE

22. RESOLVED

(a) that the offer of the owner of the premises in Duck Street, Mousehole, recently occupied by the Unionist Association, to let the premises for use as a Wardens' Post at a rent of £6 10. 0. a year as from 25 December 1940, exclusive of rates, be accepted;

(b) that Mr R. Pentreath be appointed as caretaker of the premises at £3 per year;

(c) that the offer of the Unionist Association to allow their furniture, including a billiard table, to remain on the premises for the use of the members of the A.R.P. Services, be accepted with thanks.

MILITARY ACTIVITY IN MOUNT'S BAY

There was a lot of activity in Mount's Bay, which was patrolled by boats and minesweepers, and consequently there were a number of military bases in the area. A battalion of soldiers was stationed in Mousehole at one time at the top of Raginnis Hill, on Love Lane. Derek recalls that the children used to go there to try and get badges and buttons from the soldiers, and also that an occasional Bren Gun carrier would go through the village. There were also soldiers stationed at the bathing pool in Penzance, and Derek believes that some heavy guns installed there were manned by soldiers in the army camp at Raginnis. Jack Waters was also aware of soldiers stationed in Penzance:

'I went to work during the war; I started serving my time in Penzance at Taylor's Garage, which was right near the bathing pool, and we had the soldiers billeted in the top of the garage, because there were two floors. They had their guns in the bathing pool to combat any invasion or anything. We had all British soldiers there, and then they went and we had Americans. They left their mark – two little babies! Oh yes, one or two, but that was life during the war.'

There was a lot of unusual traffic in the Bay and Frances remembers watching the ships pass by:

'I used to watch the convoys, these black ships which passed every few days, they looked big although they were on the horizon, one after another. That's how I knew the Atlantic was there, someone said they went out into the Atlantic.'

Marian remembers one particularly shocking incident:

'Well, things happened out in the Bay. I remember coming out of chapel one beautiful Sunday morning, with the sea like a millpond, and there was this dreadful explosion. It was a minesweeper which blew up because it had hit a mine, just off Penzance, so we knew German U-boats had come in during the night and laid mines.'

The minesweeper was the *Royalo* – a steam trawler – which was blown up in September 1940,[4] not very long after the arrival of the evacuees. The mines were a constant hazard to all boats in the Bay, and during southerly gales mines came ashore on the rocks and exploded. German planes were sometimes seen passing over and occasionally dropping bombs in the vicinity. Here is another story told by Marian:

'I can also remember being up in the middle of the night and watching a dogfight out over the sea. You would hear the noise going on and I got up to see what it was about. On one occasion there was a stick of bombs dropped on the Crackers,[5] I think it was possibly planes which came over to bomb Plymouth, and instead of taking their load back with them, they would come down west because there was nothing much down here to stop them. The stick of bombs came across all the meadows and was quite scary. I heard a whole lot of them, one after the other, bombs one after the other from an aeroplane.'

Several people spoke of the German bombers dropping their unused bombs in the Bay as they went back to Germany. As a young boy, Raymond remembers witnessing a similar

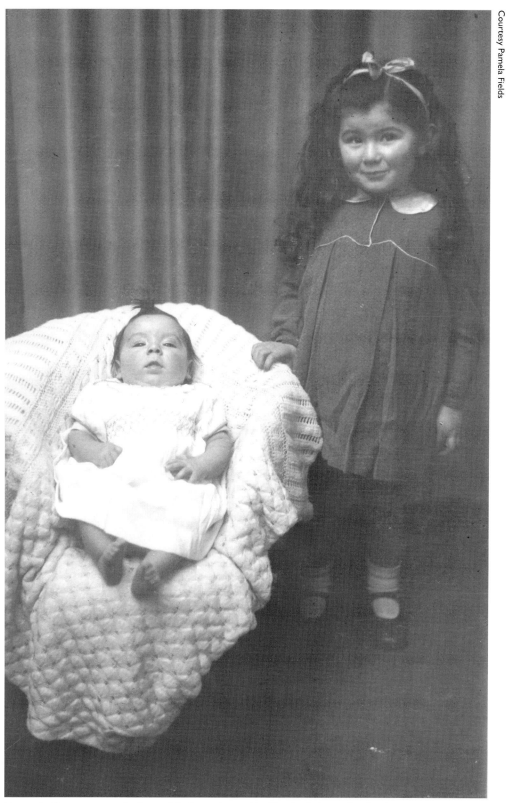

Pamela Barnes as a baby with her sister, Lydia, in Mousehole, January 1941.

Ralph and Jean Barnes in 1938.

Pamela and Lydia Barnes in front of Brookland Cottage, Foxes Lane, 1941.

Ralph Barnes, wearing his college colours, on honeymoon in Looe, Cornwall, in 1935. He was one of the few people in the group to have visited Cornwall prior to evacuation.

Lydia Barnes on a rocking horse in front of Brookland Cottage, August 1941.

Jean and Ralph Barnes, with their daughters Pamela and Lydia, taken in London in May 1942, while Ralph was on leave.

Pamela, Jean and Lydia Barnes in Penzance, June 1943.

To my darling wife, Jean, and to my sweet children, Lydia & Pamela. Ralph. Dec. 1943.

Ralph Barnes in uniform, December 1943.

Baby Pamela and Lydia Barnes with their grandparents, Mark and Lottie Ansell, their mother Jean and Aunt Theresa in Mousehole, January 1941.

Farming in Cornwall. Photograph taken by Mildred Fromovitch during a return visit to Mousehole, May 1947. Mildred and Frances worked on the farm after they left school. Left to right top row: ?Farmer Trevor Giles, Martin Trewavas, Phil Wallis, Sheila Frost née Cornish, Mary Wallis née Bailey, Ena McClarey. Seated: Lionel Wallis, John Gruzelier and Earnest McClarey, Ena's father.

Formal opening of the new JFS at Kenton on 14 October 2002, when the principal guest was Prime Minister Tony Blair. Ralph Barnes, centre, was also a guest and was the only surviving male teacher of the original Jews' Free School.

Pamela Fields, née Barnes, and Susan Soyinka in April 2009.

Jack Marks' fruit shop, Old Montague Street, 1945. Notice on the vegetable box, left: 'BANANAS ON SALE HERE AT 12:30PM SUNDAY 12TH MARCH.' These were the first bananas in the East End since the war began in 1939. The smiling young man in the front is Cyril Hanover, Jack Marks' son, who was evacuated to Mousehole with his brother Malcolm. (Springboard Education Trust)

Jack Marks' new shop in Brick Lane, 1950s. Jack Marks was the trade name of Jack Hanover, seen here with his wife.

Jack Marks with the Beverley Sisters, 1950s. He was well-known in celebrity circles at that time, and there are other photographs of him with Gracie Fields, Bob Hope and Norman Wisdom. Malcolm Hanover was the godson of the well-known wartime entertainer Bud Flanagan.

Mildred and Irene Fromovitch on the south quay, Mousehole, December 1946.

The Fromovitch sisters with their mother when they visited Mousehole after the war, May 1947. Left to right, Irene, Mrs Fromovitch, Mildred and Ada.

Joan Ladner's Auntie Lizzie Keates, née Ladner, in Warren's Cafe (now the Cornish Range), holding up a harvest festival loaf, 1960s. Lizzie and her father, Ernest Ladner, were foster parents to Elaine and Desirée Frischman.

A *Mezuzah* found recently on a door post in Mousehole, 2009.

Elaine Pomeransky, daughter of Frances Pomm, with Lord St Levan of St Michael's Mount. She met him when carrying out research for a book.

Edwin Madron fishing, late 1940s. Edwin was the sweetheart of Frances Fromovitch when she was in Mousehole.

Bertha Pomeroy being crowned Miss Cornwall, 1949.

Edwin Madron with his sister Stella in the late 1940s. Jose Marks stayed with the Madron family.

Jeanne Harris née Waters in front of her home in Mousehole, February 2009.

Joan Richards née Ladner at her home in Mousehole, February 2009.

Frances Pomm née Fromovitch, March 2009.

Jack Goldstein, photographed shortly after his 80th birthday, March 2009.

JFS Mousehole Reunion, 25 October 2009. Left to right, top row: Eddie Lazarus, Connie Stanton née Mellows, Ted Leigh/Labofsky, Maurice Powell/Podguszer, Frances Ayrton née Cohen, Arnold Powell/Podguszer, Cyril Hanover, Betty Posner, Estelle Kaye née Esther Posner, Malcolm Hanover, Sid Leader/Solly Lederman, Shirley Drazin née Spillman. Seated, left to right: Frances Pomm née Fromovitch, Mildred Moore née Fromovitch, Susan Soyinka, Pamela Fields née Barnes, Renee Rosenthal née Labofsky.

Marian Harris, just outside her front door, from which she has a spectacular view of Mousehole harbour, February 2009. This is where Leonard Marks and Bernie Warman were billeted with Marian's Auntie Florrie.

Photograph of Leonard Marks and his family in London, 1995, which has pride of place on the mantelpiece in Marian Harris's home. It was this photograph, first seen by the author in May 2008, which led to her discovery of this evacuation story.

incident when down on the front one lovely evening. He describes the bombs dropping from the aeroplane as being like bottles coming away from it. Melvia Cornish witnessed the same incident from the cliff in Newlyn, describing the bombs as 'little things coming down diagonally'. The most frequently talked about episode was the machine-gunning of St Clement's Island by a German plane, which everyone believed had mistaken the island for a ship. Jose Marks remembers she was standing by the telephone booth at the time, and Jeanne Waters also remembers the incident:

'I was down on the harbour front one evening and a German plane strafed the island out there from end to end with machine-gun fire. I think they must have thought it was a boat which was anchored there. I was really frightened. I was down by the harbour side when it happened and crouched in a doorway. It didn't come anywhere near the land, it was all on the rocks there, but I can quite understand Germans thinking in half-light or evening light that it was a ship which was anchored there.'

Several people recall the incident occurring in the evening or night time, as does Derek Harvey, who also remembers the consequences:

'We ended up having about 200 dead gulls floating around. But Lord Haw-Haw,[6] he announced the following morning that a battleship had been sunk in Mount's Bay, but it wasn't a battleship at all, it was an island, and the island was still there.'

Marian remembers an incident, likely to have been the same one as described above, which was witnessed by her Aunt Florrie's evacuee Lenny Marks, who came home white faced:

'I'm not quite sure whether it was August Bank Holiday Monday in 1940 or 1941, remembering in those days August Bank Holiday was the beginning of August, because our boys were only here for two August Bank Holidays. One of them, Lenny, was down on the Old Quay, fishing off the end of it. Uncle Vivian had fixed him up with hooks and lines. And I think it must have been a German plane, which came down low and machine-gunned the beach on the far side of the village, and swept down and machine-gunned the end of the quay. But he didn't actually hit the quay. Now, whether he intended to or intentionally missed it and was just giving everybody a fright I don't know, but that was the only time when somebody deliberately machine-gunned from a German plane. We think they possibly were aiming at St Clement's Island.'

A few bombs were dropped on Penzance and Percy recalls that his father was very much involved with bomb repair, as he was in the building business. The nearby village of Paul was also hit in January 1942, an incident which directly affected Myra Phillips:

'In Paul, on a Sunday night, we had bombs that fell in the field up behind the pub, the King's Arms, and a little cottage was wrecked. There were 15 Belgians that were living in the house and every one of them got out uninjured, I believe. And then, that night my mum went upstairs and came down crying. She said, "Our ceilings are down on the bed." We had our windows in as well. It didn't hit our roof, it was the blast that came right across from the bombing, and our ceilings inside came down. And also we had unexploded bombs in the field opposite the school, and Paul was cordoned off for a couple of days. A team of lads came down and detonated the bombs, we were very lucky it didn't affect the school or anything.'

The nearest heavy bombing took place in Plymouth in early 1941. Although in Devon, the effects of the bombing could be seen from Mousehole some 70 miles away. Bertha remembers standing watching the fires, and Vera saw what she thought was lightning as she watched the planes going over. Maurice has particular reason to remember the occasion as one of the heavy raids on Plymouth took place simultaneously with his going down with acute appendicitis and being taken by ambulance to the hospital in Penzance. One direct consequence for Mousehole of the Plymouth bombing was the evacuation of children from Plymouth to the area.

The war activity in the Bay inevitably affected the fishermen of the area, particularly in Newlyn which, according to Derek, was targeted by the Germans:

'A lot of Belgian and French boats went out fishing every day, but they didn't stay out overnight. They would go out in the mornings, especially in the summer, early at half-past five time and were back in again seven o'clock at night. Whereas, normally, their boats would have stayed out for a week or 10 days. When they came back in after the day outing, they were all counted; they had a patrol boat called the *Valida* which used to meet them, used to see them off in the mornings, sort of counting them and making sure that all was well and then, counting them coming back, making sure they weren't lost. But apart from that, in the village we never had a lot of trouble really.'

All movements of boats, including British boats, were strictly controlled and in the early years of the war, only day fishing was allowed, from sunrise to sunset; however, by mid-1941 some restrictions were lifted and some night fishing took place.[7] Fishing was, of course, an extremely hazardous occupation during this period, due to the mining of the Bay.

THE THREAT OF INVASION

The Government feared that the Nazis might invade the country via the tip of Cornwall and Pamela recalls that her mother thought she saw General Eisenhower in Penzance, whom she believed had come from America to hold secret discussions with Churchill about possible invasion. Pamela gives an account of steps taken to counter invasion:

'My aunt was working in St Ives for a time in a munitions factory, and the thing that did amuse us when she told us about it years later was that they put coiled wire all round the beaches. And she said, jokingly, "As if that's going to keep the Germans out," but that was the rule of the day, all this barbed wire was put around all the beaches to stop people going on the beach in case the Germans were to land.'

Many of the beaches with coiled wire were also mined, but some of the local children took little notice of the warnings. Melvia remembers cycling with a friend to Marazion, where barricades had been laid across the beach. Undeterred, Melvia and her friend crawled through the spaces in between the barricades and went into the sea. Another story is told by Ted Labofsky, who thought Mousehole was about to be invaded:

'Well, once I had an experience. They thought that there was going to be an invasion and the church bells were going to go. I woke up one morning and I heard bells, might have been on the radio, and I heard a *tap, tap, tap, tap*, and I jumped out of bed, I was a bit frightened. I went down and Mrs Harvey was doing something on her sewing machine. And that's about the only experience I had.'

However, a small number of children felt the threat of invasion in a very real way and had an acute sense of the closeness of war and the way in which it might affect them and their families. Even at his young age, Arnold remembers learning of the German invasion of Russia, when listening to the radio with the Cromptons one lovely summer day. Another very serious child, Connie Mellows, also recalls her anxieties about the menacing advance of the Germans:

'The other thing that I remember distinctly, which probably added to a certain amount of discomfort being in Mousehole, was that in those days on the front of newspapers they used to print maps of the advancement or retreat of the British army and the German army. I remember there was one where it showed the German army in France and it also showed the distance across the Channel between France and England, and it was 26 miles. In my nine years of life I knew that I was more than 26 miles from Mummy and Daddy, and the Germans were nearer to my Mummy and Daddy than I was. I knew that the first place the Germans would head for if, God forbid, they happened to land in England would be London, and that would be probably the last I'd see of my mother and father, because I was aware that I was Jewish and they were Jewish. And I knew what was happening to the Jews. So you must never underestimate the workings of a nine-year-old mind.'

Indeed so. As the testimonies on these pages bear witness.

THE MOUSEHOLE WAR EFFORT

The war may have seemed distant to the children of the village, especially the evacuees, but to the older inhabitants it felt all too real. Not only were their homes and livelihoods threatened by the intermittent attacks, but more importantly for them, their husbands, sons and fathers were away at war, as Jack Waters here describes:

'A lot of the locals were away in the Army, the Navy and the Air Force and were probably doing a very good job. Some months before the war, they all joined the Territorials and thought it was a great thing. Then the war came, and right away the village became quite dead. One of my brothers went away, but the other brother, Sidney, was working on the land, so he got exempt. Land workers got exempt.'

The sudden departure of so many men in the village even impinged upon the younger children, such as Raymond:

'I was just four years old at the outbreak of war. I can just remember some of the men that were going to war coming to see me in hospital because I had my appendix out at the end of 1939. Owen Ladner and Godfrey Ladner were going off to war and they came in to see me in the hospital. I always remember that. Apart from that, in the war years, we played soldiers and we had a good life down here really, away from most things.'

All too quickly, the reality of war became clear for Marian and the other villagers:

'Three weeks after the war started HMS *Courageous* went down and there was somebody from the village on her, Edwin Cornish. So that hit us straightaway, and several young men from the village died so each time that happened, being a close-knit village, of course, we were certainly reminded of it.'

Melvia Cornish remembers that Edwin was only 19 years old, and that Mrs Cornish (no relation to Melvia) stayed indoors, in mourning, for 10 years. Melvia recalls that Mrs Pentreath also lost a son on the HMS *Courageous*, as well as her only other son later in the war, and that Mrs Cotton lost her husband on the *Rawalpindi*, another ship destroyed early in the war. Melvia remembers being asked by her mother to go and keep the widow company.

One of the early events to bring the war home to Mousehole was the evacuation of Dunkirk, which took place from 27 May to 4 June 1940. Thousands of Allied troops had become stranded on the beaches at Dunkirk on the north coast of France and were cut off from escape by the German army. The Government made a plea to anyone owning a boat along the south coast to take part in a massive rescue operation, in which a number of Mousehole men participated with enthusiasm. Mr Cornish, father of Melvia, made four trips to Dunkirk, which he later described to his daughter as 'like sailing into hell'. His graphic descriptions of the horrific scenes on the beaches made a lasting impression on Melvia and, no doubt, others in the village.

The Mousehole men returned home just a few short days before the arrival of the evacuees on 13 June 1940. It is likely that the coinciding of these two events, the return of the men from Dunkirk and the arrival of the evacuees, had a significant psychological impact on the village. The returning heroes and the victims of war were both welcomed into the bosom of the village and showered with love and care.

One of the newly arrived evacuees, Ted Labofsky, was to witness the immediate aftermath of Dunkirk when he went on a trip to Falmouth with the Harvey family:

'I also went to Falmouth and saw the boats just come back from Dunkirk. They'd been back and they were washing down all the blood off the decks of the boats. I can remember that well.'

A tragedy involving other returning troops took place in November 1940, when the Paddington to Penzance train crashed near Taunton, killing 26, including 13 Navy men, and injuring many others. One of the passengers on the train was Mr Levene, one of the evacuee teachers. According to one report,[8] the compartment he was originally in suffered most of the damage and injuries, but after sitting there for a while, something had made him get up and move. The incident was all the more poignant because the train driver, a London man, had had an impeccable record of service for 40 years, but he made an error, according to an inquiry, due to the strain of knowing that his home had been damaged and because of working in the blackout.[9] Such incidents are among the hidden consequences of war.

Many of the older evacuees, particularly the girls, were also aware of the absence of the young men of the village, some of whom they had befriended before their departure. Frances and Evelyn remember hearing about the 'boys at sea' and were greatly saddened, along with the villagers, when some of them got killed in action. One of the evacuee teachers, Mr Barnes, also went away to war, as his daughter Pamela remembers:

'My father left right at the end of December 1940. I have a photograph of him already in uniform taken in January 1941 in Worthing where he was doing his initial training, there and in various other places, until finally he set sail. His serving career took him away. It was quite extraordinary, once he was up and away, and he ended up in the Desert Rats at El Alamein, the 8th Army, the Monte Cassino campaign, and went right through the Middle East, Palestine, Egypt, Iraq, Iran and South Africa. He just never got the opportunity to have leave, except once when we went up to London to see him.

'It's like my mum said, you never knew from one day to the next what was going on, and everything was heavily censored. You didn't know where he was, you didn't know what arena he was in, and things would come months later, it wasn't like the instant communication of today. You just had to wait for the post, and that could take weeks getting there. She was writing very regularly, that much I do know. They exchanged a lot of letters and cards which she kept, and we always had his photographs up. She talked about him a lot, to keep him alive for us, but you know, I sometimes wonder how women like her got through the war because they didn't know from one day to the next what was going on.'

An article about Ralph Barnes' active service appeared in *The Jewish Chronicle* in October 1941,[10] when mention was also made of his time spent in Mousehole.

JEWS IN THE FORCES

The three brothers Barnes and their brother-in-law, Israel Fox, are serving with the Forces. Ralph Barnes, Royal Engineers, was a teacher in the Senior section of the Jews' Free School, London, and when a party of the children was evacuated to Cornwall, he went with them. For many years he took PT with the boys, and he organised games for the Association of Jewish Youth. Before he joined the Army last year, he voluntarily took the services for the children and many parents during the Holy Days in the reception area.

Another aspect of war which had a considerable impact on Mousehole was the requisitioning of boats, which left few serviceable fishing boats in the village and only boys and older men to man them. Requisitioning was to have some tragic consequences in some instances, as described here by Percy:

'Most of the fishing fleet was requisitioned and the local fishermen were given the option by the Navy of either becoming a crew member of their own boat or to release the boat entirely and let the Navy run it. One of our lads was David Sleeman who had a boat called *Internoss,* and I remember him telling me after the event that that boat was his livelihood and he wasn't prepared to let that boat go and be used by somebody who was unused to it, so he and his brother decided that they would become members, presumably of the RNR. They operated the boat with a young naval sub-lieutenant nominally in charge, but I think he just let the people who owned the boat run it under naval instructions. Most of the fishermen went with their boats to make sure that they were looked after properly. They were often used to connect with convoys that were coming across the Atlantic. They didn't go very far out, they just carried messages.

'Now there were some older people who took the other view, and they just let the boat go to the Navy. The Navy selected their crew from the people they had available. An uncle of mine decided to do that, and his own boat, which was a fairly new one, was requisitioned and he then used an old boat, which wasn't as new or as big as his own, and did some fishing within the Bay. I don't think they were allowed to go very far. I know that he and a relative went down towards Cudden Point to catch some pilchards. They caught so many that the boat split open and he died. He was drowned just off Cudden Point, and I can remember, probably when Ted was there, my father spent the next week walking the coast and the cliffs from Marazion to the Lizard, looking for the bodies.'

Another tragic and unrecognised consequence of war. Some of the younger members of the village also became involved in the war effort in their own small way as, for example, did Joan Ladner, who together with her friends staged concerts for the Red Cross.

'I am a pianist and I started doing concerts at the age of 12 and a half at the British Legion. We got given the key to do what we wanted there, and there were 25 of us girls who used to do concerts for the Red Cross, when the evacuees had gone back, obviously. So we were very much thinking about the war and thinking about what others were doing for us. And, of course, cinema was uppermost; we went to the cinema a lot. So you saw the newsreels and it lived in your memory, the concentration camps and such like.'

Young though she was, and living in a small isolated coastal village, Joan clearly had a keen sense of some of the horrendous events taking place during the war. And that war was to have yet further impact on the village. Not only had the villagers opened their doors to 100 or so evacuees from London, followed by numerous other refugees and evacuees from far-flung places, but they now also had to contend with an influx of parents fleeing the London Blitz.

Chapter Ten

A FAMILY AFFAIR

Mrs Lazefsky and Lily Frankel sharing a bed

FAMILY VISITS FROM LONDON

The parents of the evacuees were 300 miles away in London and, naturally, they wanted to visit their children. However, this was a lengthy, time-consuming and expensive journey, and most of them would have been in work, so it would have been difficult for them to leave for any length of time. There was much correspondence, and those parents who could afford it sent parcels to their children, as Marian explains:

'Our two boys had regular communication with their parents. I can't remember Lenny's parents coming down, but he was certainly well looked after. He had clothes and parcels sent. Bernie's mother and his *Buba* came down and stayed at one point, and the *Buba* couldn't speak a word of English. I think most of our evacuees were of Polish extraction.'

Lenny's sister, Jose, does remember her parents visiting, and they, like their children, very soon participated in village activities:

'I was in Mousehole for 12 to 18 months, and we would receive letters and parcels whenever possible. Both my parents worked but managed to visit whenever the railroads were not being bombed. My parents went rabbit-hunting with Mr Johns, Marian's uncle. They used to go home with lobsters and stuff like that. It was lovely then.'

Some parents participated so enthusiastically in seaside life that they ran into difficulties, like Mildred's father:

'My mother came and she stayed for some time, and my father came down for a week or two and he went on the beach and got heat-stroke. He took to his bed, and he said, "Get me some whisky, that would help." So I went into the public house there, the Ship Inn, and got him some whisky, in a little bottle, and took it back for him. We slept in the attic at Miss Oliver's house. There were two double beds up there, where we three girls slept. But I remember when my parents came down, they slept in one of the beds and the three of us slept in the other bed.'

For the poorer parents, in particular, affording the long journey was a real struggle, and some never managed to visit at all, as was the case, sadly, with Betty and Esther Posner's parents. There may also have been, for them, an issue of travelling in what was essentially a foreign country, which they would have found daunting. Mrs Goldstein had difficulty affording to visit her children, but she did manage it on at least one occasion. Vera remembers that her mother sometimes came down on a troop train but she then had to return to work, so could not stay long. Evelyn continues the story:

'When my mother was able to afford it, she would come down to see us and stay in the Lobster Pot. I always remember going in there to see her. On the table was the butter with a little flag in for each guest, and her flag was in her butter. They were allocated one or two ounces of butter during the stay, and that was her ration. I also recall walking to the edge of the dining room and it literally seemed to be hanging over on to the sea. I thought, "My God, it must be on stilts". It was only the times that she came that we went there.'

Vera and Evelyn's brother Jack was the only evacuee to recall that some of the parents came on organised coach trips and his story illustrates how quickly the visiting parents became part of village life; indeed, Jack makes it sound almost as if the East End 'villagers' were out on a trip visiting a local village community, rather than having come on a full day's journey:

'Other people used to come on a coach from the East End because we all lived in the same neighbourhood. They used to hire a coach, the mothers and fathers that were able to come down. I don't know how they organised it all. All I know was the coach used to pull up at the bus stop which was outside our house. I was always out and about, if the weather was good. And, being a kid, I would see the other kids running there, and I saw it on quite a few occasions when it did come and the people coming out. A lot of the people knew me and I knew some of the mums and dads because I'd seen them locally when we lived in this small neighbourhood in the East End. In those days everybody lived on top of one another.

'I remember particularly the Hanover family, because they were in the fruit business, and they always had big parcels of goodies, fruit and bananas and all things you couldn't normally get. And they always used to say, "Hello" to me. I saw them on quite a few occasions.'

Mr Hanover, a well-known East End grocer, whose trade name was Jack Marks, became particularly well known in the village because of his generosity in providing fruit for everyone and is remembered by many of those interviewed, including Evelyn:

'The villagers thought very highly of the Hanovers because every so often he would bring big boxes of oranges and distribute them around the village. He would bring the fruit and he used to go to the hall with the big boxes.'

When Mrs Hanover came alone, she stayed with Mr and Mrs Sampson, the foster parents of Cyril and Malcolm, who lived in Keigwin Place; however, when she came with her husband, there was not enough room, so the couple went to stay with the Sampsons' neighbour, Mrs Nettie Pender. Cyril explains:

'There wasn't enough room for Uncle Dick and Auntie Mary to put Mum and Dad up, but I knew Mrs Pender, and she said, "Well, your parents, if they want to, could come and stay with me." Nettie Pender,[1] Sylvia's parents, and that's when my mother got quite friendly and came down and stayed there. The Penders' two boys must have been away, and her husband, Jack Snr, was in the Navy. Sylvia was a young girl.'

Sylvia Pender also remembers these visits, and her description below shows, once more, how many of the visiting parents became integrated into village life, just like their children:

'Mother was absolutely wonderful. She kept open house for any mothers who came down. We loved hearing about their way of life. Mrs Hanover came often. Mrs Sampson had room for her when she came, but not the father. When he came, mother moved from her room so Mr and Mrs Hanover could have it, and she moved to the air raid table, a sort of indoor Anderson shelter. There was a lot of interaction. Mothers would come and have a cup of tea and sit and chat. It was a two-way process. Mrs Hanover came every evening and three or four of her friends came as well.'

For the children whose parents did not come, or were not able to visit often, watching the arrival of other children's parents must have been excruciating, as Jack Goldstein here describes:

'I used to stand there waiting to see if anybody from my family was going to be on the coach, and never once was there. The Hanovers knew me by my name and they also knew my family because we lived on top of them, more or less, and my father had a fruit stall in Petticoat Lane. And I remember Mr Hanover used to say to me, "Isn't your father coming to see you?" Only my mother came down once, and I've got a picture of her with me on the beach in Mousehole, but my father never came near or by all the time we were there, never had as much as an apple from him. He never once gave me or my sisters that much. So I never had much of a good young life.'

There can be no doubt that Jack's painful childhood experiences were in sharp contrast to the love and affection he received in Mousehole, and it is for this reason that he cherishes the memories of the time he spent in the village.

For children who stayed throughout the war, especially those whose parents could not afford to visit often, and however much they were loved by their foster parents, the rather unfortunate consequence was that they became estranged from their own parents, as was the case with Shirley Spillman:

'My mother used to come down on the train, for a short while, for the weekend. She was working so she couldn't afford to come. Two or three times a year, possibly. She used to send me stuff from London, clothes and bits and pieces. I think she stayed in Penzance, I've got a feeling she stayed there. Well, she was a visitor and came with presents, and yeah, I was pleased to see her. But I can't think there was any close connection really, there couldn't have been.'

Even though most of the evacuees loved their time in Mousehole, and were quite happily integrated and secure in their village life, the arrival and then departure of their parents was an understandable wrench, a reminder of their family life back home. Frances recalls that the only time she cried in Mousehole was when, at the age of 14, her mother visited and she did not want her to go home.

HOME FROM HOME

London suffered intensive bombing during the Blitz, which took place between September 1940 and May 1941 with very heavy casualties and, for the Jewish East Enders, the loss of a number of important communal buildings. It was during this period that Jews' Free School and the Great Synagogue were destroyed. A number of the parents of the Mousehole evacuees came to stay during this period, for as much as six months or more.

Some of the visiting parents stayed in the homes of their children's foster parents, where there was room, others were found accommodation with the friends or relatives of foster parents, and yet others rented accommodation; indeed, this was quite a significant further migration from the Jewish East End, which no doubt occurred in other parts of Cornwall, to a greater or less extent, where there were Jewish evacuees. The Hanovers were one of the families to come at this time, as Cyril explains:

'My mother was invited down, she used to stay with Nettie Pender. Mother loved it so much, but she couldn't stay there indefinitely, so we eventually moved out of Keigwin Place. We must have stayed with the Sampsons, I would say, close on a year. Mother made enquiries of Mr Tregenza. He had a big house, Tavis Vor, next to the Coastguard Hotel, on the Parade. He took us in. Our sister, Marie, was a bag of nerves in London, so she came down as well, and one of my brothers, Ernie, came down to visit.'

Cyril's brother Malcolm continues the story:

'Tavis Vor was a big house, owned then by the former Mayor of Penzance, Charles Tregenza. He had a housekeeper, Gwen, who came in and looked after him, but he lived alone, in this massive house. There were about seven bedrooms, and I think we took it over for a while. I had my own dog, his dog was my dog, Slipper, and there was a big garden at the back where we used to play football with Slipper. We had our own private path running down through the garden to the beach. It was like a film star's house. It really was massive, it was a mansion, and he was a lovely man. He'd sing the songs of the old days, like *I'm Off to Tipperary in the Morning*. And I can picture him now, he wasn't very mobile, bad joints, and with a stick and rosy-cheeked, grey-haired, glasses, bowler hat; a very smart man.'

Malcolm's account shows the degree to which visiting relatives added to the general family atmosphere which existed between the villagers and the evacuees, sharing together the experience of war:

'Our father came down for a break and various cousins to get away from the bombing, and it was a haven for them, if only for a few days. Even my late Uncle Barney Ringle with his wife Dolly, they stayed at the Coastguard Hotel, so again, there was a bit of a family atmosphere. And that was a good time as well although the war was on, for us youngsters, you know, to be there and have the run of the house.'

Other villagers also went out of their way to welcome visiting parents fleeing the bombs. Mr and Mrs Waters, the parents of Jack Waters, allowed their evacuees' mother to stay, free of charge, in a cottage owned by the family:

'I remember the Reidermans, the father was from Russia. I know Mrs Reiderman came down and we put her in one of our cottages. Celia went to stay with her mother and Rosita stayed with us. It was a three-room cottage with a cellar underneath in Duck Street. Father owned two lovely little cottages there, but it's all pulled down now. Well, trouble was at that particular time if you never had a front door and a back door they condemned them, and I think Father got £50 for them. They could have been utilised and made good, but there you are, they just pulled them down and there's a car park there now.'

Ted's parents, Mr and Mrs Labofsky, stayed with the brother of Ted's foster parents, Mr and Mrs Harvey:

'Well, when the bombs were really at their peak during the Blitz, my parents came down and stayed with Mr Harvey's brother, Cyril Harvey, who lived next door in a house called Clovelly. They gave them a room there for some time, and my sister, Renee, went to Miss Oliver, where the Fromovitch girls eventually stayed, she didn't come originally. Renee was very happy there. My mother and father stayed there for a couple of months, then they moved to St Ives, where my father and some other people who had come down opened a little workshop, and did a bit of work down there. They lived in the workshop, they ate in the workshop and they slept in the workshop, making clothes. My father was in tailoring, he was a tailor's presser.'

This was a clear example of the East End coming to Cornwall. Percy Harvey also remembers Mr and Mrs Labofsky, staying with his uncle next door:

'Where they all slept, Heaven knows. It must have been a pretty tight squeeze when Barney and Sarah, Ted's parents, came down. But Ted's mother was a very pleasant woman, and she used to take Ted walking up Raginnis Hill. We always used to be rather amused because when we asked her where she'd been she would say, "Up where the four winds blow." That was her phrase, and we always remembered her from that sort of comment that she used to say.'

Pamela Barnes' grandparents and Aunt Theresa visited and became well acquainted with the local community. Theresa stayed for some time, and took work in St Ives:

'My maternal grandparents came down, and I've got a photograph of my grandmother holding me when I was three months old. And my grandfather, bear in mind he was Russian-born, loved going along the harbour, he loved that harbour and talking to the fishermen.

'My mother had one sister, Theresa, who was nine years her junior, so she was about 18 when war broke out, and she was requisitioned to do war work. She came down for some time to Mousehole, which she absolutely adored, and got friendly with girls of her age. Obviously they were teenagers, and she was working over at St Ives doing war work of some kind. They used to go over to Penzance where there was a dance hall, and there were American soldiers based there, she quite enjoyed that, and again, she had lovely memories of Mousehole, and talked about it over the years.'

Other East End parents found ways, like Mr Labofsky and Theresa, of making a financial contribution, as is clear in the story which Marian tells:

'Joan Young [née Trembath] at the end of the street, I can't remember the name of her evacuees, she had two girls, but the family home in London was bombed, flattened, and the mother just turned up here one evening off the train, with nowhere to go, and she came down here and lived with Joan's family for a long time. Joan told me only yesterday that her evacuees' mother, she was a lovely lady, was an expert tailoress, a wonderful tailoress. She sort of earned her keep here by doing a lot of sewing, because I think Joan's family had a machine.'

This story shows, like so many of the others, the extraordinary generosity of the people of Mousehole in accepting people who arrived virtually destitute and without forewarning. There clearly was a sense of everyone pulling together at a time of war. The two evacuees in question, staying with Joan Young's family, were Miriam and Lily Roar.

Inevitably, the overcrowding of the village resulted in some tensions. Joan Ladner, whose evacuees were Dan Frankel and Harold Lazefsky, tells this story of two of their visitors who had difficulties getting on with each other:

'Lily Frankel, Dan's sister and Mrs Lazefsky, Harold's mother, they came down in the Blitz. Mrs Lazefsky was rather a large lady, dear lady, and Lily was my height, a little soul, so Mother and I shared a single bed because we only had three bedrooms. We had the single room, Dan and Harold had the front bedroom, and Lily and Mrs Lazefsky, they were in the third bedroom in the back bedroom, looking at the island really. And in the midst of it, they fell out. They didn't like each other very much. Well, Mum said, "You've still got to sleep in the same bed, you'd better sleep back to back." And they did. They went to sleep back to back. They were there for six months like that while the Blitz was going on.'

The image of two people quarrelling and sleeping back to back while the bombs were flying around is rather an amusing one. So much for good relations! In some instances, quite extended family networks came to stay in the locality, as was the case with Maurice Podguszer's family:

'To begin with we saw very little of our family, and afterwards when the air raids on London began to get very heavy, my mother came down and she, with her mother and sister, rented a house in Newlyn. Grandmother Sarah Cohen was a very religious woman who was responsible for bringing emancipation teaching to Jewish women. She could write and speak several languages. My other grandmother stayed with the Nathans for a period in Mousehole on Raginnis Hill.'

Arnold continues the story:

'Once the bombing started in London proper, by the end of 1940, my father acquired a house in Newlyn, and there my mother came with other members of the family. My mother was staying there with my youngest brother, Michael, and my older sister Gloria. With her, in the same cottage, was her mother, Sarah Cohen, an elderly lady at that time, in her late 70s. There were also my mother's sisters, Minnie Ross and her children Geoffrey and Alan. And my mother's other sister, Hannah Kosky, with her children Julius and Pearl. So, there were four cousins, together with my brother Michael and my sister, Gloria.

'In addition to that my mother's brother had taken accommodation for his children in Mousehole as well, David, Frances and Michael Cohen, and there was a much younger child, Gloria Cohen, who stayed with another family. The cousins living nearby, we seldom visited or ever saw them. I remember seeing them perhaps once. Mother left in September or October 1941. Maurice must have left by then.'

Gloria Cohen, born in 1938, was extremely young at the time she was billeted with Mrs Osborne at Brynmyr on Raginnis Hill. She believes that she did not come with the original party, but that her mother found the accommodation for her. Although so young, she remembers that Mr Osborne died the day before her fourth or fifth birthday, and that in spite of her loss, Mrs Osborne nevertheless proceeded with her birthday party the next day. Gloria has always remembered this kindness.

Unlike his cousin, Arnold, who did not have access to books, Julius Kosky remembers that it was while in Cornwall that he learnt the pleasure of reading. One of the rooms in the house where his family stayed in Newlyn was lined with bookcases filled with hundreds of books, many of which he read.

Somewhat surprisingly, Arnold and Maurice did not see a great deal of their mother while she was staying in Newlyn. Maurice remembers only visiting her occasionally, while Arnold remembers sometimes visiting at the weekend. In any event, it would have been difficult for them to go to Newlyn during the week, as they were attending school. Once Maurice left, probably in September 1941, his younger brother Michael took his place in the Crompton family home, which created a new situation for Arnold, who by now had become established in his life in Mousehole and 'knew the ropes':

'I think that my older brother felt that I was a bit of an encumbrance, because I can remember trailing after him saying, "Wait for me, wait for me." So now, instead of me trailing after my older brother, it was now my younger brother trailing after me, saying the same thing, and younger brothers tend to be a bit of a nuisance.'

A LONDONER GROWS UP IN MOUSEHOLE

Pamela Barnes' experience was different from that of the other evacuees, because she was born in Penzance and spent the first five years of her life living in Mousehole, after many of the other evacuees had left. Like many wartime children, she did not really know her father until 1946, after the war ended, and it was not until then also that she knew anything of life in London. Her early childhood therefore resembled, in most respects, that of the local children in Mousehole. Even though so young at the time, Pamela has a remarkable recollection of that memorable period of her life. Several of Pamela's memories accord with those of the evacuees and villagers given in the stories above and elsewhere in this book. Moreover, in its richness of detail and in the evocative nature of its content, Pamela's description of her childhood in Mousehole during the war years compares favourably with the reminiscences of a Mousehole childhood written by local people, and is worth therefore quoting at length:

'My earliest memories are of living in a lovely cottage in Foxes Lane with my mother and sister. Foxes Lane comes down to the harbour and, in the other direction, leads to the school. The rent cost 5s 10d.[2] I have a very early memory when I could have only been about 18 months old. I was in my pram in Brookland Cottage when a chicken landed on my pram, which caused me to scream. Mummy remembered this incident, but she never wanted to tell me so that I wouldn't be frightened of the chickens because at that time the cottage was opposite the Matthews' farm, whose daughter was Lenna Harvey.

'There was a little farmyard area and the chickens used to just run wild. Another early recollection is of being allowed to go in and see them when they were young, yellow fluffy chicks. Lenna used to make the milk and the cream and we used to go over with a jug, and I can always remember this rather big white jug that we had. We didn't have a refrigerator or anything, so you'd go over daily to get your milk.

'The farm belonged to Lenna's father and I think she had a son, Anthony, who was roughly my age. They had a few animals there, cows that went up in the fields, and a horse stabled in there. There was a ghastly thunderstorm one night, and the horse obviously had got frightened and there was this terrible neighing. He was beating his hooves against the stable and was obviously very scared.

'As I started growing up a bit, I remember all the children coming past the cottage to go to the village school. So I used to sit myself on the windowsill, which was a nice low windowsill in the front of the cottage there, and I would sit and watch them go past, longing to go to school.

'We were very close to the harbour and the beach, which was just a playground and absolutely fantastic. My sister and I were allowed to play on the beach with other kids. There were all these lovely little pools, we had little nets and we'd collect crabs and we used to bring all these bits and pieces, and shells and starfish up in buckets and empty them into a bigger bucket in the back yard, all these lovely things from our own childhood perspective that were going on. It was fantastic.

'Mummy was very well known, and a lot of people used to gather in our cottage. It was just open, you never even locked doors in those days, people just came and went. And she just got involved with a lot of the villagers and made some very good friends, and the immediate neighbours were fantastic. Our special friend was Agnes Gruzelier who was like my second mum. She was a wonderful, wonderful lady. She lived near the Keigwin Arms; just along from there is a row of cottages, and you have to go down some steps to the front door. Village life is village life, everybody knew everybody's business, and from day one practically Agnes became a good friend to my mother. She used to babysit if Mum went to London to see her parents occasionally. Raymond Pomeroy[3] was the local taxi-driver who used to run a black car. Grandmother died in February 1945 and Mum called in Agnes to look after Lydia and me. Raymond arrived in a chauffeur's hat to drive mum to the station.

'Agnes had several brothers who were all fisher-folk, and I know one or two got drowned years before. She kind of kept the family together, and looked after her father into old age. By the time the war broke out she was in her 40s. She had no children, of course, she was single. It was quite amazing that years later, in the 1960s, she actually married a widower, and she went and spent most of her latter years, before her husband Arthur died, in a bungalow up in Newlyn. And then when she got really frail, her last days were in Paul, quite close to Paul Church actually.

'Across the road from us in Foxes Lane were the Gilberts, and she was called Salome, believe it or not, and she was the most wonderful lady, very large, big-bosomed lady, who just took to my sister and I, because she'd only had sons. So she just loved these little girls and used to spoil us. Our favourite food was having mashed potato with a fried egg on top, because that's what she would do. One of her sons was Geoffrey, who was a bit of a tearaway and would tease us girls. He had a hand-made cart, like a wooden box with wheels on it, and because Foxes Lane sloped down, he'd ride the length of the hill and scare the daylights out of anybody who was there. But she was a lovely, lovely lady, always cooking, always chirpy and cheerful. I think she was a widow even then, and her life must have been quite hard, but you know, all I can think of is this beaming face.

'My mother was friendly with Miriam and Gladys Harvey, who lived on the other side of Mousehole, past the Lobster Pot side. Miriam's daughter, Heather, was exactly my age, Heather Harvey. Agnes Gruzelier had a sister, Eileen Luke. She had two children. There was Hilary Luke, my age, and her brother, Gerald, who was my sister's age. My sister used to knock around with him a bit. He was a bit of a tearaway, and one day my sister fell in the harbour because they were climbing up the steps, and, of course, my mother was very anxious. Sadly, Hilary died as a very young woman. She caught meningitis in her teens and died, it was very sad.

'I had the freedom of the village, so to speak. I was allowed to walk down on my own, so I thought I was very important. Everybody had their doors open and everybody knew who you were. I do have a recollection of wandering into people's homes, and even ending up with one of Agnes's friends in her cottage one afternoon. They were drinking tea, and this woman was reading tea leaves, which quite fascinated me. I'd never heard about this. You know, they used to drain the cup, and read the tea leaves left in the cup. My mother had got concerned and had come down looking for me and we were all sitting round this table looking at the tea leaves. I must have been quite young, three, four at the most. You could be trusted to walk, you weren't going to get lost, and there was no traffic, no cars, so it was all perfectly safe.

'We had our friendly postman that everybody knew, Bill Blewett, who would come up every day with the post and he would read it before you read it, which was always funny, but we would laugh about it. Bill Blewett was also a bit of an actor, and he ended up appearing in war-time films with Tommy Trinder. There was a love story shot in Mousehole and Penzance in 1942–43 with Margaret Lockwood, Patricia Roc, Stewart Granger and David Ferrar. A very big scene was shot at the Minack Theatre in Porthcurno. Mummy met all of these people, the stars. Once, we were sitting on a bus coming from Penzance and she saw a man and asked if he was Marius Goring. He said "What a pretty little girl". Alfred Marks was another famous actor who was in several films and he used to visit his sister, one of the evacuees in Mousehole.'

This idyllic life in Mousehole was interrupted only once, when the family went up to London to see Ralph Barnes while he was on leave. Here again, Pamela shows remarkable recall for a child of such a young age:

'I went up to London on only one occasion with my sister and Mum, and that was round about 1942. We did the train journey and my grandparents were living in Hackney with my aunt, my mother's eldest sister. We stayed longer than we wanted to because I caught quite severe measles and couldn't be moved. There was a bombing raid in Hackney in 1942, coming up to my second birthday, and my mother didn't want to leave me because I was ill. My grandmother said, "I'm older, I'm staying with the baby. You've all got to go down to the shelters." Even as a two-year-old, I do remember being cuddled by her while the bombs fell. I have a family photo taken with my father, who must have been on leave in London at this time. When I recovered, we went back to Mousehole, and I have no recollection of going back to London again in the years up to the end of the war.'

For Jean Barnes, this trip to London must have been a stark reminder of the life they would have led in London had they not been evacuated to Cornwall. A stark reminder, also, of the contrasting lifestyles. So Pamela's idyllic life continued. Like other village children, she was introduced to the local occupations of fishing and farming and started to learn how these impacted on daily life:

'I remember watching the fishing boats come in, and how they would pull in the nets, and sit on the quayside. And Agnes, because of her brothers being in the fishing fleet, could sew the nets as well which was quite an art because every time a catch came in, the nets always had to be repaired. If it was a fine day, instead of going up to the lofts, where they would spread them out, they would sometimes do it on the harbour side.

'Another big catch was crabs and lobsters, a food I personally do not eat because it's not *kosher* and I just didn't like them as a creature to look at, I suppose they reminded me of spiders. But I do remember when I was old enough, and I was allowed to, I would sometimes walk down on my own and used to be quite fascinated with the shape of these lobster pots. I always loved the shape of that woven basket. You'd see them pulling them up with the lobster or possibly a crab inside them.

'I also have a recollection of my sister and I, we must have been three or four, going on one of the harvesting trips and coming back sitting aloft the very tall pile of hay on a hay cart. And my mother was quite astonished, terrified we'd fall off, but we loved it, so obviously the farmer allowed all the kids to go up at some point and watch the hay-gathering because it was all done by hand in those days.

'My mother loved it. She always said it was like going to the end of the world. In those days, everybody looked out for everybody else. It was a country life, and we had happy times in spite of the war. It was a happy time; it was very, very good.'

After the war, the family were given the opportunity of buying Brookland Cottage for £500, but could not at that time afford it, a decision which, perhaps in later years, they came to regret.

PRAISE FOR HOST FAMILIES

While the evacuees were enjoying their new-found life and freedom in Mousehole, the Jewish authorities in London were monitoring the welfare of some 6,000 Jewish evacuees spread throughout the country in 200 centres scattered over 26 different counties, from Cumberland to Cornwall. In April 1941 *The Jewish Chronicle*[4] gave a very positive report of the way in which these children were adapting to their new environment. Interesting to note is the reference to Jewish food, discussed in chapter seven.

REACTIONS OF EVACUEE CHILDREN

Dr Nathan Morris gave an analysis of the reactions of the Jewish children to their new life under evacuation conditions at a meeting of the Religious Education Board, which was held last week at Woburn House [...]

Behind [the figures] lay a story which, in many respects, was dramatic and stirring. The majority of Jewish children at the present time were not cared for by their parents, but by strangers – by non-Jews, who had undertaken the irksome duty of bringing up other people's children. These were placed with decent English folk. A remarkable fact about it all was that in all his talks with people concerned intimately with the complex problem of evacuation, including large numbers of children, he could not recall one case of unkindness to or harsh treatment of a Jewish child. The children were unanimous about the kindness shown to them everywhere, in most cases by people who knew of Jews before only by repute.

MARVELLOUS EFFORT AT SELF-ADJUSTMENT

The English countryside has given their children a great welcome, and in their reaction to it, Jewish children had made a marvellous effort at self-adjustment. It always meant a wrench – a strange environment, unknown ways of life, different food. It had not yet been realised that the question of food was not only a matter of religious observance. Feeding habits played a psychological, and probably also a physical, part in the life of a child. Universally their children longed for Jewish food. It was a severe psychological test, but the children had come through it with a success that entitled them to a large measure of pride and self-congratulation.

The Jewish Authorities were keen for children to remain, for their own safety, in the reception areas. It is likely, therefore, that this report was intended to reassure parents back home, and to that extent, there was almost certainly some exaggeration or glossing over of the facts. Present day commentators such as Martin Parsons[5] have written extensively about the suffering experienced by many evacuees of all denominations, and Tony Kushner[6] has written of the difficult experiences of many Jewish evacuees who were mistreated because of their religion; however, the stories in these pages are clear evidence that the majority of Jewish children in Mousehole, at least, were indeed being cared for in the manner described in the article above.

Chapter Eleven

AT PLAY

'When we went to Land's End, oh, it was wonderful, I couldn't believe it. People said, "That's the last piece of England till you get to America." It was all so vast, the sea was so vast, it was so totally different to what we were used to in London, where we were all sort of packed together like sardines, no fresh air. And there we felt alive, and felt wonderful.'
Vera Goldstein

FRIENDSHIP PATTERNS

The way in which the children formed friendships was determined by their age, gender, whether or not they had siblings, who they were billeted with, and in what circumstances, and also how long they remained in Mousehole. With only one or two exceptions, the evacuee children were born between 1927 and 1935, and hence their ages at the time of their arrival in June 1940 ranged from five to 13 years. It appears, therefore, that there were three distinct age groups among them; the youngest who were five to eight years of age, a middle group of nine, 10 and 11-year-olds, and an older group of 12 and 13-year-olds.

For most of the children, their social life and social contacts seemed to revolve around the social life of the family they were living with; indeed, some of the younger children barely moved beyond this family grouping, other than to go to school. This was especially the case where there were siblings billeted together, who could play with one another, such as Betty and Esther Posner, staying with the Drews. In fact, the sisters were unaware of being part of an evacuee group, and were astonished to see themselves, 70 years later, at the front of a group photo of the evacuees taken at Paul in July 1940. Other younger children befriended one, two or, in some cases, a small group of other children of their age, and mostly of the same sex, with whom they played around the village.

Derek, one of the younger villagers, remembers that his sister Edith was very friendly with Betty Konyon and also with Frances Levene with whom she spent hours playing. However, most of the evacuees formed friendships with other evacuees who were in the same class at school, at least during the early stages. Malcolm Hanover befriended another evacuee, Johnny Wright, who although not Jewish, was attending Jews' Free School Mousehole. Arnold Podguszer got involved with a group of boys from school, though he also remembers some of girls in his class whom he befriended:

'We lived about a quarter of a mile to half a mile from the village. I had a scooter so I could scoot in and out which was wonderful, but I don't recall playing with any of the village children. We made friends with other evacuees but not with the villagers. For no particular reason other than we knew the children we were at school with.

'I remember a little girl who sat next to me, Millie Butler. And a little girl called Irene Fromovitch, who I thought was very pretty. There were five sisters. I remember talking to Irene and she said she was one of five. I said, "So am I," and it made some sort of association because of this.'

In any event, all the children mixed together on the beach. For the small number who remained in Mousehole throughout the war, such as Shirley Spillman, friendships were more likely to be with village children. Her particular friend was Pat Jeffery, whose father was the shoe-maker, while Millie Butler was friendly with Elaine Pomeroy. Shirley became so integrated into village life that she was barely aware of who was an evacuee and who was not. Towards the end of the war, one of the youngest evacuees, Gloria Cohen, was befriended by Anne Pender, the youngest of the villagers interviewed:

'My sister and I were sent up Raginnis Hill to play with a lovely little girl that Mrs Osborne looked after called Gloria. It was a very beautiful house, beautiful garden, and Mrs Osborne was a very lovely lady. Gloria, I remember, had very dark hair, and it was quite a joy to go and play in this beautiful setting up Raginnis Hill.'

An even younger Pamela Barnes did not know any of the evacuees; indeed, she has no recollection of them, so that her friendships were almost exclusively with village children.

Girls of the middle group, such as Jose Marks, were often involved in doing errands for their foster parents, which entailed moving around the village and therefore getting to know many of the villagers. Jose believes that she knew the villagers more than some of the other evacuees. There seem to have been a lot of little boys of the middle group, of whom Jack Goldstein was one, who had known one another at JFS before their arrival in Mousehole. For these, it was a question of continuing with friendships previously established at home in London, and there were therefore groups of boys this age who formed little gangs of their own, as Jack explains:

'We didn't mix with the young village children, not because they weren't very friendly, they were. It seemed as though we – I can't speak for the girls – but us boys, the friends that I had were all from the school and I noticed that most of the young boys that lived local had their own friends. But we never had any problems or any arguments or anything. They just kept to their friends and we kept to ours. My friends were all from the same school as it was before we came to Mousehole, you knew all your own class boys, didn't you? All the children that came down with us, Jews' Free School kids.'

In the latter part of the war, the young village boys did play with the remaining evacuees, as Derek Harvey remembers:

'We would all play together in the street as boys do, cowboys and Indians, all the usual things. We made our own enjoyment, boys made go-karts out of push-boxes and what they could scrounge really. When the war got on a bit and when we got a bit older, we used to play "Commandos" and we used to run the streets even with blackout. Of course, we knew this place like the back of our hand, we could lose anybody in Mousehole in them days.'

The older children also arrived with established friendships, many of them having known one another in London. Most of them were well integrated into the families with whom they were billeted and got involved in their social lives; however, they also associated with one another at school and to some degree beyond it. Interestingly, unlike the younger children, the older boys and girls mixed together. When older siblings, who had not been evacuated, visited Mousehole from London, they also became involved in this adolescent grouping. These youngsters used to gather on The Cliff in the evenings after school, where they would chat with village children of a similar age, and whom they therefore befriended, as Evelyn recalls:

'A lot of the village kids used to hang out on The Cliff, so they got to know us. The Ope was a sort of meeting place. All the boys and girls used to collect and we would talk with them for an hour or two, and then we would go in to supper and go to bed. It was just wonderful, we would be friendly with all the village boys and girls of our age group, maybe a year or two older.'

Ted was in the unusual position of living with two village boys, as well as having his own friends in the school. He thus developed a wide network of friends.

'I spent a lot of time with the boys in the family, Percy and Billy Harvey. I went about with them a lot, as much as my school friends really. Among my school friends, Maurice, who was my age, had a bike, and I learned to ride on his bike. Cyril Hanover was also my age, and I knew Lenny Marks very well. Lenny Marks and Bernie Warman, they were my immediate friends because they lived in The Gurnick just at the bottom of where I lived. I knew Lenny Marks before, and I knew his sister Jose well. There was Danny Macintosh, and Ronney Glazer was also the same age group. He lived in a farm up at the top of Raginnis Hill and delivered milk. I had another friend, Aby Baruch. The family who took him in really treated him well.

'Among the villagers, there was Bertha Pomeroy, who was very good-looking, and Richard Richards was my age. He was the last person I had a fight with. I wasn't a "goody goody". We had problems as well. The village boys and the evacuee boys were like two little gangs. No trouble, but that little anger.'

This reference to gangs is extremely interesting in the context of Percy's stories about boy gangs in the village.[1] These were hardly comparable with the gang culture of modern cities, but they did seem to be a way of ensuring that the village boys were toughened up to prepare them for their future harsh occupations on sea and land. Ted remembers that, apart from his association with the Harvey boys, he and the other evacuee boys of his age group tended not to mix a great deal with the village boys. There was occasional conflict and tension between the two groups, though on only one occasion did this actually take on racial undertones.[2] Another incident, which he describes below was, he felt, nothing more than normal 'boys stuff', and nothing to do with him being Jewish:

'Well, I was once out on the boat in the harbour, and another village boy in another boat barged into me, sort of mucking around, and then when we got off the boats he wanted to fight, and he was about a head and shoulders taller than me. He thought he was a lot bigger than me and he thought he'd get away with it. We had a fight and he hit me in the eye, and I jumped on him and pulled him down on the floor. I was going to bash him on the floor, and someone stopped us.'

One could hear the 12-year-old boy inside the 82-year-old Ted as he told this story. Ted believes that one of the reasons for these conflicts was that there were just too many boys in one small village with as many evacuees as there were village boys. This is a very good point. The fight can probably also be understood in the context of the territorial conflicts experienced by the village boys, which were part and parcel of village life. On the village side, Jack Waters also remembers that the older groups of village boys and evacuee boys tended to keep to themselves, and like Ted remembers that there were sometimes tensions between the two groups, which does not seem to have been the case with the younger boys. Perhaps the older boys, driven by their adolescent hormones, were far more conscious of their differences and were beginning to stake their territorial claims, as Jack Waters describes:

'There weren't any big frictions. There were skirmishes, you know, boys from different areas, but nothing serious. I mean, we may have resented some things that they'd got that we should have had. They sort of kept to themselves, like we did, more or less to ourselves. I mean, it was a different religion, and the rest of it, but there were no big issues about it. They were little scuffles like children would have, but nothing more than normal, not really. I think, as far as I remember, they gelled in very well.'

Even the younger boys occasionally got into minor scuffles, according to Derek Harvey, who also acknowledged that it was all part of the rough and tumble of boyhood:

'We had a few scraps up school, because some of them were a bit rough. So were we, really, I suppose. But we all got on, eventually we all got on very well, and it was quite a quiet place when they went afterwards.'

While the teenage boys tended to keep to their own groups, the evacuee girls were more likely to make friends with the village children, though there were exceptions to this. Some of the adolescent friendships among the boys stemmed from shared sporting interests, as was the case with Cyril Hanover:

'I remember a couple of village boys I was friendly with. They were footballers, Jack Waters and Jacky Gilbert; he was a friend of mine. He had a brother called Geoffrey. And Madron, one of the Madrons, they were a Mousehole family. Another boy called Torrie. And we made plenty of friends with boys by first names, you know, "Hello, Tom", "Hello, John". There was a boy called Lashbrook, we called him "Lashy". He was a friend of Jacky Waters. We all played football together. They were wonderful, friendly people. I even got friendly with one of the village girls. I was always sweet on Ada Williams, she was lovely.'

Feelings of attraction such as the one described by Cyril were bound to occur in such a gathering of young people under these circumstances. Vera remembers liking Watson Trevaskis who sadly got killed in the war, and she recalls how heartbroken she felt. As we have seen, Frances was developing a relationship with young Edwin Madron:

'We were sort of innocent sweethearts but no one knew. His father used to call him Fromovitch to wake him up in the morning.'

For those older evacuees who remained a long time in Mousehole, their friendships with the village children became solidified. Frances counts many of the villagers among her friends and recalls not mixing a great deal with the evacuees. She certainly must have had contact with other evacuees in the early days, especially when she was still in school; however, she stayed on in Mousehole until the end of the war, by which time most of the other evacuees had left, so her friendships by that time were with the older children in the village.

One interesting feature of this evacuation story was that, in addition to siblings, a number of the evacuees were related, as we saw in the previous chapter. The four Cohen children, who lived on Raginnis Hill, were cousins of the Podguszers, while Millie Butler, too, had several cousins in the village. The Podguszers also had cousins who were 'private evacuees' living in Newlyn. Although such relatives, and even siblings who lived separately, did not necessarily mix much socially as they remained within their host families, they obviously knew and recognised one another, and this added to the general feeling in the village of everyone knowing everyone else.

The older village children who attended school in Penzance, Jeanne, Marian and Percy, did not have the same opportunity as the other village children of mixing with the evacuees. Furthermore, all three of them had large amounts of homework, as a result of which they were not able to go out in the evenings. Of course, Jeanne and Percy both had an evacuee living with them, and Marian Harris visited her Auntie Florrie on a daily basis before and after school and had her meals with Lenny Marks and Bernie Warman. Furthermore, living right on The Cliff, Marian would have seen from her window the groups of children gathering in the evenings, as she did her homework.

THE BEACH AND HARBOUR

The beach was a favourite playground for all the children, but most especially the little ones. There are three beaches in Mousehole; the harbour, which at that time was largely off limits, though boys did play there; the beach below Gurnick Street, to the right of the harbour as you face it; and the beach to the left of the harbour, which is full of large rocks and pebbles. This is where most of the children played. The area you reach as you first go onto this beach is called the New Rocks by the villagers, while further down is the Cove. As we have seen from Marian's account in the first chapter, the beach was full of natural objects, which children could use in their imaginative play. Pamela Barnes is able to remember the precise rock on which she played, which was probably the same rock as that described by Lily Polgrean, on which her mother sat when she was pregnant:

'We had a favourite place, there was this rather big rock that we nicknamed "the armchair" because my mother used to like to sit with her back against it, and that's where we'd come down and have our little picnics and things, so we always called that "the armchair rock".

Lily Polgrean gives a further interesting account in her book[3] of the way in which the village children interacted with the evacuees on the beach:

We mixed with these children in the village and especially when visiting the beach. They were mostly nice children and we compared their Jewish culture with our own Methodist upbringings. In particular, I remember one of the nice boys, whose name was David Sachs.

Many other evacuees vividly recall their time spent playing on the beach, wandering around the village, or simply standing and looking out over the harbour, watching the coming and going of the fishing boats. Jose Marks even remembers collecting monies for the lifeboat by selling flags. Malcolm Hanover teamed up with Johnny Wright[4] who was:

'...my main ally, my main friend, my pal. We were two rascals together. We used to go bullfrog catching in the ponds around the rocks in the area, over the rocks towards where we eventually stayed, Tavis Vor.[5] Also we used to go out blackberry picking and come back at all hours; we used to just fend for ourselves. We went on long walks up Raginnis Hill, the steep hill by the side of the Wesleyan chapel. Or up to Paul, which was past our school playground. Even hikes to Lamorna Cove. The two of us were quite safe, you know. It was summer, the nights were light. We even mucked about in the harbour, which wasn't very nice, because the sewage came down through there. But kids of that age get up to all sorts of things. Of course, it was wartime. But again, it was lovely.'

One of the younger villagers, Raymond, remembers Malcolm getting tar on his clothes at Marazion and described him as 'a real character'. He also has a strong recollection of Billy Wright, whom he remembers as a brilliant footballer. Raymond was also friendly with Alan Paris,[6] younger brother of Tony Paris, and almost three years Raymond's junior:

'Alan was a little short boy. I have two photographs of us playing in the harbour together.[7] He used to come to our back door, but he wouldn't come in our backyard, because he was afraid of our dog. He used to shout "Raymond, are you coming out?" He pronounced my name Rymond, with his cockney accent.'

One of the boys appearing in the photographs mentioned by Raymond was Donald Waters, who in 1996 gave Raymond a written description of the photos:

I remember we were down on the harbour mud, playing 'boats' on the incoming tide, witness the bits of wood, and even using one's shoes as a boat, our boyish imaginations turning them into 'battleships' or *'Queen Marys'*.

Another little boy who loved playing on the beach was Arnold, living out at Penlee Point. Clearly a very serious little boy, he took Nanny's instructions about playing out very literally:

'Nanny insisted that when you'd finished your meal you went out to play, no matter what. I remember on one occasion getting very wet indeed because she insisted you had to go out, and we assumed that no matter what the weather was you had to stay out. Then she said, "No, if it's really bad weather you can come in again." But, you know, I took these admonitions quite seriously. I mean, we had been brought up to be well-disciplined children and I suppose as one of a large family, you had to obey instructions. My father was quite a disciplinarian. If it was during any of the summer months, we would go down to the beach. We'd have a little bent pin on the end of a line and we'd go fishing and all manner of things. The beach was a wonderful playground for children.'

Arnold often played on the beach below Penlee Point, quite a way past the Cove, where there were fewer children and he was unsupervised, although at other times he went down into the village:

'Sometimes we would go and play round the harbour, where there were lots of activities and there were other children from the school there. And, of course, there were adults there, whether they were supervising or not, you would see the fishermen mending their nets round the harbour wall and so on, which was really quite interesting and exciting. Of course, my older brother was striding off and I couldn't keep up with him. I suppose he had his own friends. There were a group of little boys at the school, a sort of little gang of us. I remember one of them was called Ginger. I suppose we roamed around as a little pack getting ourselves into mischief and so on.'

Many people commented on how safe the village and the beach were, even for unaccompanied young children. In reality, there was a lot of informal supervision, with adults engaged in tasks round and about, keeping an eye on the children, as we have seen in Arnold's account above, or older children watching out for the younger ones.

Of course, playing on the beach often included swimming in the sea, a whole new experience for some of the evacuees, like Jack Goldstein:

'According to the weather, we used to go and play on the beach and do a little bit of fishing in the rock pools, and we loved to do that. Mr Richards used to take me down to the beach when I wasn't in school, and I remember him saying, "Can you swim?" I said, "No." I'd never been in the sea, let alone swim, and he taught me to swim. He said to me, "Do what I tell you, and I'll teach you to swim, and you'll soon get the hang of it." The way he taught me to swim was he gave me a rubber ring that you put over your head. There was a little cove that everybody used to go to, a natural cove, with big rocks at this end and big rocks at that end and in the middle it was just pebble beach, so it was a convenient place to swim. He said to me, "Just walk out until you get up to there and turn round and face me. Now do this. Lean forward and kick your legs up at the back and just keep doing that. You won't go under because you've got the ring on." And it seemed, you know, natural, and he taught me to swim in no time.'

The older children also loved swimming, and some of them, unlike Jack, had already learned to do so before they went to Cornwall. Frances had learned to swim while at Buxton Street Junior School in the East End:

'You'd go to Goulston Street in Aldgate. That's where the pool was, and they'd teach you. Then you got certificates for 25 yards, 50 yards, 100 yards. It was near Petticoat Lane market, near there somewhere.'

On one remarkable occasion, Mildred and Frances swam all the way to St Clement's Island. Mildred begins the story:

'We always seemed to wander round the harbour, and the beach was wonderful because I loved swimming. Well, I may have gone to Southend, but Cornwall was so different. We were always on the beach collecting shells and I made a lovely necklace, I often wonder what happened to that, out of little tiny shells. Frances and I swam to the island. How mad was that! When you think back, it was frightening. But I'm always proud of myself for doing that.'

Frances continues:

'Oh, it was lovely in this clear water, and we'd jump off the rocks near the beach but quite deep. Dive in the water, swim between Mildred's legs and she'd do it to me, and we'd dive in to this beautiful clear water. It must have been nice if we swam to the island. I don't know whose idea it was, all I remember is walking to the edge of the water and getting in and getting off at the island, and there were birds on the island, seagulls. When we got on to the island we could hear the evacuees clapping and cheering from the beach. Oh, if a master had seen us, we would have got *what-for*. But then we sat there, and I looked in the water and there were all these little fish swimming around. Oh my God! Mildred said, "Come on, we've got to go back, we can't stay." We got in, and then this fisherman in his boat was shouting, shaking his fist. I think we might have gone over his nets, I didn't think they put nets out so near to land. But we got back, thank God!'

Another person who swam to the island was Vera Goldstein, on a separate occasion. And Vera did get *what-for* from her teacher!

'There was a little island just off Mousehole beach called St Clement's Isle, and I remember one day I played "hookey" from school with a girl – I can't remember which girl – and I swam to the island, and Mr Levene looked through his binoculars and he saw me on it. When I got back I got a very heavy reprimand. That stands out.'

THE LURE OF THE SEA

Many of the books about Mousehole tell of the days when fishermen walked back and forth on The Cliff. It was said that The Cliff was the length of a boat's deck. Nettie Pender[8] described it this way:

> In my early remembrances, up to the time of World War One, one would have a job to walk along The Cliff [...] Men of different age groups would be walking to and fro, covering only a few yards. This would happen, of course, if the weather was too bad for them to go out to sea. The older men would be talking about bad storms they had encountered [...] Each man had his own story to relate; even the youngsters who had not long gone to sea could relate one to another their experiences, and what they would do.

This custom had clearly not entirely died out by World War Two, as is apparent from this description by Jack Goldstein:

'Mr Richards was a retired fisherman and he used to tell me about the places he'd been. He'd also spent years, like most of the fishermen in those days, in the Merchant Navy, and they were very proud of their connection with various shipping lines. The old-timers used to wear a long-sleeved pullover, all navy blue, I don't remember seeing them in anything else, with the shipping company's name across the front, like the Cunard Line, the P & O line. All the old-timers used to walk up and down the front there, on The Cliff, for hours, walking up and down chatting about years ago, when they went here, there and everywhere.'

One of the most exciting activities of village life for the evacuees was going out on the boats. While it was mainly the boys who did this, some of the girls also had the opportunity to do so, though generally as passengers rather than as budding fishermen. In the case of the Fromovitch sisters, this was to have unfortunate consequences as we saw in a previous chapter. Evelyn and Vera Goldstein had much more pleasant trips out with Johnny Drew, on his boat, the *Bonny Lass*. They particularly enjoyed seeing the seagulls nesting on the island. Just like the village boys, and many of the other evacuee boys, it was not long before their brother, Jack Goldstein, was in a boat:

'And then, when we got to be known, there were several people had little rowing boats, "punts" they used to call them. They used to have an oar, one oar only at the stern end and they had a little place where the oar went. And they let us use the boat. First of all the fishermen, when they weren't working, would teach us how to row; they used to what they called *scull* them. You sculled with one oar from the stern end, and you'd go like this, and like this, and the boat used to go along very quickly, and we got proficient at it.'

Asked if this had been exciting for a little city boy, Jack responded with feeling:

'I should say! When the sea was calm they let us go outside the harbour, but they wouldn't let us go out if it was rough because it was dangerous. But we used to love doing that. It was a marvellous place.'

Malcolm and Cyril Hanover also went out in a boat with their foster father, Mr Sampson, as Cyril here recounts:

'Uncle Dick and his son Ronnie used to take us out on his boat and show us how to fish, and we used to go fishing down by the bed of the ocean. They took us out on a boat called *Quo Vadis*, which was their little fishing boat, 'cos he was a fisherman by profession, earning his living. Marvellous.'

These experiences and these feelings are echoed by Ted:

'It was wonderful to learn how to fish and to handle a boat, wonderful. The boys used to take me fishing. Mr Harvey had an uncle who had a boat there and we used to go out sailing on the boat. It was his Uncle Percy Laity, I think his name was. We used one oar: *sculling*, they call it. You don't row with two oars, you have one oar at the back and you make a sort of a *sculling* movement, like that, and it propels the boat along. It was a very pleasant life for someone who'd come from the slums of London, very exciting!'

Percy Harvey, who Ted was living with, describes these outings in more detail:

'There was another chap who I was called after, Percy Laity, who was a very good fisherman; a very prosperous fishermen. And when he retired, he had a small boat which I used quite a lot, both with him and without him. This boat had a small sail and we used to sail down towards Lamorna Cove, where we'd put out a few crab pots and things like that, and if I caught a lobster, this made my week because I would take it up to the hotel and get five shillings for it. So probably Ted was involved with that. When we were not out in the boat, we used to go fishing off the Cave at Mousehole, a place called the *Kettle and Pan*. The Cornish for that place was *Crib and Zawn*. We used to go out there a lot and I'm quite sure Ted came with us and we used to fish with rod, fish with lines. We fished with a *boulter*, which is like a long line. We would cast it out about 50 or 100 yards, and it had a line with strops hanging down with hooks on, with bait, and we'd throw that out and would leave it there overnight, and go out and see what was on it the next day.'

Although Maurice was living a little way outside the village, and in that respect was somewhat isolated, he nevertheless managed to have a wonderful time, helped by the fact that he received generous gifts from the Cromptons:

'I had a bicycle bought for me, so I cycled down to the village, and I was one of the only kids who had a bike. I was also bought an air rifle and encouraged to learn how to use it. I didn't know how to swim and fish at all and was taught by local kids. A local woman who lived up in Paul used to come down to the Cromptons and was a house cleaner for them, so Nanny didn't do ordinary housework. And this particular boy, the cleaner's son, used to come down. Eventually I got very friendly with him. I can't remember the name...'

According to Myra Phillips, who lives in Paul, the cleaner was Lizzie Annie Hoskin, who was friendly with the Cromptons and had an only son, John. Maurice was later able to confirm that this was indeed the boy who had played with him. Ronney Glazer also remembers playing with John Hoskin,[9] so this young man must have befriended a number of the evacuees.

'Well, there was this young man [John Hoskin] and he came down to the Cromptons' house and we would go fishing with him. He was encouraged to be friendly with us. He would be my age. He would take us to the local areas and show us the various places to fish with a piece of string. We also learnt how to fish with a bent pin and a piece of limpet attached to it.

'Then there was a local fisherman with a small sail boat who used to take out groups of boys to fish with him, and I can remember going out on this boat fishing for mackerel. On one occasion we were out, having caught the mackerel, when we then caught something bigger. We hauled in a small blue shark, which he proceeded to knock on the head to kill it whilst it was in the boat. And when we got ashore, I can remember it being dumped into the harbour sand. Of course, everybody was interested in that. He was Ladner, Lardner, something like that. He took us out. We had a great time.'

While he was recounting this story, Maurice sat with his eyes closed, and a big smile on his face, as if visualising in his mind's eye those pleasant times of long ago. The local fisherman he referred to here was almost certainly Percy Laity, who clearly took a number of young evacuees, as well as village boys, under his wing. Percy Laity's boat is shown on the cover of this book with yet more children playing in it, including Donald Waters who, in 1996, wrote this about the picture:

> Geraldine Underell FRPS, who lived in the village, took the photograph. She arranged us children in this composition of diagonals, down in Mousehole harbour. The date would have been some time during the summer of 1944 or 1945. The small yacht belonged to Mousehole fisherman Percy Laity, who lived in Fore Street.

Sadly, it seems that Percy Laity died in his boat only a few years after this photograph was taken, as Donald writes:

> This little sailboat, with Percy at the helm, was tacking out off the corner of St Clement's Isle, when a sudden slant of wind caused the boat to heel, and the mainsail boom snapped over, catching the owner across the head, and knocking him unconscious and overboard. The mishap was seen from the village by some other fisherman, who immediately got a boat out and over to the rescue. But it was too late for the old chap, who had drowned. I remember him well as a quiet, decent sort, and when he used to go out of the harbour, we boys used to vie with each other and shout and ask to come aboard for the sail. He taught several of us youngsters the art of sculling.

Such is the triumph and the tragedy of a life spent at sea.

EXPLORING THE COUNTRYSIDE

While the young children played mainly on the beach and around the harbour, the older children roamed further afield, often walking quite long distances. Even the younger ones went walking within the vicinity of Mousehole, sometimes in pairs or small groups, at other times with their host family. Esther Posner remembers walking unaccompanied with her sister through hilly paths and fields, even though they were only seven and eight years old at the time. Millie Butler was taken on walks in the locality by a friendly neighbour:

'Every week Mrs Jeannie Oliver, who lived down the street, took me for a walk to the village of Paul. She used to teach me about the plants and flowers and the birds which we saw. I remember that her husband was a fisherman and was at sea most of the time. She seemed to be lonely and she befriended me.'

Walking was a favourite leisure time activity of the villagers; indeed, there was a custom in the village of walking to Lamorna and back on Good Friday, which Marian thinks may have had some sort of ancient, religious or pagan significance. Ted remembers going out for walks with Mrs Harvey:

'We did a lot of walking with Mrs Harvey, and a favourite walk on Sunday afternoons was to Lamorna Cove, that was a walk of about a two or three miles. It was a regular walk, up Raginnis Hill, across the fields, right through the farmland and through the moors on to Lamorna. They would walk down the path and the boys and myself would usually climb down over the rocks.'

Ted also remembers roaming around with friends, either the Harvey boys or other evacuees:

'We were mostly running about and going to Smugglers' Cove. When you go up Raginnis Hill, about halfway up, there's a side path going off the hill to the left and you follow that path and it brings you right down to the coast with cliffs, lots of cliffs and Smugglers' Cove is just beyond that. From there you can look down into the cave which goes underneath the hill.'

On one occasion, Ted's adventures with his friends nearly got them into serious trouble for trespassing:

'We used to go up past Paul village and there was a big estate there which had chestnut trees, and we used to go and collect them. Once we were in the trees and got surrounded by a pack of foxhounds, and the master of the hounds came along and he said, "They won't hurt you," adding, "you should ask permission to come into the grounds." I may have been with Lenny and Bernie, but I also went with Percy and Billy Harvey.'

Maurice remembers the sense of freedom, and also the knowledge that came with walking:

'We were given very much free rein. I can remember walking up the various hills there and walking even beyond, to the huge cave which was just outside of Mousehole and having a whale of a time. We had a lot of free time on our hands and learnt a heck of a lot about the hillsides that surrounded Mousehole.'

Cyril Hanover recalls that much of this walking was done in groups of older children:

'We used to go blackberry picking in the fields and for walks in the beautiful places just outside Mousehole; Paul, Lamorna Cove was quite near, Penlee Quarry and to Sennen Cove. We used to go with friends, groups of friends, perhaps half-a-dozen or 10 of us, to these various places. It was wonderful, and they were wonderful people.'

Initially, Evelyn and Vera only went out with Mrs Harvey, or with one another, but were eventually allowed out on their own, as Evelyn here recalls.

'We used to love walking, I was healthy as anything, and Auntie used to love walking as well, but she didn't come with us that far. She first of all walked with us to Paul and towards Lamorna Cove, and then we did it ourselves. And it was always lovely; we used to see all the bluebells growing down there, just fantastic. After we were there a little while, we then began to walk along the cliffs to Newlyn, and Penzance sometimes, and all the way back. We used to love it, to feel the wind in our faces, the smell of the sea, it was just too wonderful.'

Vera remembers that some of these walks were done in groups together with other evacuees:

'We used to walk for miles, every Saturday from Mousehole to Penzance, and sometimes to Marazion. We all used to go in a group, mainly the older children. I remember going with Ernie and Cyril Hanover. It was wonderful, absolutely wonderful.'

One day, according to Evelyn, they walked all the way to Land's End, a distance of eight miles. The occasion made a lasting impression on her and she could not help but compare it with life on the streets of London, where such freedom was quite impossible:

'One particular time we came up through Paul and then went all the way to Land's End. When you get right to the top, there's a big plateau, a viewing point, and we saw the First and Last House, and looking over the Atlantic Ocean it was like the end of the world to us, you saw nothing anywhere, only sea. We went to the edge of the cliff and looked over it, across the Atlantic, and we thought: "Isn't this amazing, we've come to the end of the world."'

For those who could afford it, cycling was an ideal way of travelling around and enjoying the countryside. Marian was one of the villagers able to do this:

'I managed to buy a second-hand bike with some pocket money I'd earned when I was 15, and a friend of mine had a bicycle, and she and I would cycle around all over the place, there was very little on the roads in those days. So we used to go cycling quite a lot.'

If you had access to a car, a rare thing in those days, then you could travel even further afield. Ted was one of the few evacuees to have this privilege:

Rory's father
J.P.H.

'When I first went there, the Harveys took me everywhere. Mr Harvey was a builder and had a little car, a small Austin, one of those baby Austins, and he had a petrol allowance. Every weekend we'd go out somewhere, somehow, and it was very, very nice. I can remember going to lots of places: St Ives, and different beaches, Praa Sands, Marazion and St Michael's Mount. Maybe it's because when you've got something to show someone you go out more yourself.'

Maurice and Arnold's exploration of the environment led, on one occasion, to an incident with potentially the gravest of consequences. This story is all the more surprising, and, dare one say, amusing, because the Podguszers were particularly well brought-up little boys. Arnold gives his version of events:

'I do remember one terrible event. Just above where we lived there was a large quarry and above that there was gorse and ferns, and I don't know who was playing with the matches but we set it alight and we couldn't control the fire. I remember running back to

Nanny to tell her and she said, "Well, just go down to the beach and don't say anything to anybody," which is what we did and it just burnt itself out. You know, I don't know who was playing with the matches or why we were doing it, but little boys do these things and it got out of hand.'

Maurice here gives his side of the story:

'It was the life of old Riley there really, and we got up to mischief. There was a disused quarry, though I should add it wasn't entirely disused, as there was a hut there, used for the storage of dynamite for the big quarry which was further up. I can remember one day we were there and we started to play with matches. It was very dry and the bracken caught light and it started to burn. We knew what we'd done and we made ourselves scarce. We ran down to the beach and there were huge, black clouds of smoke and we were waiting for a big bang to take place because we knew what was behind there. Nothing happened, and the next day we decided to go and see what we'd done and everybody was very fortunate. The powder keg or dynamite store, what we didn't know was that in front of it was a stream and that the fire had burnt itself right out, right up to the stream. We might have inadvertently brought part of the cliff face down on Penlee lifeboat!'

Or blown up part of Mousehole itself, in echoes of the Spanish Raid of 1595!

SOCIALS AT THE BRITISH LEGION

Much of the social life of the village revolved around the chapel, from which stemmed a love of music and singing, which spread beyond the confines of chapel life. For many villagers singing was a major leisure activity, as was the case with Jeanne Waters:

'Then there was choir practice, there was the chapel choir, there was the male voice choir and there was a mixed choir in the village as well, and singing was something we all enjoyed. There used to be children's concerts and things like that, which were lovely when some of the evacuees joined in. One of them was Danny Macintosh, he was a very fair boy and I can distinctly remember what a wonderful boy soprano voice he had, so he must have come and sung either in church or Sunday School in the little concerts or I wouldn't have known about it. Beautiful voice.

'There were some socials at the chapel, what they called the Junior Guild, and they could go along there. I think there was a nice little bit of entertainment put on at the British Legion. They used to have films sometimes there and musical evenings, a bit of dancing and so on. I think for the younger ones there wasn't quite so much available, but when they became teenagers I think that's when they would find more to do in the way of social activities.'

Danny Macintosh was 'sweet' on Bertha Pomeroy and tried to use his good singing voice to woo her during one get-together at the British Legion, as Bertha recalls:

'He was very nice-looking and he was a lovely singer. Well, he sang to me once, at the Legion, in a concert. The song was *Who's Taking You Home Tonight?* And he looked at me all the time. Mind, we weren't very old, 12 or 13. Just budding.'

Frances recalls the pleasure of attending the social get-togethers:

'We often had socials at the British Legion Hall, which we liked very much. Most people would go, the locals and the evacuees, the older children, whoever wanted to go. We had dancing, which we liked, and there was one of the Gilberts who lived next door to the farm entrance, I used to dance with him.'

Even some of the younger children, including 10-year-old Jose Marks, attended the organised events:

'Once in a while, the Legion Hall would put on musicals and plays or we had get-togethers. I was in a musical, there was a whole group of youngsters at the time and parents came to watch. One of the evacuee girls called Marion was a contortionist. She could move her body in different ways. She performed on stage during a get-together. I would sing and dance. I had to sing *A Nightingale Sang in Berkeley Square*. The sleeve on my dress split, and I was very upset.'

The event which Jose here refers to was almost certainly the Christmas Concert Party which took place on 26 December 1940. It was hoped that this was to be a big occasion, so in order to raise funds for it another programme was arranged some weeks beforehand, which was reported in *The Cornishman* on 4 December 1940:[10]

MOUSEHOLE ENTERTAINMENT

Mousehole residents intend to give the youngsters – evacuees and locals – a real good time during the coming Christmas. Members of the Women's Section of the British Legion [...] arranged a capital programme in the Legion Hall on Tuesday of last week to secure funds. An appreciative audience assembled, and the capable chairman was Mr Barnes, one of the visiting schoolmasters.

Items of a miscellaneous character were contributed by young visitors from London, and local boys and girls as follows: Betty Shaffer, Hilda Carl, Jack Joseph, Peter Coker, Ralph Plots, Celia Reiderman, Clarice Hoffman, Anita Godfrey, Ada Williams, Monica Gray, Elaine Frischman, Joe Gilbert; Mrs Godfrey, a London visitor, and Mrs Mary Sampson and Clara Vogel also contributed. Mrs A. Sampson, accompanied.

The Government had in fact provided funds for the Christmas entertainment of evacuees, part of a plan to encourage them to remain in the reception areas. An interesting note to this effect is reported in the minutes of the West Penwith Rural Council in December 1940,[11] where it was felt that funds should also include the local children:

ENTERTAINMENT OF EVACUEE CHILDREN AT CHRISTMAS

The Clerk reported that the sum of £96 had been allocated by the L.C.C. for the entertainment of these children during Christmas and that the hope had been expressed that local children would also be entertained in a like manner, that he had asked the W.V.S. to arrange for the treats, and that he had apportioned the money to the respective Parishes on the basis of approximately 1/- per head.

The meeting went on to agree that the council should contribute the sum of one shilling per head for each local child attending school. The WVS was asked to assist in the entertainment with the help of school teachers. This was a wise decision as, if evacuees alone had been entertained, this could have caused resentment in the local communities. In the event, the combined funds for local and evacuee children were considerably enhanced by the generous provision of Mr Jack Marks, father of Malcolm and Cyril Hanover, as Cyril here recounts:

'My father came down and gave a big party; this was Christmas-time 1940. He got in touch with a comedian and a songstress from Plymouth and brought them down on the train, with boxes of apples, oranges, bananas, sweets and chocolates for the evacuees and local kids. You couldn't get nothing like that, but my father had a bit of sway up here. You know, everything was on ration then, and they thought it was wonderful.'

This was indeed a very big occasion, which was reported at some length in *The Cornishman* in January 1941.[12] The reported number of 400 evacuees is incorrect, the figure having been close to one quarter of that amount, and probably refers therefore to the total number of people present.

CHRISTMAS CONCERT PARTY

LAUGHTER AND GAIETY AT MOUSEHOLE

A grand concert and Christmas party were given by Mr Jack Marks, of London, assisted by many willing helpers, to 400 evacuee children in Mousehole British Legion Hall on Boxing Day.

During the first part of the afternoon there was community singing, followed by numbers given by the following children: Celia Reiderman, Clarence Hoffman, Jose Marks, Clara Vogel, Phyllis Barnes, Edwin Madron, Frederica White, Betty and Doris Fishman, and Gerald Landeau.

Tom Leslie's concert party contributed to the second half of the afternoon, each artist performing in first-class style topical and popular selections, all of which were in harmony

---

with the occasion. They won unstinted applause, and the whole entertainment was thoroughly enjoyed by young and adults alike.

At the conclusion every child was given a bag containing cakes, fruit and confectionery, including a large saffron bun. The fruit and confectionery were gifts from kind-hearted Mr Marks. All had a great time, and those who attended were parents down from London to see their children over Christmas, and many people from the village itself. During the interval, Mr Marks, who is interested in education and other public work (and whose children are evacuated to Mousehole) said he was very pleased to have travelled the 600 miles to give these evacuees a treat, which they so much enjoyed. He realised that many were away from their parents for the first time, and to help in giving enjoyment to the little ones he felt he was doing his bit towards a worthy cause, and promised that he would do all in his power to return to Mousehole in the early part of the New Year and give them another treat. Before closing he thanked most warmly the ladies of the British Legion Committee for helping to make the party such a success: also, the men of the British Legion and everyone concerned in doing anything possible to brighten the lives of the children.

All parents of boys and girls are deeply grateful to the foster-parents, who so readily opened their hearts and homes to all evacuees.

Such events at the British Legion Hall became quite a feature of Mousehole social life at that time, and another fundraising entertainment was reported in *The Cornishman* only a few weeks later.[13] Once again, the names of many local and evacuee children are mentioned who feature in the pages of this book. Mrs Janie Ladner, an accomplished pianist, was the mother of one of the villagers interviewed, Joan Ladner. According to Joan, her grandfather, Ernest Ladner, the butcher, was also the reporter for the Mousehole column of *The Cornishman* at this time.[14]

MOUSEHOLE JUVENILES' EFFORTS

During recent months, Mousehole British Legion Hall and premises have accommodated numerous refugees, mainly from the Metropolis, who have been enabled to meet and enjoyed many happy hours daily.

The time for spring cleaning the premises has arrived, and to acquire the necessary funds three young girls Malvina and Maureen Johns, and Monica Gray, determined to get together some local and evacuee children to provide selections of various kinds. They approached Mrs Janie Ladner, who undertook to help, and duly prepared the young artistes, all of whom, with the greatest enthusiasm, acquitted themselves most creditably in action songs, and other items, which gave considerable pleasure, the occasion being the variety entertainment on Friday evening, when the hall was filled to capacity. Mr Edwin F. Madron presided, and contributed most creditably several pieces evidencing much talent. In addition to the concerted selections by the little ones, older boys and girls singing solos and duets included Phyllis Barnes, Jose Marks, Elaine Pomeroy, Marion

Hewson, Doris and Betty Fishman, Clara Vogel, Frederica White, young Edwin and Joe Madron, in clever contributions. Miss Stella Madron, daughter of the Chairman, was at her best in choice songs. Mr Johnson charmed old and young with his manipulation of the piano accordion; a duologue by Ida Selner, and M. Hewson was very effective [...] Lieut E.G. Pentreath, MC [...] offered congratulations to the Misses M. and M. Johns and M. Gray, Mrs J. Ladner (who so ably contributed to the repertoire, and accompanied throughout), and to all who had taken part.

Another form of entertainment was going to the cinema in Newlyn. Shirley remembers that on a Saturday, a small group of children would go on the bus, as in those days the cinemas had a children's show. Connie Mellows also remembers doing this, even though she was only three months in Mousehole. Interestingly, it was Mrs Rose's maid who took them, so it is clear that some consideration, at least, was given to their needs:

'I can remember going on the bus to Newlyn to go to the pictures, and when we used to come out of the pictures there was a fish and chip shop opposite, and we used to go there with the maid and buy chips and eat them on the way home.'

Frances also remembers going to the cinema, as no doubt did many of the other evacuees, as this was a common form of entertainment in those days and also a means of obtaining the news:

'Saturday we went to the pictures, about thru'pence each it was, in Newlyn. There was a Meadery there; I don't know if it is still there, that's where the cinema was. When you come down from Penzance, on your right is the Meadery. Or it was. So we'd go there for pictures and all the village boys came because we went.'

As mentioned by a number of evacuees, they were not only able to watch films in the cinema, but also had the privilege of watching films being made in Mousehole. Jose Marks, for example, remembers watching Tommy Trinder and Robert Newton making a war movie.

A few of the older children, including Mildred and Frances, remember venturing further afield than the British Legion and going to a dance hall in Penzance on Saturday nights. This was probably towards the end of the war when they were much older. Mildred remembers dancing with a man who worked on a ship, and when he came into Mount's Bay, he would toot the foghorn to let her know he was in town!

A SPORTING LIFE

Cyril Hanover was a keen footballer and described himself as an 'all-round sportsman'. Together with another evacuee, Mark Deswarte, he played for local football teams, one of these being an evacuee team. He proudly presented the cuttings, displaying his football prowess, which he has kept for 70 years:

'I've got a cutting here. I was very good at football, and I was chosen to play. This was an evacuee XI playing Penzance Schools XI, and you can see my name mentioned a few times. We were all selected from different schools evacuated from London to play the Penzance XI. Can you see it halfway down there somewhere? "And two people played for Mousehole, a boy called Deswarte and Hanover", me!'

The boyish pride was clear in Cyril's voice as he recounted this story. There was also a combined Mousehole and Jews' Free team for which Cyril and Mark played, and, again, their successes were reported in the local press.[15]

ADDISON GARDENS 0, MOUSEHOLE AND JEWS' FREE 0

For the first time this season, the lads from Mousehole were visitors to St Clare where they opposed Addison Gardens. Addison Gardens attacked strongly, and Cole and Rabin were unfortunate with several good attempts. The visitors, however, made some strong raids, which allowed Decerf to distinguish himself in goal.

On the changeover, Mousehole attacked and forced numerous corners, all of which were cleared. Just on time, Addison Gardens obtained an abortive corner but a goalless draw was an equitable result.

For Addison Gardens, Rabin, Cole and Ball were outstanding, while Mousehole were well served by Hoskin in goal, Hanover and Deswarte.

MOUSEHOLE AND JEWS' FREE SCHOOLS 3, GAINSBOROUGH 1

A combined team from Mousehole and the Jews' Free Schools visited the St Clare ground and defeated Gainsborough by a margin of two goals in a very enjoyable game. Almost immediately from the kick-off, Gainsborough went through for their outside right, NOBBS, to score. The lads from Mousehole were heavy and fast, and soon drew level when DESWARTE netted. Gainsborough tried hard to draw level but fell further behind when HANOVER again beat their 'keeper. The visitors continued to attack, but were unsteady at times. They succeeded in finding the net once more to win an excellent game by 3–1.

The latter article displayed a league table showing that the Mousehole and Jews' Free team had gained a creditable position, in spite of only playing three games. It is interesting to note the way in which evacuees have been included in these teams; Millbank must have been an evacuated school based at Madron, while Gainsborough must also have been an evacuated school, along with several others of those mentioned. Combined teams, fully local teams and teams consisting only of an evacuated school were all placed alongside one another, indicating the degree to which evacuees had become integrated into and accepted by the local population. Hence this football league table can be regarded as a symbol of the success of evacuation in this area.

THE LEAGUE TABLE

	P	W	D	L	F	A	Pts
County School	7	7	0	0	41	8	14
Addison Gardens	9	6	2	1	12	8	14
Millbank and Madron	7	2	4	1	7	8	8
Gainsborough	9	2	4	3	10	12	8
Lescudjack	9	2	3	4	4	16	7
Mousehole and Jews' Free	3	2	1	0	6	1	5
St Paul's	6	2	1	3	7	11	5
Calvert and Montague	7	2	1	4	9	13	5
Hugh Myddleton	5	0	2	3	0	6	2
R C and Sacred Heart	5	0	0	5	6	18	0
Heamoor and Gulval	0	0	0	0	0	0	0

Chapter Twelve

AT PRAYER

'And they knew now in Mousehole that the blessing and the promise will be fulfilled.'[1]

RELIGIOUS EDUCATION FOR JEWISH EVACUEES

Following the second evacuation in June 1940, the Jewish authorities became increasingly concerned about the spiritual welfare of Jewish children now scattered throughout the country. At a meeting of the Joint Emergency Committee for the Religious Education of Jewish Children, held in December 1940, it was agreed to hold a consultation entitled *Jewish Education under War Conditions* in early 1941.[2] Also at the meeting, a Mr J. Halpern reported on the position of the new reception areas and gave a fascinating account of negotiations with the appropriate authorities in Cornwall.

CONSULTATION ON RELIGIOUS EDUCATION

The most interesting point, he said, was that as the result of visits to the education authorities in Cornwall, the Jewish children could now receive instruction by their resident teachers in school hours, with the goodwill and co-operation of the local and evacuee headmasters [...]

In this connection, Mr Halpern said that the helpfulness of the chairman of the Methodist body in Cornwall was very much appreciated.

As a result of such efforts in Cornwall, South Wales and the Home Counties, more than 1,000 children who had not hitherto been receiving any organised religious instruction would now be receiving tuition [...]

They were striving, in very trying circumstances, to keep alive in these scattered children, their sense of identity with the larger Jewish life from which they had been torn, to preserve among them the habit of education, which [...] might die altogether if neglected.

The reference to the involvement of the Methodist body in Cornwall is particularly relevant, given that Mousehole was a Methodist community. It is probable that some of the discussions undertaken related specifically to the children in Mousehole, since this was the largest grouping of Jewish children in Cornwall. The Jewish authorities were, of course, well aware of the grave situation with regard to Jewish people on the Continent, hence their anxiety about keeping alive the Jewish faith and Jewish identity. One issue that concerned them was the possible lack of understanding of Jewish matters in the reception areas. In

January 1941,[3] Mr Max Clapper, an evacuee teacher based at Porthleven in Cornwall, wrote to *The Jewish Chronicle* to thank Dr Myer Fisher for his delivery of 'three impressive lectures' at Porthleven and Helston, aimed at promoting 'a better understanding of the Jews' as well as 'a more harmonious relationship between the Jew and his neighbour'. Mr Clapper urged his colleagues in reception areas to organise similar meetings.

Another difficulty in providing religious education for the Jewish evacuees was the lack of suitable personnel, as many ministers were now serving as chaplains in the forces. Someone calling himself 'An English Jew' wrote to *The Jewish Chronicle*[4] to suggest that the board of deputies should introduce a kind of 'conscription scheme' to enforce each Jewish minister not engaged in army work to spend at least one day a week on spiritual work in a reception area. While it is unlikely that such a scheme would have been workable, or even desirable, the fact that the suggestion was made at all displays the level of anxiety surrounding the issue of the religious education of Jewish evacuees.

Nor was the concern for the evacuated children only. For the large number of Jewish children remaining in London, their religious education had also been disrupted by the evacuation, due to the departure of Jewish teachers to the reception areas and the shortage of ministers. The organisation of religious educational activities was hampered by the fact that prior to the war, individual religious bodies had been responsible for their own arrangements. It was felt that a much greater degree of coordination was now required. These issues were discussed at a meeting of the Joint Emergency Committee in May 1941,[5] when Dr Isodore Fishman, the Education Officer of the Union of Hebrew and Religion Classes, said that regional conferences of teachers in the reception areas were being arranged in Cornwall, Cardiff and other places, where a day would be devoted to a discussion of the organisation of Hebrew classes and other educational issues.

The regional conference in Cornwall took place in Par in June 1941 and was attended by, among others, Mr Levene from Mousehole. This conference was probably held in the home of Professor Charles Singer, son of the author of the Singer prayer book,[6] and an eminent and internationally renowned doctor in his own right. He had retired to Par and took an active role in the welfare of Jewish evacuees in Cornwall. The meeting was reported in *The Jewish Chronicle*.[7]

TRAVELLING TEACHERS

Jewish Education in Cornwall

Jewish teachers in Cornwall, who daily travel many miles to the various evacuee centres, came together at Par last week, to confer, under the auspices of the Joint Emergency Committee, on educational matters.

Dr Isodore Fishman, Education Officer of the Union of Hebrew and Religious Classes, who presided, said that in Cornwall there were 20 centres where some 300 Jewish evacuees received religious instruction. Three resident teachers, as well as seven day-school teachers, who had gone out with school parties, had been appointed by the Joint Emergency Committee.

During a session devoted to organisation, Mr H.E. Salomons (Porthleven, Helston, Marazion, and Penzance) gave an account of the work done at these centres. At Porthleven, Jewish pupils attending the various schools were released during the scripture period to join together at one centre for religious instruction. Mr A. Goldbloom (Truro, Connor Downs, and Pool) spoke of the eagerness with which the children looked forward to his visits.

Mr I. Nodel (Caerhuys, Nampean, Sticker, Polgooth, and St Dennis), who covers many miles in travelling to his various centres and has been provided with an auto-cycle, said that, in spite of their strange environment, many of the children clung tenaciously to their Jewish ideals. Mr D. Levene (Mousehole), appealed for a Sefer Torah. Miss Magrill (West Looe) said that she was doing her utmost to prevent the children being taken to church.

[...] Dr Fishman, in summing up [...] paid tribute to the local authorities and headteachers for their ready co-operation.

It is interesting to note that many Jewish children scattered throughout Cornwall were being provided with religious instruction by itinerant teachers. One person who remembers Mr Nodel on his motorbike is Sonya Harris who, together with her sister Irene, was evacuated first to Polgooth, then Hewas Water near St Austell. She recalls that he came twice weekly to give Hebrew classes in a shed in the playground, and that arrangements were made for the Jewish children to celebrate festivals in a local church. She even remembers that he played the *shofar*, a horn which is sounded at Rosh Hashanah, the Jewish New Year.

Mousehole was in a different situation, because of the numbers of Jewish children grouped together, and because of having its own school and staff. If the figures relating to the number of Jewish evacuees in Cornwall are correct then, astonishingly, one third of them were based in Mousehole. Mr Levene's brief contribution to the meeting was to have significant consequences, as we shall see later in this chapter. There was an amusing response to this article the following week.[8]

PEDDLING HEBREW

There is something rather appealing about the report [...] of the way Jewish teachers in Cornwall travel many miles daily round various evacuee centres to give Hebrew lessons, especially when one learns of the enthusiast who goes round by auto-cycle. The name of the place where the local education conference was held tempts a colleague to remark that Jewish education must be good stock for investment now that the teachers have reached Par!

THE SYNAGOGUE AT PAUL

The effect of these deliberations in London and elsewhere was felt in North and mid-Cornwall, possibly because of the presence of Professor Charles Singer in the area, but seems to have created only an echo in distant Mousehole. Many of the youngest members of the group have only the vaguest of recollections of Jewish religious practise while they were there; however, it is clear that efforts were made to establish a Jewish way of life for the evacuees. Mr Levene had been involved in religious education in Soham and it is probable that he took the lead in these matters in Mousehole. In Jews' Free School in London, Jewish education would have been part of the daily school curriculum; indeed, the whole curriculum would have revolved around Jewish life as it was lived throughout the day, the week and the seasons, and would have incorporated Jewish history, festivals and prayer. In Mousehole School, Jewish worship must have taken place at least once a week during the time allocated for religious instruction. For the Jewish boys in particular, the teaching of Hebrew was an important part of their education, which was carried out not just in school, but also in *Cheder* as we have seen in Ted's earlier account. It is certain, therefore, that by the time JFS Mousehole was established, and when permission was granted for evacuated Jewish children to receive religious instruction in school, there would have been at least some Jewish element to the daily curriculum. This is confirmed in Evelyn Goldstein's description of helping out at school:

'We used to sing Hebrew songs and learn when the Jewish holidays were. I would sing with the children, not actually teaching, and do some poetry with them, verses, things like that, and they would repeat.'

Several of the evacuees remember having Hebrew lessons either in school or at someone's home in Mousehole, which would suggest that some form of *Cheder* was set up at some point. Connie Mellows is sure she had Hebrew lessons, even though she was there for only three months, while Shirley Spillman, who was there much longer, recalls going to the home of one of the teachers but that this 'fizzled out'. She thinks that the teacher may have been Mr Levene, but that there also may have been a visiting teacher for a brief time. Jack Goldstein also thought there was a *Cheder* of some kind which he likened to the one he had attended at JFS in London:

'I used to go to a *Cheder* in London on Sundays because if you belonged to the Jews' Free School you had to go, it was in the premises. There must have been one there, in Mousehole.'

Among the older boys, Ted does not remember being taught Hebrew in Mousehole, but Maurice believes that Hebrew was taught:

'I was expected to read and understand Hebrew, too. No question, there had to be, the continuation had to take place in Mousehole. It must have been at school. We would have been having a separate service of our own when the local children were having their Christian education, although I recollect this only very vaguely.'

In fact, one of the villagers, Melvia, remembers that religious assembly in Mousehole School took place on a Friday, lasting about half an hour, but that the Jewish evacuees did not participate in this. They must therefore have gone to another part of the school for their own worship.

Of course, as well as establishing some form of religious education in school, there was also the question of services on the Sabbath. Even before the establishment of the school, efforts had been made to set up regular Sabbath services. An informant wishing to remain anonymous says that Mr Levene went to a lot of trouble to arrange synagogue services in Paul Church Hall with the vicar of Paul. Interestingly, one of the group photographs, taken in July 1940, was identified by several of the villagers as being in front of 'Paul pub', which is the King's Arms adjacent to Paul Church Hall. The photograph was taken on what was then the village green, but is now a car park and includes 48 boys and girls of all ages together with Mr Barnes. Given its location, the photograph must have been taken on a Saturday on the occasion of a Sabbath service. At that stage, therefore, many of the children were involved in attending services, or at least that particular service; however, not all the children continued to attend on a regular basis, most particularly the younger children and the older girls. Jeanne Waters believes there was no element of compulsion for the younger children at least:

'Frederica didn't attend the Saturday morning synagogue school at Paul. We were quite aware of it, but she didn't make any move to go at all, so whether it wasn't a very strict Jewish family, I don't know. I don't think there was any pressure from their teachers to say they must go. I don't ever remember her saying, "Oh, I must go, I have to go. Mr Nathan says I must do." No pressure either from us or from the teachers.'

One of the younger boys, Arnold, remembers something of the services, probably because he attended with his older brother Maurice:

'Certainly on a Saturday, we walked up a very steep hill to Paul. There was a Church Hall and that's where we had a Saturday morning service. I just remember there were services, and singing in them, but nothing else. I couldn't read Hebrew. I don't recall being taught Hebrew at that period. I do remember on one occasion my father came down to visit us and actually went to a service there with us, and this must have been somewhere in 1941.'

For other children, particularly the middle age range of boys, the village held far greater attractions, as Jack here points out:

'I don't remember anything about it because I never went. I heard about it but I never went. Well, I was never asked to go. Some boys mentioned to me about they'd been, but nobody ever came to me and said "Would you like to come?" or "You have to come." I didn't bother, because on the weekends we were so busy playing in the lovely surroundings and that's all we wanted to do. Or I did, anyway.'

Some of the older girls also felt that they had more interesting things to do; Vera cannot remember ever going to the services at Paul, though she must have done on at least one occasion as she features in the photograph. Her sister Evelyn does remember attending some services, but she thinks these took place in Mousehole School:

'We used to have Hebrew classes on Saturday in Mousehole, I think in the school hall. I can remember singing *Adon Olam,* that's a Hebrew song, and Mr Levene would just do a little service, not too long. And Saturday afternoon we would come home and then we'd go to town with Auntie.'

Mildred and Frances went to some of the services, but Frances tells this story, showing there was some encouragement for them to attend:

'Miss Cohen once came down Paul Hill and I was cleaning the windows with a squirter. It was fun, I liked doing that. I hadn't been to Saturday school! Oh, dear! She told me I should have come.'

Cyril recollects a time when both boys and girls attended services:

'I can remember Mr Levene taking the Jewish children, giving them some sort of Sabbath service to keep us well-informed with the faith, and we did that most Saturday mornings. Just some Hebrew services on Saturday morning. I think it was boys and girls.'

Other accounts show that the older boys, at least, were expected to attend. Lenny Marks and Bernie Warman were staying with Marian Harris's Aunt Florrie, and Marian recalls that:

'They had a service which they had to attend, every Saturday. Whether it was in the Church Hall at Paul, or in the school here, I'm not sure. But they definitely had synagogue on a Saturday morning, which was compulsory.'

This is confirmed in the account given by Ted, where he gives details of the kind of service held:

'We had a synagogue at Paul, in Paul Church room opposite the church. There was a small hall and we had our services there every Saturday morning. I went every Saturday, all the time I was there. It wasn't a proper, full service, it was an abridged version of the service, with Mr Levene. We followed the Jewish festivals, but it was limited. We knew we were Jewish and that's about it. I mean, I never had a Barmitzvah, I was 13 there. You know what a Barmitzvah is, of course. It's just really the first calling, your first time you're allowed to be called up to read from the Sefer Torah. We never had a Sefer Torah.'

Ted's account implies that the reason he had no Barmitzvah was because there was no Sefer Torah, the hand-written biblical scroll containing the first five books of the Bible in Hebrew. Cyril also remembers that there was no Torah. He returned to London for his Barmitzvah, though Ted, as a consequence, never was 'Barmitzvahed'. However, it seems that there were several Barmitzvahs in Mousehole, even though there was no scroll. Solly Lederman reached his 13th birthday in March 1941, and a short while after that held his Barmitzvah. He recalls that several other boys, possibly as many as four or five, also held their Barmitzvah within a week or two of his. In preparation for the event, they were taught after school hours to read the appropriate portion of the Bible in Hebrew. Because no Torah was available they read from the Chumash, which is the printed version of the Torah. Solly believes that his Barmitzvah took place in Mousehole School hall, rather than in Paul.

The only other person to remember the services in Paul in any great detail is Maurice Podguszer, who recalls that Mr Haffner, as well as the teachers, became involved in running the synagogue and services. He confirms that the expectation to attend was largely in relation to the boys:

'We were expected to go up the hill to Paul and to attend a Saturday service in what was a makeshift synagogue. Certainly the boys were; there was no question about that. We had to go. I attended throughout my time in Mousehole. The services were simple but they took the normal Jewish liturgical service. I can remember Rosh Hashanah being kept at Paul, in the first September there.'

This would have meant that, by virtue of attending the services, those children involved would have been taken through the Jewish year and participated, to that extent, in the Jewish festivals. It is likely that this also happened for all the children within the context of Jews' Free School Mousehole, that is to say, there would certainly have been some teaching of the Jewish festivals throughout the year, even though most evacuees do not remember this. Their memories have been occupied by images far more exciting than school!

Maurice is alone in remembering that a small Ark was installed at some stage at the synagogue in Paul and that there was a scroll in the Ark. Given that the departure of Cyril and Ted was most likely to have taken place in July 1941, when they left school, the scroll must have been brought after that date. Maurice remembers the appearance of the Ark in surprising detail:

'I can remember the Ark. It was a dresser cupboard standing about 5ft high, with the open shelves at the top removed. The prayer books were stored in the bottom and a scroll in the top, where there was a curtain with a *Magen David*, a Star of David, on it. The doors on it were locked when not in use.'

The Ark and scroll were of particular significance to Maurice as he is the only evacuee in Mousehole known to have held his Barmitzvah there using a scroll, an event which Ted and Cyril do not remember, even though they attended services. When first recounting the story, Maurice thought the event took place in September 1940 as that was the time of his 13th birthday. However, on later reflection, he realised it must have been a year later, as it took place after his hospitalisation in May 1941. He describes the event:

'It was just part of Saturday service. There was a small Ark that was there, and the scroll was produced. I was expected to go up and just say the blessings of the Lord. That was about it; it was very, very simplified.'

Maurice is sure that he was not the only boy to read from the scroll as he remembers others doing so during the Saturday services held there each week. Though some of these could have held their Barmitzvah earlier using the Chumash, like Solly, Maurice feels sure, in the circumstances, that there were others who read their Barmitzvah portion from the scroll. He also recollects that Mr Haffner had some hand in bringing the scroll to Mousehole. The mystery of how it arrived will be revealed later in this chapter.

Had Maurice held his Barmitzvah during normal times, his family would have been involved (possibly this is the occasion when his father came) and a celebration of some sort would have been held to mark the special occasion. It is the custom for Jewish boys holding their Barmitzvah to receive gifts from their family. Maurice received a gift from his foster mother, Mrs Crompton:

'She was extremely nice, very friendly, and I can remember friendly to the point where, when I was Barmitzvahed, she bought me a rolled gold propelling pencil. And I'll go beyond that, when I went swimming at Marazion beach, the other side of Penzance, I managed to lose that pencil in the sand. Far from being angry with me, however, she bought me another replacement in jade, a green jade propelling pencil.'

What is remarkable about Mrs Crompton's kind act, especially given that the Cromptons were not religious, is that she was clearly aware of the significance of the event and of the customs associated with it. Maurice thinks that this was possibly because of the Crompton family connections in the upper echelons of society, before the couple came to Mousehole. Most of the people of Mousehole had probably never encountered Jews before, but there would have been some aspects of biblical Judaism that the Cornish people would have been familiar with, as they were steeped in the Old Testament. Myra Phillips, living in Paul, and whose evacuee was Anita Godfrey, makes this comment:

'Well, I just remember that my dad respected her Sabbath on a Saturday. I can't tell you how, why, but things were different in the home on a Saturday when Anita lived with us, to what they were before.'

Joan Ladner remembers the evacuees going to their own services on a Saturday and that they were not allowed to eat pork. Asked if the villagers respected these practices, she replied feelingly:

'Oh yes, yes. I would have thought there would have been ultimate respect for anything that was to do with their culture.'

The Barmitzvah celebrated by Maurice and the other boys in Mousehole were not the only ones to take place in Cornwall. In April 1941 four boys celebrated their Barmitzvah together in Helston, attended by local dignitaries.[9] To these four Barmitzvahs were added six more, which took place at Porthleven, not far from Helston, supervised by Mr Clapper,[10] whose letter to *The Jewish Chronicle* is quoted earlier in this chapter.

JEWISH FESTIVALS

Judaism is often described as a way of life which, for Orthodox Jews, impacts on every aspect of daily and family living, in the way homes are kept, in the way meals are taken, in the way festivals are conducted and, of course, in daily prayer. A traditional Jewish life of this kind was not possible for the evacuees, even had they wished it; though, as we have seen, a Jewish life was provided to a limited degree through the services in Paul and by means of some Jewish religious education in school. Jewish observance is all-embracing in its nature, as is here expressed by Jack Goldstein, even though his own participation was very limited:

'Among those who attended, they kept everything that normally happened in Jewish surroundings in London. Those that were eager to go to the Sabbath services in Paul would have kept the festivals. You couldn't do one bit and not the other. If you attended, it followed that you did all of the bits and pieces.'

The first major festivals to occur after the arrival of the evacuees were Rosh Hashanah, the Jewish New Year, followed by Yom Kippur, the Day of Atonement, which is a day of fasting. These festivals began that year on the evenings of 2 and 11 October 1940[11] respectively, by which time children had spent almost four months in Mousehole, much of it on holiday, making the most of their new environment. This must have made it difficult for them to pull themselves back to a former way of life. Not surprisingly, therefore, some children did not keep the fast on Yom Kippur, as in the case of Vera, who 'just blended in with what was happening'. Others tried to keep the fast, with varying degrees of success. Marian Harris here tells the story of Lenny and Bernie's attempts to fast:

'There's a day of fast, Yom Kippur. Well, Bernie stuck it out, which was rather difficult being in a household where everybody else was eating and drinking. Lenny managed to refuse food in the house, but went for a walk to get away from it and stuffed himself with blackberries instead and had a bad tummy ache as a result. He didn't quite make it, he couldn't last out; he was so hungry.'

Mildred and Frances remember spending a day fasting on the beach at a time their parents were visiting. 'We didn't eat all day. We fasted.' The success of the girls in keeping to the fast on this occasion was probably due to the presence of their parents.

The first Passover in Mousehole took place in April 1941. Prior to that date, strenuous efforts were made by the Jewish authorities in London to ensure that the festival could be observed by evacuees in the reception areas. A Passover Committee for Evacuees was formed, chaired by Mr D. Goldblatt, who wrote the following heartfelt appeal in February 1941.[12]

PASSOVER AND EVACUEE CHILDREN

Sir,

The war has created for us our own 'Refugees' in the form of 8,000 evacuee children whose billets can be found in villages in Cornwall, in Cumberland, in Norfolk and other counties; in all, about 250 centres. I do not pretend that they are homeless or hungry, but it is certain that, during the years, which must judge them in their future approach to the faith into which they were born, they are cut off almost entirely from those formative influences which are all important. In this body of youth lies our future. We can either tend it or discard it [...]

[...] My committee refuses to believe that Jewry, conscious that their forebears [...] have celebrated the Passover as a proof of their belief in freedom and the rights of man, will, when England is 'taking it' in support of that self same principle, slough off its responsibility and decline to keep alight the torch of liberty for its own next generation.

Here once again, we see the enormous anxiety displayed at the prospect of Jewish youth losing its faith and its identity. This letter was followed up by a further letter from Mr Goldblatt appearing in April 1941.[13] Here he reported that provision had been made for Jewish children spread throughout the country to celebrate Passover, either in *kosher* canteens or by participating in a Seder, the Passover meal, organised by the Jewish Evacuation Committee. Furthermore, every child was to be provided with 'a token parcel of matzoh', the unleavened bread eaten during the period of Passover when leavened bread is forbidden.

Mr Goldblatt's efforts bore fruit in Constantine in Cornwall, not far from Helston, where Passover celebrations were held.[14] There appears to have been a substantial Jewish community which had established itself in this area. Quite why there was such a large contingent of Jewish adults here is not clear, though possibly they were private evacuees.

CONSTANTINE (Cornwall)

About 100 Jews, 30 of them children, are living in the village and district of Constantine, in Cornwall. At Passover, there were communal Sedarim, led by Mr Harry Rubein, who conducted the services also and is religious teacher to the children. Mr Rubein is, in addition, secretary of the local Allotments Association and he is Quartermaster Sergeant in the Home Guard.

A communal Seder was also held in Par that year at the home of Professor Charles Singer, who invited Jewish evacuees living in the area. One of these was Ingrid Rosenbaum,[15] a German Jewish refugee, by this time seven years old. She remembers that on this occasion she was given an anglicised version of the Hebrew prayer, the *Shema*,[16] to enable her to read it. When she took this piece of paper back to her foster home, it was used by an English lady, who did not of course read Hebrew, to teach her to recite the *Shema*.

Despite the staunch efforts to ensure that evacuees were able to celebrate Passover, not a single Mousehole evacuee interviewed remembers participating in a communal Seder. Given the encouragement from London, and the fact that there were a large number of children and several teachers still remaining in Mousehole at this time, this is astonishing, and can only be explained in terms of something having happened to prevent it. One possibility is that because so many parents were living there at the time during the Blitz, Passover was celebrated within the families. The parcels of matzoh did, however, arrive in Mousehole. Millie Butler recalls that Mr Levene distributed these at school and made certain that the children ate at least some matzoh during Passover. Sadly, not all of the matzoh were used in the manner intended, according to Arnold:

'This must have been 1941, each child was given a box of matzoh. It was given out at school by Mr Levene, and I remember taking them home to our foster parents who said these would make splendid cheese biscuits. And that's the last we saw of them. I wasn't aware of a communal Seder or anything else, there might have been but I didn't know of it.'

Pamela Barnes remembers that her mother Jean made efforts to keep a Jewish life and a *kosher* home, while living in Mousehole during the war years:

'From the food point of view, it was certainly a *kosher* home, nothing that would be called *traif* went through the doors. *Traif* is anything that's like pork, unkoshered meat that has to be killed a special way. And as I say she gave her bacon and meat coupons away, she didn't even use them. I know she lit candles on the Sabbath, because we had a brass pair of candlesticks on the mantelshelf, and I can recall that even now.'

GOING TO CHAPEL

Almost all the children attended chapel with their foster parents, most especially the girls. There were a number of reasons for this. In the first instance, going to chapel was a way of life in Mousehole at that time, and since the majority of children had been absorbed into the families, they simply did what the family did. Secondly, the chapel was the centre of village social life, in effect a community centre as well as a place of worship, and it was natural that the children should want to join in with this. In both these respects, Methodism was not dissimilar to Judaism, which is also a way of life and where the synagogue is the centre of communal life. Another respect in which the life of the village resembled a Jewish way of life was the degree to which religious life and family life were entwined, with the family being at the heart of everything, as Jeanne describes:

'We were very family-orientated and I can't remember anybody in the village who wasn't. Family life was very, very precious in the village, and everyone realised that we enjoyed a happy family life and what happened was we just tagged on one or two more children, that's all. There was a close-knit feeling between adults and children even in the wider, extended family; my grandmother, for instance, lived next door with an unmarried aunt and they were all part and parcel of one huge family.'

Another reason for the evacuees attending chapel was that it simply would not have been possible for foster parents to leave young children at home, and it certainly would not have been reasonable to expect them not to conduct their normal way of life in order to accommodate the evacuees. While it is understandable that the Jewish authorities in London would wish evacuees not to attend church or chapel, there were some respects in which this was an unreasonable expectation in the circumstances. People in reception areas were very generously accepting children into their homes, and in Mousehole, at any rate, this was done with goodwill. One could not expect them, in so doing, to change their own way of life. It is probably for all these reasons that Mr Levene and the other teachers apparently allowed the children to go to chapel with their foster families or, at the very least, turned a blind eye to this practice. But where apparently he drew the line was when the children started going round singing Christmas carols. Marian Harris, who attended St Clement's Chapel, on Raginnis Hill, explains:

'A lot of the children were taken to Sunday School and went regularly to chapel with their host families, because in those days the chapel was always full on a Sunday night and quite full on Sunday morning. Everybody had their seats where they sat, because people paid seat rent in those days. It was very elitist, and if a stranger came and sat in their seats, well nobody liked that. But, yes, they went and Mr Levene didn't object to any of that because he saw that his children were well-fed, well-dressed and happy.'

St Clement's was the largest chapel and therefore the one that most evacuees attended. Percy Harvey and Derek Harvey attended the other chapel. Percy remembers that his evacuee, Ted, went to chapel 'as part of the family', while Derek explains that:

'Up Mount Zion, some of the evacuees, Betty Konyon and Deborah, came to Sunday School with my sister and me. They went to synagogue on a Saturday, otherwise they'd have been out on the street, because all my people went to chapel. They went, and we had various sorts of functions, Christmas time, socials and all the rest of it, and they came as one of us.'

Joan Ladner's family attended both chapels, and here explains why, in her view, the evacuees participated in chapel life:

'In fact I went to both because my father had been an organist at the other one, so I spent equal time more or less at the other one. I was really a member of the Wesleyan but we always helped out at both.

'Well, all I can say is that I know if they wanted to go, they would go, even Lily and Mrs Lazefsky on occasion, because there were always seemingly either male voice concerts or something going on in the chapel. So it was a matter of interest that they went more than anything really. They probably shouldn't have gone to chapel, I expect, but they often did go with us if there was anything on, and they went to Paul for the synagogue on Saturday, though I have heard that Mr Levene didn't really like them going carol-singing. He drew the line at that but he closed an eye a bit on what they did, because they joined into the social life of the Sunday School and anything that went on. They joined in everything really.'

Jeanne Waters here describes how her evacuee attended chapel with her, as part of the family:

'Frederica came to Sunday School and to chapel with us always. She even sang in the choir. We would go to chapel in the morning and Sunday School in the afternoon. She never, ever said "I mustn't" or "I don't want to do that", she just was absorbed into our life really and seemed to be very happy to do so. That was our way of life and she came along with it, but her parents certainly didn't write and say she wasn't to go.'

The degree to which the evacuees went to chapel as part of their social and family lives is illustrated in the stories told by Evelyn and Vera. For them it was a matter of joining in with the family and having fun. Evelyn described the services as 'nothing really strongly religious' and even felt that the hymns they sang were similar to those they sang in JFS. For Vera:

'Well, we used to go to church with Mrs Harvey even though we were Jewish, but Mr Levene said that we could. Oh, it was wonderful. Mrs Harvey donned us both in these old-fashioned hats, which we thought were very trendy at the time, and she had Evelyn on one arm and me on the other. We used to go to the Wesleyan church and we used to listen to all the prayers and the singing and we quite liked it. We joined in the singing, the songs that we knew.'

The two teenage girls did not feel they were compromising their Jewish faith. For Shirley, a much younger child, it was a different story:

'I went to chapel every week, twice a day on Sundays. My Jewishness fell away, I didn't know I was Jewish, I was just like anybody in the village. Down there I was one of them. Social life emanated from the chapel, dependent on which chapel. The Wesleyan was the biggest and strongest. But there was definitely this distinction between that chapel and the other one on the way to Paul. I went to chapel, I went to Sunday school. I was taught at Sunday school.

'It was very well attended, and you had to put on your best bonnet and clothes. We had a choir master, and there was a choir. The big festival was harvest festival, in the summer, which sticks in my mind with the beautiful flowers and the fruit, that's round about September time.

There were some others during the year, and one flowed into the other, which flowed into the other. Christmas, I think, was quite big as well. There were social events in the church hall and you used to go around collecting for various charities, but you just flowed one to the other, I didn't know anything different. It was what I did. That was the routine.'

Shirley became particularly involved in chapel life because of her young age and the fact that she remained in Mousehole for most of the war. In fact, such was her integration into village life that a few of the villagers did not realise she was Jewish, even though they knew she was an evacuee. Ted also became involved in chapel life with the Harvey family, and unusually he went also to other places of worship outside Mousehole:

'Wherever the family went, I went. Actually I went to chapel with them every Sunday and sometimes we'd go into Truro to the big cathedral there. We went to both because Mrs Harvey was a chapel lady and Mr Harvey was a churchman. They split up sometimes but mostly went to chapel because it was so local. But sometimes, we'd walk up to the church in Paul.'

Very few people in Mousehole worshipped outside the village, though, as we have seen from Ted's account, Mr Harvey did from time to time. Percy had not remembered that his father went to church in Paul until hearing Ted's story, and he was astonished that Ted should have remembered the story rather than himself. He then went on to give some of the family history:

'Oh, yes. My father used to go quite often. He wasn't a great Methodist, he tended to prefer Church of England. Occasionally on a Sunday morning, if it was fine, my father would walk up through the fields to Paul. Now, I would go with him occasionally and Ted would come with us. My father never went to church that often, but some of his family were church people. There was a relative of mine who won the first VC in Cornwall, in the Crimean War. He was called Joe Trewavas, a Navy man, and he was staunch Church of England, so I think that a lot of my family tended to follow him, the Trewavases, to Paul Church.'

Just as a small number of Mousehole people went to Paul Church, some of the Paul villagers also attended chapel in Mousehole during the war, as Myra Phillips here explains:

'When I was a little girl, during the war we used to come down to Mousehole because we didn't have any blinds and weren't allowed to have the lights on in Paul Church, so our service was at four o'clock in the afternoon, and then I used to come down to Mousehole with my parents and either go to the little chapel at the bottom of Mousehole Lane or the Wesleyan Chapel for evensong. The Mousehole people always made us welcome, it was lovely. I loved all the singing and the choir.'

Jack Waters makes the interesting comment that while Rosita Reiderman attended chapel with his family, her older sister Celia, who was living in the village with her own mother, did not attend chapel. Jack believes that this was because she was under the more Jewish influence of her mother, though it is interesting that Mrs Reiderman did nothing to prevent her younger daughter from attending chapel. Presumably she was happy for her daughter to participate in the activities of the family she was living with.

The Fromovitch sisters became equally involved in chapel life and raised some interesting issues in relation to the similarity between going to chapel and going to synagogue.

Frances: 'We used to go to the Methodist church. Irene and I sat upstairs in the Matthews' own pew. I enjoyed it. I don't think I sang because I didn't know any of the songs, but I loved listening to the choir. Stella Madron and Lenna Matthews were in the choir and so was Lenna's boyfriend, Edwin Harvey. We went there more often than to the synagogue. Years later, Lenna said they shouldn't have made us go to church, being Jewish.'

Mildred: 'I sat upstairs, always in the same seats with Mr Warren and sometimes Mrs Warren. It's funny, isn't it, there was an upstairs. Because in the synagogues, there's an upstairs, isn't there, for the ladies.'

The fact of having their own pews and of being upstairs, rather like in the ladies' gallery of a synagogue, made both of them feel that attending chapel was rather like attending synagogue. Although their mother did not attend chapel during her visits, Frances remembers that some of the visiting mothers did so:

'It just shows you what people did in the war, going into a church, being Jewish. One mother who came down was leaning over the balcony and waving to someone. You'd think she was in the pictures or something, and she was calling to people. That's what they do in the synagogue very often. They don't stop talking. It's true.'

Cyril and Malcolm recall that for them, attending chapel was a way of showing respect to their foster parents, so in that sense they did not see it as going against their own religion, as Malcolm recalls:

'I remember going to the Wesleyan Chapel at the foot of Raginnis Hill with Auntie Mary and Uncle Dick. Very nice, lovely old chapel, nice harvest festival. You'd say "Going to chapel, see you chapel this Sunday." We lived in their houses, ate their food, we went to pay our respects. Even though it wasn't our religion, we still went.'

Jack Goldstein was one of the few evacuees not drawn to the chapel in the way that most of the other evacuees were. This was largely because he had far more exciting things to do. He nevertheless appreciated the sense of inclusion on those occasions that he did attend chapel:

'They used to ask me to go to chapel, and I went with them a few times but I wasn't very interested or keen. They didn't press me to go but I did go with them a few times. And they were very good on that, I mean, when we went there nobody looked at you as though to say, "Hello, what are they doing here?" That kind of attitude. They just took it for granted, if you walked in with the people you were living with and sat down, and listened or took part in the service, they just accepted you as one of the locals. You became like one of the locals, that's how they took you in.'

Interestingly, the evacuees staying with outsiders to the village appeared to have been the only ones not to attend chapel at all, as was the case with Connie Mellows, staying with Mrs Rose. Arnold is also clear that he did not attend chapel or participate in any of the Christian activities during his stay in Mousehole, though he remembers once being taken to listen to a concert, which he did not enjoy. Arnold is very unusual in not having enjoyed the singing in the village, as this is one aspect of village life which seems to have been universally loved; indeed his brother Maurice did join in singing activities with the local children:

'We integrated with the children quite readily and easily. It got to a point where we were even attending the local Wesleyan Chapel's children's evenings. The children that would go to the Wesleyan church were singing in their choirs, and, of course, the Jewish children joined in. I think the Jewish children were making more musical noise than the local children.'

However, Maurice is also clear that he did not attend chapel and believes his foster family, the Cromptons, were not interested in religion:

'I didn't go to chapel on a Sunday, it was only in the evening, when they were singing. I only went for the choir. All the other kids used to go there and I joined in. I went with whoever it was I was friendly with at the time. I didn't go with the family, that's certain.'

Very few of the evacuees have recollections of celebrating Christian festivals such as Christmas with their families. Probably the reason for this is that such festivals in those days were celebrated in the chapel, not in the home, as in today's secularised society. Again, this bears an interesting comparison with Judaism. Shirley's description of festivals flowing one into the other at chapel, could equally be applied to synagogue services.

Modern-day Mousehole is beautifully lit up at Christmas time, but this would in any event not have been possible during the war due to the blackout. Neither was there any strong tradition of Christmas trees in those days. There was a limited tradition of giving gifts at Christmas, which were modest in the extreme in comparison with what today's children receive. For example, Ted describes receiving 'thru'penny bits in the Christmas pudding'. Vera and Evelyn both received gifts of autograph books which they still have in their possession, as Evelyn here describes:

'Minnie Harvey gave me an autograph book at Christmas 1940. I have in it a poem I wrote which was published in *The Cornishman* in Penzance. Minnie thought it was so good she took it down to Penzance and they wrote to say they are going to print it. Willy Brick did the cartoons in my autograph book and Mrs Ladner from the paper shop wrote in it: "Learn to make the most of life, lose no happy day, Vanguard House, April 18th 1941".

Living throughout the war in Mousehole, it was inevitable that Pamela Barnes and her family should become involved in the social life of the village, and therefore in the life of the chapel:

'We did get involved in village life inasmuch as we went down to the chapel, not specifically for services. Maybe once or twice, I might have got swept along with my schoolmates or something like that. It was very much the community centre, and my sister got involved because she was older, she was in the pantomime, and we used to go to the pageants and parades and used to sing in the choir. That chapel is what you call low church anyway, very laid back, they were not Bible-banging people, and there was a very simple service because it's very Wesleyan. And I've got quite a lot of time for that, because you know, they were God-fearing people, and village people particularly who relied so much on the seasons and nature, being fisher-folk and farm-folk. God was quite close to them, you were so aware of God.'

CHRISTMAS CAROL SINGING

During Christmas 1940, many of the older evacuees became involved with the local children in going around the village singing Christmas carols. The younger children were not involved in this as young children were not allowed out in the dark winter evenings. The Podguszers also were not allowed by Nanny to join in the carol singing. Whether Nanny felt this was not appropriate for Jewish children, or whether she felt it was too far from Penlee Point on a winter night, is not known, but Maurice does recall Mr Levene's displeasure at the event. The children who went found it great fun, as Mildred here recalls:

'We thought it was lovely. Frances and I used to go. Funnily enough there was more than Frances and I; there may have been a small group. We'd knock on the door and sing away, and yes, even though I couldn't sing, somebody paid me. Yes, we sang Christmas carols.'

In addition to the sheer enjoyment of the occasion, the fact of being paid was most definitely an extra bonus, as Evelyn has reason to remember:

'Also we used to love to go around at Christmas and sing the carols, we thought it was such fun. We would sing outside and they'd call us in, the villagers, because they knew us so well. They used to say, "Now come in, me dears, don't be afraid, come in." And I remember we used to collect a few pennies, and we'd be thrilled to bits. We used to save up the pennies to buy something, because we never had anybody give us anything, no money. My mother couldn't afford it, you see, and we never had anything really, big parcels, nothing like that, like the other children had.'

For Jose, saving was not what was on her mind; she remembers exactly what she spent the money on:

'At Christmas time we would go around singing Christmas carols and then take whatever money we got and go right to the fish and chip shop.'

Marian remembers how the Christmas carolling came about, and describes with great insight Mr Levene's reaction and the way he might have felt about the situation:

'There was a Boys Brigade, which was a Methodist youth club, and some of the older evacuee lads were friendly with some of the boys in the Boys Brigade. I think it must have been the first Christmas that they were here, they went around singing carols in the village with the Boys Brigade. But when Mr Levene heard about that he had them all into his office and they were told he was turning a blind eye to them going to Sunday School, or to chapel, but he would not tolerate them singing carols at Christmas. I suppose because Christmas was celebrating the birth of Christ, it was a particularly Christian time. I think he found it difficult because he realised that it would be very difficult for the host families to function if they had children who weren't allowed to go to chapel. I think it must have been quite a strain for him and quite a struggle with his conscience. But he didn't object to the children being taken to chapel. The welfare of the children was of prime importance rather than going to chapel. He probably thought that when they went back home they could become good Jewish children again.'

ON BEING JEWISH

Each of the villagers and evacuees were asked individually whether the fact of the evacuees being Jewish had any effect on their relationship. The answer on both sides was a resounding 'no'. There was some initial curiosity, and some recognition of difference, but this very quickly settled down. The early talk of Jews having horns, mentioned by four people, soon dissipated, as two of the evacuees explain:

'One child asked "where are your horns?" It was a one off and never happened again.'

'Being Jewish did not affect our relationship with the villagers; however, it was there that we first heard the expression "I thought Jews had horns!" The villagers had never come across Jews before. I do remember someone asking me about that, right at the beginning, but there was no malice.'

What Ted describes as 'a bit of aggravation' between the gangs of boys also resulted, on at least one occasion, in what might be described as a racial incident. One of the evacuees made a comment in Yiddish to one of the village boys, probably in response to something said to him. The village boys realised, even though they didn't understand what the word meant, that it was probably an insult. They were right. Yiddish is a very expressive language, which can sometimes be understood from the tone alone. Ted relates the incident:

'Well, I was sorted out once. Someone else, not me, made a Jewish remark, a Yiddish remark, and the group surrounded me and asked me what it meant, and it wasn't very nice. But I sort of knew I couldn't tell them the actual translation, so I just smoothed over it.'

It seems clear that there was some fault on both sides. Ted believes this incident occurred because most of the villagers had not known Jews before, and that the occasional conflict between the evacuee boys and the village boys was more 'the sort of thing that goes on with normal boys', rather than anything to do with being Jewish. Certainly nothing of this nature appears to have happened among the girls. For most of the villagers, any differences first noted were of no consequence and the evacuees simply became a part of the village, the following comments being typical:

Marian: 'Well, we thought it rather odd at first because we had never had any experience of being cheek by jowl with Jewish people, but as happens with children, they play together and forget about it. Children are quite accepting of each other when left to their own devices. Apart from the fact that they had cockney accents, and didn't know about things relating to the sea and the countryside, there was nothing to remind us that they were anything different.'

Jeanne: 'It never made any difference that they were Jewish. They were just children and were treated as members of the family. The elderly people just absorbed them into the family. We were more than happy to welcome them, we were so appalled at the thought of them being bombed, so we just wanted them to be happy in our lives and in the quiet way we lived.'

Derek: 'Not at all really, children were all children together. Like I said, when we were told about it, we weren't told they were Jewish, we were told that children were coming down. And when they came we just treated them all as children, we didn't know what creed, that didn't seem to worry us. Sometimes if you get two people with two different religions, it can clash, can't it, but it never seemed to. The evacuees disappeared Saturday to the synagogue and came back whatever time. And from then on to the next Saturday it was just ordinary.'

Joan: 'It didn't make any difference at all. I just think they were wonderful. They were mostly loveable children, and the older girls were really special, the Fromovitches, and Vera and Evelyn that lived around the corner here. I don't think there was anybody that would ever hurt them in any way, shape or form, because they were so nice.'

These views were echoed by the evacuees themselves. It is illuminating to compare these comments with the accounts of their previous evacuation experiences. Again, the following comments are typical of many similar ones made by all the evacuees:

Maurice: 'Very easy and pleasant, easy-going relationship. There was no friction whatsoever.'

Jack: 'It was never mentioned, as far as I know. Nobody ever showed any anti-Semitism whatsoever. And I think most people will tell you the same.'

Evelyn: 'None whatsoever. It was never pointed out that we were any different to anybody else. We never even gave it a thought, never.'

Millie: 'The villagers understood and respected the fact that we had been brought up in a different religion and cultural background.'

Pamela: 'The thing that stuck in my mind was how they embraced everybody. We were just accepted. I was never called names, it's something you would remember. I don't think I even heard the word "Jew". We were just part of village life. My mother kind of integrated into the society, in their day-to-day life. Her recollection was that it was one of the happiest times of her life. That just shows it.

'A lovely story my mother related, was about a Mrs Downing, who lived in Foxes Lane. I think she was a widow of many years standing and quite a devout, religious person. She used to have a rather large Bible, and on a fine day would sit outside her cottage reading it. One day she actually came over and said how privileged she was to meet Jewish people.'

THE TORAH COMES TO MOUSEHOLE

During the time that the JFS evacuees were enjoying themselves in their village safe-haven, a remarkable event was unfolding in London which was to have significant repercussions in Mousehole. During her research, the author discovered an article in *The Jewish Chronicle*, dated September 1941, entitled *The Torah returns to Penzance*,[17] a reference to the fact that there was once a thriving Jewish community in Cornwall. She had the greatest difficulty accessing this article as the online archives rendered it largely unreadable, and apart from the title she was only able to discern a few key words, including *Mousehole* and *Maurice*. Her first thought was that this must have referred to Maurice Podguszer, though this proved not to be the case. Original copies of that issue appeared to have been lost, but she was finally able to read the article at the end of July 2009, the day before Tisha B'Av,[18] the significance of which will become apparent below. This is an important date in Jewish history, which commemorates the destruction of the Temple and the scattering of the Jewish people. Other significant events in Jewish history have often been known to occur on that same date. The day after reading the article, and with the story still echoing around her mind, the author listened to a Jewish speaker describing the occasion on Radio 4's *Thought for the Day:*[19]

> This evening traditional Jews will start a day-long fast, from sunset to sunset. The fast of the Hebrew month of Av is the saddest day in our year. It marks the destruction

of both of the Temples in Jerusalem, and the loss of national independence. We remember these events even though they happened thousands of years ago.

Here is that article which the author read for the first time on the eve of Tisha B'Av:

THE TORAH RETURNS TO PENZANCE

OUT OF THE MIDST OF FIRE

There is a Sefer Torah today in Mousehole, only five miles from that spot called Land's End, where this island of Britain falls into the Atlantic Ocean.

Mousehole is near Penzance and years ago Jews lived in Penzance. One shop in the town still has a *mezuzah* on its door, though it has been in Gentile hands for generations. On the other side of Penzance is Marazion, and here too you will find evacuee Jews today.

How did the Sefer Torah get to Mousehole?

Ask Maurice. Last Pesach he was 13 years old, and he had his Barmitzvah at the Great Synagogue. He was a little chap for his age, and he was rather attracted by the little Sefer Torah from which he read his portion. The Warden had laughingly commented on it.

The Warden had more to say on a certain night last May, though no longer laughingly. Neither will Maurice forget that night quickly. Both his parents were killed by the blast of a bomb in the street. Fortunately, he did not know it at the time. But a great feeling of horror crept over him as he saw the Great Synagogue, his Shool burning. He must never let his Sefer Torah be destroyed.

'Stop him. He's mad,' the firemen shouted.

But they couldn't stop Maurice. The Ark was ablaze, and men and women shut their eyes, unable to bear the thought of the little nipper being roasted alive.

A miracle. Maurice was in the street again, crawling on his hands and knees, and pushing in front of him, without letting it touch the ground, his Sefer Torah. It was the only one that had been saved. How he had achieved it even Maurice could not tell you.

What was to be done with it? The United Synagogue wanted to send it to a safe deposit in the country. 'Let us have it,' asked the Joint Emergency Committee. 'We often get requests from our teachers for the use of Sefer Torah in reception areas.'

And so the Sefer Torah found a temporary home in the basement of Woburn House.

A new complication. Maurice would not part from the Sefer Torah. He had nothing left to live for. His parents, his home, all had gone. That is why for days, you would find Maurice hanging around Woburn House. At night he would sleep in the shelter in the basement. He refused to be taken away. How he managed to live was a mystery.

Some weeks ago, a message came to the Joint Emergency Committee. The teacher at Mousehole needed a Sefer Torah.

'Will you allow yourself to be evacuated to Mousehole, if we send your Sefer Torah there?'

'Oh yes sir. And please, sir, let me take it there myself?'

So the problem of the Sefer Torah, and of Maurice's evacuation were settled at one and the same time.

You should have seen the excitement on Maurice's face when he was seated in the taxi, clutching the Sefer Torah. At Paddington Station, he would not allow the porter to touch that brown paper parcel.

'Wot is it, a time bomb?' one porter jokingly remarked.

The whole way to Mousehole, Maurice sat rigidly in his corner seat, the parcel held tightly in his hands. Only when it was safely in the newly-made Ark in the school in Mousehole did Maurice utter a deep sigh, as if to say 'I can breathe again at last.'

They read from the Sefer Torah for the first time on Tisha B'Av.

'When thou art in tribulation, and all things come upon thee, even in the latter days, if thou turn to the Lord thy God, and shalt be obedient unto His voice, (for the Lord thy God is a merciful God), He will not forsake thee neither destroy thee, neither forget the covenant of thy fathers, which He swore to them.'

And they knew now in Mousehole that the blessing and the promise will be fulfilled.

Little could the children listening to the words read from their new Torah have known that on this very day in 1941, SS Commander Heinrich Himmler formally presented his plan to the Nazi Party on the Final Solution for the extermination of Jews.[20] Truly, the children of Mousehole, loved, cared for, and safe out of harm's way, were blessed on that day.

Chapter Thirteen

DEPARTURE AND AFTERMATH

When Stepney goes from Cambridgeshire,
And men make peace again,
Both Town and Country boy will share
A balm for parting's pain.
The memory of their mingled life
Will serve them to the end
As proof that Town and Country boy
Can comrade be and friend.

S.M. Rich [1]

SUPERVISION OF DEPARTING EVACUEES

Shirley Spillman remained in Mousehole until June 1945, and when being interviewed about her ultimate departure, she raised an extremely interesting question relating to the manner in which the evacuation scheme was operated and organised:

'Who kept tabs on who was left and who was not left? I don't know. My parents obviously knew I was there but I could have stayed there. And there was no inspection either. That's very surprising. Nobody came around, say once a year, to say, "How are you?" or "What's been happening? Are you treated well or are you being knocked around?" Nobody came to inspect.'

These issues were in fact considered but not, it seems, until well into the operation of the scheme, as is here evident in the minutes of the Welfare and Evacuation Committee which met in Penzance in September 1941. [2]

VISITING OF UNACCOMPANIED CHILDREN

The committee considered an enquiry dated 8 August 1941, from the Senior Regional Officer, Ministry of Health, asking that the arrangements for visiting unaccompanied children should be reviewed so as to ensure that such arrangements are adequate and suitable.

A general discussion ensued from which it appeared that in those cases where there was a helper attached to the school there was no cause for complaint but that where schools have been disbanded since their arrival in Penzance and the party leaders have gone back to London there was a lack of organised and periodical visiting of these children.

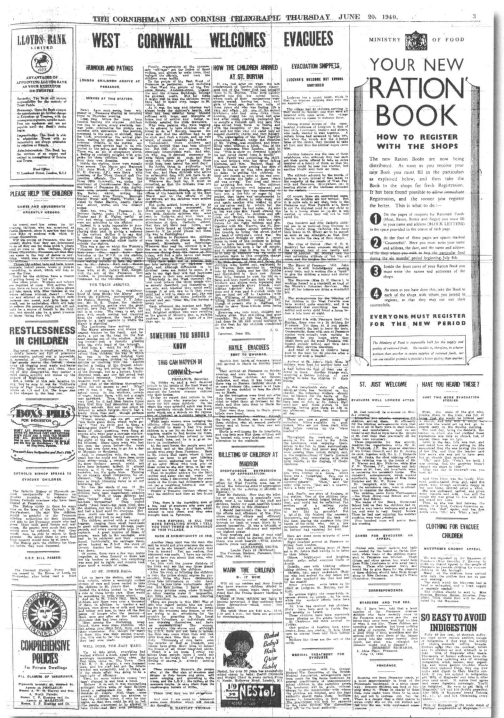

'West Cornwall Welcomes Evacuees', *The Cornishman*, 19 and 20 June 1940.

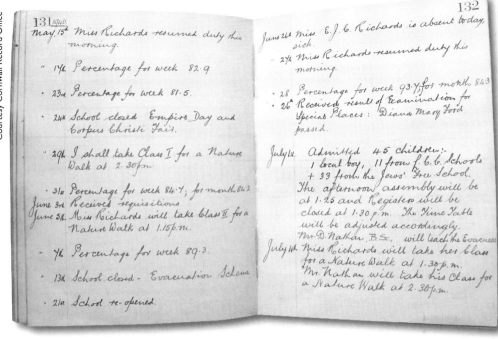

Extract from log book of Paul Church School, showing admission of evacuees on 1 July 1940. Mr Nathan joined the staff to teach the evacuee children.

Extract from log book of Paul Church School, showing that some of the JFS evacuees were transferred from Paul Church School to Mousehole School on 1 October 1940, in order to rejoin the rest of the group.

Mousehole School Admission Register, showing the names of 10 children who transferred from Jews' Free Mousehole to Mousehole School in January 1942, after Mr Levene had left and JFS Mousehole had closed down. Frances and Michael Cohen are the cousins of Maurice and Arnold Podguszer.

14

ADMISSION.

ADMISSION.	Date of Admission.			Date of Re-admissi'n			NAME IN FULL (Enter Surname first).	Date of Birth.			Whether Exempt from Religious Instructi'n	NAME OF PARENT OR GUARDIAN.
	D.	M.	Year	D.	M.	Year		D.	M.	Year		
2081 ✗	5	1	42				Fishman, Doris	25	2	29	Yes	Mrs. Waten
2082 ✗	5	1	42				Fromovitch. Irene	30	1	34	Yes	Miss Oliver
2083 ✗	5	1	42				Fromovitch. Mildred	27	11	28	Yes	"
2084 ✗	5	1	42				Godfrey, Anita	29	1	30	Yes	Mrs. Phillips
2085 ✗	5	1	42				Godfrey, Irvine	7	4	33	Yes	
2086 ✗	5	1	42				Hewson, Marion	2	12	28	Yes	Mrs. Trembath
2087 ✗	5	1	42				Levene, David	21	1	34	Yes	Mr. Harding
2088 ✗	5	1	42				Levene, Frances	5	4	35	Yes	Mrs. Lugg Harry
2089 ✗	5	1	42				Levene, Ralph	1	12	31	Yes	Mrs. Lugg
2090 ✗	5	1	42				Paris. Thomas	1	11	31	No	Mr. C. Teffery
2091 ✗	5	1	42				Reiderman, Celia	4	9	29	Yes	Miss Hicks
2092 ✗	5	1	42				Reiderman, Rosita	24	2	35	Yes	Mr. S. Watts
2093 ✗	5	1	42				Selnes, Ida	16	12	28	Yes	Mrs. Webbs
2094 ✗	5	1	42				Selnes, Mea	5	5	31	Yes	Mr. Webbs
2095 ✗	5	1	42				Swages, Phyllis	3	5	36	Yes	Mrs. Swages
2096 ✗	5	1	42				Swages, Sylvia	1	7	29	Yes	"
2097 ✗	5	1	42				Spillman, Shirley	2	8	33	Yes	Mr. R. Shadue
2098 ✗	5	1	42				Wright, Betty	24	10	31	No	Mrs. Bennett
2099 ✗	5	1	42				Wright, John	26	3	35	No	"
2100 ✗	9	1	42				Podguszer Arnold	16	4	32	Yes	Mrs. Chamberlain
2101 ✗	9	1	42				Podguszer Michael	6	3	34	Yes	"
2102 ✗	27	1	42				Taylor, Walter Ernest C	28	11	31		Mrs Grazelier owner Mrs. Taylor Tenant
2103 ✗	3	3	42				Stephens. Rona	22	12	32		Mrs. Williams
2104 ✗	3	3	42				Stephens. Peter	16	5	34		"
2105 ✗	9	3	42				Thomas, Jean E	7	2	'28		Mrs. R.H. Sampson
2106 ✗ 2084	26 5	1 1	42 42	9	2	42	Fromovitch Frances Godfrey Anita	13 29	3 1	24 30		Miss Oliver Miss Oliver
2107 ✗	1	4	42				Harvey Marline	18	6	35	No	John Harvey.
2108 ✗	13	4	42				Symons Anthony Wm	12	12	36		Wm John
2109 ✗	13	4	42				Giles Thomas Derek	8	2	37		Thos. Trevor
2110 ✓	13	4	42			X	Cary Bryan	25	3	38		John Henry
2111 ✓	13	4	42			X	Gartzell, Wm Arnold Roby	22	12	37		Wm Arnold Gartzell
1790 ✗	7	9	36	18	4	42	Jenkin James	5	1	30		James Jenkin
1859 ✗	31	1	38	13	4	42	Jenkin Ronald	26	1	34		James Jenkin
1944 ✗	26	6	40	13	4	42	Cattran June	15	6	36		Isabel C. Cattran
2112 ✗	20	4	42			X	Quick Ann Yvonne	17	4	38		James

Mousehole Admission Register, showing the names of 21 more children transferring from JFS Mousehole to Mousehole School in January 1942. Frances Fromovitch reappears on the register on 26 January 1942. Five of those listed have been interviewed for this book:

WITHDRAWAL.

ADDRESS.	NAME OF LAST SCHOOL.	D.	M.	Year	CAUSE OF LEAVING.	REMARKS (Character, &c.)
Mount View, Paul 151 Wentworth Bldgs, Wentworth St. E.1	Jews Free Mousehole	9	1	42	Ret'd to London	OS TYED/38/5
Commercial Rd. Dwellings Mousehole	" "	27	7	45	Retd	OS DVAM/139/5
8, Brady St Bdgs, London E.1, Commercial Rd	" "	18	5	45	Returned	OS DVAM/139/8
Oakland Cottage Park 65 Bellham E.1	" "	16	1	42	Ret'd to House E.1	OS TCAC/191/4
	" "	30	7	43	Retd to London	OS TCAC/191/5
Regent Tce 20 Rothschild Bdgs, Flower & Dean St E.1	" "	16	1	42	Retd to London	OS TOAG/16/5
King's Arms, Paul 11, Fournier St E.1	" "	20	10	42	Trans. to Paul	OS AISL/229/7
The Wharf E.1	" "	28	8	44	Trans to Gory	OS AISL/229/8
Wellington Place	" "	17	4	42	Gone to Hotel	OS EMLA/130/1
Fore St, 123 Brady St Bdgs E.1	" "	26	3	43	Retd to London	OS DM.GE/11/4
Duck St. 121 Rothschild Bdgs, Flower & Dean St E.1	"	15	6	46	" "	OS TCBB/108/5
St. Clements	"	15	6	45		OS CTSU/108/7
Vivian Ho. Vivian Tce 17 Toynbee St., Wentworth St E.1	"	6	12	42	Retd to London	OS TDAK/77/2
"	"	6	2	42	" "	OS TDAK/77/3
1 Gurnick St.	"	30	1	42	Ret'd to London	OS TREG/225/3
"	"	30	1	42	Retd to London	OS TREG/225/2
Vanguard Ho. 8, Nant Rd. Childs Hill N.W.2.	"	15	6	45	" "	OS AIAC/171/5
Fore St. 26 Quaker St. Bdgs London E.1	"	?	?	?	Retd.	OS TBSE/165/4
"	"	?	?	?	Retd.	OS AVPF/60/3
Pardoe Point 18 Heddon Court Cockfosters Herts	"	30	1	42	Retd home	OS AFVB/220/4
"	"	30	1	42	Retd home	OS AFVB/220/5
Sea View, Chapel Street	Trebanos Mixed Pontardawe S.Wales	21	5	43	Scholarship Boys County &	OS NSKJ/14/5 13, Eylam Rd. Plaistow West Ham E.15
Trevethoe Villa M.H	Lescudjack Girls	0	3	42	Returned to Pz.	Temporary Visitor
"	Boys	10	3	42	Returned to Pz.	
Lower Salt Ponds	Tregony Ch.M	24		42	Exemption	
Commercial Rd. 8, Brady St. Bdgs, London E.1	LCC Central Sch. Pz	18 17	6 4	44 42	Retd to London Returned to London	OS
Salt Ponds Mousehole	Paul Council	1	4	42	Returned to Paul	
Middle Kempell	None	22	12	44	Trans. Paul	
Asphodel Raginnis	"	28	7	48		
Florence Place	"	?	?	?	Pz Grammar.	
Duck Street		✓				
Mylor The Parade	Lamlash I. of Arran	?	?	?		
Mylor The Parade	"	6	4	44	Trans. to Lescudjack	
Millpool	Blackpool Inf	5	11	43	Removed to Wales	Temporary
Keigwin Place	None	✓				

Francis and Mildred Fromovitch, Anita Godfrey, Shirley Spillman and Arnold Podguszer.

28/8/41.

I had the greatest time of my life living with Uncle Vivian and Aunt Flo for fourteen months. To say that they treated me as a mother and father would not be far wrong. Their kindness that they bestowed upon me came from their hearts, and from the hearts of a mother and father. My own parents were hundreds of miles away from me, but here under this very roof I found a new mother and father, who have treated me as their son. I cannot express in words the lovingly way in which I have been treated as one of the family. I even found new Aunts & Uncles in Mousehole, and most of all a loving Granny. I have greatly respected Granny Johns because I feel that she has helped to make me happy, and because I think that she is as good as my Granny. Marian is a fine girl and if she carries on at school like she has been doing I am sure that she will grow up into a fine, clever young lady. I bless all those who have made me happy here.

Bernard Worman,
246 Amhurst Rd.,
Stokenewington,
London
N.

P.S.
I sure will miss Aunt Flo's cooking.

Letter from Bernie Warman to Florrie and Vivian Johns, his foster parents, when he left Mousehole in August 1941. Florrie was Marian Harris's great aunt.

Before leaving, Bernie and Lenny carved their initials on the wall of Auntie Florrie's home, which is now the home of Marian Harris.

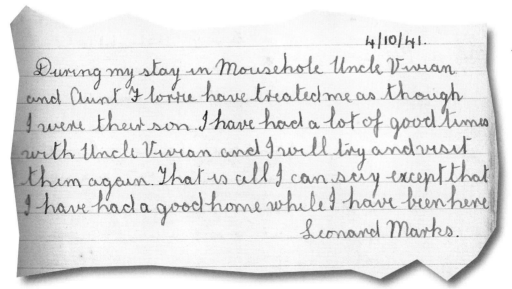

4/10/41.

During my stay in Mousehole Uncle Vivian and Aunt Florrie have treated me as though I were their son. I have had a lot of good times with Uncle Vivian and I will try and visit them again. That is all I can say except that I have had a good home while I have been here

Leonard Marks.

Letter from Lenny Marks to Florrie and Vivian Johns, his foster parents, when he left Mousehole in October 1941.

Courtesy Joan Richards

Letter from Desirée Frischman to her foster parents, *c*.1942–43.

Courtesy Joan Richards

Letter from Elaine Frischman to her foster parents, *c*.1942–43.

Evelyn Goldstein's autograph book, which was given to her by her foster mother, Mrs Harvey, in December 1940. This page shows a poem written by Evelyn and published in the local newspaper.

From an Evacuee

Among our evacuees is a loetess, if that is not too Victorian a word. Evelyn Goldstein, aged fifteen-and-a-half, of "Waterbury," Mousehole, sends me some pretty verses, and in congratuating her I should like to say that her clear and attractive handwriting is pleasant to come upon in these days o illegible scribbles and ornate flourishes. Here is her poem:

LONDON NOISES.

Leave no litter if you're found
Shelter in an Underground;
Pick up what's been left by you
And by other people, too.

Sirens have to make a nois—
Do not heed them girls and boys.
In a raid run helter-skelter
For the nearest public shelter.

If you're wakened by a warning
Don't be fretful in the morning;
Others too have lost their sleep,
There are plenty who could weep.

Very charming.

Evelyn Goldstein's autograph book, showing an entry in Hebrew written by Mr Levene in December 1940.

arising before the actual position has been approved.

2. INSTRUCTIONAL EQUIPMENT: The Clerk reported that the
equipment for the use of the L.A.G.C. Instructors
had been despatched from London and that at the moment
he had arranged for the same to be held on the Council's
Order by the G.W.R. Company at their Penzance Goods
Depot pending the arrangement of a proper store, that
he had with Mr.Rose inspected the store at Penzance,
by the courtesy of the Chief Constable, and that the
proposals to use the shed at the rear of the Office
were of no avail as the same did not provide anything
like the space required, that he had endeavoured to
find other premises near the Office without success
and that as a last resort he had consulted with
Mr.Fenton who could arrange for the Council to rent
a suitable store at Stable Hobba, the property of
Cornish Fish Products Ltd. at a rental of £10 a year
and that having inspected the store with Mr.Rose, the
same appeared to be very suitable for the purpose and
that arrangements could be made for the supervision of
the equipment and proper disinfection etc. after use,
in conjunction with Mr.Fenton and his Company, and
that the Company were prepared to erect the necessary
fittings in accordance with those found most suitable
by the Penzance Corporation.

The Committee decided to take the store on the terms
indicated and requested Mr.Fenton to make the necessary
fittings available as soon as possible and to report in
due course as to the remuneration to be paid to the
Storekeeper, and as to the proper terms of the tenancy.
They ask that their action be confirmed.

3. GOVERNMENT EVACUATION SCHEME: The Clerk produced the
instructions issued by the Ministry of Health as to the
duties devolving upon the Council in this matter and
reported that the suggestions of the Ministry in the
first instance were that a preliminary letter should be
sent to each Householder in the District setting out
the proposals, and that following this, a Register of
all houses, hotels, camping grounds etc. had to be prepared, followed by books for use of visitors who would
visit each house and record what accommodation was
available on the standard basis of one person per
habitable room, after which the visitors books had to
be returned and carefully preserved for use in case of
an emergency arising, the necessary records having also
to be recorded in the Register, and a return made to the
Ministry and the County Council by the 28th February
next, the Council having on the information then available to make a provisional decision as to:-

    (a) the number of unaccompanied children

    (b) the number of teachers and helpers

    (c) the number of others

which each house could accommodate.

The Committee discussed the suggestion of the Minister
that the best result was likely to be obtained by a
judicious combination of skilled official personnel
and of voluntary effort, but came to the conclusion
that the best method in this District would be for the
Register and Books and permanent Records to be prepared
by the Office Staff and the Visiting done by the Rating
Officers and such assistance as they themselves might
arrange for.
Expenditure properly incurred in carrying out the survey

Minutes of West Penwith Rural Council, outlining household
survey, 26 January 1939.

5. HAYLE WATER COMMITTEE: Mr.T.H.Hodge was elected to fill the vacancy on the Water Committee caused by the resignation of Mr.H.W.Turner.

6. WATERWORKS AT HAYLE: The Chairman again raised the question as to whether or not the Contractor on the Water Scheme was employing the stipulated number of Hayle men in carrying out the Contract, and it was resolved to ask the Clerk of the Rural District Council if he would get the information for the Committee.

                              (Sgd.) R.J.Hammill

                                   Chairman.

RESOLVED - That the Report be received and adopted.

CIVIL DEFENCE
COMMITTEE

The Report of the Committee of the 29th February, 1940 was read as follows:-

                              29th February, 1940

        Minutes of a Meeting of the Civil Defence Committee held at the Council Chambers, Chapel Street, Penzance, on Thursday the 29th February, 1940 at 11.15 a.m.

            Present:- Mr.W.B.C.Tregarthen (Chairman)

                   Messrs E.G.Shovel, G.W.Fenton,
                   J.Laity, W.Richards, F.S.Harvey,
                   M.T.Mann, W.Trewern, Col.C.H.Paynter.

1. GOVERNMENT EVACUATION SCHEME: The Clerk produced his correspondence with the Ministry of Health, The Rural District Councils Association and the Cornwall County Council relative to the new Evacuation Scheme adopted by the Government and reported that the quota of unaccompanied children to be sent to this area in the event of further evacuation taking place after the development of air attack was 2,000 and a duty now devolved upon the Council to make plans for the reception of this number, but that it should be borne in mind that the new plans are designed to be put into operation only when serious air attack appears certain.

The Clerk reported that the County Council deemed this matter urgent and had called a Conference of Billeting Officers to be held at the County Hall to-day, to discuss the following:-

        (1) De-training arrangements
        (2) Road transport to dispersal points
        (3) Billeting arrangements
        (4) Educational arrangements
        (5) Co-operation between Billeting and Education
             Authorities
             as
and that/Mr.Warren, the Assistant Clerk, had been attending to the present Scheme he had arranged for him to attend the Conference and to receive the necessary instructions.

Minutes of West Penwith Rural Council, outlining preparations for receiving evacuees, 29 February 1940.

An apology for non-attendance was received from Mr.W.Jeffery.

1. GOVERNMENT EVACUATION SCHEME: A letter dated 7.3.40 was read from Mr.H.V.Warren stating that it was financially impossible for him to accept the decision of the Council on Thursday last and setting out the facts relating thereto.

The Officers having retired, the Committee fully discussed the position and unanimously recommend that Mr.Warren be paid immediately the sum of £25 to cover the cost of putting his car on the road and a sum of 3d per mile travelling expenses in respect of same; the whole cost to be charged to the Ministry of Health Evacuation Scheme Account. The Committee having power to act authorised the issue of the cheque accordingly.

As most of the preliminary work will of necessity have to be done after Office hours, the Committee recommend that Mr.Warren be paid at the rate of 1/6d per hour for this work and that he be empowered, if found necessary, to employ additional assistance at the following rates:-

1/6d per hour for a male and 1/3d per hour for a female.

The Committee considered the Report prepared by Mr.Warren as to the County Conference held at Truro on Thursday last together with an explanation of the further details necessary and particulars of the Billeting Scheme which would be based on the education facilities available.

The Committee decided to leave the details in the hands of the Clerk and Mr.Warren, as Chief Billeting Officer, to confer with the W.V.S., and to prepare the necessary Scheme.

> They RECOMMEND - That an emergency Committee be appointed to deal with urgent matters and to assist the Clerk, if necessary. The Committee to consist of the Chairman (Mr.W.B.C. Tregarthen), Col.C.H.Paynter and Messrs F.S.Harvey, J.J.Oliver and W.A.Eddy.

> RESOLVED - That the name of Mr.B.G.Smart be added to the Civil Defence Committee.

(Sgd.) W.B.C.Tregarthen

Chairman.

RESOLVED - That the Report be received and adopted.

OFFICES
SUB-COMMITTEE

The Report of the Sub-Committee of the 14th March, 1940 was read as follows:-

14th March, 1940

Present:- Mr.W.Jeffery (Chairman)

Messrs E.G.Shovel, S.B.Olivey and S.B.Humphrys.

Minutes of West Penwith Rural Council, showing payment of workers, 28 March 1940.

Juvenile Employment. **CONFIDENTIAL REPORT CARD.**

Surname *Fromovitch*

Other Names *Frances*

Address *Commercial Rd Mousehole*
Penzance

Date of Birth *13. 3. 24* School *Mousehole*

Is Industrial Supervision Necessary ?

Voluntary Organisation

Wishes of parent with regard to employment ....

Occupation of parent *Warden - full time. LCC*

Occupation obtained and name of firm

Medical Report. Indicate " Normal " or defects, *e.g.*, hearing, eyesight, or physique.

EDUCATIONAL REPORT.

Standard, form or class reached *Class I is top*

Time in (a) Advanced Course*

(b) Secondary Course

Certificates gained

Good Subjects *Needlework*

Average Subjects *English & Arithmetic*

Weak Subjects

Any instruction in Manual Training (Boys) Domestic Subjects (Girls) *No*

Head Teacher's General Report. *Polite & Reliable*

Occupation Recommended *Dressmaking* Signature *A. J Elford* Date *15. 6. '42*

Remarks. (For use at Juvenile Exchange).

E.D. 210. * For completion in Scotland only. (95) *M.5592/1154. 3/38. 250,000. (3) A.H.661-2.

Frances Fromovitch's school report card from June 1942, signed by the headmaster, Mr Elford.

Government Evacuation: Roll of persons received into district of Local Authority, in Truro. This contains very little detailed information and was clearly written in a hurry.

Sample of an evacuee record form. Leonard Rogers appears to have lived with five different foster parents in Truro, some of them on more than one occasion. Records show that he continued to live with Mrs Colliner until 1946.

Government Evacuation: Roll of persons received into district of Local Authority, in Truro. According to this, there was only one teacher with this party, a Mr Chivers, and no helpers or other adults!

Sample of a householder's billeting record. Records show that Mrs Colliner accomodated at least 12 other evacuees at her home in Truro, in addition to Leonard Rogers.

A LONDON EXTRA supplement on readers' evacuation memories 50 years after the outbreak of war

Your tales of kindness, sadness and separation

JEWS' FREE SCHOOL EVACUATION NEWS SHEET

ISSUE NO.1.   NOVEMBER,1939

Printed under direction of Mr D.R. Isaacs at the Evacuation Headquarters of the Jews' Free School School Farm, Ely Jewish Boys' Home, 57 St Mary's Street, Ely

As war was declared on September 3, 1939, hundreds of thousands of children were sent out of London and major industrial areas.

Stations were filled with children, some tearful, some excited, all carrying a bag, a name label, and a gas mask slung around their necks.

Within six months, the number of Jewish children among them was estimated at 11,000 but 3,000 had already slipped back home.

In London's East End, together with nearby Hackney and the slightly further afield Stamford Hill, well over half the Jewish children left town.

Some 75 per cent of Stepney children were evacuated, including the pupils of the Jews' Free School, Robert Montefiore Schools, Buxton Street and Commercial Street Infants School.

Self-control

Miriam Moses, the great social worker and former Mayor of Stepney, praised the mothers for their self-control when letting their children go.

Although for some children, the experience would be a great adventure, their parents knew that they were leaving a Jewish home and environment for the quietly stolid atmosphere of the English countryside with its small towns and villages.

Rabbis and communal leaders at the Board of Deputies made huge efforts to maintain the continuity of Jewish education and kosher food supplies.

Appeals were sent to cover the cost of sending books and teachers to reception areas, any one of which might hold between 1,000 and 5,000 Jewish children.

Speakers were sent to address the Jewish pupils of schools like Hackney Downs, billeted in Kings Lynn, Norfolk. The Jewish boys evacuated from Owen's School at the Angel, Islington, to Bedford, were particularly well looked after.

Leading Jewish educationist Arnold Harris made his home in Bedford a centre of Jewish life and learning.

Severe winter

It was easier to keep one's Jewish identity when a whole school was evacuated. The Jews' Free School in Bell Lane moved out to Ely in Cambridgeshire. Children were billeted with families in the surrounding villages, but school attendance provided a focus of Jewish life.

A teacher appealed for warm clothing to protect the children of Robert Montefiore School, who were sent to Chatteris, Cambridgeshire, from "the severe winter weather of this Fen district." The Stepney Jewish Primary School moved to Windsor in Berkshire and the Solomon Wolfson Jewish School went from Bayswater in West London to Broughton Gifford in Wiltshire.

The Jewish Secondary Schools Movement evacuated from Amhurst Park, North London, to Shefford in Bedfordshire. The Jewish Orphanage in West Norwood moved to Worthing; the West Hampstead Boarding School to Lewes, Sussex.

The Residential School for Jewish Deaf Children in Wandsworth, South-West London, moved out to Brighton in February, 1940. But in September it moved again to Marlborough in Wiltshire.

Autumn term, 1940, also saw the popular Brighton Jewish boarding schools, which mopped up London's better-off schoolchildren, move out en bloc. Until then, Brighton had been officially designated a safe zone.

The private Jewish schools, Mansfield College, Whittinghame College, Macaulay House College, Aryeh House School and Beaconsfield College, all with premises in Brighton, Hove or Cuckfield, Sussex, moved to North Wales, Cornwall and Gloucestershire.

Habonim, the Jewish youth movement, took over the organisation of the High Holy Days and Passover for children who were far removed from the centres of Jewish life.

Their network was one of the main conduits for Jewish observance and education in remote areas. They set up South Devonshire hostels, in Exmouth, Dawlish and Teignmouth, for the new concentrations of Jewish children.

Air raids

They also took care of the older group of over-16s who worked on training farms (called hachsharah). Bachad and Habonmer Hatzair were the two other Jewish youth movements, religious and non-religious respectively, involved in the agricultural war effort.

The "phoney war," which facilitated the return of large numbers of Jewish evacuees — much to the dismay of the Board of Deputies — came to an end with Hitler's air raids, which started on August 13, 1940.

Anticipating the Battle of Britain, the Government decided to send children to safe havens in North America. One of the factors in this short-lived policy was the hospitality offered by overseas families, including the Jewish communities of Canada and America.

The scheme came to an end with the torpedoing of the liner, City of Benares, on September 17, when 306 people, including 77 children, died.

Despite the Blitz, many families preferred to stay together in the familiar surroundings of their London homes.

On October 4, 1940, the "JC"

reported: "It seems incredible that even last week children were returning to London from reception areas. Moreover, Jewish children have been returning in relatively larger numbers than non-Jewish children."

Each of the following evacuation stories sent in by readers is unique. Whether they tell of kindness, cruelty or strangeness, they all show how the experience of separation from parents deeply affected a whole generation.

ABOVE: A Habonim group photograph

RIGHT: Horseplay. The teenagers cutting each other's hair with garden shears

BELOW: Singing by a camp fire

PHOTOS: COURTESY OF SPRINGBOARD EDUCATION TRUST

The day war broke out

The wedding photo. Minnie Gurovitch and Harry Hyman who married on September 3, 1939. They lived at first in Stamford Hill, and later in Hendon. On the left: the bride's parents, Katie and Beaie Gurovitch. Right: Sarah and Max Hyman, the groom's parents

Norwood child's disappointment

SIMON JACOBS was nine years old when he travelled with a party from the Jewish orphanage in West Norwood to Worthing.

The orphans were taken around the town in groups to try to find billets.

"Believe me, there were plenty who slammed the door in our faces," Mr Jacobs was eventually billeted.

"I was treated with great kindness and was looked after like a son. Unfortunately, this did not last long as the Germans were at Dunkirk and they had to move us away from the coast."

He was sent to Hertford, only about 20 miles from London.

"This was a very unhappy period for me right up to the end of the war. I used to run away to London, but they always brought me back. When I was an evacuee in Hertford, my sister, Hannah, and myself lived in filthy conditions, often going hungry.

"The only time I felt happy was at Worthing. I still keep in touch with the people with whom I was billeted.

"I visit them two or three times a year. They are now well into their 80s."

Looking for horns in Norfolk

Rita Symons, née Frieda, formerly of Hackney, was evacuated, aged 12, together with her younger sister Estelle, aged 10, with her school, Dalston Grammar, to Norfolk:

We were taken to a ramshackle hall and distributed to local families. My sister and I were accompanied to our billet by a local teacher, who ran ahead to our family to warn them that we were Jewish children.

Our welcome was very memorable — no sooner had I arrived, when the wife began examining my very long hair.

When I remonstrated and said that I did not have nits, she replied that she wasn't looking for nits, but for horns!

'Your tales of kindness, sadness and separation', from *The Jewish Chronicle*, 1 September 1989, when a series of articles were reproduced to mark the 50th anniversary of the original evacuation.

The reference to schools being disbanded is relevant to this story as the evidence is that JFS Mousehole was closed in December 1941, and at least some of the teachers returned home at that point, in spite of the fact that a substantial number of evacuees remained behind. The evidence is also that some of the teachers remained, most probably Mr Nathan and Miss Cohen, though for how long is not known. It seems likely from what is said in the minutes above that the continued presence of some of the JFS teachers in Mousehole would have meant that no supervision was felt to be necessary. The issue resurfaced towards the end of the war, when it became apparent that arrangements would need to be made for any remaining unaccompanied children to be returned to their homes. In most instances, of course, it was the parents of evacuees who made the necessary arrangements to ensure the safe return of their children, though to what extent they liaised with the appropriate authorities in so doing is not known.

The minutes of the Welfare and Evacuation Committee held in April 1945[3] show that, somewhat belatedly, a temporary post of welfare officer was established in connection with the visiting and supervision of all unaccompanied children billeted in private households in the borough, and that a Mr E.T. Fulford was appointed to the post at a salary of £200 per annum plus war bonus, the appointment taking effect from 26 April 1945. The committee was also asked to send representatives to a conference of reception authorities in the county, which had been arranged for the same day. Among the matters to be considered were the welfare of unaccompanied children and any residual problems consequent upon the return home of evacuees.

It seems extraordinary that the welfare and supervision of evacuees should have been considered at such a late stage of the war, so Shirley is probably quite right that no one in a position of authority ever visited her to check that she was being properly looked after. In her case, of course, she was cared for very well, but for the authorities to assume that this was always the case was quite wrong.

At the end of the war, in July 1945, the Welfare and Evacuation Committee[4] produced an interesting breakdown of evacuee numbers showing that the vast majority of evacuees in the borough came from London.

BILLETING OF EVACUEES

The Chief Billeting Officer reported that from 1939 to June 1945, the number of evacuees billeted in the Borough of Penzance was 8,761, excluding Devonport High School boys and persons accommodated in requisitioned houses, made up as follows:-

London area	4,636
East Coast	365
Plymouth	661
Scilly	133
Tunbridge Wells	228
Other areas	745
Brixham Belgians	89

Nurses and Helpers	92
Workers	415
Local	1,397
Total	8,761

Two years later, the Welfare and Evacuation Committee[5] noted that there were now so few evacuees remaining in the majority of reception areas that the billeting work arising from their continued presence was negligible, and hence the committee was disbanded.

EARLY DEPARTURES

It is probable that a number of evacuees in Mousehole returned home within a short while after their arrival in June 1940. This would have been some of the younger children who were missing their parents and unable to settle, and also a small number who found themselves in unsuitable billets. A cousin of Millie Butler, evacuated from JFS Infants' School, remembers that he was billeted in:

'...a dodgy old dirty cottage. I was one of the unlucky ones, Millie had a fantastic time. But we survived.'

When his parents learned of the conditions he was living in, they quickly came to collect him. Connie Mellows was living in far better circumstances on a material level, but nevertheless her stay was also short lived, for very different reasons:

'Mrs Lewis was very concerned that the Cornish people didn't realise the danger of bombing and that they had made no provision for air raid shelters as we had in London. And she wrote to my parents saying that she really thought that the children would be safer in London where there was the proper provision against air raids and bombs. And so my mother came down to see what it was all about and while she was there she discovered that all our washing and laundry was done by the maid's mother in their home and the maid's little sister had scarlet fever. As a consequence my mother took me back to London very quickly. Of course, I didn't mind. I was going home to Mummy and Daddy. Mousehole had been like a very nice summer holiday.

'I think if Mrs Lewis thought we were going to be safer in London, then all I can say is she must have been very ignorant, and number two, perhaps she wanted to be rid. I don't know, but the consensus of opinion in my family was it was such a stupid thing to say.'

One cannot help but sympathise with the views of Connie's family. Connie returned to London at the height of the Blitz, by which time a bomb had destroyed a neighbour's home, so her family had been obliged to move to the flat of Connie's grandmother. An elderly couple living nearby had lost several members of their family when the V2 bombs fell on Hughes Mansions in Vallance Road. After a brief and unsuccessful evacuation to Norfolk, Connie was then sent to live with a young couple in Oxford with whom she happily remained until the end of the war. When she returned from Oxford, Connie joined the Brady Club, where she also met Ted Labofsky and Celia Reiderman, though it was not until years later that she realised they had been in Mousehole together. At the Brady Club, she joined the drama group, which was the beginning of a lifelong involvement in the performing arts.

When Connie left Mousehole, her co-evacuee was left alone in the Rose household. It appears that it was inconvenient for Mrs Rose and her daughter to cater for a child on her own and they therefore sent her to live with the maid. It is doubtful whether this would have been done on an official basis, since Mrs Rose had plenty of room, not to mention resources, and would not have been able to argue that she could not take anyone in. Obviously, by comparison, the maid lived in much reduced circumstances, and when the girl's parents discovered what had happened to her, they came to take her home.

Betty and Esther Posner's stay in Mousehole was also curtailed, though they remained for about 18 months. They had to leave because Mrs Drew became pregnant and her daughter Margaret Dillon Drew was born in 1942. The girls were sad to leave but did not have a great deal of time to think about it as they were re-evacuated twice, first to Bury St Edmunds, where they were looked after by several housekeepers in one year, and then to Whittlesea near Peterborough. In spite of Mousehole having been their first evacuation, it is the one which the sisters remember most vividly. Nevertheless, there are huge gaps in their memory, not the least being that they do not remember being part of the JFS group. The most probable reason for their poor memory of these events is that their moves to different parts of the country, and their being cared for by so many different people, resulted in one event merging into the other, so that the whole period, in effect, became a complete blur.

Jeanne Waters also recalls that her evacuee, Frederica White, left unexpectedly:

'I think she was here about 18 months, but her mother took her away for a little holiday and then wrote and said that Frederica wouldn't be coming back. They were away from London now and she didn't see it was necessary for her to stay down here. We never heard from her again and I'm sad about that because I would love to have known how she grew up and what she did. Father always wanted to know how she had turned out.'

Just after the war, Jeanne came tantalisingly close to finding Frederica. A lady called Pearl Jenkin, who was the wife of the manager of the firm for which Jeanne's husband worked, met Frederica in a big store in London, while on a visit there. She contacted Jeanne on her return to tell her what had happened:

'I had a phone call one evening from Pearl and she told me that the young lady who was the shop assistant said, "Excuse me, but do you come from Cornwall?" And Pearl said, "Yes, I do," and she said, "Do you know Mousehole?" "Yes," said Pearl, "I know Mousehole quite well really." "Do you know anyone called Jeanne Waters? I was her evacuee." I nearly jumped out of my chair, I really did. We were so thrilled to think we were going to have some contact with her and then Pearl said "Oh dear, I can't remember which shop we were in." It was a very great regret.'

SCHOOL LEAVERS

Many of the evacuees were born in the year 1927, and so in 1941 reached the age of 14, which was the school leaving age at that time. This meant that they had to leave Mousehole School and look for work. A few remained to work in the area, for example, according to Joan Ladner, Willy Brick worked at a shoe shop in Penzance. But for most of the school leavers, this was the time they returned to London. Ted was one of those to leave Mousehole School in 1941, and he received an attractive offer of employment:

'When I was 14, I was offered a job on a fishing boat. I asked the Harveys and they said I'd better get my parents' permission. So when I wrote home to my mother and father saying that I'd got a job on the fishing boat, they said, "We're coming to get you." They thought it was safer in London with the bombs than on a fishing boat! I would love to have done it. But at that age you don't have a lot of choices. You've got a family, and my father said "You've got to come home". Simple as that.

'When I got to Paddington I felt terrible, the smell, especially with the steam and the smoke. We all slept in one room and at that age we were getting bigger. So my father and myself slept in the bedroom and my sister and my mother slept in a put-u-up in the front room. I went to work. We were very capable of getting over things. You had to get over things; one thing's over, another thing starts.'

Ted went back to visit Mousehole with Lenny Marks in 1943 when they were both 16 and they stayed for a week at Auntie Florrie's house. They were also invited to the Harveys' for tea. In later years, Ted took his children, and introduced them to the Harveys. During that first return visit, Ted remembers that he and Lenny went to the pictures with Marian, who remembers the outing well:

'Ted and Lenny both took me to the cinema and they were rather proud doing it, I think, because by that time they'd got jobs and earned a bit of money. They came back on holiday and took me to the Ritz cinema in Penzance to see *Gone with the Wind*. And yes, I was rather pleased, I had two boyfriends, not just one.'

Marian here describes the departure of Aunt Florrie's evacuees, also school leavers:

'Well, they left in ones and twos. They just went home as they grew up and came to school-leaving age. Auntie Florrie had a visitors' book she used from 1934 onwards because she did bed and breakfast for people who came here on holiday. Bernie wrote in the visitors' book on 28 August 1941, and Lenny wrote on 4 October 1941. It was when they had come to school-leaving age and went home. When they left, I felt a bit lonely really, I missed them. I really did because I'd got so used to having them around. Well Bernie was what, five days older than me actually, and Lenny was about three months younger than me so they weren't exactly like big brothers. But it was nice, I felt

I had brothers. And that was an experience I had never had, and I enjoyed it. It was lovely to have brothers.

'Bernie did come down once, but Auntie Florrie was full up with visitors, and he was very disappointed he couldn't stay. After that, he didn't maintain very much contact but Lenny always kept in touch with Auntie Florrie and Uncle Vivian. Uncle Vivian died in 1944, and I think after that I was the one who wrote the letters and kept in touch. After Lenny got married in 1949 he brought his wife Blanche down here to see where he'd stayed, and then they brought the children down.'

Lenny loved Mousehole so much that he and Blanche continued to visit every year until the mid-1990s, staying in various places in Cornwall, but always finding time to spend at least one day in Mousehole. Another villager who thought of her evacuees as brothers was Joan Ladner, who like Marian was an only child. Joan was hugely upset when they left:

'I remember when Harold and Dan went, it just broke my heart, and I remember where I was that day because Mother had me go to stay with a relative near Goldsithney. She wanted to see that I wasn't too upset. I remember sitting on the step and the house was called Windermere, and crying my eyes out. It was awful when they went. I was just 10 and terribly upset, thinking, you know, it's part of your family gone, really. I just loved them.'

Joan was 10 in March 1942, which suggests that that was around the time that Harold and Dan left, although their names do not appear on the January 1942 register. Joan visited the boys after the war and went to Daniel Frankel's shop in Commercial Road. Harold visited Joan and her mother several times, but eventually lost touch. They never heard from Daniel but he recently contacted the author and Joan has been put back in touch with him.

Vera and Evelyn left Mousehole in the summer of 1941, again because Vera left school at that time, and before their departure Auntie Minnie gave each of them a painting by a local artist. Having been so happy in Mousehole, they both found it difficult to readjust to life in London, but were nevertheless determined to make a success of it. Vera tells the story:

'I did not want to leave. Evelyn and I both left together, I was 14 and Evelyn 16, and when we arrived in London everything was dirty and sooty, and I couldn't breathe. We were most unhappy, and my mum said, "I can see that you're not settling down here." We just couldn't get to grips with being in this horrible atmosphere of London at that time. She said, "You know, if you're not happy, go back," which we did. We went back to Mrs Harvey and we stayed with her for a couple of weeks, and I think she pointed out to us, "As much as I'd love to have you, you have got your mum, and you must try and get back there and make a life." And that's what we did.

'Readapting was very, very difficult, because we were used to this lovely little house, with the sea air and breeze and everything. But in London we lived in a house with two or three rooms and no bathroom. I made up my mind I'd got to be a success and, wherever I worked,

I decided to stay there for a short while, pick up what I can, knowledge of the business, and move on, which I did. My desire for success stemmed from being in Mousehole, seeing how life could be, and how it was in reality, and I didn't like the reality.'

Evelyn continues:

'We hated going back to London, because we didn't know what life was going to be like. We knew it would be different, we would miss Mousehole, we would miss the tranquillity, we'd miss the seagulls, we'd miss the easy life that we'd had there, the lovely food and everything else. But once we went back to Mousehole, we realised, it's lovely, but we needed to get back into the real world and start looking for jobs because we needed to help our mother. We came back and I then started to learn to be a machinist and Vera started to learn to be a saleslady.

'Then, once we started to work, Vera and I made sure that we saved up, the two of us, and put money together and we went to a furniture shop in Whitechapel, and first of all we made sure that we had a nice little dining room table and chairs. We bought the dining set first so that if we had any friends coming in we had somewhere nice for them to come. Then we bought a settee and two armchairs, and we bought a big square carpet, I remember, with lino going around the edge, and gradually we got the home together, the two of us, from working.'

Both Vera and Evelyn eventually went into the jewellery business in which they were very successful. It is astonishing that two young Jewish girls from the East End of London should have gained their aspirations for success in life from an isolated and remote fishing village.

Cyril also left Mousehole when he was 14, probably during the summer of 1941, leaving behind Malcolm and his mother, who by this stage were staying at Tavis Vor. Although it was a wrench to leave his foster family, Cyril did not experience the difficulty in readapting to life back home that some of the other evacuees did, partly because of his age, but also because of his easy-going personality.

'I was very sad, because I'd had a wonderful time, and now I was coming back to London. But, it wasn't hard. I wasn't there long enough. The only thing I was scared of was the bombs. I had a delayed Barmitzvah in Great Garden Street Synagogue.'

Malcolm went home a few months after Cyril but before the end of 1941, as he does not appear on the Mousehole School register of January 1942. The family went to live in Pinner, because the East End had been bombed so badly, though their father carried on working there every day in his grocer's shop. Business as usual, as Cyril said. Malcolm describes the atmosphere:

'We came back and had to face the consequences, the bombs were coming non-stop, V1s and V2s, people were getting killed, losing other people we knew in the East End.'

In spite of his fond memories of Mousehole, Cyril never returned; however, every Christmas for many years after the war, their father sent large boxes of fruit, one to Nettie

Pender and one to Mrs Sampson. Malcolm remembers taking the parcels to the Red Star office in Paddington, where they were put on the train to Penzance. Sylvia Pender remembers receiving these parcels. Malcolm returned to Mousehole several times to visit his former foster parents, the Sampsons, perhaps because, having been much younger than Cyril, he had a greater sense of them having been second parents to him. He visited them in the early 1950s with his mother, and returned a year later on his own, now about 20. One particular episode stands out, which he calls his 'infamous adventure with an unlicensed bookmaker in Penzance'. On this second visit, he met Mr Haffner, father of one of the teachers, who, it seems, had remained in Mousehole.

'Haffner was there and we teamed up. He was an elderly gentleman. He looked to me about 80, easy. I met Haffner on the bus going to Penzance, it was a Friday lunch-time and the bus was parked up top, near the Coastguard. He told me he was going to have a bet and he knew all the race courses. So we go to Penzance and we find where Dyson's illegal betting shop was taking bets.[6] Dyson had a little office in Penzance, off Market Jew Street. And we bet a few shillings. I didn't have much money in those days but I was well versed with gambling because I was working on the *Greyhound Express* at the time, which was a sports' daily.

'All of a sudden some plain-clothes policemen appeared just to nick Dyson. Dyson turned white and Haffner was deaf, of course, quite a bit deaf. So I said to him, "It's the police." He said, "*What?*" I said, "*It's the police.*" "Well," he said, "I'll wait for you outside." As he moved to leave, they grabbed him, took us round to the local police station in Penzance, and we were interviewed. They said to us, "What property have you got on you?" And Haffner said, "Jar of stomach powder," because he had ulcers, that's what he declared. We were charged and asked to come up another time and the police then released us. The funny thing is, Haffner's punch-line, when we got out the court to get the bus back, he said, "We've still got time for a couple of Guinnesses!"

'When I went back and told Auntie Mary, I was very upset about what Mum and Dad would say, and she was shrieking with laughter. Uncle Dick and Auntie Mary thought it was very funny. And I got a letter a bit later from Dyson, he wrote to me saying

"You were found guilty of haunting a house in an illegal area, and fined 6s 6d, which I paid.' And that was the episode of my infamous time in Penzance.'

Later, Malcolm started writing the story for the *Sporting Life*, and actually contacted Mr Haffner's daughter. Apparently, she was quite dismayed at her father's illegal activities! Malcolm also remembers that Raymond and Elaine Pomeroy came to stay in London, and that he took them to see *London Laughs* at the Adelphi, with Jimmy Edwards. Raymond Pomeroy also remembers this occasion very well:

'Millie Butler was a friend of my sister, Elaine. We went to see her in the 1950s, she lived just off Petticoat Lane. We also went to see Malcolm Hanover at his father's flat just off the Edgware Road. The Hanovers had fruit shops in London, and I remember looking out the window of Millie's flat and you could see one of their shops. And the Hanovers, they were very friendly with the Crazy Gang, and the night we went there, Malcolm's father was a big chap, I can see him now, and he said, "Would you like to go and see the Crazy Gang?" I thought we should never get in to see the Crazy Gang that late in the day, but he just picked up the phone and said, "Hello Doll," to this lady on the end of the line, "I want three stalls," and that was it, he just got them. I remember Malcolm took a cheque for some charity that they were involved in, and after the show we went and had a meal on the way back from the theatre, that stuck in my mind.'

TRANSFERS TO OTHER SCHOOLS

Maurice left Mousehole in 1941, as he was awarded a scholarship to a technical school in Luton which eventually became the North Western Polytechnic. He had taken the entrance exam just before war started.

'To be very truthful, I was pleased because it meant that I could do something I wanted to do, engineering. It was just farewell and I was then off to another adventure. I think I went back with my father on the night train from Penzance to London. It was near the start of the school year, which would be September 1941. I went back with my father to Cockfosters because immediately after the war had started, he had bought a house there. From there he took me on to Luton where I was found a billet. The North Western Polytechnic was totally different from what had gone on in Mousehole. I mean, here there was actual formal education.'

Maurice found himself in completely different circumstances because on the one hand he had a much better education, but on the other hand, not such a wonderful leisure life. Although he found his new school very pleasant, he did not enjoy his first day there because he was punished in a manner reminiscent of Arnold's punishment in Mousehole School:

'I wound up being taken to a class that was an engineering workshop. And having arrived in the class as the new boy, a number of the boys there were throwing around little bits of folded tin, and one piece was thrown at me. I proceeded to pick it up and threw it back. Just as I did that the teacher, a Mr Jones, saw this, and said to me "Come here, that boy, you know the rules." I said, "I don't know any of the rules, I'm here just this afternoon for the first time." He said, "Well, everybody knows the rules." And he sent for the punishment book and the cane and I got six of the best across my backside.'

This is another example of the kind of discipline practised in schools during that era. Maurice re-visited Mousehole once or twice, while on leave from the army when stationed at Bodmin. He remembers staying at the Lobster Pot and meeting villagers he had known. Arnold left a few months after Maurice, with his brother Michael. He was pleased to get back to his family and to start receiving a proper education:

'We left somewhere about Easter 1942. I suppose basically that much of the heavy bombing had stopped by then. My parents had acquired a home out in Cockfosters which was 10 miles from the centre of London so it was a much safer venue. In the city area we had no garden, but suddenly there was a house with a lovely garden and lots of green spaces around us. I suppose our parents wanted their children home as much as we as children wanted to go back to our parents, so I think I was happy to go home. During Christmas 1941, I remember going back to London with my brother, Michael, and then went back to Cornwall. I think that was a very unsettling thing to happen because, while we were away we got used to being away, we were quite content. Now suddenly you go home for a holiday and that was a mistake because now this made matters worse again. I suppose we then wanted to go back home.'

This must have been a common experience for many evacuees, to settle in their foster homes, but then to become unsettled when they went to stay for brief holidays with their parents. This is not to say that they should not have visited their parents, but it is another example of the way in which the Government had not recognised the need of children for stability and had not thought through the impact of moving children from one place to another. Arnold's major concern on his return was catching up with his missed education:

'Well, the biggest experience was readapting to school. I don't know if I was a bright or a dull child academically, but certainly once I went to school in London I was at the bottom of the class, and we were doing things that I'd never done before which were quite strange to me. It was very difficult for me initially to catch up, and I think it was equally difficult for my brother, Michael. At 11 you had to take the 11-plus examination, which I failed, and I felt it very deeply. I suppose my parents were disappointed, but I felt rather humiliated that I couldn't do better.

'One of the main things I was able to do once we got back home was to go to a public library and I was encouraged to read and could start taking books out. I was able to join the Boy Scouts and it was a much more normal family life. The life that we had with the Cromptons – don't misunderstand me – was a good life, and I think in many respects it stimulated me, because we lived with a non-Jewish family and in a completely non-Jewish environment, which I think was to our benefit. But, as I say, they weren't our parents and there were certain things lacking as a consequence through no fault of theirs. But gradually my education caught up. I started to be able to read and a normal life resulted, apart, of course, from the war that was still on.

'I think that the period in which we were evacuated during the war fragmented my life to the extent that I never felt bad about leaving home. You were torn away once and you cried a few tears, but you couldn't keep crying the same tears and you got used to it. Throughout one's life, one was constantly leaving home and it didn't matter any more.'

Arnold returned only once to Mousehole, and did not maintain contact with anyone; however, by an extraordinary coincidence, he met the stepson of his childhood friend Millie Butler at a very small wedding party in Hawaii, and was able to get back in touch with her.

Jack Goldstein left Mousehole in very difficult circumstances, like Maurice, to attend another school, but in this case entirely against his own wishes. This was probably after the summer of 1941:

'I didn't want to leave. In 1939 before the war, I sat the preliminary exam in JFS, but it took quite a while before the results came. If you passed you went to JFS Central. We all forgot about it as it was done over a year before. One day some education official came into the class in Mousehole and said they had only just managed to sort out the results. He said the people on his list should have been in JFS Central School, and then he called out the names of the boys who had passed, I think there were three or four of them. He read out my name and said "You are to be sent to JFS Central School". It never occurred to me where it was.

'Well, he must have told Mr and Mrs Richards. She knew about it but she didn't tell me. She wasn't very happy. So anyway, the day comes and Mrs Richards took me to Penzance railway station. She was crying all the way there. When I saw her crying, I was crying, I didn't know why. It never occurred to me where I was going, nobody said anything. I didn't even know I was going on the train, all I knew was that we were going to Penzance, to the station. I didn't even think about going on a train because after I'd gone on that train coming down, I didn't want to know about trains. Anyway, a train comes in, she puts me on, kisses me goodbye, and away I went. She was crying all the way home, I suppose.'

Following his arrival in London, Jack's mother tried to persuade him that the change of school would benefit him and he was put on another train the next day, still without any idea of where he was going.

'It was the same railway station where we went for the first evacuation to Cambridge. But it still didn't register where I was going. Then I learned it was Cambridge. I nearly went potty. Of all the places in the world, I didn't want to go there. Then I was put with some horrible people, who were anti-Semitic. I didn't like them, can't remember their name, and I can't picture them because I wanted them out of my mind. I hated the place and I hated these people.'

It seems likely that, however he was treated by his new foster parents, Jack was so devastated by leaving his beloved Mousehole that there was no way that he could have adapted to his new environment. The complete lack of information about where he was going simply added to his distress. He soon learned that he had, in fact, been sent to Isleham, where JFS Central School was based at the time. The other boys in the school had already been there for a year and were well established. Jack quite liked the school, but to add to his difficulties, soon found that, having lost a year, he was well behind the others educationally. He was determined not to stay in a place which he hated so much and managed to return to London on a coach which had brought visiting parents from Spitalfields. He refused to go back to Isleham and was eventually sent to another school in King's Lynn, which he describes as even worse, and he ran away again. As a consequence, he went to a local school in London, left at 14 and missed out on his opportunity of gaining a good education.

'That was the end of my education. I didn't want to leave Mousehole. I would love to have stayed in Mousehole more than one year. I can't tell you how upset I was. I was shattered, absolutely shattered. They couldn't have got me out of there for all the money in the world if I'd have known where I was going. That's probably why they didn't tell me because they knew I probably wouldn't want to go.'

This was the evacuation scheme at its worst: decisions taken about children's futures without any consideration for their thoughts or feelings, without any explanation, which might have helped them to understand what was happening to them. Then putting them on trains, sending them from one place to another, without telling them where they were going, so that they could not in any way prepare themselves for what was to come.

Jack returned to Mousehole for the first time in 1999. He had wanted to go before, but his wife preferred to travel abroad. When he became widowed, he decided to take one of his daughters and her family and booked a cottage in Gurnick Street.

'When I got down there it seemed as though I'd been there the day before, although it was 60 years later. But I couldn't see anybody who had any connection with the evacuation. That really upset me and I cried. Nearly every place in Mousehole was changed into an artist's studio or a souvenir shop, and it was nothing whatsoever like it used to be. No fishing boats, no fishermen, and I couldn't see anybody that I knew.

'And then by chance I met up with this lady, Greta, I met her the day before I was coming back. I thought she was a local, so we got talking and I told her, "I haven't been here since 1941." So she said, "Oh, you must be one of the evacuees." I said, "That's right. I'm trying to find somebody from then that might know something about the evacuees." So she said to me, "I wasn't born here, I came to live here after the war. But now I'm considered to be one of the locals, it takes you about 50 or 60 years before they accept you as a local. But I know somebody who has lived here all her life and knows everything about it. She lives over there in Gurnick Street."

'I was staying in Gurnick Street. All the week I didn't know about Marian and that she lived about four doors along. Anyway, in the evening, I told my daughter and we went there and knocked on the door. This is the part that amazes me, she actually opened the door and she hadn't seen me for 60 years and when I explained I was an evacuee, and told her who I was billeted with, she said, "You're Jacky Goldstein." Can you believe that? She confirmed who I was by just looking at me after all those years.[7]

'Marian lived on the other corner from Mr and Mrs Richards, and all the time I was there I didn't know her. She's like a book, she's amazing. She knew all about me and my sisters. I was a little boy running around with boys in my class, and she must have looked at me millions of times. So that's how me and Marian have got to be friends and that brought it all back, and we've been in touch ever since.'

Jack's comment about Marian confirming who he was would seem to suggest that his identity, his very being even, was in some way inextricably tied up with Mousehole. When asked about this, he tearfully replied:

'Well, I suppose it was the best part of my childhood. Previous to that I never had a minute's happiness, not one.'

LATER DEPARTURES

The departure of so many evacuees left the village feeling empty as Derek here describes:

'They seemed to disappear quick, it seemed there was no sort of warning. Suddenly they were there and suddenly they'd gone. Well, it left a space really, and all of a sudden we had loads of room. I don't know what happened to all the extra desks, I suppose they were all took away.'

Many of the evacuees had been so loved by the villagers that a number of them wanted to adopt them, apparently a common evacuation experience throughout the country. Mildred remembers that Mr and Mrs Warren wanted to adopt her, and it seems Mrs Osborne wanted to adopt Gloria Cohen. Joan recalls that Mrs Rouffignac wanted to adopt Sheila Brick. The desire to adopt was felt particularly strongly in the case of childless couples, especially those whose evacuees stayed with them throughout the war, and with whom they therefore became very close. Marian here describes one such case:

'Frances Levene was with Mr and Mrs Harry of Wharf House. I think they absolutely adored her because they'd never had children. They were an elderly couple, well-to-do by village standards. She came for years after the war, when she was quite grown up, and they absolutely adored her. She never seemed to lose touch with them.'

Records show that although Frances left Mousehole School in July 1945, she was readmitted in July 1946, with no indication of when she finally left. Celia and Rosita Reiderman also remained in Mousehole throughout the war until June 1945. When the girls left, Jack and Bertha Waters remember that they remained in contact for some time:

'We kept in touch with Rosita for a little while. We went up and visited them. Rough area, but they had a nice little flat, it was well done, and they had a television. She was ever so nice. But it was a rough area. When we came away in the dark, they said they'd come with us to make sure, which was a bit frightening to us, who were used to Mousehole. But then, as I say, we never heard anything from them any more.'

According to accounts from other evacuees who met the girls at the Brady Club after the war, one of the girls married while the other emigrated with her parents to America, possibly Philadelphia. Millie went home during 1941 but returned to Mousehole during the bombing, and stayed for the rest of the war:

'I finally left when I was about 11 years of age when the bombing of London had nearly stopped. I was one of the last evacuees to leave Mousehole. I had mixed feelings about leaving. On the one hand I was leaving the Tonkins who had been so very kind and wonderful to me, but on the other I was going to my mother and my home in London. It was going to be a new experience for me and so it was very exciting. I went back regularly when the war was over, to visit with the family that had cared for me, and also to meet their friends.'

Shirley was one of the children to stay the longest in Mousehole. Having arrived there in 1940 aged seven years, she left in June 1945 at the age of 12. During these five years, very significant years of her life, she did not return to London at all, and her mother only visited occasionally. As a consequence, by the time of her departure she had become totally integrated into the Ladner family and into village life. For her, the return to London meant going back to a life with which she was no longer familiar, and she found the process of reintegration into her own family traumatic in the extreme.

'I didn't want to leave. Well, I didn't know where I was going to, really. I didn't know anything else. I can't even remember how I got back. It must have been by train, but I don't remember anybody taking me. I was a very, very unhappy person. Very unhappy, emotionally, and in every which way. It was a totally different lifestyle; totally, totally different. I missed Mousehole to begin with, probably for 12 months or so.
'Home life was also totally different, not so structured, because my mother was working and things were still on ration. Food was not that easy to come by. I remember she bought Jewish food, Jewish meat. She used to go out very early in the morning before she went to work to queue up at the Jewish butcher, because there was a quota. There was a quota with sweets, and with some other food, and you had a ration book. You see I didn't realise about all this. Well, I never saw a ration book in Mousehole, what did I know about ration books?'

School life was to prove particularly traumatic, and not just because she was behind educationally. No longer could she walk round the corner to the local school she knew so well with her little group of friends. At 12, she was at a particularly difficult age for making new friendships and had no sibling with whom she could share her experiences:

'I had to settle in at school, and I think I was disadvantaged because I really hadn't had a proper education. I think I was in Wessex Gardens Primary first and then Copthall Secondary School. You had to make friends through the school and it wasn't that easy. We were much more spread around. I would live here, they would live there, not necessarily have children in your turning who you went to school with. You walked on your own, you didn't go in a group because everybody was spread around.'

Although Shirley did not find it particularly difficult to relearn a Jewish lifestyle, as she was now surrounded by a large extended family, what she found particularly distressing was the anti-Semitism she met with, of which she had had absolutely no experience in Mousehole.

'The Jewish side of things didn't seem to be quite so bad. I had aunts and uncles and cousins so they came into it more. I think I picked up a Jewish way of life as I went along. You went with the flow. I didn't learn it. I didn't sit down and study it, no. But obviously I was Jewish. Anti-Semitism was quite rife, I think, and it seemed to be more rife when I was a teenager. I remember going once to the films with my mother and we wanted to buy some chocolate, and the lady said to us, not realising we were Jewish, "I'll give you some because you're not Jewish but if it was a Jew I wouldn't give them the chocolate." I had just not come across that kind of thing in Mousehole.'

For Shirley, then, in spite of gradually socialising and making friends among Jewish people, the period during which she was evacuated was a happy one, but the consequences of that evacuation were devastating, tearing her, as it did, from her normal family life, to which she then had the greatest difficulty readjusting. She was billeted with a family which was totally different from her own in every respect, not just in terms of religion, but also in with regard to class. She was pampered and idolised by her foster parents, and learnt from them to appreciate the finer things in life.

'I came from a working-class background and I went back to a working-class background and I had been spoilt. There was a huge difference between what I had had in Mousehole and what I came back to. I had to get to know my mother and father all over again. That was what the war did.'

Indeed, that was what the war did. Shirley's experience was not at all uncommon. Many evacuees returning home found themselves having to adjust to a life and to a family that was no longer familiar to them and, like Shirley, found this a most traumatic experience.

Frances and Mildred believe they stayed in Mousehole initially for two or three years but then went home. According to Frances' school report card, she left Mousehole School in June 1942 at the age of 15, somewhat unusually as the normal school leaving age at that time was 14. She then returned to London, leaving behind her childhood sweetheart, Edwin, and believes she worked as a dressmaker for a while. Mildred probably left school the following year, and also then returned to London, where she met her future husband Eric at the age of 15. During this time, their younger sister Irene remained alone in Mousehole, a situation she was not too happy about, though their other sister, Ada, visited her on holiday at one time. Ada later told her sister Frances:

'I felt so sorry for Edwin. He was standing at the harbour and you'd gone home. I felt so sorry for him.'

When the Doodlebug raids began in June 1944, Mildred and Frances returned to Mousehole, again to Miss Oliver's, and spent a year working on the land, first at Jack Mitchell's farm and then later for Farmer Giles, both near Raginnis Hill. Their tasks on the farm involved hoeing, weeding and picking flowers, which were sent up to London. Frances remembers that they earned 27 shillings a week.[8] An abiding memory for both of the sisters is watching the ships in the Bay as they worked:

'Where we worked was overlooking the Bay, so as we picked we looked out to sea. It was beautiful. And then we'd see ships come in from somewhere. We were on the cliff, high up, with the daffodils and the violets, and we could see them coming in.'

Mildred remembers that they finally left shortly after VE Day, which was 8 May 1945. She remembers it particularly because, for the first time during the war, the lights were put on in Raginnis Hill. Frances remembers her departure for a very different reason, as she had to leave Edwin for a second and final time:

'He asked me to stay with him in Mousehole but I couldn't because of our different religions.'

Having loved Mousehole so much, readapting to life back in London was difficult for the girls, not so much for Mildred, who now had a new love, but certainly for Frances, who found the transition very painful:

'I didn't want to go. Because I loved Mousehole. I didn't want to go to the East End of London. It doesn't matter even if it was a mansion that we lived in, I wanted to stay in Mousehole. I couldn't. I suppose we readapted because you have to, haven't you, you've got to get used to it again. That's the terrible thing. No, I missed the sea, and the lovely water, and the quiet. See, I like it quiet, I could just sit on the pension seat, looking at the sea, and I wouldn't want anything else. That was enough. I missed the people as well, because I'd got to know a lot of them.'

And, of course, she missed Edwin. A terrible tragedy followed which was to affect Frances for the rest of her life. Edwin died in a boating accident in 1951.

'Edwin drowned. I think he was 24. We were both 24. They went fishing, they had a big boat, the *Renovelle*, with Mr Madron at the wheel. I read it in *The Cornishman*, we used to have that. He was out on his father's boat, with Jimmy and Joey, his brothers, and apparently Joey was washing the deck and fell in the sea. And Edwin, who couldn't swim, jumped in to save him, and Jimmy saw them both. He jumped in and apparently grabbed them both by the hair. I don't know how he kept afloat, I really don't, but he grabbed them, got them on deck, but Edwin died. Their parents were devastated. Stella, his sister, told me that several young men carried the coffin all the way up the hill to Paul.'

Edwin was a popular young man, and at his funeral the streets of Mousehole were packed with mourners. A lorry was needed to transport the 147 wreaths to the cemetery in Paul. In March 1957, Mr Madron and his family appeared, without Edwin, on the television programme *This Is Your Life*, one of the few episodes which Frances missed.

'I couldn't go back to Mousehole for 21 years. His death was like a shadow over me, because I'd known him from when he was 13, sitting on his bike. Edwin wasn't there and I think that was one of the main things – I couldn't go back because Edwin wasn't there. I loved Mousehole, but for me Edwin was Mousehole.'

THE BARNES FAMILY RETURNS TO LONDON

Jean Barnes, and her daughters Lydia and Pamela, were the only Jewish family unit to remain in Mousehole throughout the war. They had become so integrated into village life that, as Pamela tearfully remembers, departure was particularly difficult for them:

'Oh, I was quite sad when we left because I remember waving goodbye to everybody. Agnes was there just crying her eyes out. It was horrible coming back, imagine coming from beautiful Cornwall to London, I mean, Hackney was like the actual dregs of London at that time. These ghastly, filthy buildings and rough people, which I wasn't used to, and no green spaces, and obviously more traffic than I was used to. I just hated it.'

Many of the evacuees have commented on this contrast between the open scenery of Mousehole and the oppressiveness of London, which struck them most forcibly on their return. The family immediately encountered the kind of problem that was to face many returnees to London at the end of the war. The Barnes' home in Palmers Green had been requisitioned by the Government and they had to go to court to evict the people who had moved into it. In the meantime, the family went to live with Pamela's grandfather and aunt in a flat in Hackney. At this stage, Ralph Barnes had not returned from the war, and Pamela believes they went back to Mousehole while awaiting his return.

'My mother's heart was always in Cornwall, her heart was set on that place. I think she would have liked my father to get a teaching job down there. And I think we were there for another few months until he finally got demobbed in early 1946. So I was five and a half when I actually saw him again. All I can remember is sitting in the flat in Hackney the day he was due to come home, and he came in with a kitbag. Well, it was weird, and my words to him were, "Are you real?" I think it was all a bit strange for us because we suddenly had this man in our presence who we were not used to.'

This was a common experience for children who had not seen their father throughout the period of the war. Getting to know her father again was not the only difficulty experienced by Pamela in her new life in London:

'It was a cultural shock. I started school, and the kids were taking the mickey out of me because I had a Cornish accent. They were just rough, these kids. Like everything else, you adapt, quicker than you probably realise as kids, but I hated that school, I just hated it.'

Pamela also has a vivid memory of going to the synagogue in Hackney for the first time. She remembers this as a 'totally alien experience' where people were dressed up, the air was heavy and hot, and the women were sitting separately from the men. But what struck her most particularly were the disputes over where people sat. Her mother sat in a seat that was not allocated to her, and she was 'very rudely asked to move'. Although she has been to synagogue over the years, Pamela feels that that initial reaction never went away from her. As we have seen in an earlier chapter, there was in fact a similar allocation of seats in St Clement's Methodist Chapel in Mousehole.

On his return, Ralph Barnes was not able to teach at his former school, JFS, as it had been bombed, and he went instead to teach at Islington Green School where he remained until his retirement. The family eventually moved back to the house in Palmers Green where they remained, except for a year spent in a large house in Chiswick in 1948, when Ralph and Jean Barnes became responsible for the care of a number of displaced Jewish children, refugees from Europe who had all lost their parents in the Holocaust. In this way, the family reconnected with the Jewish community, and although not ultra Orthodox they returned to a Jewish way of life. Pamela subsequently became acquainted with other Jewish girls in the grammar school she attended and became increasingly involved in Jewish issues:

'Then I had my Zionist streak after that and I was in the FZY, which is Federation of Zionist Youth, and then I went on to Israel, but that's another story.'

The return to London did not prevent the family from retaining strong links with Mousehole and Cornwall. The Barnes family visited Mousehole every year for many years, each time renting cottages in the village, but later in other parts of Cornwall also. Initially they travelled down by train, but then Mr Barnes bought a car when Pamela was in her teens and she remembers the excitement of driving down for the first time. With the car, they were able to explore Cornwall, but Mousehole remained the base. Agnes Gruzelier was always the link and the family stayed with her on numerous occasions, and always kept in touch with her. Pamela continued to holiday with her parents in Cornwall until she was 18.

When Ralph Barnes retired in the late 1960s, he and his wife moved to Penzance and bought a house at Lydden Crescent in Alverton, where Pamela also lived with them, off and on, for the first three years, from 1969 to 1971. She returned to work in London, but continued to make frequent visits to her parents in Penzance. Even though now officially retired, Ralph Barnes spent several years throughout the 1970s working as a supply teacher at a school in St Just, something he greatly enjoyed. The Barnes became actively involved in the local community and had many visitors, including a number of former evacuees and the Chief Rabbi. Sadly Mrs Barnes became ill in the late 1970s and they had to return to London so that she could receive treatment, but she died in 1984. Somehow, the Cornish connection died at the same time. Thus, a remarkable chapter in Cornish and Jewish history came to an end.

Chapter Fourteen

LOOKING BACK

THE VILLAGERS

Jeanne Richards née Waters

Jeanne became an uncertificated teacher until she married at 21 and had one son. She later joined the civil service, working in the national insurance offices in Penzance, where she remained until retirement. She is widowed and has one grandson and a great-grandson. Jeanne has lived in Mousehole her whole life, all but 10 years in the same house.

'I think it reminded us very much of how different life was for other people in big cities, and it made us appreciate the comparative safety we experienced here. We got on well. There wasn't this Jewish and Christian attitude at all. They were just people and we learnt to live together, work together and play together, the children particularly. The children were just children, they weren't evacuees, they were kids and they could run about on the beach and have a whale of a time.

'I'm very pleased that they came. It was just a good time really, a good experience to have met people from a different way of life altogether from ours, very different and yet to find that we could get on well together. I think that's good to feel that you can have two quite diverse backgrounds and get on so well together.'

Marian Harris

Marian worked for a bank until 1953 and then underwent secretarial training, ultimately obtaining a job as secretary in the hospital service in Exeter, where she spent seven happy years. Sadly, her mother died suddenly in 1962, and she had to return to Mousehole, when she went to live with her Aunt Florrie on Gurnick Street. She then spent 14 years working as a medical secretary in Penzance, with her friend, Greta Lewis. She nursed Aunt Florrie for seven years before her death in 1983. In spite of some ill-health, Marian remains an active member of the Mousehole community.

'It only could have brought good because it opened my eyes that people were different. In a way I suppose we were rather naïve here, almost at the end of the country at Land's End, because none of us was well travelled. I think it broadened our outlook because we became aware of the East End of London, and it brought it on to our own doorstep. We didn't really know very much about Jewish people, and I became aware of what the Old Testament was about really and I did buy a book by Herman Wouk on Judaism, *This is my God*.

'We just gradually gelled. There was the odd fight, because there were the aggressive ones in the village and there were aggressive boys among them. But after a time, nobody noticed whether they were Jewish or not. I think the Jewish children who were here for some time and were dearly loved by the families were very loyal to those families when they went back to London and have remained intensely loyal to Mousehole.

'I'm glad they came. And they did make a difference to us because they made us realise that there were other people, leading other lives in other places, which didn't have a view like Mount's Bay, and the children had never known the freedom that we had here. I think that probably rubbed off on the evacuees, and went into their characters and they've never forgotten it.

'Another advantage from my point of view was the experience of having siblings, from being an only child to having two "brothers". I loved that. It was being a real family.'

▸ Percy Harvey
Percy became a railway civil engineer, working in many parts of the UK. He is a Fellow of the Institution of Civil Engineers. He has written a book on the history of Mousehole and is a Bard of the Cornish Gorsedd. He has two sons and five grandchildren. He retired to Penzance where his home overlooks Mount's Bay. Mysteriously, there is a *mezuzah* on the doorpost of his home.

'The two communities got on very well together. No question. I would say that it opened their eyes more than it opened ours, and my feeling about the evacuees at this moment in time, is that it was a useful experience for everybody. We got on with Ted, no question about it. Ted was part of the family and we never forgot him.'

Jack Waters and Bertha Waters née Pomeroy
After a period in the Army (REME), Jack became a motor mechanic and car salesman, working at Taylor's Garage in Penzance for 35 years. He then bought his own garage on the roundabout at Longrock, near Marazion, where he remained for 10 years until retiring.

Bertha became Mousehole Carnival Queen in 1949 and was crowned Miss Cornwall that same year. Jack and Bertha started 'walking out' just after they left school, married in 1952 and have two children and three grandchildren. Bertha worked for 16 years selling ice cream at the drugstore on The Cliff in Mousehole, for the last four of which Jack joined her following his retirement. Over the years, the two of them must have sold ice cream to many thousands of visitors to Mousehole. They have lived in Mousehole all their lives.

Jack: 'I was very pleased really, because we always were given the idea that the East End of London was a poor environment, and then they came down here to the way we lived, and the scenery, the openness of it all. I thought, well, that that should do them a bit of good, I think. I was happy they'd come. We got on very well with Celia and Rosita.'

Bertha: 'There was a war on, and I think people were just glad to help.'

Melvia Williams née Cornish

Melvia was a sales assistant for several years, before marrying and having four children. She lived for many years in Newlyn but returned home to Mousehole in the mid-1980s when she remarried. She is now a widow and has six grandchildren.

'Well, it made a terrific interest. For a start we knew nothing about London except that it was the capital of England. They seemed strange at first but we got to know them pretty well and I think we got on all right. I'm sure there was no animosity like you hear now with different races. No, we got used to them and we chatted to them, they taught us a lot and they extended our horizons. And they talked eventually about their lives up there and we told them about ours. So really they integrated very well, they were very nice. Nothing was ever the same again because after the war, Mousehole had been discovered and we got a lot of people coming in.'

Myra Ellis née Phillips

Myra has lived in the same cottage in Paul since the age of nine months. She was a hairdresser for 43 years, mainly in Newlyn. She is now widowed and has one son, two grandchildren and two great-grandchildren.

'All my neighbours made Anita feel welcome. They treated her just like they treated me.'

Joan Richards née Ladner

Joan worked at the grocery next to the Ship Inn for four years, then married at 19 and had four sons. Her husband was a shipwright and ran the Mousehole football club for almost 50 years. Joan is a pianist and for several years was the deputy pianist for the Mousehole Male Voice Choir. She is widowed and has nine grandchildren and 13 great-grandchildren who keep her very happy and very busy. She has lived in Mousehole all her life.

'I think it was good for us, I really do. It was a wonderful experience and even rationing was a good experience because I still think that half a pound of butter is marvellous. I think it keeps you grounded and I think you're just thankful to be alive. Well, I just felt sorry for them having to leave their parents basically. I suppose we all did. It must have been very hard from their point of view, and I think probably the people that we all loved in Mousehole would have done their utmost to help them integrate and be welcomed. They became like part of us, really. I loved them very much.'

Derek Harvey

Derek served his apprenticeship as a carpenter with the same firm as his father, staying there until he did his National Service. He worked for the Local Authority as a carpenter for 30 years, then became self-employed for 15 years until his retirement. He has been a member of the Mousehole Male Voice Choir since 1950. He remains a very active member of the community; for example, he drives people to hospital. He is married and has two children and two grandchildren. His daughter is the post-lady in Mousehole. Derek has lived all his life in Mousehole.

'We got on well, because they were children and children can get on well together, can't they? It was a bit strange for the first few weeks, having different names to remember, but they seemed to integrate and fit in. We used to play loads of street games and all the things that normal kids do. It was the children who all mixed together and we all just carried on as if we were all in one class. Everybody knew everybody else. It was an era really, wasn't it? It's all history now, but it was nice to know them all.'

Raymond Pomeroy

Raymond trained as a mechanic before doing his National Service in the REME, when he briefly met his former school friend and evacuee, Alan Paris. Raymond then worked for the Western National Bus Company for 32 years, 21 of which was as a foreman in the garage. He is married with one daughter and has lived in Mousehole all his life.

'The war wasn't the happiest of times but we were all in the same boat. We got on well together, playing soldiers in the street or in boats down the harbour, which children can't do now.'

Anne Beeton née Pender

Anne was originally brought up in London but spent part of the war in Mousehole. Her family returned to live in Mousehole in 1952 when she was 14. She trained as a nurse at West Cornwall Hospital in Penzance, married and went to live with her husband in Bournemouth, where they raised four children, always spending holidays in Mousehole. Anne and her husband retired to Mousehole and have nine grandchildren.

'The people who housed the evacuees have lots of memories and became very, very fond of the children, whom they just treated as their own children, they were just part of the village. It's been part of the history of the village always.'

THE EVACUEES

Evelyn Edelman née Goldstein

Evelyn visited Mousehole only once, but she corresponded with Auntie Minnie until she died. Evelyn got married in 1948 and set up a jewellery business with her husband, eventually manufacturing as well as selling. They have two sons and five grandchildren, two of whom attend JFS. For many years, Evelyn and her husband owned a flat in Marbella and lived there for six months of the year.

'It made us different people, I think. We just took on a different way of life in Cornwall. We saw how very well Auntie lived. She had this beautiful home, and life was so different. So we always wanted to do that same sort of thing, have our own home, entertain people. I think she educated us, Minnie, being a school teacher, and I think it must have moulded the other children as well, maybe indirectly.

'Auntie loved us to bits. And she was very particular the way we looked and the way we conducted ourselves, the way we stood and everything else. "Be upright, girls," you know, "Come on, girls, head up, be proud," and that's how we were. And, of course, when we came back we missed all that. I think it was wonderful, just wonderful. I've never forgotten it, never, and I don't think I ever will.'

Vera Lubin née Goldstein

Vera visited Mousehole many times and had a little car she called *Minnie* when she passed her driving test, which she drove all the way back to Mousehole. Vera got married, and with her husband opened a jewellery shop which one of her two sons now owns and runs. Vera still helps out in the shop, between three and six days a week. She has three grandchildren and continues to be very active, travelling extensively.

'That community there, they were the most wonderful people you can ever imagine. I have a lot of affection, I've never forgotten them. I'm a Cornish girl at heart. Such charming, wonderful people. When I came back I decided I was going to make something of myself. Auntie Minnie was instrumental in so many things in my life. I still think of her daily. We were absolutely adopted by our Auntie, she was our other mother. It made me realise also how you can mix with other people, apart from being Jewish, that didn't come in the equation. And it's held me in good stead all through my life, not to sort of only mix with one type.'

Frances Pomm née Fromovitch

Frances became a dressmaker and also worked as a hospital receptionist. She married in 1952, having met her husband at the Brady Club. They lived in Mile End for several years and had one daughter. She and her husband lived in Clacton-on-Sea for 20 years until he died in 1994. Frances started visiting Cornwall again in the 1970s and went to live there after her husband died, first in Budock Water and then in Redruth, though she would have preferred Mousehole. She left Cornwall in 2000, which she feels was the worst thing she ever did, and now lives with her granddaughter. She still hopes to return to Cornwall.

'Well, all I can say is that I thought it was wonderful. It affected my life so much that I didn't want to go home to London, I really didn't. There was something magical there. What could be nicer than seeing that sea every day, and the pier and the harbour. Sometimes you can't find the words. I could just stand at the harbour for hours, looking. A wonderful, wonderful place and the people were very kind and really friendly.

'When I left Mousehole it was as though my life was over. I left my heart in Mousehole, that's all there is to it. I am in love, and I'll always be the same, in love with Mousehole. I wish I was 13 again.'

Cyril Hanover

Cyril spent a year in the Army and then worked for many years with his father in the grocer's shop which by this time had moved to Brick Lane. When betting became legal in 1961, he became a clerk in the betting industry for several years. Cyril now lives with his brother, Malcolm.

'A lovely, wonderful memory, we were very fortunate my brother and I. We saw things you could never dream about. People moving out their homes, giving up their beds for us, parents, for me, for Malcolm. Giving us spending money, taking us and board and lodging us and clothing us. The money they got was a pittance. They treated us like their own children.

'It broadened our outlook and, of course, I hope it broadened theirs as well. Did any of these other evacuees say anything different? I'm sure they all put them on a pedestal, didn't they? It was wonderful, wonderful, I'll never forget it as long as I live.'

Ted Leigh formerly Labofsky

Ted's first job was with a manufacturing optician making frames. He worked there for nine months, together with his friend Danny Macintosh, who was making the lenses. Ted then went into the forces, and subsequently became a tailor for 25 years. However, he saw that the trade was declining so he became a licensed taxi driver until his retirement. He is married with two children, four grandchildren and one great-grandchild. Having missed his first Barmitzvah, he is to hold his second Barmitzvah in 2010 at the age of 83.

'Oh, it affected my life all right. Gave me a different sort of outlook because when I went in the forces, I'd been away from my parents, I could look after myself. I knew how to handle myself with other people. I knew how to handle a boat. I was stationed in Gibraltar for two years and I had a little boat there. That was very nice. I think if we had to go anywhere in the world that was the finest place. I thought it was wonderful that they took us in, wonderful, wonderful experience, and I've got nothing but praise for them, nothing but good thoughts about them.'

Maurice Powell formerly Podguszer

Maurice became a teacher and was then called-up into the Army for two years, serving in the Royal Army Educational Corps. He taught for a year, but left teaching and set up a business in advertising and marketing which he ran until the late 1980s. He also developed a group of advertising agencies. He is married with three children and two grandchildren.

'It was an adventure. It enabled me to see some of the more beautiful things that were about and around; the sea, the fields, that type of thing. It put me in touch with nature, if you like. In the way in which I met people in Mousehole, related to them, it was very pleasant. I think they were very, very generous to the evacuees. But I feel it could have been a closer relationship had we not have been billeted at Penlee Point. I would have preferred to be more part of the community.'

Mildred Moore née Fromovitch

Mildred married her childhood sweetheart Eric and they had three children. She became a dress machinist on her return to London and, later in life, worked in an office where she learned to operate a computer. She is now widowed and has two grandchildren, one of whom attends JFS.

'Well, it showed you life that you didn't know anything about. I was born in Whitechapel, there was no lovely sea, no countryside. It was a different life altogether. It was wonderful. You get to know people, different ways of life, and you get friendly with the people and hear their life stories. They were lovely people, to open up their homes to us like that. It's a one-off, I think, Mousehole. It was a magic place, and how can you thank people. When you're a child, you don't realise what they're doing. I wish them all well.'

Jack Goldstein

Jack became an apprentice to a press photographer in Fleet Street, who was involved in processing and developing top secret war photographs, some of which he displayed on his bedroom wall. At 16 he joined the Merchant Navy and travelled the world for five years, after which he became a manager for 20 years in his sister's jewellery factory. He then spent 25 years as a taxi driver. He is widowed with two children and four grandchildren.

'It taught me a lot about people, and how some people were brought up and took it for granted and didn't have a clue how other people lived in other places. A lot of people loved the East End but it wasn't so much the bricks and the buildings and the views. What they loved was the type of people, because the people that were living in that area in those times were all on the same level and all having to live a kind of existence that a lot of people never knew about.

'Well, the people who lived in Mousehole, were naturally like they were, they didn't put on no airs and graces for us or didn't pretend nothing, just like us. They took us in as though we were family, even more so. Absolutely marvellous. Well, looking at it from a young boy's point of view, that was the best time of my life. I never had a good time until I went there. Of course, afterwards I met my wife, had my own children, and it was a whole different thing. But as a child, that was the best part of my life. I get emotional about it because it was something that really affected me, it was so good.'

Jose Kirby née Marks

Jose has remained in contact with several of the villagers and has visited Mousehole many times. After the war, she held several jobs including working as a secretary at a film studio. At the weekends she volunteered to work on the wards at the Jewish Hospital. Jose met her future husband in London but they married in the USA after emigrating there in 1955. They have two sons. Her last position in the USA was director of finance at a large hospital.

'Mousehole was the quiet time in my life, away from war and devastation. I will always be grateful to the people of Mousehole for their kindness and caring at a difficult time. I miss the saffron cake and Cornish pasties and blackberry pie and I hope to return once more if possible. Great, great memories. I just loved being there, I loved the people. Cornwall will always be in my heart. Most of the people who went there felt that way.'

Anita Cohen née Godfrey

Anita became a telephonist/receptionist, working for several companies, including 16 years at a Jewish charity. She married in 1968 and lives with her husband in Bournemouth. She visited Cornwall in 1976 and spent an enjoyable evening with Mr and Mrs Barnes in Penzance.

'I just enjoyed living there amongst the people. They were so kind, friendly and understanding, and I don't know what we would have done without them.'

Connie Stanton née Mellows

Connie married and had two children and six grandchildren, two of whom attend JFS. She became a solicitor's clerk and later a PA to a lawyer, but she has spent her entire life performing as an 'unpaid' singer, dancer and comedienne. She met her husband doing shows and together they have staged many performances to raise money for charity. They ran a group at one time called the Spotlighters and currently have a group called the Pantaloons, which tours the Jewish Care homes to perform for the elderly and frail residents.

'It probably gave me a sense of independence that I hadn't known before, because I had to look after myself. I was happy up until I knew what was happening with the war. For me, being in Mousehole was like a summer holiday at the seaside. It's a lovely place. I've been back once since. Strange, but I remembered the shop, I found the house. I went and spoke to the lady who now lives in the house who was very welcoming and insisted that I have tea with her, and she asked me to show her which was the bedroom that we had. And it was lovely, I thoroughly enjoyed it and in fact I'd like to go back again.'

Miriam Conway née Roar

Miriam became a hairdresser, married and had two children, six grandchildren, two step-grandchildren and one great-grandchild.

'They respected our religious beliefs and treated us as if we were their own. They didn't seem to judge us in any way, they just accepted us. I feel better for knowing them and I am grateful for everything they did for us and for showing us such warmth and hospitality.'

Arnold Powell formerly Podguszer

Arnold went to medical school in Sheffield and became a doctor. He married and emigrated with his wife to North America for five years, working first in Baltimore, then in a remote area of the Canadian prairies. His single-handed practice in Canada covered an immense area where he was the only doctor. He returned to London to set up home for his young family, which now included three children. Together with his wife, he developed Springdene Nursing and Care Homes, and since retirement from general practice he has embarked on a new career as an author. They have eight grandchildren.

'I think it affected my life for the better, strangely enough. It exposed me to a way of life that I might not have experienced. It was a very picturesque, pretty village. It was a part of my life that I thoroughly enjoyed. There was a dichotomy – on one side one felt homesick and one missed one's parents. On the other hand, it was such a lovely environment, a place where one could explore to one's heart's content. It was a wonderful period for a child to be left without parental supervision to explore and enjoy. But unfortunately when it came to giving you marks at an examination, it didn't count for very much. But so far as life was concerned it did, so maybe that didn't matter at the time.'

Betty Posner and Estelle Kaye née Esther Posner

After the war, Betty and Esther went to visit the Drews, who also visited them in London. Esther has recently been in touch with their daughter Margaret. Betty worked for the United Synagogue in the East End, largely in the Jewish Institute Advisory Centre. She now does charity work visiting Jewish patients at the Royal London Hospital. Esther became a teleprinter operator. She married and has two children and four grandchildren.

Betty: 'I felt this extraordinary excitement when I saw the evacuee appeal in *The Jewish Chronicle*. We had quite a happy time, we enjoyed it. The Cornish episode was the most vivid of our evacuation experiences, in terms of colour, after London's East End, to be near the sea and the views.'

Esther: 'They were very friendly, kind people. Living in Mousehole made us what we are today; independent and happy at what we have achieved in life, never forgetting our Jewishness and the hard life our parents had.'

Millie Shulman née Butler

Millie went into the fur trade, first as an apprentice then as a fur buyer. In 1964, she emigrated to the USA, where she worked in the fashion industry. With her first husband she owned and operated a successful fashion retail business. She has one daughter and two grandsons. After her husband died she remarried, and she now lives with her second husband in Florida.

'I maintained contact with the Tonkins and some of my villager friends. I have returned to Mousehole on many occasions and always with fond memories of the village and the villagers and the way they welcomed us with open arms and made us feel one of them. They could not have been kinder. The Tonkins used to come to London to visit me and we remained very close.

'The whole experience of evacuation was a warm one for me. On the one hand I had to leave my family, but the way in which I was welcomed and taken care of was quite fantastic. I often think of Mousehole and the years I spent there growing up, and I realise how lucky I was to be sent there away from the dangers of London during the war and to be looked after by such loving people. The whole village made us very welcome and were wonderful to us. I know of nobody in our group who was unhappy.'

Shirley Drazin née Spillman

Shirley maintained regular contact with her Mousehole school friend, Pat Jeffery (later Ellis), who has sadly died. She has continued to exchange occasional cards and letters with Pat's family. Shirley married and became a company secretary in finance.

'I loved the character of the place. It was lovely, wonderful. They accepted us with open arms and I was very well looked after. It showed me another side of life. It gave me a dimension and an insight which I would never have had otherwise. I never knew really about non-Jewish people to that extent and their way of life. And they had a code, as chapel-goers, which I think I picked up on. There is right and there is wrong, and there were consequences. The way you treat people, the way you are with people. It's there in the background: you never tell a lie, you mustn't steal. I would have got these from the Jewish religion, I'm sure, as well, but those kinds of values stuck with me.

'In that way it was a positive influence, but there were other downsides as well, when I came back. I was taken out of what would have been my normal environment, for a very long time and I didn't want to come back. The problem was when I returned to London, I found it emotionally and culturally difficult to readjust. But, yes, the experience itself was a very happy experience.'

Malcolm Hanover

Malcolm worked as a journalist with the *Sporting World* which closed after two years, and he then joined the *Greyhound Express* for 14 years. His third paper was the *Sporting Life* from which he retired in 1993 but was kept on as a freelance boxing writer until the paper closed in 1998. He then took up more freelance work with the Press Association until 2002. He still keeps up with his sporting interests. He lives with his brother Cyril.

'Well, it was a time when people got together. It was a wonderful time, a sad time, and they tried to make our sadness a bit lighter by being so caring, loving and kind. These villagers, who weren't moneyed people, some in business, some just ordinary fisher-folk. It was just the care, love and devotion they gave to these waifs and strays that had come over 300 miles from the East End of London.'

Elizabeth Barber née Vogel

Elizabeth, who emigrated to Victoria, Australia, had a sister Clara and a brother Henry, who were evacuated with her to Mousehole. She was not interviewed for this book, as the author was unable to trace her. However, in June 2008, she wrote the following letter of thanks to *The Cornishman*:

'To the wonderful people of Cornwall, and especially Penzance and Mousehole, I want to take this opportunity to thank you. I know it's over 70 years, but better late than never. My thanks to you for the shelter and comfort given to us Londoners, to the people who gave us their homes, to the British Legion, who made sure us kids had a lunch. My memories are of arriving in Penzance with my brother, my sister and a horde of other children, each with a label, a gasmask and little else. Mum and Dad and my baby brother were still in London. My brother, sister and I were separated and billeted in separate homes. The loving care we received, even though fear was prevalent was something I cannot describe. So, once again to you wonderful Cornish people, my friends, a heartfelt thank you!'

Pamela Fields née Barnes

Pamela spent many years working in advertising, sometimes appearing in television commercials. She married an Israeli in the early 1960s, spent two years living on a *kibbutz* in Israel and on her return to the UK resumed her advertising career. She divorced in the late 1960s at the time her parents moved to Cornwall. She returned to live with them and worked as a legal secretary in Penzance. On her return to London she worked for a car rental company and remarried, introducing her second husband to Cornwall. Tragically, Pamela's husband died suddenly in 1990, after which she did not return to Cornwall. Following the death of her husband Pamela worked for 15 years at *The Jewish Chronicle* until her retirement in 2005. Sadly, she lost her sister Lydia in July 2008, only nine months after losing her father also. Pamela has one niece, Karen.

'I've always been rather proud of seeing Cornwall on my birth certificate. In my heart I am Cornish, though really I am not, it was an accident of birth.

'Although it was wartime, we just all had these happy memories, because we weren't being bombarded, we didn't know drastic shortages, the people were fantastic to us and every day was sunny. There were just never any problems. Anti-Semitism did not rear its ugly head, they were welcoming from day one. The villagers all rallied round and for my mother, it was just a very happy period of her life.

'They just seemed to us such wonderful, welcoming people; they had no attitude, no pre-conceived ideas about anything, just a wonderful, wonderful community. Perhaps it is because of the geography of the place, its earthiness, its openness, the fact that it is as far as you can get away from London, fisher-folk who were very worldly in their outlook. I remember my grandfather saying, "They may not be bookwise, these people, but they certainly know." You could have very intelligent conversations with them, very wise people, full of humour as well, always ready to tell a joke, just wonderful, wonderful people. Just lovely, lovely memories!'

Maurice and the Scroll

The fate of Maurice who brought the scroll to Mousehole remains a mystery, for none of the evacuees remembers him, even though the scroll and the ark are remembered by his namesake, Maurice Podguszer. However, his story remains a symbol of the entire episode, for the children evacuated to Mousehole did indeed escape from 'out of the midst of fire' and the manner in which they were received and treated by the people of Mousehole was nothing short of a miracle.

AFTERWORD

It has been my hope in writing this book to bring to life an era in our history, to shine a light on the human stories behind the headlines, behind the facts, the figures and the government statistics. The Government Evacuation Scheme of World War Two is a well-known episode in British history, but, apart from the people who participated in it, the public's knowledge of it is generally limited to what they learn from the occasional documentary or from television news reports, where former evacuees speak briefly about their experiences. Rarely are these experiences explored in depth. It is this in-depth exploration that I have hoped to achieve in these pages.

There can be no doubt that the Government Evacuation Scheme, by removing children from the danger zones, helped to avoid the loss of life of thousands of people, and in this respect, it has to be considered a success. From an organisational perspective, the scheme was an unparalleled achievement. To have managed the movement of three and a half million civilians around the country, and within the context of a limited communication system, was astonishing.

A common criticism of the scheme, however, is that it did not take account of the thoughts and feelings of the individuals involved, nor of the human impact of such a massive movement of people. Planned along military lines, government officials appear not to have considered, for example, the emotional impact on the thousands of people gathered at railway stations, where children were torn away from their parents and taken to an unknown destination for an unknown period of time. Or of the trauma for children of being crowded into a room, selected by strangers and taken to an unfamiliar environment. Once billeted, there was no adequate supervision to ensure the children were properly cared for. The billeting of children brought to light a range of social difficulties and frictions, not least because of the different lifestyles of town and country people, but also differences along the lines of class and religion.

There was a lack of foresight, also, regarding the long-term impact on children of being separated from their parents and siblings, of disrupted family lives and missed educational opportunities. Many children experienced the greatest difficulty readjusting to their former lives; indeed, it is now recognised that a substantial proportion of evacuees have suffered life-long trauma as a direct consequence of their evacuation experiences.

It is against this backdrop that the evacuation of Jews' Free School to Mousehole is so remarkable, for it is difficult to imagine two more different groups of people. Certainly there were a few unhappy stories, but for the vast majority of evacuees and villagers, this was a story of love and, for many, of lifelong friendship. Why was this particular evacuation story such a success?

Despite their outward differences, there were many respects in which the villagers and evacuees were quite similar. For both communities, religious and family life were closely intertwined and a high value was placed on children and the elderly. Connected with their respective religions, there was for both, a rhythm to each day, each week and each season, throughout the year. And perhaps most significantly, both communities also had suffered, in their very different ways, significant tragedy and loss. As a consequence, there was, on both sides, a recognition of the preciousness of human life and a raw earthiness and sense of humour, which they had developed to help them cope. As so aptly expressed by Jack Goldstein, 'the people who lived in Mousehole were naturally like they were, they didn't put on no airs and graces for us or didn't pretend nothing, just like us'. In this respect, it seems almost that the people of Mousehole unconsciously recognised in the evacuees and their families a kindred spirit, making it easy for them to be accepted as part of the village. This story, then, is a triumph of the human spirit, and one which holds many lessons for today's divided world.

APPENDIX ONE

LIST OF CHILDREN KNOWN TO HAVE BEEN EVACUATED TO MOUSEHOLE WITH JEWS' FREE SCHOOL

NAME OF EVACUEE	NAME OF HOST	ADDRESS OF HOST
David AULMAN	Mr and Mrs Halse	Corner Shop
Lydia and Pamela BARNES	Miss Humphrys	Brookland Cottage, Foxes Lane
Aby BARUCH	Mrs Batten	St Clement's Terrace
Sheila and Woolf (Will) BRICK	Mrs C. de Rouffignac	Chapel Street
Millie BUTLER	Mrs Tonkin	Duck Street
Hilda CARL		
Philip and Rose CHAPMAN	Mrs Tregenza	Dumbarton Terrace
Peter COKER	Mrs Amelia Tregenza	Dumbarton Terrace
David, Frances and Michael COHEN	Mrs Richards	Raginnis Hill
Gloria COHEN	Mrs Osborne	Raginnis Hill
Ruth COLEMAN		
Max DAVIS	Mr and Mrs Praed	Gurnick Street
Maurice DELEW		
Mark DESWARTE		
Harry FIREMAN and brother		
Betty and Doris FISHMAN	Mrs Waters	Mount View, Paul
Daniel FRANKEL	Mrs Janie Ladner	Mill Pool Terrace
Jacky FREEMAN		
Desiree and Elaine FRISCHMAN	Ernest and Lizzie Ladner	Brook Street
Frances and Irene FROMOVITCH	Wright Matthews	Matthews' Farm, Commercial Road
	Miss Oliver	Commercial Road
Mildred FROMOVITCH	Mr and Mrs Warren	Commercial Road
	Mr W. Jeffery	South Cliff
	Miss Oliver	Commercial Road
Ronney GLAZER	Mr Luther Pender	Raginnis Hill
	Mr Thomas	Raginnis Hill
Anita GODFREY	Mr and Mrs Phillips	Oakland Cottage, Paul
Irvine GODFREY	Mr and Mrs Taylor	Todden Coath Farm, Paul
Evelyn and Vera GOLDSTEIN	Mrs Minnie Harvey	Waterbury, Duck Street
Jack GOLDSTEIN	Joe and Lylie Madron	Raginnis Hill
	Mr and Mrs G. Richards	Duck Street
Barnie GREEN		
Cyril HANOVER	Mr and Mrs Sampson	Keigwin Place
Malcolm HANOVER	Mr and Mrs Sampson	Keigwin Place
	Charles Tregenza	Tavis Vor, The Parade
Marion HEWSON	Mrs Trembath	Regent Terrace
Clarence HOFFMAN		
Jack JOSEPH		
Betty KONYON	Mrs Katie Harry	Cherry Garden Street
Deborah KONYON	Mrs Blewett	Cherry Garden Street
Ena KOSKY	Mrs Minnie Harvey	Waterbury, Duck Street
Ted LABOFSKY	Mr and Mrs Percy Harvey	Floriana, Chapel Street
Gerald LANDEAU		
Eddie LAZARUS	Mrs Matthews	Arosfa, The Parade

Harold LAZEFSKY	Mrs Janie Ladner	Mill Pool Terrace
Lew LAZARUS	Mr (?Dr) Sharpe	?Paul Lane
Solly LEDERMAN	Mr and Mrs Bill Pomeroy	Wayside
David LEVENE	Mr and Mrs Harding	King's Arms, Paul
Frances LEVENE	Mr and Mrs Harry	The Wharf
Ralph LEVENE	Mrs Lugg	Wellington Place
Joyce and Maureen LEVENE	Mr and Mrs Thomas	Wellington House
Danny MACINTOSH	Mr and Mrs Richard Ladner	Chapel Street
Jose MARKS	Mr and Mrs Madron	Vivian Terrace
	Mrs Trembath	Regent Street
Lenny MARKS	Mr and Mrs Johns	Gurnick Street
Connie MELLOWS	Mrs Rose	Cave Lane
Betty and Margaret MERRITT	Mrs Jukes	The Parade
Alan and Thomas PARIS	Kate and Charlie Jeffery	Fore Street
Monty PIRELLY and brother	Mr and Mrs J. Madron	Raginnis Hill
Ralph PLOTS	Mrs Amelia Tregenza	Dumbarton Terrace
Arnold, Maurice and Michael PODGUSZER	Mr & Mrs Crompton	Penlee Point
Betty and Esther POSNER	Johnny and Pauline Drew	St Clement's Terrace
Celia REIDERMAN	Mr and Mrs Waters	St Clement's Terrace
		Duck Street
Rosita REIDERMAN	Mr and Mrs Waters	St Clement's Terrace
Lily ROAR	Mrs Trembath	Portland Place
	Mr and Mrs Eddy	Commercial Road
Miriam ROAR	Mrs Trembath	Portland Place
	• Mr and Mrs Harvey	Commercial Road
Alfred ROTTENBERG	• Percy Laity	Fore Street
David SACHS	Mr and Mrs Harris	Wesley Square
Ida and Max SELNER	Mrs Webber	Vivian Terrace
Betty SHAFFER		
Ronnie SMOLOVITCH		
Shirley SPILLMAN	Mr and Mrs Ladner	Vanguard House, The Cliff
Israel STEINHART	Mrs Pollard	Coronation Villas
Phyllis and Sylvia SWAGER	Mrs Swager	Gurnick Street
Eric TEJADA		
Leila TOUCHINSKY		
Clara VOGEL		
Elizabeth VOGEL		
Henry VOGEL		
Jean and Wally WARBERG	Mrs Emmie Williams	The Parade
Bernie WARMAN	Mr and Mrs Johns	Gurnick Street
Frederica WHITE	Mr and Mrs Waters	The Parade
Peggy WHITE	Mr and Mrs Williams	Dumbarton Terrace
Sidney and Shirley WOOLF	?Mrs Cobb/Mrs Lobb	?Regent Terrace
Betty and John WRIGHT	Mrs Bennett	Fore Street
J. William (Billy) WRIGHT	Mrs Blewett	The Parade
	Mr and Mrs Oliver	Duck Street

The following older siblings visited Mousehole and in some instances stayed during the Blitz: Betty Butler, Lily Frankel, Ada and Marie Fromovitch, Rene Glazer, Ernie and Marie Hanover, Renee Labofsky, Alfred Marks and Gloria Podguszer.

? Actor/Comedian?
TV/Radio

APPENDIX TWO

THE TORAH RETURNS TO PENZANCE

Courtesy *The Jewish Chronicle*

ROSH HASHANA

Issued by the Joint Emergency Committee for Jewish Religious Education and by "The Jewish Chronicle" in collaboration

SEPTEMBER, 1941 TISHRI, 5702

A TALK ON THE HOLY DAYS

The Lessons They Teach

There is an old story of a king whose son, once full of promise, left his father's kingdom and going abroad lived a wild and useless life.

Later he became ill and his thoughts then turned homewards. He felt doubtful, however, whether his father whom he had wronged greatly would receive him, but he remembered his loving-kindness and plucked up courage to send him a message saying that he was laid low with sickness and longed to be at home again.

The king, who was merciful, rejoiced at this message and sent word saying, "Tell him to come but a little way and I myself will go and meet him."

This little tale is full of meaning for this solemn time. It is a parable and, as some of you know, a parable is a story which enshrines a great truth.

Rosh Hashana

Rosh Hashana, our Jewish New Year, which commences next Sunday, is the beginning of the Ten Days of Penitence which are a preparation for the holiest day in our Hebrew Calendar—Yom Kippur, the Day of Atonement. The Rabbis teach us that if we are truly sorry for our misdeeds and ask God to help us to do better, He will show us the right way. It is as if He came to meet us, for He gives us strength to overcome our faults.

This Rosh Hashana will seem very different from New Years in the past. Some of you may not be able to attend a service and hear the blowing of the Shofar; but you will be able to read many of the beautiful prayers which belong to this solemn time. The Shofar is a reminder, an "Alert" to warn us, as do the prayers, of our great responsibilities as Jews and Jewesses, and as citizens of this beautiful, free country.

New Year, which is also called the Day of Memorial, tells us to think about our conduct. It bids us to consider whether our behaviour is of such a kind that it will bring happiness to our parents and to the community to which we belong. Have we been absolutely truthful in thought and word and deed and are we living so that the people can feel that Judaism is a great and noble religion because the children who are brought up in it are unselfish and helpful, upright in all that they do, of cheerful comradeship to their friends and neighbours and especially to the kind foster-parents who are granting them hospitality?

"Young Ambassadors"

It may not have been always easy for young Londoners to accustom themselves to country life and country ways, but you, like the boys and girls who have crossed the Atlantic, can be "young ambassadors," encouraging good feeling and better understanding between town and country and between Jews and their fellow citizens.

This is, of course, a great task, but it is a task which nobody must shirk. When our ancestors were rescued from Egyptian slavery, God told them through Moses that they were to be a "kingdom of priests and a holy nation." Later came the message through one of the greatest of the prophets, that they were called to be God's witnesses and His servant. This meant that the glorious duty would fall upon them of teaching the world about God and goodness.

Our part is to show that we are not unworthy of this heritage. It may be only a small part to play, but if we take our share quietly and not priggishly we can be of use. Some of you may have heard the story of the discontented taper. The taper felt sore because it could only show a tiny light and it wanted to throw out brilliant beams like one of the great lamps in the lighthouse. One night a big storm was blowing up but the taper kept alight and presently the lighthouse keeper took it aloft and with the little light kindled all the great lamps which then shone out to sea and protected the ships from foundering on the hidden rocks. The

Continued on page 3, foot of col. 2

A Message from the Chief Rabbi

My dear young friends,

Once again you are spending Rosh Hashana and Yom Kippur away from home. But I am sure that you will all do your utmost to keep these Solemn Festivals as you did when you were happily living with your parents, and that you will attend a Synagogue Service wherever it is possible for you to do so.

When I think of all the thousands of Jewish evacuee children going to these new places of worship, I am reminded of the old Rabbi who said that every Kol Nidre eve, as he entered the Synagogue, a Voice from Heaven greeted him with the words, "Welcome to your Father's House." Such a greeting awaits every one of you as you enter your House of Prayer during the High Festivals. Not only because your father, and his father before him, wished you, as their child, to be truly Jewish in Faith and in the observance of the *Yomim Noroim*, but because God, the Father of us all, blesses with His Divine Presence any place in which His children come together to pour out their hearts unto Him in prayer. And our Heavenly Father loves with a special love the sound of prayer that issues from the lips of the young, if they call upon Him in truth. These Sacred Days remind you how in the past year you have many times done things that you should *not* have done, and failed to do many things that you *should* have done. We must all be filled with sorrow and regret because of our failings and shortcomings.

May God who lovingly forgives all who are truly sorry for their sins, hear your prayers and fulfil your heart's desire. May He send victory and peace to our beloved country, and inscribe you and your dear ones in the Book of Life for a Happy New Year.

J. H. Hertz

Chief Rabbi,

4, Creechurch Place, Aldgate.

Ellul 11, 5701.

THE NEW YEAR: IN BIBLE TIMES AND AFTER

The New Year Festival, Rosh Hashana, holds a very high place in Israel's calendar. Next to the Day of Atonement (Yom Kippur) it is the most solemn day of the year when we should attune our hearts and minds to serious thoughts and reflections on our spiritual and moral well-being.

"A new year," say the Rabbis, "should be the starting-point of a new life." There is thus something characteristic about the Jewish idea of a New Year. While passing across the threshold of time, from one year to another, we should do so not in riotous revelry but in religious resolve to do better with the new than we did with the old, to make amends therein where amends are needed.

New Year's Day, therefore, appropriately begins the season of renewal, repentance, and the return of the Jew to God. Fundamental religious ideas underlie the various phases of Rosh Hashana. The inspired voice of the Bible and of post-Biblical literature reveals and illumines the nature and importance of this Festival in the life of Israel.

The Joy of Religion

Rosh Hashana is celebrated by Jewish communities all over the world for two days. It begins in the evening before the first day of Tishri, the seventh month of the religious year. Its characteristic symbol is the Shofar, the ram's horn. The Bible makes reference to it in these words: "In the seventh month, on the first day of the month, shall be a solemn rest unto you, a memorial of blowing of trumpets, a holy convocation." And again, "In the seventh month, on the first day of the month, ye shall have a holy convocation: ye shall do no servile work; it is a day of blowing of trumpets unto you."

In Palestine, in ancient times, Israel thronged to Jerusalem, the religious centre, to celebrate the Festival. "And when the seventh month came, and the children of Israel were in the cities, the people gathered themselves together as one man to Jerusalem."

In the time of Ezra, the reading of the Torah characterised and enhanced the observance of the great day. "And all the people gathered themselves together, as one man, into the street that was before the water gate; and they spoke to Ezra the scribe to bring the Book of the Law of Moses, which the Lord had commanded to Israel; and Ezra the priest brought the Law before the congregation both of men and women, and all that could hear with understanding, on the first day of the seventh month."

We are further told that on that occasion the people were moved to tears by what they heard. The imperishable words of the Divine Law uttered by the great leader warmed their hearts and filled them with a deep consciousness of the solemnity of the day.

But solemn and awe-inspiring as was the day it was not to lack the message of gladness. It was meant to be also a day of joy, the joy of a deep religious experience. Therefore Ezra tried to calm the people's grief and to restore the festive spirit. "This day is holy unto the Lord your God; mourn not, nor weep. . . . Go your way, eat the fat, and drink the sweet, and send portions unto them for whom nothing is prepared; for this day is holy unto our Lord; neither be ye sad; for the joy of the Lord is your strength."

The Clarion Call

In Scripture times the Shofar was used on all important occasions to announce great events. It announced the New Moon and solemn feasts. It proclaimed the year of release. It was also frequently employed as the signal-horn of war, as the alert in time of approaching danger. As the Prophet said: "Shall the horn be blown in a city, and the people not be afraid?"

On Rosh Hashana the shrill and heart-searching sounds of the Shofar evoke the penitent mood. A medieval Rabbi has suggested many reasons for the sounding of the Shofar on New Year's Day: the Creation, the Binding of Isaac, the Revelation on Sinai, the proclamation of God's kingship, the final Day of Judgment, the Resurrection, and the Messianic Redemption. All these sublime ideas are associated in the Bible with the Shofar.

But the famous Maimonides saw a higher purpose in the Shofar. He writes: "Besides its Scriptural object, the New Year's trumpet has a deep meaning. It says: 'Awake, ye that sleep, up, ye that slumber; examine your actions and repent.'" The Shofar sounds are an alarm to the whole House of Israel to rally its ranks, to strengthen itself for the fight against the foes that assail it on every side. They speak of the history of the Jew. They tell of the martyrdom of Israel's sons and daughters in ages gone by. But they also speak of the present. They echo the cry of the poignant pain of brother Jews suffering under the heavy yoke of oppression and tyranny. They summon us to rally round the ancient standard that has encouraged us in many a previous struggle.

Never was there need of a greater demonstration of Jewish solidarity than to-day. Never was it more urgent that we should

Continued on page 4, col. 1

THE TORAH RETURNS TO PENZANCE

Out of the Midst of the Fire

There is a Sefer Torah to-day at Mousehole, only five miles from that spot called Land's End where this island of Britain falls into the Atlantic Ocean.

Mousehole is near Penzance, and years ago Jews lived in Penzance. One shop in the town still has a mezuzah on its door, though it has been in Gentile hands for generations. On the other side of Penzance is Marazion, and here too you will find evacuee Jews to-day.

How did the Sefer Torah get to Mousehole?

Ask Maurice. Last Pesach he was thirteen years old, and he had his Barmitzvah at the Great Synagogue. He was a little chap for his age, and he was rather attracted by the little Sefer Torah from which he read his portion. The Warden had laughingly commented on it.

The Warden had more to say on a certain night last May, though no longer laughingly. Neither will Maurice forget that night quickly. Both his parents were killed by the blast of a bomb in the street. Fortunately he did not know it at the time. But a great feeling of horror crept over him as he saw the Great Synagogue, *his* Shool, burning. He must never let *his* Sefer Torah be destroyed.

* * *

"Stop him. He's mad," the firemen shouted.

But they couldn't stop Maurice. The Ark was ablaze, and men and women shut their eyes, unable to bear the thought of the little nipper being roasted alive.

A miracle. Maurice was in the street again, crawling on his hands and knees, and pushing in front of him, without letting it touch the ground, *his* Sefer Torah. It was the only *one* that had been saved. How he had achieved it, even Maurice couldn't tell you.

What was to be done with it? The United Synagogue wanted to send it to a safe deposit in the country. "Let us have it," asked the Joint Emergency Committee. "We often get requests from our teachers for the use of Sifre Torah in reception areas."

And so the Sefer Torah found a temporary home in the basement of Woburn House.

* * *

A new complication. Maurice would not part from the Sefer Torah. He had nothing left to live for. His parents, his home, all had gone. That is why for days you would find Maurice hanging round Woburn House. At night he would sleep in the shelter in the basement. He refused to be taken away. How he managed to live was a mystery.

Some weeks ago a message came to the Joint Emergency Committee. The teacher at Mousehole needed a Sefer Torah.

"Will you allow yourself to be evacuated to Mousehole, Maurice, if we send your Sefer Torah there?"

"Oh, yes sir. And please, sir, let me take it there myself."

So the problem of the Sefer Torah and of Maurice's evacuation were settled at one and the same time.

* * *

You should have seen the excitement on Maurice's face when he was seated in the taxi, clutching the Sefer Torah. At Paddington Station he would not allow the porter to touch that brown paper parcel.

"Wot is it, a time-bomb?" one porter jokingly remarked.

The whole way to Mousehole Maurice sat rigidly in his corner seat, the parcel held tightly in his hands. Only when it was safely in the newly-made Ark at the School in Mousehole did Maurice utter a deep sigh as if to say, "I can breathe again at last."

* * *

They read from the Sefer Torah for the first time on Tisha b'Av.

"When thou art in tribulation, and all these things come upon thee, even in the latter days, if thou turn to the Lord thy God, and shalt be obedient unto His voice (for the Lord thy God is a merciful God), He will not forsake thee, neither destroy thee, nor forget the covenant of thy fathers which He sware unto them."

And they know now in Mousehole that the blessing and the promise will be fulfilled.

APPENDIX THREE

LETTER TO THE AUTHOR REGARDING THE FATE OF HER AUNT SONYA

	SERVICE INTERNATIONAL DE RECHERCHES
	INTERNATIONAL TRACING SERVICE
	INTERNATIONALER SUCHDIENST

Bad Arolsen, 20th September 2000
gei/Hy

Re: Your inquiry concerning your family members
Mr Yoschi WEINBERGER, born around 1900, Ms Sonya SMETANA,
born in 1927 and Mrs Bertha SMETANA nee WEINBERGER,
born in Vienna on 9.1.1896

Dear Ms Soyinka,

referring to your previous letters we advise you that based on the
particulars given by you a check was made of the documentary material available here.

The following particulars could be taken from the records available
here:

     SMETANA, Sonia, Nationality: Austrian
     (no further personal data)

     and

     SMETANA, Berthe, Nationality: Austrian
     (no further personal data)

     were confined to Camp Drancy by the "Befehlshaber der
     Sicherheitspolizei und des Sicherheitsdienstes Frankreich"
     (date not indicated) and transferred to Concentration Camp
     Auschwitz on September 2, 1942.
     Category: "Jüdinnen"

SONYA'S ENTRY ON THE YAD VASHEM WEBSITE

יד ושם
Yad Vashem
Яд Вашем

Full Record Details for Smetana Sonia

Source	Namentliche Erfassung der oesterreichischen Holocaustopfer, Dokumentationsarchiv des oesterreichischen Widerstandes (Documentation Centre for Austrian Resistance), Wien
Last Name	SMETANA
First Name	SONIA
Key to Transport	Transport 27 from Drancy to Auschwitz on 02/09/1942
Type of material	List of victims from Austria
Language	German
Victims' status end WWII	Perished

APPENDIX FOUR

GERALDINE UNDERELL: A TRIBUTE
1911–2003

Geraldine Underell lived in Mousehole during the 1940s, becoming a Fellow of the Royal Photographic Society in 1941. At that time she was living in Florence Place, an address she shared with her husband, also a Fellow of the Society. Strangely, no one in Mousehole remembers her husband, and it seems likely, therefore, that he was away at war, possibly killed in action, since there are no further records of him at the Society after 1947. The Society records show that in the 1950s and early 1960s, Geraldine appears to have lived in London, but moved to Yorkshire in the late 1960s. She then went to live in the USA in the early 1970s but it is not known how long she remained there. Her final address was in Crail, Fife, Scotland, where she died in 2003.

Geraldine is remembered by many of the older residents of Mousehole. Writing in connection with two of her pictures, Donald Waters describes her as:

> A pleasant type of person, and devoted to her photographic art. She would often oblige with a snapshot of this or that to people, and so, outside of more serious work, and at a time when cameras were not an 'everymans' possession, she provided something of a time capsule of the various facets of everyday living in a small Cornish village.

A young Margaret Perry remembers admiring Geraldine so much that she tried to emulate her when taking photographs of Mousehole during the late 1940s. It was Margaret who discovered Geraldine's wonderful photographic record of Mousehole entitled *A Cornish Portfolio*. The book is undated, and does not include the name of a publisher, therefore, it appears to have been a private collection which did not resurface until after Geraldine's death. Margaret's copy of the book is in pristine condition, looking as if it has never been used. The author managed to track down one further copy of the book, in equally new condition, to a book dealer in Scotland. The collection of photographs in Geraldine's book beautifully captures a particular era in Mousehole history, and it has been a pleasure to include some of these photographs in this book.

In her foreword to *A Cornish Portfolio*, Geraldine describes Mousehole as a 'photographer's paradise'. She recalls having spent many happy years in Cornwall as a child, some members of her family having been artists in the Newlyn and St Ives schools. She turned to photography, rather than painting, which she realised was a way of 'drawing in light'. She brought two small cottages overlooking the harbour in Mousehole and turned the cellar of one cottage into a darkroom, where she processed her own photographs. She writes:

> Oh the joy of waking up early in the morning and looking out of the window and seeing the morning light acting like a spotlight on the busy fishermen in their boats preparing to go to sea, or shining into the alleyways between the cottages and picking out the children scurrying to school or if early enough, a quick paddle before school. The girls and boys always provided wonderful natural models at all times, especially as the harbour was their playground [...] The older natives being so used to the local artist in their midst paid no heed to the camera.

It had been Geraldine's intention to spend her life in Mousehole, but she became disenchanted when the village became transformed by the invasion of visitors. She remained in the village for a while after the war, developing the use of diagonal composition, which would come to identify her work, but eventually left to study the latest techniques in colour photography. Her foreword ends with these words:

> They say you should never go back to a place you loved when young. And how right they are. Thank goodness I have so many pictures to remind me of those days. If there is a moral in this let it be that if you have a personal photographic paradise then photograph it while it exists, in years to come it may be gone. If it has a name like 'Mousehole' I think it best to avoid it, you'll never want to share it with the hordes that descend on it.

Let us hope that Geraldine would approve of the manner in which her wonderful photographic memories are now being shared.

APPENDIX FIVE

THE SPRINGBOARD EDUCATION TRUST

The work of Geraldine Underell is beautifully complemented by the atmospheric photographs of the old Jewish East End, reproduced from the books of the Springboard Education Trust, with the kind permission of editors Aumie and Michael Shapiro.

Established in London in 1979, the Springboard Education Trust set itself the task to produce stimulating, educational programmes for the elderly and disadvantaged. The success of the programme encouraged Springboard to extend its innovative approach by producing audio-visual and video educational programmes for teenagers and adults.

Today, Springboard's programmes, together with its series of *Memory* books and other printed materials, are in use in many parts of the world, notably in the UK, Israel and the USA.

ACKNOWLEDGEMENTS

I have been quite overwhelmed by the huge amount of help, encouragement and support I have received from a wide range of people who have taken a keen interest in my project. This book would never have come about had I not met Marian Harris in Mousehole in May 2008, for it was Marian who first told me about this extraordinary story. Since our first meeting, she has been an endless source of information and encouragement. I was first introduced to Marian by the wonderful Greta Lewis, who sadly died in January 2009, just two weeks after I began my research. I am deeply indebted to both of them.

My thanks go also to the many other people in the locality who have been so extremely helpful and supportive. Margaret Perry, a Mousehole historian, has provided me with invaluable information, as well as photographs and postcards of old Mousehole, and has most generously acted as my consultant on all matters Mousehole. It was through Margaret that I first learned of the work of photographer Geraldine Underell, some of whose atmospheric photos of Mousehole appear in these pages. Margaret also introduced me to the wonderful Steph Haxton, whose illustrations add so much to this book, and I am most grateful to both of them. Judy Joel, owner of The Little Picture Gallery in Mousehole, and creator of an interactive CD on Mousehole history, has kindly copied and sent me photographs which villagers have passed to her. Frank Granger, a former Mayor of Penzance who originates from London's Jewish East End and has had a life-long love affair with Mousehole, has also lent his support.

I am most grateful also to Peter Waverly, another Cornish historian, who has carried out a search for me of newspapers of the era, and has unearthed some fascinating articles, many of which are quoted in this book. I was able to gain access to newspaper stories of the times through the Cornwall Centre at Redruth whose staff, led by Kim Cooper, were most helpful. Members of staff of the Cornwall Record Office, in Truro, most especially Sophie Trembath and Deborah Tritton, have also been most helpful in locating and sending me copies of archival documents and in helping me with my own searches when I visited them.

Professor Charles Thomas, first Director of the Institute of Cornish Studies from 1971 to 1991, showed great interest and provided some useful contacts. Garry Tregidga, Assistant Director of the Institute of Cornish Studies and Director of the Cornish Audio Visual Archive (CAVA) loaned me recording equipment to record the stories of the Mousehole villagers, and has given much support and advice. At his suggestion, copies of all my recordings have been placed in CAVA so that they can be accessible for future educational and research purposes. Through Garry, I was also put in touch with Mary Vidal who, to my utter amazement, offered to transcribe the recordings I had made on a completely voluntary basis. Transcription is a lengthy, time-consuming and skilled task which I could never have done myself, so in a very real sense, this project would never have come to fruition without Mary's hard work and dedication. I am deeply grateful to her.

Keith Pearce, co-author of *The Lost Jews of Cornwall*, has given me some useful insights into the Jewish history of Cornwall. Members of Kehillat Kernow, the current Jewish community in Cornwall, have shown great interest in my project, most especially Pat Lipert who kindly published an article in their newsletter. *The Cornishman,* the newspaper serving West Cornwall, has kindly published two articles about my project in January and September 2009, and BBC Radio Cornwall broadcast an interview with me in October 2009.

One of my primary sources of information has been the current JFS, in the person of David Lerner, Public Relations and Alumni Officer. David has shown a great deal of interest and enthusiasm from the outset, and has given me a number of useful contacts. He also offered to host a reunion at the new JFS site in Kenton, which took place on 25 October 2009. Through David, I also learned of the work of Dr Gerry Black, a Jewish historian, from whose books on the history of JFS and on Jewish London I have quoted extensively in Chapters Two and Three. Many wonderful photographs of the Jewish East End are contained in the Springboard *Memory* book series, edited by Aumie and Michael Shapiro. Aumie not only gave me permission to use some of these photographs, but also offered useful help and advice on the Jewish East End. Some of the archive articles from *The Jewish Chronicle* proved difficult to obtain, so my particular thanks go to Sue Greenberg at the *JC* who helped me to track down the article entitled *The Torah returns to Penzance.* Members of staff at several Nottinghamshire libraries and the British Library have also helped in obtaining copies of *JC* articles, as did my friend, Shirley.

I have received invaluable assistance from James Roffey, Founder of the Evacuee Reunion Association, and from Martin L. Parsons, Director of the Research Centre for Evacuee and War Child Studies at Reading University. Dr Parsons is the foremost expert on war-time evacuation and has generously offered advice on evacuation issues. Through the staff at Ely Museum, I was able to contact Christina Rex and Dennis Adams, both of whom have written about the original JFS evacuation to Ely and they have both been most encouraging.

Considerable thanks go to my publishers DB Publishing (originally Breedon Books), particularly Steve Caron, Managing Director; Michelle Harrison, who signed me up; Alex Morton, Publishing Manager; Steven Brown, Designer; Jon Hoggard, Editor; and Jo Rush, Marketing and Publicity, all of whom have shown great commitment to and faith in my project. I have been particularly impressed by their patience in answering my endless questions and by their flexibility in allowing me huge input to the final layout and design.

Of course, I could not have completed this project without the encouragement and support of my family, my husband, Kayode, and my children, Lara, Bambo and Alex. Particular thanks go to Alex who proofread the book for me, and in so doing learned much of his own history. My brother Steve and his wife Sue have made me very welcome in their home whenever I have visited Cornwall to conduct my research, and Steve has shown endless patience in downloading my recordings and in resolving the many technical issues about which I had no clue. A warm thank you goes to my wonderful grand-children, Joshua, Faith, Joel and Leon, who have provided me with hours of laughter and fun in between the hard work of writing this book.

Finally, my biggest thanks go to the Mousehole villagers and former evacuees whose names are listed at the front of the book and who gave me so much of their time to share with me their memories, as well as their precious photographs. Their stories are told in these pages.

CREDITS

The following authors have kindly given me permission to quote from their books:

Margaret Perry, Percy Harvey and Lily Polgrean Grose for their books on Mousehole. Sylvia Johns has given permission to quote from the book of her mother, Nettie Pender.

Dr Gerry Black for his books on Jewish London and the history of JFS and Dennis Adams for his document on the first JFS evacuation.

Martin Parsons for his books on evacuation.

It has not been possible to trace the copyright owners of *The Cry of a Bird*, by Dorothy Yglesias and *Harbour Village*, by Leo Tregenza, as the publisher for both books, William Kimber, no longer exists.

Permission to quote from archival documents, newspapers and radio broadcasts has kindly been given by:

Deborah Tritton of the Cornwall Record Office.

Jacqui Walls, Editor of *The Cornishman*.

Richard Best, Editor of *The West Briton*.

Richard Burton, Managing Editor of *The Jewish Chronicle*.

David Lerner, for the use of the JFS website, including the Evacuation News Sheets.

Gary Haines, Whitechapel Gallery, for the Avram Stencl poem at the beginning of Chapter Two.

Margaret Perry for the poem at the beginning of Chapter Nine.

BBC Radio 4, for the *Thought for the Day* broadcast of 29 July 2009 by Rabbi Laura Janner-Klausner.

Permission to reproduce photographs has kindly been given by:

English Heritage, for the aerial photograph of Mousehole.

Aumie Shapiro, for the photographs of the Jewish East End. For more about Springboard, see Appendix 5.

Tower Hamlet Archives, for the Back Yards photo in Aumie Shapiro's book.

Dr Parsons for the photograph depicting the evacuation of Robert Montefiore School, reproduced from his book, *I'll Take That One*. Every effort has been made, unsuccessfully, to find the original copyright holder of the photo.

Andrew Ball for the photograph of the author.

Despite all efforts to trace the copyright owners of Geraldine Underell's work, this has proved impossible and I therefore give tribute to her in Appendix 4.

Credit for the many personal photographs reproduced in the book is given alongside each photograph and in the list of illustrations.

BIBLIOGRAPHY

CORNWALL AND MOUSEHOLE

Brock, Elizabeth, *The Jewish Community of Penzance, A brief account of their history*, Elizabeth Brock, 1998

CAVA, Cornish Audio Visual Archive, Institute of Cornish Studies, University of Exeter, Director, Dr Garry Tregidga, www.cava.studies.org

The Cornishman archive articles dated 1939–41, 1951, 1961, 1967–68

The Cornwall Record Office, Truro
- BT-188-1, Truro Evacuation Records, Unaccompanied Children, 1
- BT-672, Truro Evacuation Records, Evacuee Record Form
- CC1-23-2, Cornwall County Council, Minutes, Civil Defence Committee, 1939–1945
- DC-PEN-192/193, Penzance Borough, Minutes, Welfare and Evacuation Committee, 1941–1947
- DCWP 209/210, West Penwith Rural District Council, 1939–1940
- SPAU1-2-4, Mousehole County Primary School, Admission Records, 1940–1946
- SR-PAU-4-3, Paul Church Town Council School, log book, 1933–1950
- SRA-PENZ-5-7, Penzance County School for Boys (later Penzance Grammar School for Boys), Admission Records, 1935–1941
- SRA-PENZ-8-6, Penzance County School for Girls (later Penzance Grammar School for Girls), Admission Records, 1938–1941
- X866/84, Evacuation: Why and How? Issued from the Lord Privy Seal's Office, July 1939

The Golowan Trust, *The Mousehole Trail, A Walk around Mousehole and to Paul*, The Golowan Trust, 2006

The GPO Classic Collection, Thirties Britain, *The Saving of Bill Blewitt* (sic), volume 2, VHS

Grose, Lily Polgrean, *Mousehole Childhood, 1928–1950*, Landfall Publications, 2008

Harvey, Percy, *Mousehole alias Porthennis, Chronicle of a Seafaring Community*, privately published manuscript, 1994, available at Morrab Library, Penzance

Ince, Catharine, editor, *Life in Cornwall 1939–42, Extracts from the West Briton Newspaper*, Truran, 2001

Lewington, Sue, *Mousehole*, Truran, 2003

Mousehole Carnival 2008, *Mousehole Heritage*, an interactive CD researched and compiled by Judy Joel, 2008, available from The Little Picture Gallery, Mousehole, 01736 732877, www.littlepicturesmousehole.co.uk

Pearce, Keith, and Fry, Helen, editors, *The Lost Jews of Cornwall: from the Middle Ages to the Nineteenth Century*, Redcliffe Press, 1999

Pender, John J., *A Mousehole Man's Life Story*, Sylvia Johns, 1982

Pender, Nettie Mann, *Mousehole, History and Recollections*, Sylvia Johns, 1970

Perry, Margaret, E., *Mousehole, A Brief History*, Margaret E. Perry, Newlyn, 1998

Sagar-Fenton, Michael, *About Penzance, Newlyn and Mousehole*, Bossiney Books, 2000

Stevenson, William, edited by Margaret Perry, *Growing up with Boats*, William Stevenson, 2001

Tregenza, Douglas, *Departed Days, Mousehole Remembered*, Truran, 1984

Tregenza, Leo, *Harbour Village, Yesterday in Cornwall*, William Kimber & Co., 1977

Underell, Geraldine, *A Cornish Portfolio*, privately published, undated

The West Briton, archive articles dated 1939–1940

Yglesias, Dorothy, *The Cry of a Bird*, William Kimber & Co., 1964

JFS AND THE JEWISH EAST END

Adams, Dennis, A., *Exodus to Ely, the Evacuation of Jewish Women and Children from Spitalfields in London to the Isle of Ely during the Second World War 1939–1945*, privately published in 2001, obtainable from Ely Museum

Black, Dr Gerry, *Jewish London, An Illustrated History*, Breedon Books, 2003

Black, Dr Gerry, *J.F.S., The History of the Jews' Free School, London since 1732*, Tymsder Publishing, 1998

Glinert, Ed., *East End Chronicles*, Allen Lane, Penguin, 2005

The Jewish Chronicle, archive articles dated 1939–1941, 1984, 1989, 2007

JFS alumni website, Alumni Officer, David Lerner, www.jfsalumni.com
- History of JFS
- Memories
- *Evacuation News Sheets*, 1940-44

Lerner, David, editor, *JFS Alumni*, April 2008 and September 2009 editions

Lichtenstein, Rachel, *On Brick Lane*, Penguin Books, 2007

Powell, Arnold, *Raging Against Time,* AuthorHouse, 2007

Shapiro, Aumie and Michael, editors, *Guide Map to the Jewish East End,* Springboard, 1985

Shapiro, Aumie and Michael, editors, *Memories of the Jewish East End,* Springboard, 1985

Shapiro, Aumie and Michael, editors, *More Memories,* Springboard, 1987

Shapiro, Aumie and Michael, editors, *When We Were Young,* Springboard, 1988

Shapiro, Aumie and Michael, editors, *Jewish Eastenders,* Springboard, 1992

Shapiro, Aumie and Michael, editors, *Jewish Londoners,* Springboard, 1993

Shapiro, Aumie and Michael, editors, *The Jewish East End, Then and Now,* Springboard, 1994

Shapiro, Aumie and Michael, editors, *The Jewish East End,* Springboard, 2003

Shapiro, Aumie, *Going down the Jewish East End with Aumie Shapiro*, dvd, Springboard Education Trust, 2006

WORLD WAR TWO EVACUATION

Evacuee Reunion Association, Chief Executive, James Roffey, www.evacuees.org.uk

Kushner, Tony, *Horns and Dilemmas: Jewish Evacuees in Britain During the Second World War*, in *Immigrants and Minorities*, Frank Cass, Volume 7, November 1988, Number 3

Parsons, Martin, *Evacuation, The History Detective Investigates Britain at War*, Hodder Wayland, 1999

Parsons, Martin L., *'I'll Take That One' Dispelling the Myths of Civilian Evacuation, 1939–45*, Beckett Karlson, 1998

Parsons, Martin and Starns, Penny, *The Evacuation, The True Story*, BBC Radio 4, DSM, 1999

Rex, Christina, *Doodlebugs, Gas Masks and Gum, Children's Voices from the Second World War*, Amberley Publishing, 2008

Robins, Phil, editor, *Can I Come Home, Please? The Second World War-by the children who lived through it,* Scholastic, in association with the Imperial War Museum, 2009

Research Centre for Evacuee and War Child Studies, University of Reading, Director, Dr Martin L. Parsons, www.extra.rdg.ac.uk/evacueesarchive

Starns, P. and Parsons, M., *Against Their Will: The Use and Abuse of British Children during the Second World War*, in Marten J., editor, *Children and War,* New York University Press, 2003, pp. 266-278

GLOSSARY AND ABBREVIATIONS

Adon Olam: *Lord of the World*, a popular Hebrew hymn.

Ark: cupboard in a synagogue containing the Torah scrolls.

Ashkenazim: (adj. Ashkenazi) Jews of Central and Eastern European origin (Yiddish).

Bard of the Cornish Gorsedd: The Cornish Gorsedd, whose members are called Bards, is dedicated to the preservation of Cornwall's Celtic heritage. The title 'Bard' is awarded to someone for their outstanding commitment to the county.

Barmitzvah: ceremony for a Jewish boy on his 13th birthday (Hebrew).

Board of Deputies (of British Jews): The representative organisation of British Jewry.

Boulter: long line used for catching large fish.

Buba: Grandmother (Yiddish).

Bullcats: small fish found in rock pools.

Challah/cholla: plaited bread used during Jewish celebrations (Hebrew).

Cheder: a room or school where Hebrew is taught (Hebrew).

Crackers: The local name given to a cart track leading to the coast from the top of Raginnis Hill.

Down-chapel/downtown: Mousehole expression used to denote the chapel or part of town south of Fore Street.

Frum: Yiddish term for a very religious person.

Erev: the eve of, the day before, e.g. Erev Shabbat, the eve of Sabbath.

Gap: the space between the two quays in Mousehole through which boats enter and exit the harbour.

Halvah: Jewish and Middle Eastern sweet made from sesame paste.

Kashrut: Jewish food laws (Hebrew).

Kehillat Kernow: name of the Jewish community in Cornwall today, Kehillat being the Hebrew word for community and Kernow being the Cornish word for Cornwall.

Kibbutz: settlers' community and co-operative in Israel.

Kindertransport: name given to the rescue mission prior to the outbreak of World War Two when the UK took in nearly 10,000 predominantly Jewish children from Nazi Germany and the occupied territories of Austria, Czechoslovakia and Poland. The children were placed in British foster homes, hostels, and farms.

Kosher: in accordance with Jewish food laws.

Magen David: Star of David (Hebrew).

Matzoh: unleavened bread used at the time of Passover (Hebrew).

Menorah: nine branched candlestick used during the Chanukah Festival (Hebrew).

Mezuzah: small object fixed to Jewish door posts containing verses from Deuteronomy (Hebrew).

Mazel tov: 'congratulations', 'good luck' (Hebrew).

Mitzvah: good deed (Hebrew).

Ope: Cornish expression for narrow opening between houses.

Pesach: Passover, commemorating the exodus of the Hebrews from Egypt, where they had been enslaved (Hebrew).

Pilchard drivers/drift boats: 30 to 40ft fishing boat used to catch pilchards using a drift net. Mackerel drivers were larger boats, some 50ft long.

Porth, pronounced por: port or harbour (Cornish).

Private evacuees: These were self-funded evacuees who made their own arrangements and were not therefore part of the official Government Evacuation Scheme.

Punt: a small boat designed for use in shallow water.

Rosh Hashanah: Jewish New Year, usually in September.

Shabbat/shabos: Sabbath, weekly day of rest and worship in Judaism (Hebrew).

Scull: n. oar, v. to propel a boat forwards using one or more sculls.

Seder: meal and ceremony conducted on the eve of Passover (Hebrew).

Sefer: book (Hebrew).

Sefer Torah: hand-written scroll containing the first five books of the Hebrew Bible.

Sephardim: (adj. Sephardi) Jews of North African and Spanish origin (Hebrew).

Shema: the most important Jewish prayer, in Hebrew, which religious Jews recite twice daily. It is included in almost every synagogue service.

Shofar: ram's horn used in announcing festivals (Hebrew).

Shool/shul: synagogue (Yiddish).

Shoot: an open water pipe fed by local springs, where villagers used to obtain their water. There used to be several of these in Mousehole.

Siddur: Jewish daily prayer book written in Hebrew.

Singer's Prayer Book: This is the widely used and standard prayer book for most orthodox Jews in Great Britain.

Split: Cornish expression for scone or bread bun.

Talmud: written rabbinic commentary on Jewish law (Hebrew).

Talmud Torah: elementary Jewish school with special emphasis on religious education (Hebrew).

Traif: not *kosher*, i.e. not in accordance with Jewish food law.

Up-chapel/uptown: Mousehole expression used to denote the chapel or part of town east of Fore Street.

Yad Vashem: The Holocaust Memorial Centre in Israel. Yad Vashem has a website listing the names of all those known to have perished in the Holocaust .

Yiddish: a Germanic language with elements of Hebrew, spoken throughout the world, mainly by Ashkenazi Jews.

Yom Kippur: Day of Atonement, the most holy day of the Jewish calendar (Hebrew).

Zaide: Grandfather (Yiddish).

Zawn: deep cleft in the cliffs (Cornish).

ARP: Air Raid Precautions.

BCE: Before the Christian Era, or Before the Common Era, alternative version of BC, Before Christ.

BEF: British Expeditionary Force.

CE: Christian Era or Common Era, alternative version of AD, Anno Domini.

CFS: Central Foundation School.

CRO: Cornwall Record Office.

GWR: Great Western Railway.

JC: *The Jewish Chronicle.*

JFS: Jews' Free School.

LCC: London County Council.

LDV: Local Defence Volunteers.

NUT: National Union of Teachers.

REME: Royal Electrical and Mechanical Engineers.

RNR: Royal Naval Reserve.

WVS: Women's Voluntary Service.

NOTES

Chapter One: Mousehole

1. Poem written at the age of 81 by Augustus Mann, who left Mousehole for London in 1859, aged 25. He was the great-uncle of Nettie Pender, who quotes the poem in her book, *Mousehole, History and Recollections*, S. Johns, 1970, p.49.
2. Except where otherwise stated, most of this section is based on Margaret Perry's book, *Mousehole, A Brief History*, Margaret E. Perry, Newlyn, 1998, and on conversations with her during 2009. *The Mousehole Trail, A walk around Mousehole and to Paul*, The Golowan Trust, 2006, which Margaret was involved in writing, has also been a useful source of information, as has Percy Harvey's *Mousehole alias Porthennis, Chronicle of a Seafaring Community*, privately published manuscript, 1994.
3. Margaret Perry, op.cit.p.5.
4. According to Peter Pool, in his book, *The Place-Names of West Penwith*, privately published, Pool, P.A.S., 2nd Edition, 1985, p. 59, there were many variations of the spelling of Mousehole between the 13th and the 15th centuries.
5. Nettie Pender, op.cit.p.7. Other variations exist, including 'Moeshayle' (also Nettie, p.7), an abbreviation of 'Moweshayle', and also 'Mowse hal', meaning 'women's stream', found in *The Mousehole Trail, A walk around Mousehole and to Paul*, op.cit.p.5.
6. Margaret Perry, op.cit.pp.10–13.
7. Ibid.pp.15–17.
8. Nettie Pender, op.cit.p.16. Nettie is the mother of Sylvia Pender, one of the villagers interviewed, and of Jack Pender, a well-known artist.
9. Ibid.pp.35–36.
10. Margaret Perry, op.cit.pp.31–32.
11. Ibid.p.35.
12. Ibid.p.7.
13. Quoted in Leo Tregenza's book, *Harbour Village, Yesterday in Cornwall*, William Kimber & Co., 1977, p.74.
14. Margaret Perry, op.cit.p.39.
15. Nettie Pender, op.cit.p.57.
16. Many of the streets in Mousehole were, and still are, known by several names for historical reasons, making the job of the postman very difficult. According to Derek Harvey, 'There is no sign for my street, Wellington Place, and on my rates, it's called 6 North Street. Number 1 North Street is 14 houses away and is called Vivian Terrace.'
17. Percy Harvey, op.cit.p.96.
18. Ibid.p.162.
19. Ibid.p.232.
20. See 21 and 25 below.
21. Dorothy Yglesias, *The Cry of a Bird*, William Kimber & Co., 1964, the Country Book Club Edition p.17.
22. Percy Harvey, op.cit.p.150.
23. Ibid.pp.269–270.
24. Ibid.pp.275–276.
25. Dorothy Yglesias, op.cit. This book tells the story of the Mousehole Wild Bird Hospital.
26. Margaret Perry, op.cit.p.41.
27. Leo Tregenza, op.cit.p.69.
28. A *mezuzah* is a small object containing verses from the Bible which is affixed to the doorpost of Jewish homes.
29. Nettie Pender, op.cit.pp.58–59.
30. Percy Harvey, op.cit.p.145. Three pence, equivalent to just over one penny in today's money, but still beyond the reach of many villagers at the time.
31. Ibid.p.145.
32. Ibid.p.149.
33. Ibid.pp.318–319.
34. A half-crown was 2 shillings and 6 pence, about 12½p in today's money.
35. Mr Harvey Senior chose the name Floriana because his new house, like the town, had a lot of steps leading up to it.
36. Leo Tregenza, op.cit.p.22.
37. Three pounds ten shillings.

Chapter Two: The Jewish East End
1. Poem entitled *Whitechapel Britain*, written by Avram Stencl and translated by Miriam Becker. By kind permission of Whitechapel Gallery, Whitechapel Gallery Archive.
2. The information in this section is drawn almost entirely from the book by Dr Gerry Black, *Jewish London, an Illustrated History*, Breedon Books, 2003.
3. Ibid.pp.10–13.
4. Commemoration of the anniversary of the destruction of the First and Second Temples in Jerusalem, and the scattering of the Jewish people.
5. Gerry Black, op.cit.pp.15–16.
6. Ibid.p.19.
7. Ibid.pp.21–25.
8. Ibid.pp.28–32.
9. Ibid.p.38.
10. Ibid.p.76.
11. Ibid.p.56.
12. Ibid.p.62.
13. Ibid.p.78.
14. Ibid.pp.86–95.
15. Ibid.pp.95–103.
16. Ibid.pp.106–115.
17. Ibid.p.119.
18. Ibid.pp.141–144.
19. Ibid.pp.150–154.
20. Ibid.pp.154–156.
21. Aumie and Michael Shapiro, *The Jewish East End, Then and Now*, Springboard, 1994 pp.28–29.
22. This section is based largely on information taken from the JFS website, and the book by Dr Gerry Black, *JFS, The History of Jews' Free School, London since 1732*, Tymsder Publishing, 1998.
23. Ibid.p.1.
24. Aumie and Michael Shapiro, op.cit.p.8.
25. Communication with David Lerner, JFS, September 2009.
26. Gerry Black, *JFS, The History of Jews' Free School*, op.cit.p.76.
27. Ibid.p.113.
28. Ibid.p.123.
29. Ibid.p.4 This whole paragraph has been taken from the JFS website.
30. Ibid.pp.46–54.
31. Ibid.p.51.
32. *Goldlink*, Alumni magazine of Goldsmiths College, January 2003.
33. Lydia Graham née Barnes sadly passed away in July 2008, less than a year after her father Ralph Barnes who died in October 2007.
34. Quoted from *Going down the Jewish East End with Aumie Shapiro*, dvd, Springboard Education Trust, 2006.

Chapter Three: Preparations for Evacuation and Evacuation One
1. Quoted in *Evacuation News Sheet* number 1, December 1939, JFS Alumni website, www.jfsalumni.com.
2. This section is based largely on information provided in Dr Martin Parson's book, *I'll Take That One: Dispelling the Myths of Civilian Evacuation, 1939-45*, Beckett Karlson, 1998, and on Dr Parson's website for the Research Centre for Evacuee and War Child Studies, University of Reading, www.extra.rdg.ac.uk/evacueesarchive. The author has also made reference to the book Martin Parsons co-authored with Penny Starns, *The Evacuation, The True Story*, BBC Radio 4, DSM, 1999.
3. Martin Parsons, op.cit.p.23.
4. Martin Parsons and Penny Starns, op.cit.p.23.
5. See 14 below.
6. Martin Parsons, op.cit.p.36.
7. Ibid.p.40.
8. Ibid.pp.49–51.
9. Ibid.pp.55–56.
10. Martin Parsons, *Evacuation, The History Detective Investigates Britain at War*, Hodder Wayland, 1999, p.8.
11. Quoted from Dennis Adam's book, *Exodus to Ely, the Evacuation of Jewish Women and Children from Spitalfields in London to the Isle of Ely during the Second World War 1939–1945*, Ely Museum, section 4.
12. Martin Parsons and Penny Starns, op.cit.p.108.

13. Communication with Martin Parsons, September 2009.
14. Martin Parsons and Penny Starns, op.cit.p.55.
15. Martin Parsons, *I'll Take That One*, op.cit.pp.59–60.
16. Ibid.pp.15–16.
17. This section is based on information drawn from the chapter on evacuation in Dr Gerry Black's book, *J.F.S., The History of the Jews' Free School, London, since 1732*, Tymsder Publishing, 1998, pp.176–185, and also on Dennis Adams' book (see 11 above).
18. Written in 1939 by Mr J. Bourn, one of the JFS teachers evacuated to Ely, and published in an early number of the JFS *Evacuation News Sheet*, quoted in Gerry Black's book, op.cit.p.179.
19. This is the widely used and standard prayer book for most orthodox Jews in Great Britain.
20. Gerry Black, op.cit.p.176.
21. Dennis Adams, op.cit. section 6.
22. *The Jewish Chronicle*, 29 September 1939, p.16.
23. Ibid.13 October 1939, p.25.
24. Quoted by Dennis Adams, op.cit. section 10.
25. *The Jewish Chronicle*, 8 December 1939, p.11.
26. Quoted by Dennis Adams, op.cit. section 10.
27. Ibid. section 9.
28. *Evacuation News Sheet 11*, November 1940, JFS Alumni website.
29. Quoted by Dennis Adams, section 11.
30. Ibid. section 11.
31. Gerry Black, op.cit.p.181.
32. Dennis Adams, op.cit. section 19.
33. *Evacuation News Sheets 16*, April 1941 and 17, June 1941, JFS Alumni website.
34. Gerry Black, op.cit.p.184.
35. *Evacuation News Sheet 12*, December 1940, JFS Alumni website.
36. Sir Nicholas Winton, MBE, (born 19 May 1909) organised the rescue of 669 mostly Jewish children from German-occupied Czechoslovakia on the eve of World War Two in an operation later known as the *Czech Kindertransport*. Winton found homes for them and arranged for their safe passage to Britain. The event was re-enacted on 1 September 2009, using a 1930s train, with several surviving 'Winton children' and their descendants who were to welcomed by Sir Nicholas in London.
37. *Kindertransport*, also known as the Refugee Children Movement, is the name given to the rescue mission that took place in the months prior to the outbreak of World War Two. The United Kingdom took in nearly 10,000 predominantly Jewish children from Nazi Germany and the occupied territories of Austria, Czechoslovakia and Poland. The children were placed in British foster homes, hostels and farms.
38. *Evacuation News Sheet 4*, March 1940, JFS Alumni website.
39. *Evacuation News Sheet 1*, December 1939, JFS Alumni website.
40. *Evacuation News Sheet 2*, Spring 1940, JFS Alumni website.
41. Goldsmiths College alumni magazine, *Goldlink*, January 2003.

Chapter Four: Journey to Cornwall

1. Cornwall Record Office (CRO), DCWP 209, West Penwith Rural District Council, 1939–1940, 26.1.1939, p.B398.
2. Ibid. 27.4.1939, p.B470. This figure was for the Penzance Borough, not the whole of Cornwall.
3. *The Cornishman*, 30 August, 1939, p.8. *The Cornishman* newspaper covers the Western tip of Cornwall from Hayle to Land's End, though at that period, there was also a Camborne/Redruth edition.
4. Ten shillings and six pence, worth just over 50p in today's money. One shilling was equivalent to 5p, five shillings to 25p. There were 12 pennies in one shilling, so 6d, or 6 pence, was worth 2½p.
5. There were 20 shillings in one pound, so 21 shillings was £1 and 1s, or £1.05 in today's money.
6. *The West Briton*, 4 September 1939, p.3. The West Briton newspaper covers the middle part of Cornwall.
7. *The Cornishman*, 6 September 1939, p.7.
8. *The West Briton*, 7 September 1939, p.2.
9. *The Cornishman*, 6 December 1939, p.7.
10. H. Hartley Thomas worked for *The Cornishman* from 1918 to 1967, becoming director and manager of the company in 1944 until his retirement. An article reporting his retirement appeared in the paper on 7 December 1967. He was a very high profile figure in the community and holder of many offices. The article also states that during the war, he took an active role in supervising the welfare of evacuees and service personnel.
11. CRO, CC1-23-2, Cornwall County Council, Minutes, Civil Defence Committee, 1939–1945, 22.2.1940, p.6.
12. CRO, DCWP 209, op.cit., 29.2.1940, p.C149.

13. The figure was in fact 2,500, as later became apparent, but 2,000 is the figure that appeared in these minutes.
14. *The West Briton*, 4.3.1940, p.2.
15. Mr Hanuy's name was spelt Hannuy in the later edition on 6.3.1940.
16. *The Cornishman*, 6.3.1940, p.4.
17. Ibid. 13.6.1940, p.8.
18. CRO, DCWP 209, op.cit., 28.3.1940, p.C158.
19. 1/6d is another way of writing 1s and 6d, or one shilling and sixpence.
20. Information given to the author by Percy Harvey when she interviewed him in May 2009.
21. *The Cornishman*, 3.4.1940, p.3.
22. Ibid.12.6.1940, p.4.
23. Ibid. Mousehole column, p.5.
24. *The Jewish Chronicle*, 14.6.1940, p.10. The paper appeared once weekly, and articles were therefore written in advance.
25. *The West Briton*, 13.6.1940, p.4.
26. Martin Parsons confirmed that this was indeed the case in a communication to the author on 16.6.09. This was also confirmed by the National Railway Museum, who stated that it was possible to travel from Liverpool Street via Farringdon to Paddington at that time on the underground railway network.
27. Two other female teachers appear in the photograph, Miss Haffner and Miss Levene. Since Ralph Barnes wrote that there were two female teachers who went on the journey to Cornwall, this would imply that Miss Cohen was not with them at that time.
28. *Goldlink*, the Alumni magazine of Goldsmiths College, January 2003.
29. CRO, SRA-PENZ-5-7, Penzance County Boys' School admission register.

Chapter Five: Arrival

1. *The Cornishman*, 19 and 20 June 1940, p.3.
2. Jeanne remembers that a boy called David Sachs stayed with her future parents-in-law, Mr and Mrs Richards who lived in Wesley Square.
3. Marian remembers that a boy named Max Davis, a very Orthodox boy, was billeted in another home on Gurnick Street, and that Aby Baruch stayed with Mrs Batten at St Clements' House, on St Clements' Terrace.
4. Other boys known to have arrived that day were Solly Lederman, who had been a pupil at JFS Central School and stayed with Mr Bill Pomeroy, Raymond Pomeroy's uncle. Also, Eddie Lazarus, billeted with Mrs Matthews, owner of the sweet shop, and his younger brother Lew Lazarus who stayed with a Dr? Sharpe. Solly and Eddie came to the author's attention when they attended a reunion held at JFS on 25 October 2009. Alfred Rottenberg was billeted with Percy Laity on Fore Street, but only stayed a few weeks.
5. Joan's grandparents Mr and Mrs Williams, living in Dumbarton Terrace, hosted Peggy White, while nearby in The Parade, her aunt Emmie Williams took in Wally and Jean Warberg, where Miss Humphrys also stayed to make room for the Barnes family in her own home. Joan also remembers that Mrs Christiana Rouffignac had Sheila and Willy Brick.
6. Lily Polgrean Grose, *Mousehole Childhood, 1928–1950*, Landfall Publications, 2008, p.29.

Chapter Six: First Impressions

1. *The Cornishman*, 19 and 20 June, p.3.
2. *The Cornishman*, 26 June 1940, pp.2 and 8.
3. Ibid.p.2.
4. Ibid.p.2.
5. Ibid.p.5, Mousehole column.
6. *The Cornishman.*, 19 and 20 June 1940, p.3.
7. Ibid.p.3.
8. *The Cornishman.* 26 June 1940, p.8.
9. Tony Kushner, *Horns and Dilemmas: Jewish Evacuees in Britain During the Second World War*, in *Immigrants and Minorities*, Frank Cass, Volume 7. November 1988, Number 3.
10. Dorothy Yglesias, *The Cry of a Bird*, William Kimber and Co., 1964, the Country Book Club edition, p.75.

Chapter Seven: Village Life

1. According to Margaret Perry, on the whole girls either had pigtails or short bobbed hair and a fringe. Cut by Mr Ladner of course!
2. During the war, there was a limit placed on the purchase of certain foods and household items, and every individual was given a ration book with coupons, so that they could only buy the amount they were allowed.
3. *Halvah* is a sweet made of sesame paste.

4. This is mentioned in Mrs Barnes obituary appearing in the *Jewish Chronicle* on 20 July 1984, p.9.
5. Information given to author by Margaret Perry.
6. Dorothy Yglesias, *The Cry of a Bird*, William Kimber and Co., 1964, the Country Book Club edition, p.75–76.
7. *The Cornishman*, 19 June 1940, p.3.
8. Cornwall Record Office (CRO), SR-PAU-4-3, Paul Church Town Council School, log book, 1940, p.133.
9. Percy Harvey, *Mousehole alias Porthennis, Chronicle of a Seafaring Community*, privately published manuscript, 1994, available at Morrab Library, Penzance, p.279.
10. *The Cornishman*, 14 August 1941, p.8.
11. There is some evidence that the Mousehole Cave was mined in ancient times for copper, according to Margaret Perry.
12. Leo Tregenza, *Harbour Village, Yesterday in Cornwall*, William Kimber and Co., 1977, p.51.

Chapter Eight: At School

1. The children were taught first by Mrs Legge, then by Miss White, who lived on Gurnick Street. The next teacher in the main part of the school was Miss Williams, whose father was the landlord of the Ship Inn, then there was a Mrs Turner from Penzance, followed by Mr White from Newlyn and Mr Elford, the Headmaster, who lived on The Parade. During the war, Mr White was called-up and was replaced, according to Derek Harvey, by a number of young probationary teachers.
2. Miriam contacted the author in September 2009 after seeing an article about this book in the JFS alumni magazine. Until then, only Jose had spoken of going to school in Paul.
3. Cornwall Record Office (CRO), SR-PAU-4-3, Paul Church Town Council School, log book, 1940. p.132.
4. Ibid., p.137–138.
5. *The Cornishman*, 15 January 1941, p.8.
6. CRO, DC-PEN-192, Welfare and Evacuation Committee, 21.8.1941.
7. Eddie Lazarus came to the JFS Mousehole Reunion on 25 October 2009, the first time the author knew of him, other than through the story recounted by Frances. Apparently his brother Lew Lazarus, who was in Mousehole, became boxer Lew Lazar and a fight he was in was included in ITV's very first broadcast.
8. CRO, SPAU1-2-4, Mousehole County Primary School, Admission Records, 1942, pp.13–14.
9. Ibid., 1940–1946, pp.9–19.
10. Major Bryant and Miss Ross were another couple who appeared to have come to Mousehole to escape a scandal 'up country'. Major Bryant owned several properties in the village which Miss Ross inherited when he died.
11. Susan Eustace eventually inherited several properties from her aunt, one being Harbour Cottage, where the author stays when in Mousehole.
12. John and Billy Wright were born in 1935 and 1933 respectively. Malcolm Hanover had a friend Johnny Wright, who must have been one of these two brothers. Malcolm was born in 1933 and says that his friend was the same age. John Wright was two years younger, whereas Billy Wright was of Malcolm's age, so it is possible that he was Malcolm's friend rather than his brother John.
13. Like the JFS children, the Belgian children had their own school and teacher in Mousehole School, even thought their numbers were so small.
14. The 1944 Education Act introduced the tripartite system of secondary education, comprising grammar schools, technical schools and secondary modern schools. Secondary education became free.

Chapter Nine: At War

1. Poem used by the Ministry of Food to try to encourage people to eat fish they were not used to. Quoted in William Stevenson, edited by Margaret Perry, *Growing up with Boats*, William Stevenson, 2001, p.68, by kind permission of Margaret Perry.
2. Air Raid Precautions.
3. Cornwall Record Office (CRO), Civil Defence Committee, Minutes, November 11, 1940.
4. William Stevenson, op.cit.p.59.
5. The Crackers was the local name given to a cart track leading to the coast from the top of Raginnis Hill.
6. Lord Haw-Haw was the nickname of William Joyce, an announcer on the English language propaganda radio program *Germany Calling*, broadcast by Nazi German radio to audiences in Great Britain during World War Two.
7. Information provided by Margaret Perry.
8. The informant wishes to remain anonymous.
9. *The Cornishman*, 6 November 1940, p.3, and 1 January 1941, p.5.
10. *The Jewish Chronicle*, 17 October 1941, p.20.

Chapter Ten: A Family Affair

1. Nettie Pender is the author of *Mousehole, History and Recollections*, S. Johns, 1970, quoted in Chapter One.
2. Five shillings and 10 pence. Five shilling is equivalent to 25 pence now.
3. Raymond Pomeroy, the taxi driver, was the father of Raymond Pomeroy, one of the interviewees.
4. *The Jewish Chronicle*, 11 April 1941, p.11.
5. See Chapter Three and also bibliography.
6. Tony Kushner, *Horns and Dilemmas: Jewish Evacuees in Britain During the Second World War*, in *Immigrants and Minorities*, Frank Cass, Volume 7, November 1988, Number 3.

Chapter Eleven: At Play

1. See Chapter One.
2. See Chapter Twelve.
3. Lily Polgrean Grose, *Mousehole Childhood, 1928–1950*, Landfall Publications, 2008, p.29.
4. See note 12 in Chapter Eight. It is possible that Billy Wright rather than Johnny Wright was Malcolm's friend.
5. A large house next to the Coastguard Hotel, where Malcolm lived towards the end of his stay. See Chapter Ten.
6. Alan Paris, born in 1938, did not appear in the January 1942 school register with his brother Tony, as he had not started school by then. Had he come with the original party he would have been under two years old, so he may have joined his brother at a later stage. He started Mousehole School on 28 August 1944 and remained in the school until June 1945.
7. These are the cover photo, *The Landlubber*, which was first shown to the author by Raymond, and a second photo of boys playing in the harbour, which for this book has been entitled *More fun in the harbour*. Both the photographs were taken by Geraldine Underell.
8. Nettie Mann Pender, *Mousehole, History and Recollections*, S. Johns, 1970, p.53.
9. Sadly, John Hoskin died at the age of 17 in 1946 of septicaemia due to a poisoned finger, which he acquired when working in the local garage. Myra remembers this sad event, because another 14-year-old girl in Paul village died six weeks later of appendicitis. These were times when tragic early deaths of this kind were not uncommon.
10. *The Cornishman*, 4 December 1940, p.6.
11. Cornwall Record Office (CRO), Minutes of the West Penwith Rural Council, 19 December 1940, C319.
12. *The Cornishman*, 1 January 1941, p.5.
13. Ibid. 27 February 1941, p.3.
14. Joan tells the story that, on one occasion, her grandfather 'put in somebody's funeral when he didn't really require it!'.
15. *The Cornishman*, 13 March 13 1941, p.6 and 9 April 1941 p.8.

Chapter Twelve: At Prayer

1. *The Jewish Chronicle*, September 1941.
2. Ibid, 3 January 1941, p.6.
3. Ibid.24 January 1941, p.19.
4. Ibid.24 January 1941, p.19.
5. Ibid.9 May 1941, p.14.
6. This is the widely used and standard prayer book for most orthodox Jews in Great Britain.
7. *The Jewish Chronicle*, 6 June 1941, p.16.
8. Ibid.13 June 1941, p.22.
9. Ibid.11 April 1941, p.13.
10. Ibid.5 September 1941, p.21.
11. Like the Sabbath, Jewish festivals begin at dusk the day before. For example, Erev Yom Kippur means the Eve of Yom Kippur.
12. *The Jewish Chronicle*, 28 February 1941, p.7.
13. Ibid.11 April 1941, p.4.
14. Ibid.2 May 1941, p.14.
15. Ingrid's journey to Cornwall is described in Chapter Four.
16. The *Shema* is one of the most important Jewish prayers and one of the first prayers that Jewish children learn. Religious Jews say the *Shema* two or three times each day as part of their regular prayers, and it is included in almost every synagogue service.
17. *The Jewish Chronicle*, September 1941, Rosh Hashanah supplement, issued by the Joint Emergency Committee for Jewish Education and by *The Jewish Chronicle* in collaboration.
18. This falls on the ninth day of the Hebrew month of Av.

19.   BBC *Thought for the Day*, 29 July 2009, Rabbi Laura Janner-Klausner.
20.   'On the 7th of Av, in 1941, *SS-Obergruppenführer* Reinhard Heydrich was appointed by Goering to carry out the "Final Solution", the murder of all the Jews in Europe. Two days later, on the 9th of Av, 1941, SS Commander Heinrich Himmler formally presented his plan to the Nazi Party on the Final Solution. One year later, to the day, the plan was formally implemented.' fourquestions.us.

Chapter Thirteen: Departure and Aftermath

1.   Last verse of the poem quoted in Chapter Three, *Evacuation News Sheet 11*, November 1940, JFS Alumni website. S.M. Rich was one of the JFS teachers in Cambridgeshire.
2.   Cornwall Record Office (CRO), DC-PEN-192, Welfare And Evacuation Committee, Penzance, Minutes, 4 September 1941.
3.   CRO, DC-PEN-193, Welfare And Evacuation Committee, Penzance, Minutes, 23 April 1945, pp.33–34.
4.   Ibid. 23 July 1945, para 1371.
5.   Ibid. 24 March 1947, para 504.
6.   Apparently betting was not made legal until 1961, so Malcolm informed the author. This was the Betting Levy Act, 1961.
7.   The author was also introduced to Marian by Greta, and it was this story that started off her interest in this project.
8.   According to Margaret Perry, with the coming of war every available piece of arable land had to be used for food crops so daffodil bulbs and other flowers were dug up and thrown into hedges or on to pieces of waste ground. Market gardeners continued to pick them from there and send them to market but eventually even this was banned from November 1942. Hence it is not clear at what time and in what circumstances Frances and Mildred were doing this work.

LIST OF ILLUSTRATIONS

FRONT COVER
Percy Laity's boat in Mousehole harbour, 1944, Geraldine Underell

BACK COVER
Susan Soyinka, by Andrew Ball
The entrance to Jews' Free School in Bell Lane, Springboard Education Trust
Jews' Free School, London, 1908, Springboard Education Trust

SECTION 1: MOUSEHOLE AND LONDON'S EAST END
(BETWEEN PAGES 28–29)

Aerial view of Mousehole harbour, Aero Pictorial courtesy English Heritage
Mousehole Harbour, 1940s, by Geraldine Underell
Mousehole viewed from the Gap, 1949, by Margaret Perry
The Cliff, 1949, by Margaret Perry
Mousehole Male Voice Choir, *c.*1950, by Margaret Perry
St Michael's Mount and Its Own Cloud, by Geraldine Underell
The First Away from Mousehole Harbour, by Geraldine Underell
Taking Home Supper, by Geraldine Underell
A Mender of Nets, by Geraldine Underrell
Waiting For the Milk, By Geraldine Underell
Washday At My Backdoor, by Geraldine Underell
Mousehole School, 1936, courtesy Joan Richards
Mousehole School, *c.*1937, courtesy Jack Waters
Foxes Lane, showing Mousehole School, courtesy Percy Harvey
The 'haymarket' in Aldgate High Street, 1920s, Springboard Education Trust
Wentworth Street, 1920s, Springboard Education Trust
King George V Silver Jubilee celebrations, 1935, Springboard Education Trust
Gardiner's Corner, 4 October 1936, Springboard Education Trust
Back yards in East London, 1936, Springboard Education Trust
Brady Street Dwellings, 1960, Springboard Education Trust
The Great Synagogue, Duke's Place, 1938, Springboard Education Trust
The blitzed ruins of the Great Synagogue, 1941, Springboard Education Trust
The Fromovitch sisters, May 1937, courtesy Frances Pomm
Charlie Saunders, caretaker of Jews' Free School, courtesy Frances Pomm
Girls' Hebrew class at Jews' Free School, Springboard Education Trust
Prize Giving Day at Jews' Free School, *c.*1930s, courtesy Mildred Moore
Jews' Free School, May 1934, courtesy Pamela Fields
Jews' Free School after the bombing in 1941, courtesy Mildred Moore
Evacuation of Robert Montefiore Senior School, courtesy Martin Parsons

SECTION 2: PERSONAL PHOTOS AND MORE PHOTOS OF MOUSEHOLE
(BETWEEN PAGES 92–93)

Evacuees on the beach in Mousehole, July 1940, courtesy Pamela Fields
Evacuees at Paul, with names, July 1940, courtesy Mildred Moore
Irene and Frances Fromovitch, Mousehole, 1940, courtesy Frances Pomm
Irene, Frances, and Mildred, Fromovitch, 1941, courtesy Frances Pomm
Betty and Esther Posner, with the Drews, 1940–41, courtesy Estelle Kaye
Lily and Miriam Roar in Mousehole with their foster mother, Mrs Trembath, 1940, courtesy Miriam Conway
Millie Butler and Miriam Roar, Mousehole, 1944, courtesy Miriam Conway
Anita Godfrey and her brother Irvine, courtesy Anita Cohen
Maurice and Arnold Podguszer in Mousehole, 1940, courtesy Arnold Powell
Elaine and Desirée Frischman, 1940, courtesy Joan Richards
Joan Ladner, Harold Lazefsky and Daniel Frankel, 1940, courtesy Joan Richards
Ted Labofsky on Mousehole beach, 1940, courtesy Ted Leigh
Mr and Mrs Harvey, 1940, courtesy Ted Leigh
Ted Labofsky with the Harvey family, 1940, courtesy Ted Leigh
Rosita Reiderman, Mousehole, c. 1940, courtesy Jack Waters
Mrs Reiderman, Mousehole, c. 1941, courtesy Jack Waters
Frances Fromovitch, Mousehole, 1940, courtesy Frances Pomm
Jack Goldstein, Mousehole, 1941, courtesy Jack Goldstein
Cyril Hanover, Mousehole, 1940, courtesy Cyril Hanover
Ted Labofsky, Mousehole, 1940, courtesy Percy Harvey
Evelyn Goldstein in her late teens, courtesy Jack Goldstein
Vera Goldstein in her late teens, courtesy Jack Goldstein
Jack and Mrs Goldstein on Mousehole beach, 1941, courtesy Jack Goldstein
Jack Goldstein and Harry Fireman, 1940, courtesy Jack Goldstein
Nurse Pender, Mousehole District Nurse, courtesy Anne Beeton
School's Out, by Geraldine Underell
Pat-a-Cake, by Geraldine Underell
Men About Town, by Geraldine Underell
Sea Dreams, by Geraldine Underell
Curiosity, by Geraldine Underell
The Landlubber, by Geraldine Underrell, 1944, (also on front cover)
Sea Pups, by Geraldine Underell
Last Paddle of the Day, by Geraldine Underell
More Fun in the Harbour, by Geraldine Underell, courtesy Raymond Pomeroy
Mousehole Carnival, 1946, courtesy Joan Richards

SECTION 3: BARNES FAMILY AND POST-WAR PHOTOS
(BETWEEN PP 156–57)

Pamela and Lydia Barnes in Mousehole, 1941, courtesy Pamela Fields
Ralph Barnes on honeymoon in Cornwall, 1935, courtesy Pamela Fields
Ralph and Jean Barnes, 1938, courtesy Pamela Fields
Pamela and Lydia Barnes, Brookland Cottage, 1941, courtesy Pamela Fields
Lydia Barnes, Brookland Cottage, 1941, courtesy Pamela Fields
Barnes family, 1942, London, courtesy Pamela Fields
Pamela, Jean and Lydia Barnes, Penzance, 1943, courtesy Pamela Fields
Ralph Barnes in uniform, December 1943, courtesy Pamela Fields
Pamela and Lydia Barnes with grandparents, 1941, courtesy Pamela Fields
Farming in Cornwall, 1947, courtesy Mildred Moore

SECTION 4: ARTICLES, LETTERS AND DOCUMENTS
(BETWEEN PAGES 220–21)

DRAWINGS BY STEPH HAXTON

INDEX

276

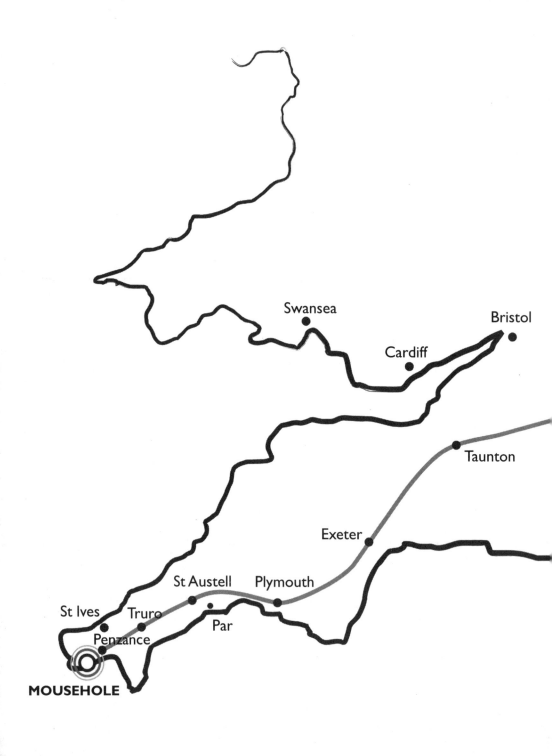